GREEK
Phrase book

David A. Hardy

Series Editor: Carol Stanley

Editor: Philippa Goodrich

BBC Books

BBC Books publishes courses on the following
languages:

ARABIC   ITALIAN
CHINESE   JAPANESE
FRENCH   PORTUGUESE
GERMAN   RUSSIAN
GREEK   SPANISH
HINDU & URDU   TURKISH

For further information write to:
BBC Books
Language Enquiry Service
Room A3116
Woodlands, 80 Wood Lane, London W12 0TT

Consultant: Alexandra Doumas

Published by BBC Books
A division of BBC Enterprises Ltd
Woodlands, 80 Wood Lane, London W12 0TT

ISBN 0 563 36293 6
First published 1992 © David Hardy

Set in Times Roman by Goodfellow & Egan Ltd,
Cambridge
Text and Cover printed in Great Britain by Clays Ltd,
St Ives Plc

Contents

HOW TO USE THIS BOOK

Communicating in a foreign language doesn't have to be difficult – you can convey a lot with just a few words (plus a few gestures and a bit of mime). Just remember: keep it simple. Don't try to come out with long, grammatically perfect sentences when one or two words will get your meaning across.

Greek can seem more difficult than some other languages because it uses a different alphabet. In fact it's not as alien as it appears at first sight, but, if you can, spend some time familiarising yourself with the Greek alphabet (see page 12).

Inside the back cover of this book is a list of All-purpose phrases. Some will help you to make contact – greetings, 'please' and 'thank you', 'yes' and 'no'. Some are to get people to help you understand what they're saying to you. And some are questions like 'do you have . . .?' and 'where is . . .?', to which you can add words from the Dictionary at the back of the book.

The book is divided into sections for different situations, such as Road travel, Shopping, Health and so on. In each section you'll find
- Useful tips and information
- Words and phrases that you'll see on signs or in print
- Phrases you are likely to want to say
- Things that people may say to you

Many of the phrases can be adapted by simply using another word from the Dictionary. For instance, take the question Είναι μακρυά το αεροδρόμιο; (*eene makrya to aerodhromyo*) – Is the airport far away? If you want to know if the station is far away, just substitute the word for

station, ο σταθμός (*o stathmos*), for το αεροδρόμιο to give
Είναι μακρυά ο σταθμός; (*eene makrya o stathmos*).

All the phrases have a simple pronunciation guide underneath based on English sounds – this is explained in Pronunciation (page 8).

If you want some guidance on how the Greek language works, see Basic grammar (page 196).

There's a handy reference section (starts on page 209) which contains a list of days and months, countries and nationalities, general signs and notices that you'll see, conversion tables, national holidays, useful addresses and numbers.

The 5000-word Dictionary (page 240) comes in two sections – Greek–English and English–Greek.

A concise list of numbers is printed inside the front cover for easy reference, and right at the end of the book is an Emergencies section (which we hope you won't have to use).

Wherever possible, work out in advance what you want to say – if you're going shopping, for instance, write out a shopping list in Greek. If you're buying travel tickets, work out how to say where you want to go, how many tickets you want, single or return, etc.

Practise saying things out loud – the cassette that goes with this book will help you get used to the sounds of Greek.

Above all – don't be shy! It'll be appreciated if you try to say a few words, even if it's only 'good morning' and 'goodbye' – and in fact those are the very sorts of phrases that are worth memorising as you'll hear them and need to use them all the time.

The language and information in this book apply to the mainland and islands of Greece. Cyprus has a distinct culture and dialect of its own, but you'll be understood there if you use these phrases.

If you'd like to learn more about Greek, BBC Books also publishes *Greek Language and People* and *Get by in Greek*. BBC phrase books are also available for the following languages: French, German, Italian, Spanish and Portuguese. Future titles include Arabic and Turkish.

The author would welcome any suggestions or comments about this book, but in the meantime, have a good trip – καλό ταξίδι! (*kalo takseedhee*).

PRONUNCIATION

You don't need perfect pronunciation to be able to communicate – it's enough to get the sounds approximately right. It's quite important to stress words in the correct place; luckily, all Greek words of more than one syllable are written with a stress mark. If you want to hear real Greek voices and practise trying to sound like them, then listen to the cassette.

Greek pronunciation is very regular – you can tell how a word is pronounced from the way it's written, once you know what sound each letter (or group of letters) represents. A pronunciation guide is given with the phrases in this book – the system is based on English sounds, as described below. Hardly any of the sounds of Greek present any difficulty.

For the Greek alphabet, see page 12.

Stress

In this book, a stressed syllable is shown in the pronunciation guide by bold type: *kaleemera, plateea*.

Words stressed on the third syllable from the end – e.g. **το αυτοκίνητο** (*to aftokeeneeto*), 'car' – get an extra stress when they're followed by a possessive pronoun: **το αυτοκίνητό μου** (*to aftokeeneeto-moo*), 'my car' (see page 203).

Vowels

	Approx. English equivalent	Shown in book as	Example	
A, α	a in 'cat'	a	γάλα	*gala*
E, ε	e in 'ten'	e	έχετε	*ekhete*
H, η	ee in 'feet'	ee	στάση	*stasee*
I, ι	ee in 'feet'	ee	όχι	*okhee*
unstressed and before another vowel	y in 'yet'	y	παιδιά	*pedhya*
O, o	o in 'hot'	o	πολύ	*polee*
Y, υ	ee in 'feet'	ee	κύριος	*keeryos*
Ω, ω	o in 'hot'	o	ευχαριστώ	*efkhareesto*

Vowel combinations

	Approx. English equivalent	Shown in book as	Example	
AI, αι	e in 'ten'	e	παιδί	*pedhee*
EI, ει	ee in 'feet'	ee	είμαι	*eeme*
unstressed and before another vowel	y in 'yet'	y	ασφάλεια	*asfalya*
OI, οι	ee in 'feet'	ee	πλοίο	*pleeo*
unstressed and before another vowel	y in 'yet'	y	Ομόνοια	*omonya*
AY, αυ	af in 'after'	af	αυτός	*aftos*
or	av in 'have'	av	αυγά	*avga*

EY, ευ	ef in 'left'	**ef**	εύκολος	*efkolos*
or	ev in 'ever'	**ev**	φεύγω	*fevgo*
OY, ου	oo in 'moon'	**oo**	γειά σου	*yasoo*

Note

αυ and ευ are pronounced 'av', 'ev', except when the following letter is one of θ, κ, ξ, π, σ, τ, φ, χ, ψ, in which case they are pronounced 'af', 'ef'.

Consonants

	Approx. English equivalent	Shown in book as	Example	
B, β	v in 'voice'	**v**	βάζω	*vazo*
Γ, γ	g in 'sugar'	**g**	αυγά	*avga*
or	y in 'yes' (before the sounds 'e' and 'ee')	**y**	γειά σου	*yasoo*
Δ, δ	th in 'this'	**dh**	εδώ	*edho*
Z, ζ	z in 'zoo'	**z**	βάζω	*vazo*
Θ, θ	th in 'thick'	**th**	Αθήνα	*atheena*
K, κ	k in 'king'	**k**	κύριος	*keeryos*
Λ, λ	l in 'long'	**l**	καλά	*kala*
M, μ	m in 'man'	**m**	μέρα	*mera*
N, ν	n in 'not'	**n**	κάνεις	*kanees*
Ξ, ξ	x in 'box'	**ks**	έξι	*eksee*
Π, π	p in 'pit'	**p**	πολύ	*polee*
P, ρ	r in 'parade' (lightly rolled)	**r**	καλημέρα	*kaleemera*
Σ, σ/ς	s in 'sit'	**s**	σήμερα	*seemera*
or	z in 'zoo'*	**z**	κόσμος	*koznos*

*when followed by one of β, γ, δ, ζ, μ, ν, ρ

10

T, τ	t in 'top'	t	φέτα	*feta*
Φ, φ	f in 'fat'	f	καφέ	*kafe*
X, χ	Scottish ch in 'loch'	kh	χωρίς	*khorees*
Ψ, ψ	ps in 'lapse'	ps	ψωμί	*psomee*

Consonant combinations

	Approx. English equivalent	Shown in book as	Example	
ΓΓ, γγ	ng in 'England'	ng	Αγγλία	*angleea*
ΓΚ, γκ	ng in 'England'	ng	αγκώνας	*angonas*
or	g in 'go'	g	γκαράζ	*garaz*
ΓΧ, γχ	nh in 'inherent'	nkh	έλεγχος	*elenkhos*
ΜΠ, μπ	mb in 'slumber'	mb	εμπρός	*embros*
or	b in 'bat'	b	μπύρα	*beera*
ΝΤ, ντ	nd in 'bend'	nd	πάντα	*panda*
or	d in 'dog'	d	ντους	*doos*
ΤΖ, τζ	dz in 'adze'	dz	τζατζίκι	*dzadzeekee*

Note

μπ, ντ, γκ are normally pronounced 'b', 'd', 'g' at the beginning of a word, and 'mb', 'nd', 'ng' in the middle of a word. They also represent 'b', 'd', 'g' in the middle of words imported into Greek from other languages – e.g. αντίο (*adeeo*).

Some consonant sounds change slightly when two words come together: e.g. την πόλη – *teem-bolee* (not *teen polee*). This happens in particular where the final ν of the word 'the' – τον or την – or of the negative δεν is followed by κ, π or τ. E.g.: τον κατάλογο (*ton-gatalogo*, not *ton katalogo*); την πλατεία (*teem-blateea*, not *teen plateea*); την Τρίτη (*teen-dreetee*, not *teen treetee*).

THE GREEK ALPHABET

Although the Greek alphabet may seem very 'foreign' at first, it has a lot in common with the Latin alphabet used in English. The Latin alphabet, in fact, is derived from the Greek, and many Greek letters, especially the capitals, have familiar shapes.

Spelling

How is it spelt?
Πώς γράφεται;
pos grafete

Capital letter	Small letter	Name	Name pronounced
Α	α	άλφα	*alfa*
Β	β	βήτα	*veeta*
Γ	γ	γάμμα	*gama*
Δ	δ	δέλτα	*dhelta*
Ε	ε	έψιλον	*epseelon*
Ζ	ζ	ζήτα	*zeeta*
Η	η	ήτα	*eeta*
Θ	θ	θήτα	*theeta*
Ι	ι	ιώτα	*yota*
Κ	κ	κάππα	*kapa*
Λ	λ	λάμδα	*lamdha*
Μ	μ	μυ	*mee*
Ν	ν	νυ	*nee*
Ξ	ξ	ξι	*ksee*
Ο	ο	όμικρον	*omeekron*
Π	π	πί	*pee*
Ρ	ρ	ρω	*ro*

Capital letter	Small letter	Name	Name pronounced
Σ	σ/ς*	σίγμα	*seegma*
Τ	τ	ταυ	*taf*
Υ	υ	ὑψιλον	*eepseelon*
Φ	φ	φι	*fee*
Χ	χ	χι	*khee*
Ψ	ψ	ψι	*psee*
Ω	ω	ωμέγα	*omega*

*σ is used at the beginning and in the middle of words, and ς at the end of words

Note

The Greek question mark (;) is like the English semi-colon.

GENERAL CONVERSATION

● The phrases **καλημέρα** (*kaleemera*), **καλησπέρα** (*kaleespera*) and **καληνύχτα** (*kaleeneekhta*) are used at different times of day. **Καλημέρα** means 'good morning' (or literally 'good day') and is used up to lunchtime – Greek lunchtime that is. Between lunch and the early evening, Greeks often take a siesta. If you meet anyone during this time, say **χαίρετε** (*kherete*) – hello! From about 5.30 p.m. onwards, use **καλησπέρα**, and to say goodnight, **καληνύχτα**.

Χαίρετε (*kherete*) and **γειά σας** (*yasas*) are both used for 'hello', and also 'goodbye'. Both are formal. The informal version of **γειά σας** is **γειά σου** (*yasoo*).

Αντίο (*adeeo*) is another word for 'goodbye'.

You'll often hear **καλημέρα, καλησπέρα, καληνύχτα** and **αντίο** followed by **σας** (*sas*) e.g.: **καλημέρα σας** (*kaleemera-sas*) etc.

● Greeks often shake hands or kiss each other on both cheeks when they meet and when they say goodbye.

● Greeks use the words **κύριος** (*keeryos*), **κυρία** (*keereea*) and **δεσποινίς** (*dhespeenees*) far more often than English-speakers say 'sir', 'madam' or 'miss' – it isn't as formal-sounding in Greek.

● When you're talking to someone in English you vary your tone of voice and your way of saying things depending on whether you're addressing them formally, showing respect, or in a more casual way (as with a friend or member of the family).

In Greek, there's an extra way of making this distinction – by using different words to say 'you' and different parts of verbs. One way is more formal, the other more casual. There's a further explanation of this on page 201, but all you need to be aware of is that in this book we have used the more formal way, on the assumption that you will mostly be talking to people you don't know. The formal word for 'you' is εσείς (*esees*) or σας (*sas*).

People may address you in the informal way (this is quite general among younger people). The informal word for 'you' is εσύ (*esee*) or σε (*se*) or σου (*soo*).

● Greeks use many facial and hand gestures to communicate without actually speaking. You should look out especially for the gesture meaning 'no': the head is tilted upwards and backwards, though this is often reduced to a raising of the eyebrows. For 'yes' the head is tilted downwards and to one side. When the head is shaken from side to side, rather like the English 'no' gesture, this implies a question: this gesture is often accompanied by a rotating of the hand, with the thumb and first two fingers extended.

Greetings

Hello	Goodbye
Γειά σας	**Αντίο**
yasas	*adeeo*
Good morning	See you later
Καλημέρα	**Θα τα ξαναπούμε**
kaleemera	*tha ta ksanapoome*
Good evening	(Hello) how are you?
Καλησπέρα	**(Χαίρετε) πώς είστε;**
kaleespera	**(*kherete*) *pos eeste*
Goodnight	How do you do?
Καληνύχτα	**Τι κάνετε;**
kaleeneekhta	*tee kanete*

Fine, thanks
Καλά, ευχαριστώ
kala efkhareesto

And you?
Εσείς;
esees

Introductions

My name is . . .
Με λένε . . .
me lene . . .

This is . . . (*male*)
Αυτός είναι . . .
aftos eene . . .

This is . . . (*female*)
Αυτή είναι . . .
aftee eene . . .

This is Mr Brown
**Αυτός είναι ο κύριος
   Brown**
aftos eene o keeryos Brown

This is Mrs Clark
Αυτή είναι η κυρία Clark
aftee eene ee keereea Clark

This is my husband/son
**Αυτός είναι ο άντρας μου/
   ο γιος μου**
*aftos eene o andras-moo/
   o yos-moo*

This is my boyfriend/fiancé
**Αυτός είναι ο φίλος μου/
   ο αρραβωνιαστικός μου**
*aftos eene o feelos-moo/
   o aravonyasteekos-moo*

This is my wife/daughter
**Αυτή είναι η γυναίκα μου/
   η κόρη μου**
*aftee eene ee yeeneka-moo/
   ee koree-moo*

This is my girlfriend/fiancée
**Αυτή είναι η φιλενάδα μου/
   η αρραβωνιαστικιά μου**
*aftee eene ee feelenadha-moo/
   ee aravonyasteekya-moo*

Pleased to meet you
Χαίρω πολύ
khero polee

Talking about yourself and your family

(*see* Countries and nationalities, *page 216*)

I am English
Είμαι Αγγλος (*if you're a man*)
eeme anglos
Είμαι Αγγλίδα (*if you're a woman*)
eeme angleedha

I am Scottish
Είμαι Σκωτσέζος/Σκωτσέζα
eeme skotsezos/skotseza

I am Irish
Είμαι Ιρλανδός/ Ιρλανδέζα
eeme eerlandhos/ eerlandheza

I am Welsh
Είμαι Ουαλλός/Ουαλλέζα
eeme walos/waleza

I live in London
Μένω στο Λονδίνο
meno sto londheeno

We live in Newcastle
Μένουμε στο Newcastle
menoome sto newkasel

I am a student
Είμαι φοιτητής (*m.*)/ **φοιτήτρια** (*f.*)
eeme feeteetees/feeteetrya

I am a nurse
Είμαι νοσοκόμος/νοσοκόμα
eeme nosokomos/nosokoma

I work in . . .
Δουλεύω σε . . .
dhoolevo se . . .

I work in an office/factory
Δουλεύω σε γραφείο/ εργοστάσιο
dhoolevo se grafeeo/ ergostasyo

I work for a computer company
Δουλεύω σε μια εταιρεία για κομπιούτερς
dhoolevo se mya etereea ya kombyooters

I am unemployed
Είμαι άνεργος/άνεργη
eeme anergos/aneryee

I am single
Είμαι ελεύθερος/ ελεύθερη
eeme eleftheros/eleftheree

I am married
Είμαι παντρεμένος/ παντρεμένη
eeme pandremenos/ pandremenee

I am separated
Είμαι χωρισμένος/
χωρισμένη
eeme khoreezmenos/
khoreezmenee

I am divorced
Έχω πάρει διαζύγιο
ekho paree dhyazeegyo

I am a widower/widow
Είμαι χήρος/χήρα
eeme kheeros/kheera

I have a son/a daughter
Έχω ένα γιο/μια κόρη
ekho ena yo/mya koree

I have three children
Έχω τρία παιδιά
ekho treea pedhya

I don't have any children
Δεν έχω παιδιά
dhen ekho pedhya

I have one brother
Έχω έναν αδελφό
ekho enan adhelfo

I have two brothers
Έχω δύο αδελφούς
ekho dheeo adhelfoos

I have one sister
Έχω μία αδελφή
ekho meea adhelfee

I have three sisters
Έχω τρεις αδελφές
ekho trees adhelfes

I'm here with my husband/
with my wife
Είμαι εδώ με τον άντρα μου/
με τη γυναίκα μου
eeme edho me ton andra-moo/
me tee yeeneka-moo

I'm here with my family
Είμαι εδώ με την
οικογένεια μου
eeme edho me teen
eekoyenya-moo

I'm here on holiday
Είμαι εδώ για διακοπές
eeme edho ya dhyakopes

I'm here on business
Είμαι εδώ για δουλειά
eeme edho ya dhoolya

I speak very little Greek
Μιλάω πολύ λίγα Ελληνικά
meelao polee leega eleeneeka

My husband/My wife is . . .
Ο άντρας μου/Η γυναίκα
μου είναι . . .
o andras-moo/ee yeeneka-
moo eene . . .

My husband is a bus-driver
**Ο άντρας μου είναι οδηγός
λεωφορείου**
*o andras-moo eene
odheegos leoforeeoo*

My wife is an accountant
**Η γυναίκα μου είναι
λογιστής**
*ee yeeneka-moo eene
loyeestees*

My husband/My wife works
in . . .
**Ο άντρας μου/Η γυναίκα
μου δουλεύει σε . . .**
*o andras-moo/ee yeeneka-
moo dhoolevee se . . .*

My son is five years old
**Ο γιος μου είναι πέντε
χρονών**
*o yos-moo eene pende
khronon*

My daughter is eight years
old
**Η κόρη μου είναι οχτώ
χρονών**
*ee koree-moo eene okhto
khronon*

You may hear

(see page 201 about ways of saying 'you')

Χαίρετε
kherete
Hello; goodbye

Πώς σας λένε;
pos sas lene
What is your name?

Από πού είσαστε;
apo-poo eesaste
Where are you from?

Τι δουλειά κάνετε;
tee dhoolya kanete
What do you do?

Τι σπουδάζετε;
tee spoodhazete
What are you studying?

**Είσαστε παντρεμένος/
παντρεμένη;**
*eesaste pandremenos/
pandremenee*
Are you married?

Εχετε παιδιά;
ekhete pedhya
Do you have any children?

Πόσων χρονών είναι;
poson khronon eene
How old is he/she/are they?

Είναι πολύ όμορφος
eene polee omorfos
He is very good-looking

Είναι πολύ όμορφη
eene polee omorfee
She is very pretty

Εχετε αδέρφια;
ekhete adherfya
Do you have any brothers
    and sisters?

**Αυτός είναι ο άντρας σου/
    ο φίλος σου;**
*aftos eene o andras-soo/
    o feelos-soo*
Is this your husband/
    your boyfriend?

**Αυτή είναι η γυναίκα σου/
    η φιλενάδα σου;**
*aftee eene ee yeeneka-soo/
    ee feelenadha-soo*
Is this your wife/
    your girlfriend?

Πού πάτε;
poo pate
Where are you going?

Πού μένετε;
poo menete
Where are you staying/
Where do you live?

Talking about Greece and your own country

I like Greece (very much)
Μ'αρέσει (πολύ) η Ελλάδα
maresee (polee) ee eladha

Greece is very beautiful
**Η Ελλάδα είναι πολύ
    όμορφη**
*ee eladha eene polee
    omorfee*

It's the first time I've been
    to Greece
**Είμαι για πρώτη φορά στην
    Ελλάδα**
*eeme ya protee fora steen
    eladha*

I come to Greece often
Ερχομαι συχνά στην Ελλάδα
erkhome seekhna steen eladha

Are you from here?
Από'δώ είσαστε;
apodho eesaste

Have you ever been to
    England?
**Εχετε πάει ποτέ στην
    Αγγλία;**
*ekhete paee pote steen
    angleea*

To Scotland/Ireland/Wales
**Στη Σκωτία/στην
    Ιρλανδία/στη Ουαλλία**
*stee skoteea/steen
    eerlandheea/stee waleea*

Did you like it?
Σας άρεσε;
sas arese

You may hear

Σας αρέσει η Ελλάδα;
sas aresee ee eladha
Do you like Greece?

**Εχετε ξανάρθει στην
    Ελλάδα;**
*ekhete ksanarthee steen
    eladha*
Have you been to Greece
before?

Πόσο θα μείνετε;
poso tha meenete
How long are you here for?

Τι νομίζετε για . . . ;
tee nomeezete ya . . .
What do you think of . . . ?

**Τι νομίζετε για την
    Πελοπόννησο;**
*tee nomeezete ya teem-
    beloponeeso*
What do you think of the
Peloponnese?

Μιλάτε πολύ καλά Ελληνικά
meelate polee kala eleeneeka
Your Greek is very good

Likes and dislikes

I like . . . (*one thing*)
Μ'αρέσει . . .
maresee . . .

I like . . . (*more than one
    thing*)
Μ'άρεσουν . . .
maresoon . . .

I like it
Μ'άρέσει
maresee

I don't like it
Δεν μ'αρέσει
dhen maresee

I like them
Μ'αρέσουν
maresoon

I don't like them
Δεν μ'αρέσουν
dhen maresoon

I like football
Μ'αρέσει το ποδόσφαιρο
maresee to podhosfero

I don't like beer
Δεν μ'αρέσει η μπύρα
dhen maresee ee beera

I like swimming
Μ'αρέσει το κολύμπι
maresee to koleembee

I don't like playing tennis
**Δεν μ'αρέσει να παίζω
τένις**
*dhen maresee na pezo
tenees*

I like strawberries
Μ'αρέσουν οι φράουλες
maresoon ee fraooles

Do you like it?
Σας αρέσει;
sas aresee

I don't like . . . (*one thing*)
Δεν μ'αρέσει . . .
dhen maresee . . .

Do you like ice cream?
Σας αρέσει το παγωτό;
sas aresee to pagoto

I don't like . . . (*more than
one thing*)
Δεν μ'αρέσουν . . .
dhen maresoon . . .

Talking to a child

What's your name?
Πώς σε λένε;
pos se lene

Do you have any brothers
and sisters?
Έχεις αδέρφια;
ekhees adherfya

How old are you?
Πόσων χρονών είσαι;
poson khronon eese

Invitations and replies

Would you like a drink?
Θα πάρετε ένα ποτό;
tha parete ena poto

Yes, please
Ευχαρίστως
efkhareestos

I'd love to
Πολύ ευχαρίστως
polee efkhareestos

No, thank you
Οχι, ευχαριστώ
okhee efkhareesto

That's very kind of you
**Είσαστε πολύ ευγενικός/
ευγενική**
*eesaste polee evyeneekos/
evyeneekee*

Please leave me alone
Παρακαλώ, αφήστε με
parakalo afeeste me

You may hear

Μήπως θέλετε . . .
meepos thelete . . .
Would you like . . . ?

Μήπως θέλετε κάτι να πιείτε;
meepos thelete katee na pyeete
Would you like a drink?

Μήπως θέλετε κατί να φάτε;
meepos thelete katee na fate
Would you like something
to eat?

Τι θα κάνετε απόψε;
tee tha kanete apopse
What are you doing
tonight?

**Μήπως θέλετε να πάτε
στον/στη/στο . . . ;**
*meepos thelete na pate ston/
stee/sto . . .*
Would you like to go
to . . . ?

**Μήπως θέλετε να πάτε στο
σινεμά;**
*meepos thelete na pate sto
seenema*
Would you like to go to the
cinema?

Μήπως θέλετε να πάτε στη συναυλία;
meepos thelete na pate stee seenavleea
Would you like to go to the concert?

Μήπως θέλετε να φάμε μαζί;
meepos thelete na fame mazee
Would you like to come to dinner?

Μήπως θέλετε να πάμε να χορέψουμε;
meepos thelete na pame na khorepsoome
Would you like to go dancing?

Τι ώρα θα συναντηθούμε;
tee ora tha seenandeethoome
What time shall we meet?

Πού θα συναντηθούμε;
poo tha seenandeethoome
Where shall we meet?

Μήπως έχετε φωτιά;
meepos ekhete fotya
Have you got a light?

Good wishes and exclamations

Congratulations!
Συγχαρητήρια!
seenkhareeteerya

Happy Birthday!
Χρόνια πολλά!
khronya pola

Merry Christmas!
Καλά Χριστούγεννα!
kala khreestooyena

Happy New Year!
Καλή Χρονιά!
kalee khronya

Happy Easter!
Καλό Πάσχα!
kalo paskha

Good Resurrection! (*on Easter Saturday*)
Καλή Ανάσταση!
kalee anastasee

Christ is risen! (*after Easter*)
Χριστός ανέστη!
khreestos anestee

He is truly risen! (*response to 'the above'*)
Αληθώς ανέστη!
aleethos anestee

May you live (a long life)! (*at weddings*)
Να ζήσετε!
na zeesete

May they live (a long life)! (*when talking of someone's children*)
Να σας ζήσουν!
na sas zeesoon

Good luck!
Καλή επιτυχία!
kalee epeeteekheea

Enjoy yourself!
Καλή διασκέδαση!
kalee dhyaskedhasee

Have a good journey!
Καλό ταξίδι!
kalo takseedhee

Welcome!
Καλώς ήρθατε!
kalos eerthate

I have found you well (*response to 'Welcome!'*)
Καλώς σας βρήκα!
kalos sas vreeka

Cheers!
Στην υγειά σας!
steen eeya-sas

Enjoy your meal!
Καλή όρεξη!
kalee oreksee

Bless you! (*when someone sneezes*)
Γειά σας!
yasas

Get well soon!
Περαστικά!
perasteeka

If only!/I wish I could!
Μακάρι!
makare

What a pity!
Τι κρίμα!
tee kreema

Talking about the weather

The weather's very good
Ο καιρός είναι πολύ καλός
o keros eene polee kalos

The weather's very bad
Ο καιρός είναι πολύ άσχημος
o keros eene polee askheemos

It's hot
Κάνει ζέστη
kanee zestee

It's cold
Κάνει κρύο
kanee kreeo

Phew, it's hot!
Πω πω, ζέστη που κάνει!
po po, zestee poo kanee

I (don't) like the heat
(Δεν) μ'αρέσει όταν κάνει ζέστη
(dhen) maresee otan kanee zestee

It's very windy
Φυσάει πολύ
feesaee polee

Is it going to rain?
Θα βρέξει;
tha vreksee

ARRIVING IN THE COUNTRY

• Whether you arrive by air, road or sea, the formalities (passport control and Customs) are quite straightforward; the only document you need is a valid passport.

• You will probably not need to say anything in Greek unless you are asked the purpose of your visit, or have something to declare at Customs. If you need to say what you have to declare (rather than just showing it), look up the words you need in the Dictionary. EC duty-free allowances apply – you can get a leaflet with the details at your point of departure. Valuable items, such as TVs, stereos and other electrical and electronic goods, may be entered in your passport; you will then have to bring them back with you when you leave, or pay the import duty.

You may see

ΑΛΛΑ ΔΙΑΒΑΤΗΡΙΑ Αλλα διαβατήρια	Other passports
ΔΗΛΩΣΗ ΣΥΝΑΛΛΑΓΜΑΤΟΣ Δήλωση συναλλάγματος	Currency declaration
ΔΙΑΒΑΤΗΡΙΑ ΧΩΡΩΝ ΤΗΣ ΕΟΚ Διαβατήρια Χωρών της ΕΟΚ	Passports of EEC countries
ΕΙΔΗ ΠΡΟΣ ΔΗΛΩΣΗ Είδη προς δήλωση	Goods to declare
ΕΛΕΓΧΟΣ ΔΙΑΒΑΤΗΡΙΩΝ Ελεγχος διαβατηρίων	Passport control
ΕΟΚ	EEC

ΚΑΛΩΣ ΗΛΘΑΤΕ Καλώς ήλθατε	Welcome
ΜΕΤΑΒΙΒΑΖΟΜΕΝΟΙ **ΕΠΙΒΑΤΕΣ** Μεταβιβαζόμενοι επιβάτες	Transfer passengers
ΟΥΔΕΝ ΠΡΟΣ ΔΗΛΩΣΗ Ουδέν προς δήλωση	Nothing to declare
ΤΕΛΩΝΕΙΑΚΟΣ ΕΛΕΓΧΟΣ Τελωνειακός έλεγχος	Customs control
ΤΕΛΩΝΕΙΟ(Ν) Τελωνείο(ν)	Customs

You may want to say

I am here on holiday
Είμαι εδώ για διακοπές
eeme edho ya dhyakopes

I am here on business
Είμαι εδώ για δουλειά
eeme edho ya dhoolya

It's a joint/group passport
Είναι κοινό/ομαδικό
διαβατήριο
eene keeno/omadheeko
dhyavateeryo

I have something to
declare
Εχω κάτι να δηλώσω
ekho katee na dheeloso

I have this
Εχω αυτό
ekho afto

I have two bottles of whisky
Εχω δύο μπουκάλια ουίσκυ
*ekho **dheeo** bookalya*
weeskee

I have two cartons of
cigarettes
Εχω δύο κουτιά τσιγάρα
*ekho **dheeo** kootya tseegara*

I have a receipt (for this)
Εχω απόδειξη (γι'αυτό)
ekho apodheeksee (yafto)

You may hear

Το διαβατήριό σας, παρακαλώ
to dhyavateeryo-sas parakalo
Your passport, please

Τα χαρτιά σας, παρακαλώ
ta khartya-sas parakalo
Your documents, please

Ποιος είναι ο σκοπός της επίσκεψής σας;
pyos eene o skopos tees epeeskepsees-sas
What is the purpose of your visit?

Είσαστε εδώ για διακοπές ή για δουλειά;
eesaste edho ya dhyakopes ee ya dhoolya
Are you here on holiday or business?

Πόσο θα μείνετε στην Ελλάδα;
poso tha meenete steen eladha
How long are you going to stay in Greece?

Ανοίξτε αυτή την τσάντα, παρακαλώ
aneekste aftee teen-dsanda parakalo
Please open this bag

Ανοίξτε αυτή τη βαλίτσα, παρακαλώ
aneekste aftee tee valeetsa parakalo
Please open this suitcase

Ανοίξτε το πορτ-μπαγκάζ, παρακαλώ
aneekste to port-bagaz parakalo
Please open the boot

Πρέπει να ψάξουμε το αυτοκίνητο
prepee na psaksoome to aftokeeneeto
We have to search the car

Εχετε άλλα πράγματα;
ekhete ala pragmata
Do you have any other luggage?

Πρέπει να πληρώσετε φόρο γι'αυτό
prepee na pleerosete foro yafto
There is duty to pay on this

Ελάτε μαζί μου/μαζί μας
elate mazee-moo/mazee-mas
Come with me/with us

DIRECTIONS

● Some general maps are available from the Greek National Tourist Office (address, page 235). A range of road maps are obtainable from kiosks and bookshops.

● When you need to ask the way somewhere, the easiest thing is just to name the place you're looking for and add 'please', e.g. **Αθήνα, παρακαλώ;** (*atheena parakalo*) – 'Athens, please?' Or you can start with 'where is . . . ?': **Πού είναι . . . ;** (*poo eene*).

● The question 'Where is the nearest (petrol station/ bank)?' is not commonly used in Greek, so instead just ask 'Is there (a petrol station/bank) around here?': **Υπάρχει (βενζινάδικο/τράπεζα) εδώ κοντά;** (*eeparkhee venzeena-deeko/trapeza edho konda*).

● If you're looking for a particular address, have it written down. In Greece, addresses are written with the street name first and the number afterwards, e.g. **Οδός Πλάτωνος 4** (*odhos platonos tesera*). Very often, the word for 'street' (**οδός**) is left out, and it becomes just **Πλάτωνος 4**.

● When you're being given directions, listen out for the important bits (such as whether to turn left or right), and try to repeat each bit to make sure you've understood it correctly. If you can't understand anything, ask the person to say it again more slowly, e.g. **πιο αργά** (*pyo arga*), prompting with **πάλι** (*palee*) – 'again', if necessary.

You may see

ΔΗΜΑΡΧΕΙΟ(N) Δημαρχείο(ν)	Town hall
ΔΙΑΒΑΣΗ ΠΕΖΩΝ Διάβαση πεζών	Pedestrian crossing
ΕΚΚΛΗΣΙΑ Εκκλησία	Church
ΚΑΣΤΡΟ Κάστρο	Castle, fortress
ΛΕΩΦΟΡΟΣ Λεωφόρος	Avenue
ΜΗΤΡΟΠΟΛΗ Μητρόπολη	Cathedral
ΜΟΥΣΕΙΟ(N) Μουσείο(ν)	Museum
ΟΔΟΣ Οδός	Street
ΠΕΖΟΔΡΟΜΟΣ Πεζόδρομος	Pedestrian precinct
ΠΕΖΟΙ Πεζοί	Pedestrians
ΠΛΑΤΕΙΑ Πλατεία	Square
ΣΤΟΝ/ΣΤΗ/ΣΤΟ . . . Στον/Στη/Στο . . .	To the . . .
ΥΠΟΓΕΙΑ ΔΙΑΒΑΣΗ ΠΕΖΩΝ Υπόγεια διάβαση πεζών	Subway

Excuse me (please)
Συγγνώμη (παρακαλώ)
seegnomee (parakalo)

Pardon?
Ορίστε;
oreeste

Can you repeat that,
please?
Ξαναπέστε το, παρακαλώ
ksanapeste to parakalo

More slowly
Πιο αργά
pyo arga

Again
Πάλι
palee

I've lost my way
Έχασα το δρόμο μου
ekhasa to dhromo-moo

Where are we?
Πού είμαστε;
poo eemaste

Where does this road/street
lead to?
Πού βγάζει αυτός ο δρόμος;
poo vgazee aftos o dhromos

Is this the right way to
Larisa?
Για τη Λάρισα καλά πάω;
ya tee lareesa kala pao

Can you show me on the
map?
**Μπορείτε να μου δείξετε
στο χάρτη;**
*boreete na moo dheeksete
sto khartee*

The airport, please?
Το αεροδρόμιο, παρακαλώ;
to aerodhromyo parakalo

The (town) centre, please?
**Το κέντρο (της πόλης),
παρακαλώ;**
*to kendro (tees polees)
parakalo*

The road to Thessalonica,
please?
**Το δρόμο για τη
Θεσσαλονίκη, παρακαλώ;**
*to dhromo ya tee
thessaloneekee parakalo*

How do I get to . . . ?
Πώς πάω στον/στη/στο . . . ;
pos pao ston/stee/sto . . .

How do I get to Nafplion?
Πώς πάω στο Ναύπλιο;
pos pao sto nafplyo

How do I get to the
airport?
Πώς πάω στο αεροδρόμιο;
pos pao sto aerodhromyo

How do I get to the beach?
Πώς πάω στην παραλία;
pos pao steem-baraleea

Where is/are . . . ?
Πού είναι . . . ;
poo eene . . .

Where is this address? (*if you've got it written down*)
Πού είναι αυτή η διεύθυνση;
poo eene aftee ee dhyeftheensee

Where is the tourist office?
Πού είναι το γραφείο τουρισμού;
poo eene to grafeeo tooreezmoo

Where is the post office?
Πού είναι το ταχυδρομείο;
poo eene to takheedhromeeo

Where is this office/room?
Πού είναι αυτό το γραφείο/δωμάτιο;
poo eene afto to grafeeo/dhomatyo

Where are the toilets?
Πού είναι οι τουαλέτες;
poo eene ee twaletes

Is it far?
Είναι μακρυά;
eene makrya

Is the airport far away?
Είναι μακρυά το αεροδρόμιο;
eene makrya to aerodhromyo

How many kilometres?
Πόσα χιλιόμετρα;
posa kheelyometra

How long does it take (on foot/by car)?
Πόση ώρα κάνει (με τα πόδια/με αυτοκίνητο);
posee ora kanee (me ta podhya/me aftokeeneeto)

Is there a bus/train?
Υπάρχει λεωφορείο/τραίνο;
eeparkhee leoforeeo/treno

Can I get there on foot?
Μπορώ να πάω με τα πόδια;
boro na pao me ta podhya

Can I get there by car?
Μπορώ να πάω με αυτοκίνητο;
boro na pao me aftokeeneeto

Is there . . . ?
Υπάρχει . . . ;
eeparkhee . . .

Is there a bank around here?
Υπάρχει τράπεζα εδώ κοντά;
eeparkhee trapeza edho konda

Is there a supermarket in the village?
Υπάρχει σουπερμάρκετ στο χωριό;
eeparkhee soopermarket sto khoryo

You may hear

Κάνατε λάθος *kanate lathos* You've made a mistake	**Ίσια, ευθεία** *eesya, eftheea* Straight on
Εδώ είμαστε *edho eemaste* We are here	**Το πρώτο (στενό, δρόμο)** *to proto (steno, dhromo)* The first (turning, street)
Εδώ *edho* Here	**Το δεύτερο (στενό, δρόμο)** *to dheftero (steno, dhromo)* The second (turning, street)
Εκεί *ekee* There	**Το τρίτο (στενό, δρόμο)** *to treeto (steno, dhromo)* The third (turning, street)
Από'δώ *apodho* This way	**Στα δεξιά** *sta dheksya* On the right-hand side
Από'κεί *apokee* That way, Along there	**Στα αριστερά** *sta areestera* On the left-hand side
Δεξιά *dheksya* (To the) right	**Στο τέλος του δρόμου** *sto telos too dhromoo* At the end of the street
Αριστερά *areestera* (To the) left	

Στην άλλη πλευρά της πλατείας
steen alee plevra tees plateeas
On the other side of the square

Στη γωνία
stee goneea
On the corner

Κάτω
kato
Down; downstairs

Επάνω
epano
Up; upstairs

Κάτω από
kato apo
Under

Πάνω από
pano apo
Over

Πριν από τα φανάρια
preen apo ta fanarya
Before the traffic lights

Μετά από τη Μητρόπολη
meta apo tee meetropolee
After/Past the Cathedral

Απέναντι από
apenandee apo
Opposite

Μπροστά στον/στη/στο
brosta ston/stee/sto
In front of

Πίσω από
peeso apo
Behind

Δίπλα στον/στη/στο
dheepla ston/stee/sto
Next to

Κοντά στον/στη/στο
konda ston/stee/sto
Near, Close to

Είναι στην κεντρική πλατεία
eene steen-gendreekee plateea
It's in the main square

Οταν φτάσετε στην Ακαδημίας
otan ftasete steen akadheemeeas
When you get to Akadimias street

Προς τη Μητρόπολη
pros tee meetropolee
Towards the Cathedral

Μέχρι τη διασταύρωση
mekhree tee dhyastavrosee
As far as the crossroads

(Δεν) είναι μακρυά
(dhen) eene makrya
It's (not) far away

Πολύ/Αρκετά μακρυά
polee/arketa makrya
Very/Quite far

Είναι κοντά
eene konda
It's close by

Πολύ/Αρκετά κοντά
polee/arketa konda
Very/Quite close

Είναι πέντε λεπτά από'δώ
eene pende lepta apodho
It's five minutes away

Είναι είκοσι χιλιόμετρα από'δώ
eene eekosee kheelyometra apodho
It's twenty kilometres away

Πρέπει να πάρετε το λεωφορείο/το τραίνο
prepee na parete to leoforeeo/to treno
You have to catch the bus/ train

Είναι στον τρίτο όροφο
eene ston-dreeto orofo
It's on the third floor

Η πρώτη/δεύτερη πόρτα
ee protee/dhefteree porta
The first/second door

Πάρτε το ασανσέρ
parte to asanser
Take the lift

You may also hear words like these:

Πηγαίνετε . . .
peeyenete . . .
Go . . .

Συνεχίστε . . .
seenekheeste . . .
Carry on . . ., Go on . . .

Κατεβείτε . . .
kateveete . . .
Go down . . .

Ανεβείτε . . .
aneveete . . .
Go up . . .

Στρίψτε . . .
streepste . . .
Turn . . .

Πάρτε . . .
parte . . .
Take . . .

Ακολουθήστε . . .
akolootheeste . . .
Go along/over . . .

Περνάτε . . .
pernate . . .
Cross . . .

ROAD TRAVEL

● Consult the motoring organisations or Greek National Tourist Office for information on driving in Greece. An international driving licence and Green Card insurance may not be technically necessary, but check their advice; you must carry your vehicle registration document with you.

● You drive on the right in Greece. Traffic from the right has priority on roads, even on roundabouts. Seatbelts are compulsory.

● Speed limits are generally:
50 km per hour in towns, 100 km per hour on ordinary roads, and 110 km per hour on some motorways.

● You have to pay a toll – διόδια (*dhyodhya*) – on some motorways. The surface of roads in rural areas can be very variable, and mountain roads can be dangerous in winter. Mainland Greece is mountainous so roads are often twisty – journeys can take considerably longer than you'd think from looking at a map. On some of the smaller islands, like Υδρα (*eedhra*), there are no roads for cars, and on others very few, so it's worth checking before taking a car.

● The main grades of petrol are σούπερ (*sooper*) – 4-star – and απλή (*aplee*) – 2-star. Unleaded petrol – αμόλυβδη βενζίνη (*amoleevdhee venzeenee*) – is becoming more widely available. Diesel – ντήζελ (*deezel*) or πετρέλαιο (*petreleo*) – is easily obtainable.

Petrol stations are not generally self-service, so you'll need a few words of Greek. Outside towns, petrol stations can be few and far between, so fill up whenever possible. Few petrol stations accept credit cards.

- Parking in towns and cities can be difficult because of traffic congestion. Some car parks have an attendant, and there are meters and underground car parks in some cities.

The penalty for illegal parking may be the removal of your number plates: to retrieve them you'll have to contact the police – αστυνομία (*asteenomeea*) – and pay a fine.

- In Athens, as an anti-pollution measure, cars are often restricted or banned from entering the central zone – δακτύλιος (*dhakteelyos*).

- There are many car hire firms in Greece, and the larger ones have offices at airports (and there will often be someone who speaks English). Look for the sign ΕΝΟΙΚΙΑΣΕΙΣ ΑΥΤΟΚΙΝΗΤΩΝ. You may be able to hire mopeds and bicycles, especially in tourist areas.

- In case of breakdown, there are two efficient emergency assistance and rescue services: ΕΛΠΑ (*elpa*) and EXPRESS SERVICE. You can phone either of them for assistance – the numbers are 104 for ΕΛΠΑ and 154 for EXPRESS SERVICE.

If you have to tell a mechanic what's wrong with your vehicle, the easiest way is to indicate the part affected and say 'this isn't working': αυτό δεν λειτουργεί (*afto dhen leetooryee*). Otherwise, look up the word for the appropriate part (see page 50).

You may see

ΑΔΙΕΞΟΔΟΣ Αδιέξοδος	Cul-de-sac, No through road
ΑΝΑΨΤΕ ΤΑ ΦΩΤΑ Ανάψτε τα φώτα	Use headlights (in tunnel)

ΑΠΑΓΟΡΕΥΕΤΑΙ Η ΕΙΣΟΔΟΣ	No entry
Απαγορεύεται η είσοδος	
ΑΠΑΓΟΡΕΥΕΤΑΙ Η ΠΡΟΣΠΕΡΑΣΗ	No overtaking
Απαγορεύεται η προσπέραση	
ΑΠΑΓΟΡΕΥΕΤΑΙ Η ΣΤΑΘΜΕΥΣΗ	Parking prohibited
Απαγορεύεται η στάθμευση	
ΑΡΓΑ	Slow
Αργά	
ΑΡΧΗ	Beginning (of restriction, etc.)
Αρχή	
ΑΥΤΟΚΙΝΗΤΟΔΡΟΜΟΣ	Motorway
Αυτοκινητόδρομος	
ΑΦΗΣΤΕ ΠΡΟΣΒΑΣΗ	Allow free access
Αφήστε πρόσβαση	
ΒΑΡΙΑ ΟΧΗΜΑΤΑ	Heavy goods vehicles
Βαριά οχήματα	
ΓΚΑΡΑΖ	Garage
Γκαράζ	
ΔΑΚΤΥΛΙΟΣ	Central Zone (Athens)
Δακτύλιος	
ΔΙΑΒΑΣΗ ΚΛΕΙΣΤΗ	(Mountain) pass closed
Διάβαση κλειστή	
ΔΙΑΒΑΣΗ ΠΕΖΩΝ	Pedestrian crossing
Διάβαση πεζών	
ΔΙΑΝΥΚΤΕΡΕΥΕΙ 5, 15, 25	Open all night 5th, 15th, 25th of the month
Διανυκτερεύει 5, 15, 25	
ΔΙΕΛΕΥΣΗ ΖΩΩΝ	Cattle crossing
Διέλευση ζώων	
ΔΙΟΔΙΑ	Toll (road, point)
Διόδια	

ΔΡΟΜΟΣ ΑΝΩΜΑΛΟΣ *Δρόμος ανώμαλος*	Uneven road surface
ΔΡΟΜΟΣ ΚΛΕΙΣΤΟΣ *Δρόμος κλειστός*	Road closed
ΔΩΣΤΕ ΠΡΟΤΕΡΑΙΟΤΗΤΑ *Δώστε προτεραιότητα*	Give way
ΕΘΝΙΚΗ ΟΔΟΣ *Εθνική Οδός*	National Road
ΕΚΤΕΛΟΥΝΤΑΙ ΕΡΓΑ *Εκτελούνται έργα*	Road works
ΕΝΟΙΚΙΑΣΕΙΣ **ΑΥΤΟΚΙΝΗΤΩΝ** *Ενοικιάσεις αυτοκινήτων*	Car hire
ΕΞΟΔΟΣ *Εξοδος*	Exit
ΕΞΟΔΟΣ ΕΡΓΟΣΤΑΣΙΟΥ *Εξοδος εργοστασίου*	Factory exit
ΕΞΟΔΟΣ ΚΙΝΔΥΝΟΥ *Εξοδος κινδύνου*	Emergency exit
ΕΞΟΔΟΣ ΦΟΡΤΗΓΩΝ *Εξοδος φορτηγών*	Lorry exit
ΕΠΙΚΙΝΔΥΝΗ **ΔΙΑΣΤΑΥΡΩΣΗ** *Επικίνδυνη διαστάυρωση*	Dangerous crossroads
ΕΠΙΚΙΝΔΥΝΗ ΣΤΡΟΦΗ *Επικίνδυνη στροφή*	Dangerous bend
ΖΩΝΗ ΑΣΦΑΛΕΙΑΣ **ΥΠΟΧΡΕΩΤΙΚΗ** *Ζώνη ασφάλειας* *υποχρεωτική*	Seatbelt compulsory
ΚΕΝΤΡΟ ΠΟΛΕΩΣ *Κέντρο πόλεως*	Town/city centre

ΚΙΝΔΥΝΟΣ	Danger
Κίνδυνος	
ΛΙΠΑΝΣΗ	Greasing
Λίπανση	
ΜΟΝΟΔΡΟΜΟΣ	One-way street
Μονόδρομος	
ΟΡΙΟ ΤΑΧΥΤΗΤΑΣ	Speed limit
Οριο ταχύτητας	
ΟΣΕ	Greek Railways
ΠΑΡΑΚΑΜΠΤΗΡΙΟ(N)	Deviation
Παρακαμπτήριο(v)	
ΠΑΡΚΙΓΚ	Parking
Πάρκιγκ	
ΠΕΖΟΔΡΟΜΟΣ	Pedestrian precinct
Πεζόδρομος	
ΠΕΖΟΙ	Pedestrians
Πεζοί	
ΠΕΡΙΟΡΙΣΜΕΝΗ ΣΤΑΘΜΕΥΣΗ	Limited parking
Περιορισμένη στάθμευση	
ΠΡΑΤΗΡΙΟ(N) ΒΕΝΖΙΝΗΣ	Petrol station
Πρατήριο(v) βενζίνης	
ΠΡΟΣΕΧΕΤΕ	Caution
Προσέχετε	
ΠΡΟΣΟΧΗ	Beware
Προσοχή	
ΠΡΟΣΟΧΗ ΤΡΑΙΝΑ	Beware of the trains
Προσοχή τραίνα	
ΠΡΟΤΕΡΑΙΟΤΗΤΑ ΔΕΞΙΑ	Priority to the right
Προτεραιότητα δεξιά	
ΠΡΩΤΕΣ ΒΟΗΘΕΙΕΣ	First-aid post
Πρώτες βοήθειες	

ΣΙΔΗΡΟΔΡΟΜΙΚΗ ΓΡΑΜΜΗ	Level crossing
Σιδηροδρομική γραμμή	
ΣΤΑΘΜΕΥΣΗ ΑΥΤΟΚΙΝΗΤΩΝ	Parking
Στάθμευση αυτοκινήτων	
ΣΤΕΝΗ ΓΕΦΥΡΑ	Narrow bridge
Στενή γέφυρα	
ΣΤΟΠ	Stop
Στοπ	
ΣΥΝΕΡΓΕΙΟ(Ν) ΑΥΤΟΚΙΝΗΤΩΝ	Repair shop
Συνεργείο(ν) αυτοκινήτων	
ΣΥΝΕΧΗΣ ΧΡΗΣΗ	In constant use
Συνεχής χρήση	
ΣΥΝΕΧΙΖΕΙ	Continues (restriction, etc.)
Συνεχίζει	
ΣΧΟΛΕΙΟ(Ν)	School
Σχολείο(ν)	
ΤΕΛΟΣ	End (of restriction, etc.)
Τέλος	
ΤΕΛΟΣ ΑΥΤΟΚΙΝΗΤΟΔΡΟΜΟΥ	End of motorway
Τέλος αυτοκινητοδρόμου	
ΤΕΛΩΝΕΙΟ(Ν)	Customs
Τελωνείο(ν)	
ΤΗΡΕΙΤΕ ΔΕΞΙΑ	Keep right
Τηρείτε δεξιά	

You may want to say

Petrol

Is there a petrol station around here?
Υπάρχει βενζινάδικο εδώ κοντά;
eeparkhee venzeenadheeko edho konda

4-star
Σούπερ
sooper

2-star
Απλή
aplee

Unleaded petrol
Αμόλυβδη βενζίνη
amoleevdhee venzeenee

Diesel
Ντήζελ/πετρέλαιο
deezel/petreleo

20 litres of 4-star, please
Είκοσι λίτρα σούπερ, παρακαλώ
eekosee leetra sooper parakalo

1000 drachmas' worth of unleaded, please
Αμόλυβδη ένα χιλιάρικο, παρακαλώ
amoleevdhee ena kheelyareeeko parakalo

Fill it up with 4-star/2-star, please
Γεμίστε σούπερ/απλή, παρακαλώ
yemeeste sooper/aplee parakalo

A can of oil, please
Ενά κουτί λάδι, παρακαλώ
ena kootee ladhee parakalo

Water, please
Νερό, παρακαλώ
nero parakalo

Can you check the tyres?
Μπορείτε να μου ελέγξετε τα λάστιχα;
boreete na moo elenksete ta lasteekha

Can you change the tyre?
Μπορείτε να μου αλλάξετε το λάστιχο;
boreete na moo alaksete to lasteekho

43

Can you clean the windscreen?
Μπορείτε να μου καθαρίσετε το παρμπριζ;
boreete na moo kathareesete to parbreez

Where is the air, please?
Πού έχει αέρα, παρακαλώ;
poo ekhee aera parakalo

How does the car wash work?
Πώς λειτουργεί το πλυντήριο;
pos leetooryee to pleendeeryo

How much is it?
Πόσο κάνει;
poso kanee

Parking

Where can I park?
Πού μπορώ να παρκάρω;
poo boro na parkaro

Can I park here?
Μπορώ να παρκάρω εδώ;
boro na parkaro edho

How long can I park here?
Πόση ώρα μπορώ να παρκάρω εδώ;
posee ora boro na parkaro edho

How much is it per hour?
Πόσο κάνει την ώρα;
poso kanee teen ora

Hiring a car/scooter

(*see* Days, months, dates, *page 209*)

I want to hire a car
Θέλω να νοικιάσω ένα αυτοκίνητο
thelo na neekyaso ena aftokeeneeto

A small car, please
Ένα μικρό αυτοκίνητο παρακαλώ
ena meekro aftokeeneeto parakalo

A medium-sized car, please
Ένα μέτριο αυτοκίνητο παρακαλώ
ena metryo aftokeeneeto parakalo

A large car, please
Ένα μεγάλο αυτοκίνητο παρακαλώ
ena megalo aftokeeneeto parakalo

An automatic, please
Ένα αυτόματο παρακαλώ
ena aftomato parakalo

For three days
Για τρεις μέρες
ya trees meres

For a week
Για μια εβδομάδα
ya mya evdhomadha

For two weeks
Για δύο εβδομάδες
ya dheeo evdhomadhes

From . . . to . . .
Από . . . μέχρι . . .
apo . . . mekhree . . .

From Monday to Friday
Από τη Δευτέρα μέχρι την Παρασκευή
apo tee dheftera mekhree teem-baraskevee

From 10th August to 17th August
Από τις δέκα Αυγούστου μέχρι τις δεκαεπτά Αυγούστου
apo tees dheka avgoostoo mekhree tees dheka-epta avgoostoo

How much is it?
Πόσο κάνει;
poso kanee

Per day/week
Την ημέρα/Την εβδομάδα
teen eemera/teen evdhomadha

Per kilometre
Το χιλιόμετρο
to kheelyometro

Is mileage included?
Συμπεριλαμβάνονται τα χιλιόμετρα;
seembereelamvanonde ta kheelyometra

Is petrol included?
Συμπεριλαμβάνεται η βενζίνη;
seembereelamvanete ee venzeenee

Is insurance included?
Συμπεριλαμβάνεται η ασφάλεια;
seembereelamvanete ee asfalya

Comprehensive insurance cover
Μικτή ασφάλεια
meektee asfalya

My husband/My wife will be driving too
Θα οδηγεί και ο άντρας μου/η γυναίκα μου
tha odheeyee ke o andrasmoo/ee yeeneka-moo

Do you take credit cards?
Δέχεστε πιστωτικές
κάρτες;
*dhekheste peestoteekes
kartes*

Do you take traveller's
cheques?
Δέχεστε τράβελερς τσεκ;
dhekheste travelers tsek

Can I leave the car in
Volos?
Μπορώ να αφήσω το
αυτοκίνητο στο Βόλο;
*boro na afeeso to
aftokeeneeto sto volo*

Can I leave the car at the
airport?
Μπορώ να αφήσω το
αυτοκίνητο στο
αεροδρόμιο;
*boro na afeeso to
aftokeeneeto sto
aerodhromyo*

How do the controls work?
Πώς λειτουργεί;
pos leetooryee

I want to hire a scooter
Θέλω να νοικιάσω μηχανάκι
*thelo na neekyaso
meekhanakee*

Do you have a crash helmet?
Έχετε κράνος;
ekhete kranos

Breakdowns and repairs

(*see* Car and bicycle parts, *page 50*)

My car has broken down
Χάλασε το αυτοκίνητό μου
khalase to aftokeeneeto-moo

Is there a garage near here?
Υπάρχει γκαράζ εδώ κοντά;
eeparkhee garaz edho konda

Can you telephone a garage?
Μπορείτε να τηλεφωνήστε
σ'ένα γκαράζ;
*boreete na teelefoneeste
sena garaz*

Can you send a mechanic?
Μπορείτε να στείλετε ένα
μηχανικό;
*boreete na steelete ena
meekhaneeko*

Can you tow me to a garage?
Μπορείτε να με πάτε στο γκαράζ με ρυμουλκό;
boreete na me pate sto garaz me reemoolko

Do you do repairs?
Κάνετε επισκευές;
kanete epeeskeves

I don't know what's wrong
Δεν ξέρω τι έχει
dhen-gsero tee ekhee

I think . . .
Νομίζω ότι . . .
nomeezo otee . . .

It's the clutch
Είναι η αμπραγιάζ
eene ee ambrayaz

It's the radiator
Είναι το ψυγείο
eene to pseeyeeo

It's the brakes
Είναι τα φρένα
eene ta frena

The car won't start
Δεν ξεκινάει το αυτοκίνητο
dhen-gsekeenaee to aftokeeneeto

The battery is flat
Άδειασε η μπαταρία
adhyase ee batareea

The engine is overheating
Η μηχανή έχει υπερθερμανθεί
ee meekhanee ekhee eeperthermanthee

It's losing water/oil
Χάνει νερό/λάδι
khanee nero/ladhee

It has a puncture
Έμεινα από λάστιχο
emeena apo lasteekho

I don't have any petrol
Δεν έχω βενζίνη
dhen ekho venzeenee

The . . . doesn't work
Ο/Η/Το . . . δεν λειτουργεί
o/ee/to . . . dhen leetooryee

I need a . . .
Χρειάζομαι ένα/μια . . .
khryazome ena/mya . . .

Is it serious?
Είναι σοβαρό;
eene sovaro

Can you repair it (today)?
Μπορείτε να το φτιάξετε (σήμερα);
boreete na to ftyaksete (seemera)

When will it be ready?
Πότε θα είναι έτοιμο;
pote tha eene eteemo

How much will it cost?
Πόσο θα κοστίσει;
poso tha kosteesee

You may hear

Petrol

Τι θέλετε;
tee thelete
What would you like?

Πόσο θέλετε;
poso thelete
How much do you want?

Το κλειδί παρακαλώ
to kleedhee parakalo
The key, please

Parking

Δεν μπορείτε να παρκάρετε εδώ
dhem-boreete na parkarete edho
You can't park here

Κάνει εκατό δραχμές την ώρα
kanee ekato drakhmes teen ora
It's 100 drachmas an hour

Δεν πληρώνετε
dhem-blεronete
You don't pay

Είναι ελεύθερο
eene elefthero
It's free

Εχει πάρκιγκ εκεί πέρα
ekhee parkeeng ekee pera
There's a car park over there

Hiring a car

Τι (είδος) αυτοκίνητο θέλετε;
tee (eedhos) aftokeeneeto thelete
What kind of car do you want?

Για πόσο καιρό;
ya poso kero
For how long?

Για πόσες μέρες;
ya poses meres
For how many days?

Ποιος θα οδηγεί;
pyos tha odheeyee
Who will be driving?

**(Κοστίζει) πέντε/τριάντα
χιλιάδες δραχμές**
(*kosteezee*) *pende/tryanda
kheelyadhes dhrakhmes*
(The price is) five/thirty
thousand drachmas

Την ημέρα
teen eemera
Per day

Την εβδομάδα
teen evdhomadha
Per week

**Την άδεια οδηγήσεως
παρακαλώ**
*teen adhya odheeyeeseos
parakalo*
Your driving licence, please

Τη διεύθυνσή σας;
tee dhyeftheensee-sas
What is your address?

Ορίστε τα κλειδιά
oreeste ta kleedhya
Here are the keys

**Επιστρέψτε το αυτοκίνητο
με γεμάτο ρεζερβουάρ
παρακαλώ**
*epeestrepste to aftokeeneeto
me yemato rezervwar
parakalo*
Please return the car with a
full tank

**Επιστρέψτε το αυτοκίνητο
πριν από τις έξι
παρακαλώ**
*epeestrepste to aftokeeneeto
preen apo tees eksee
parakalo*
Please return the car before
six

**Αν είναι κλειστό το
γραφείο, μπορείτε να
αφήστε τα κλειδιά στο
γραμματοκιβώτιο**
*an eene kleesto to grafeeo,
boreete na afeeste ta
kleedhya sto
gramatokeevotyo*
If the office is closed, you
can leave the keys in the
letterbox

Breakdowns and repairs

Τι έχει;
tee ekhee
What's wrong with it?

Μπορείτε να ανοίξετε το καπώ;
boreete na aneeksete to kapo
Can you open the bonnet?

Δεν έχω τα ανταλλακτικά
που χρειάζονται
den ekho ta andalakteeka
poo khryazonde
I don't have the necessary
parts

Θα πρέπει να παραγγείλω
τα ανταλλακτικά
tha prepee na parangeelo ta
andalakteeka
I will have to order the
parts

Θα είναι έτοιμο την άλλη
Τρίτη
tha eene eteemo teen alee
treetee
It will be ready by next
Tuesday

Θα κοστίσει δέκα χιλιάδες
δραχμές
tha kosteesee dheka
kheelyadhes dhrakhmes
It will cost 10 000 drachmas

Car and bicycle parts

Accelerator	Το γκάζι	*to gazee*
Air filter	Το φίλτρο αέρας	*to feeltro aeras*
Alternator	Ο πολλαπλασιαστής	*o polaplasyastees*
Battery	Η μπαταρία	*ee batareea*
Bonnet	Το καπώ	*to kapo*
Boot	Το πορτ μπαγκάζ	*to port-bagaz*
Brake cable	Η ντίζα φρενών	*ee deeza frenon*
Brake fluid	Το υγρό φρενών	*to eegro frenon*
Brake hose	Το σωληνάκι φρενών	*to soleenakee frenon*
Brakes (front/ rear)	Τα φρένα (εμπρός/ πίσω)	*ta frena (embros/ peeso)*
Carburettor	Η καρμπυρατέρ	*ee karbeerater*
Chain	Η αλυσίδα	*ee aleeseedha*
Choke	Το τσοκ	*to tsok*
Clutch	Η αμπραγιάζ	*ee ambrayaz*
Cooling system	Το σύστημα ψύξεως	*to seesteema pseekseos*

Disc brakes	Τα δισκόφρενα	*ta dheeskofrena*
Distributor	Ο διανομέας	*o dhyanomeas*
Electrical system	Το ηλεκτρικό σύστημα	*to eelektreeko seesteema*
Engine	Ο κινητήρας	*o keeneeteeras*
Exhaust pipe	Η εξάτμιση	*ee eksatmeesee*
Fanbelt	Το λουρί του βεντιλατέρ	*to looree too vendeelater*
Frame	Το σάσι	*to sasee*
Front fork	Το πηρούνι	*to peeroonee*
Fuel gauge	Ο δείκτης βενζίνης	*o dheektees venzeenees*
Fuel pump	Η αντλία βενζίνης	*ee andleea venzeenees*
Fuse	Η ασφάλεια	*ee asfalya*
Gears	Οι ταχύτητες	*ee takheeteetes*
Gearbox	Το κιβώτιο ταχυτήτων	*to keevotyo takheeteeton*
Gear lever	Ο μοχλός ταχυτήτων	*o mokhlos takheeteeton*
Handbrake	Το χειρόφρενο	*to kheerofreno*
Handlebars	Το τιμόνι	*to teemonee*
Headlights	Τα μπροστινά φώτα	*ta brosteena fota*
Heater	Το καλοριφέρ	*to kaloreefer*
Horn	Η κόρνα	*ee korna*
Ignition	Η ανάφλεξη	*ee anafleksee*
Ignition key	Ο διακόπτης	*o dhyakoptees*
Indicator	Το φλας	*to flas*
Inner tube	Η σαμπρέλλα	*ee sambrela*
Lights (front/ rear)	Τα φώτα (εμπρός/ πίσω)	*ta fota (embros/ peeso)*
Lock	Η κλειδαριά	*ee kleedharya*
Oil filter	Το φίλτρο λαδιού	*to feeltro ladhyoo*
Oil gauge	Ο δείκτης λαδιού	*o dheektees ladhyoo*

Pedal	Το πεντάλ	to *pedal*
Points	Οι πλατίνες	ee *plateenes*
Pump	Η τρόμπα	ee *tromba*
Radiator	Το ψυγείο	to *pseeyeeo*
Radiator hose (top/bottom)	Ο σωλήνας ψυγείου (επάνω/κάτω)	o *soleenas pseeyeeoo* (*epano*/*kato*)
Reverse gear	Το όπισθεν	to *opeesthen*
Reversing lights	Τα φώτα όπισθεν	ta *fota opeesthen*
Saddle	Η σέλλα	ee *sela*
Silencer	Ο σιγαστήρας	o *seegasteeras*
Spare wheel	Η ρεζέρβα	ee *rezerva*
Spark plugs	Τα μπουζιά	ta *boozya*
Speedometer	Το ταχύμετρο	to *takheemetro*
Spokes	Οι ακτίνες	ee *akteenes*
Starter motor	Η μίζα	ee *meeza*
Steering	Η διεύθυνση	ee *dhyeftheensee*
Steering wheel	Το τιμόνι	to *teemonee*
Transmission (automatic)	Η μετάδοση (αυτόματη)	ee *metadhose* (*aftomatee*)
Tyre (front/rear)	Το λάστιχο (μπροστινό/πισινό)	to *lasteekho* (*brosteeno*/*peeseeno*)
Valve	Η βαλβίδα	ee *valveedha*
Warning light	Τα φώτα προειδοποίησης	ta *fota proeedhopee-eesees*
Wheel (front/rear)	Ο τροχός (μπροστινός/πισινός)	o *trokhos* (*brosteenos*/*peeseenos*)
Window	Το παράθυρο	to *paratheero*
Windscreen	Το παρμπρίζ	to *parbreez*
Windscreen wiper	Ο γυαλοκαθαριστήρας	o *yalokathareesteeras*

TAXIS

- You can hail taxis in the street, or find them at a taxi rank. Taxis that are free have the sign **ΕΛΕΥΘΕΡΟ(Ν)**. Outside the cities, you may see the sign **ΑΓΟΡΑΙΟΝ**.

- In Athens sharing a taxi is a routine practice, so don't be afraid to hail one that's already got a passenger – and don't be surprised if the taxi you're in stops for someone else! The driver may ask you if it's okay, but it happens so commonly that he may not. If you get into a taxi that's already got a fare, make a note of the figure on the meter, so that you can check how much your own fare should be.

- Taxis have meters, but it's a good idea to ask what the fare will be approximately, especially if you are going some distance. Extras for luggage, airport pick-ups, etc. may not be shown on the meter. Between midnight and 5.00 a.m., and outside the city limits, a double tariff is charged – the driver will switch his meter from '1' to '2'.

- Write down clearly the address of your destination if it's at all complicated so that you can show it to the taxi driver. In Greek, addresses are written with the street name first and the number afterwards, e.g. **Οδός Κόνωνος 4**.

You may want to say

(see also Directions, *page 30)*

Is there a taxi rank around here?
Εχει πιάτσα ταξί εδώ κοντά;
ekhee pyatsa taksee edho konda

I need a taxi
Θέλω ένα ταξί
thelo ena taksee

Can you order me a taxi please?
Μπορείτε να μου παραγγείλετε ένα ταξί παρακαλώ;
boreete na moo parangeelete ena taksee parakalo

For right now
Για τώρα
ya tora

For tomorrow at nine o'clock
Για αύριο στις εννέα η ώρα
ya avryo stees enea ee ora

To go to the airport
Να πάω στο αεροδρόμιο
na pao sto aerodhromyo

To the airport, please
Στό αεροδρόμιο παρακαλώ
sto aerodhromyo parakalo

To the station, please
Στο σταθμό παρακαλώ
sto stathmo parakalo

To the Grande Bretagne Hotel, please
Στο ξενοδοχείο Μεγάλη Βρετανία παρακαλώ
sto ksenodhokheeo megalee vretaneea parakalo

To this address, please
Σ'αυτή τη διεύθυνση παρακαλώ
saftee tee dhyeftheensee parakalo

It is far?
Είναι μακρυά;
eene makrya

How much will it cost?
Πόσο θα κοστίσει;
poso tha kosteesee

I am in a hurry
Βιάζομαι
vyazome

Stop here, please
Σταματήστε εδώ παρακαλώ
stamateeste edho parakalo

Can you wait (a few minutes), please?
Μπορείτε να περιμένετε (δύο λεπτά) παρακαλώ
boreete na pereemenete (dheeo lepta) parakalo

How much is it?
Πόσο κάνει;
poso kanee

There is a mistake
Λάθος έγινε
lathos eyeene

It's 700 drachmas on the
   meter
**Στό ταξίμετρο γράφει
   επτακόσιες δραχμές**
*sto takseemetro grafee
   eptakosyes dhrakhmes*

Keep the change
Κρατήστε τα ρέστα
krateeste ta resta

That's all right
Εντάξει
endaksee

Can you give me a receipt?
**Μπορείτε να μου δώσετε μια
   απόδειξη παρακαλώ**
*boreete na moo dhosete mya
   apodheeksee parakalo*

For 1000 drachmas
Για χίλιες δραχμές
ya kheelyes dhrakhmes

You may hear

**Είναι δέκα χιλιόμετρα
   από'δώ**
*eene dheka kheelyometra
   apodho*
It's ten kilometres away

**Θα κοστίσει περίπου δύο
   χιλιάδες δραχμές**
*tha kosteesee pereepoo
   dheeo kheelyadhes
   drakhmes*
It will cost approximately
   2000 drachmas

**(Είναι) χίλιες οκτακόσιες
   δραχμές**
*(eene) kheelyes oktakosyes
   dhrakhmes*
(It's) 1800 drachmas

Είναι . . . επιπλέον
eene . . . epeepleon
There is a supplement
   of . . .

Για τίς βαλίτσες
ya tees valeetses
For the luggage

Για κάθε βαλίτσα
ya kathe valeetsa
For each suitcase

Για το αεροδρόμιο
ya to aerodhromyo
For the airport

AIR TRAVEL

● In addition to Athens and Thessalonica, there are airports at many of the major tourist centres. All are served by Olympic Airways domestic flights, and many also by international flights.

● At airports and airlines offices, you'll generally find someone who speaks some English, but be prepared to say a few things in Greek.

● The Athens airport has two sets of services: the West Airport – το δυτικό αεροδρόμιο (*to dheeteeko aerodhromyo*) – serves Olympic Airways flights only (both international and domestic), and the East Airport – το ανατολικό αεροδρόμιο (*to anatoleeko aerodhromyo*) – serves all other airlines. To get from one to the other, it is best to take a taxi.

● Buses connect both sets of services to the centre of Athens, and it is usually quite easy to find a taxi.

● Most internal flights go via Athens. The capital is more or less in the centre of the country, so flights from there in any direction take 35–45 minutes.

● Distances from main airports to city centres:

Athens – 10 km (6 miles)
Heraklion – 5 km (3 miles)
Thessalonica – 16 km (10 miles)

You may see

ΑΕΡΟΔΡΟΜΙΟ(Ν)	Airport
Αεροδρόμιο(ν)	
ΑΕΡΟΛΙΜΕΝΑΣ	Airport
Αερολιμένας	
ΑΛΛΑ ΔΙΑΒΑΤΗΡΙΑ	Other passports
Άλλα διαβατήρια	
ΑΝΑΧΩΡΗΣΕΙΣ	Departures
Αναχωρήσεις	
ΑΠΑΓΟΡΕΥΕΤΑΙ ΤΟ	No smoking
ΚΑΠΝΙΣΜΑ	
Απαγορεύεται το κάπνισμα	
ΑΠΕΡΓΙΑ	Strike
Απεργία	
ΑΦΙΞΕΙΣ	Arrivals
Αφίξεις	
ΑΦΟΡΟΛΟΓΗΤΑ ΕΙΔΗ	Duty-free shop
Αφορολόγητα είδη	
ΕΙΔΗ ΠΡΟΣ ΔΗΛΩΣΗ	Goods to declare
Είδη προς δήλωση	
ΕΙΣΟΔΟΣ	Entrance
Είσοδος	
ΕΛΕΓΧΟΣ ΔΙΑΒΑΤΗΡΙΩΝ	Passport control
Έλεγχος διαβατηρίων	
ΕΛΕΓΧΟΣ ΕΙΣΙΤΗΡΙΩΝ	Check-in
Έλεγχος εισιτηρίων	
ΕΝΟΙΚΙΑΖΟΝΤΑΙ	Car hire
ΑΥΤΟΚΙΝΗΤΑ	
Ενοικιάζονται αυτοκίνητα	
ΕΝΟΙΚΙΑΣΕΙΣ	Car hire
ΑΥΤΟΚΙΝΗΤΩΝ	
Ενοικιάσεις αυτοκινήτων	

ΕΞΟΔΟΣ Έξοδος	Gate
ΕΞΟΔΟΣ (ΚΙΝΔΥΝΟΥ) Έξοδος (κινδύνου)	(Emergency) exit
ΕΟΚ	EEC
ΕΠΙΒΑΤΕΣ Επιβάτες	Passengers
ΕΠΙΒΙΒΑΣΗ Επιβίβαση	Boarding
ΚΑΘΥΣΤΕΡΗΣΗ Καθυστέρηση	Delay
ΛΕΩΦΟΡΕΙΑ (ΠΡΟΣ ΚΕΝΤΡΟ ΠΟΛΕΩΣ) Λεωφορεία (προς κέντρο πόλεως)	Buses (to the town/city centre)
ΜΗ ΚΑΠΝΙΖΕΤΕ Μη καπνίζετε	No smoking
ΟΥΔΕΝ ΠΡΟΣ ΔΗΛΩΣΗ Ουδέν προς δήλωση	Nothing to declare
ΠΑΡΑΛΑΒΗ ΑΠΟΣΚΕΥΩΝ Παραλαβή αποσκευών	Luggage reclaim
ΠΛΗΡΟΦΟΡΙΕΣ Πληροφορίες	Information
ΠΡΟΣΔΕΘΗΤΕ Προσδεθήτε	Fasten seatbelts
ΠΡΟΣΔΕΝΕΣΤΕ Προσδένεστε	Fasten seatbelts
ΠΤΗΣΗ Πτήση	Flight
ΣΥΝΑΛΛΑΓΜΑ Συνάλλαγμα	Bureau de change
ΤΑΞΙ Ταξί	Taxis

ΤΕΛΩΝΕΙΟ(Ν) Τελωνείο(ν)	Customs
ΤΟΠΙΚΗ ΩΡΑ Τοπική ώρα	Local time
ΤΟΥΑΛΕΤΕΣ Τουαλέτες	Toilets

You may want to say

(see also Numbers, page 236; Days, months, dates, page 209)

Is there a flight (from Athens) to Santorini?
Υπάρχει πτήση (από την Αθήνα) για τη Σαντορίνη;
eeparkhee pteesee (apo teen atheena) ya tee sandoreenee

Today
Σήμερα
seemera

This morning/afternoon
Σήμερα το πρωί/το απόγευμα
seemera to proee/to apoyevma

Tomorrow (morning/afternoon)
Αύριο (το πρωί/το απόγευμα)
avryo (to proee/to apoyevma)

Do you have a timetable of flights to Thessalonica?
Μήπως έχετε δρομολόγιο πτήσεων για τη Θεσσαλονίκη;
meepos ekhete dhromoloyo pteeseon ya tee thesaloneekee

What time is the first flight to Thessalonica?
Τι ώρα φεύγει η πρώτη πτήση για τη Θεσσαλονίκη;
tee ora fevyee ee protee pteesee ya tee thesaloneekee

The next flight
Η επόμενη πτήση
ee epomenee pteesee

The last flight
Η τελευταία πτήση
ee teleftea pteesee

What time does it arrive (at
Thessalonica)?
**Τι ώρα φτάνει (στη
Θεσσαλονίκη);**
*tee ora ftanee (stee
thesaloneekee)*

One (ticket)/Two (tickets)
to Heraklion, please
**Ενα (εισιτήριο)/Δύο
(εισιτήρια) για το
Ηράκλειο παρακαλώ**
*ena (eeseeteeryo)/dheeo
(eeseeteerya) ya to
eeraklyo parakalo*

Single
Απλό
aplo

Return
Με επιστροφή
me epeestrofee

1st class/Business class
**Πρώτη θέση/Διακεκριμένη
θέση**
*protee thesee/dhyakekreemenee
thesee*

Tourist class
Τουριστική θέση
tooreesteekee thesee

For the eleven o'clock flight
Για τη πτήση των έντεκα
ya tee pteesee ton endeka

I want to change/cancel my
reservation
**Θέλω να αλλάξω/να
καταργήσω την κράτησή
μου**
*thelo na alakso/na
kataryeeso teen-grateesee-
moo*

What is the number of the
flight?
Τι είναι ο αριθμός πτήσεως;
*tee eene o areethmos
pteeseos*

What time do I have to be
at the airport?
**Τι ώρα πρέπει να είμαι στο
αεροδρόμιο;**
*tee ora prepee na eeme sto
aerodhromyo*

Which gate is it?
Ποια έξοδος;
pya eksodhos

Is there a delay?
Εχει καθυστέρηση;
ekhee katheestereesee

Where is the luggage from
the flight from London?
**Πού είναι οι αποσκευές
από τη πτήση από το
Λονδίνο;**
*poo eene ee aposkeves apo
tee pteesee apo to
londheeno*

My luggage is not here
**Οι αποσκευές μου δεν
είναι εδώ**
*ee aposkeves-moo dhen
eene edho*

Is there a bus to the centre
of town?
**Έχει λεωφορείο για το
κέντρο της πόλης;**
*ekhee leoforeeo ya to
kendro tees polees*

You may hear

Θέλετε παράθυρο;
thelete paratheero
Do you want a window
seat?

Θέλετε διάδρομο;
thelete dhyadhromo
Do you want an aisle seat?

Καπνίζετε;
kapneezete
Do you smoke?

**Η επιβίβαση θα
αρχίσει στις . . .** (*time*)
*ee epeeveevasee tha
arkheesee stees . . .*
Boarding will begin at . . .
(*time*)

Έξοδος αριθμός επτά
eksodhos areethmos epta
Gate number seven

**Το εισιτήριό σας
παρακαλώ**
to eeseeteeryo-sas parakalo
Your ticket, please

**Το διαβατήριό σας
παρακαλώ**
*to dhyavateeryo-sas
parakalo*
Your passport, please

**Την κάρτα επιβιβάσεως
παρακαλώ**
*teen-garta epeeveevaseos
parakalo*
Your boarding card, please

**Πώς είναι οι αποσκευές
σας;**
pos eene ee aposkeves-sas
What does your luggage
look like?

Έχετε το απόκομμα;
ekhete to apokoma
Do you have the reclaim
tag?

Announcements you may hear over the airport public address system

Words to listen for include:

Επιβάτες
epeevates
Passengers

Καθυστέρηση
katheestereesee
Delay

(Αμεση) επιβίβαση
(amesee) epeeveevasee
Boarding (now)

Της πτήσεως
tees pteeseos
Flight

Εξοδο
eksodho
Gate

Τελευταία αγγελία
teleftea angeleea
Last call

TRAVELLING BY TRAIN

• The Greek railway company is called ΟΣΕ (*ose*). The railways in Greece do not play a major role in public transport, apart from the Athens–Thessalonica line. This runs from one of the two stations in Athens, still known locally as **Σταθμός Λαρίσσης** (*stathmos lareesees*), though it is officially now called **Σταθμός Αθηνών** (*stathmos atheenon*).

The other station is **Σταθμός Πελοποννήσου** (*stathmos peloponeesoo*). This is the origin of a narrow-gauge line serving the Peloponnese. It is a convenient and very attractive way of travelling to the centres in the Peloponnese.

• It is a good idea to buy tickets in advance to secure a seat.

• There are buffets and restaurant cars on the main routes.

• First-class tickets are available for a 50% supplement, and there is a 20% discount on return tickets. For tourists there is a Greek Tourist Card, available for periods of 10, 20 and 30 days, and for use by up to five people.

You may see

ΑΙΘΟΥΣΑ ΑΝΑΜΟΝΗΣ Αίθουσα αναμονής	Waiting room
ΑΝΑΧΩΡΗΣΕΙΣ Αναχωρήσεις	Departures

ΑΠΑΓΟΡΕΥΕΤΑΙ Η ΔΙΕΛΕΥΣΙΣ ΤΩΝ ΓΡΑΜΜΩΝ	It is forbidden to cross the lines
Απαγορεύεται η διεύλευσις των γραμμών	
ΑΠΕΡΓΙΑ	Strike
Απεργία	
ΑΠΟΒΑΘΡΑ	Platform
Αποβάθρα	
ΑΠΟΣΚΕΥΑΙ	Baggage
Αποσκευαί	
ΑΦΙΞΕΙΣ	Arrivals
Αφίξεις	
ΒΑΓΚΟΝ-ΛΙ	Sleeping-car
Βαγκόν-λι	
ΓΡΑΜΜΗ	Line
Γραμμή	
ΓΡΑΦΕΙΟ(Ν) ΑΠΟΛΕΣΘΕΝΤΩΝ	Lost property office
Γραφείο(ν) απολεσθέντων	
ΔΡΟΜΟΛΟΓΙΑ ΑΜΑΞΟΣΤΟΙΧΙΩΝ	Train timetables
Δρομολόγια αμαξοστοιχιών	
ΔΡΟΜΟΛΟΓΙΑ ΤΡΑΙΝΩΝ	Train timetables
Δρομολόγια τραίνων	
ΕΙΣΙΤΗΡΙΑ	Tickets
Εισιτήρια	
ΕΙΣΟΔΟΣ	Entrance
Είσοδος	
ΕΚΔΟΤΗΡΙΟ(Ν) ΕΙΣΙΤΗΡΙΩΝ	Ticket office
Εκδοτήριο(ν) εισιτηρίων	

ΕΞΟΔΟΣ	Exit
Εξοδος	
ΕΡΓΑΣΙΜΕΣ ΜΕΡΕΣ	Mondays to Saturdays
Εργάσιμες μέρες	
ΚΑΘΗΜΕΡΙΝΑ	Daily
Καθημερινά	
ΚΑΘΥΣΤΕΡΗΣΗ	Delay
Καθυστέρηση	
ΚΟΥΚΕΤΤΕΣ	Couchettes
Κουκέττες	
ΚΡΑΤΗΣΕΙΣ	Reservations
Κρατήσεις	
ΚΥΛΙΚΕΙΟ(Ν)	Buffet
Κυλικείο(ν)	
ΚΥΡΙΑΚΕΣ ΚΑΙ ΑΡΓΙΕΣ	Sundays and holidays
Κυριακές και αργίες	
ΜΗ ΣΚΥΒΕΤΕ ΕΞΩ (ΑΠΟ ΤΟ ΠΑΡΑΘΥΡΟ)	Do not lean out (of the window)
Μη σκύβετε έξω (από το παράθυρο)	
ΟΣΕ	Greek railways
ΠΛΗΡΟΦΟΡΙΕΣ	Information
Πληροφορίες	
ΠΡΟΟΡΙΣΜΟΣ	Destination
Προορισμός	
ΠΡΟΣ ΑΠΟΒΑΘΡΕΣ	To the platforms
Προς αποβάθρες	
ΠΡΟΣ ΔΕΥΤΕΡΑΝ ΑΠΟΒΑΘΡΑΝ	To platform two
Προς δευτέραν αποβάθραν	
ΣΤΑΘΜΑΡΧΗΣ	Station-master
Σταθμάρχης	
ΣΥΝΑΓΕΡΜΟΣ	Alarm
Συναγερμός	

ΤΟΥΑΛΕΤΕΣ
Τουαλέτες

Toilets

ΦΥΛΑΞΗ ΑΠΟΣΚΕΥΩΝ
Φύλαξη αποσκευών

Left luggage

You may want to say

Information

(*see* Time, *page 213*)

Is there a train to Thessalonica?
Έχει τραίνο για τη Θεσσαλονίκη;
ekhee treno ya tee thesaloneekee

Do you have a timetable of trains to Kalamata?
Μήπως έχετε δρομολόγιο των τραίνων για την Καλαμάτα;
meepos ekhete dhromoloyo ton trenon ya teen-galamata

What time . . . ?
Τι ώρα . . . ;
tee ora . . .

What time is the train to Argos?
Τι ώρα φεύγει το τραίνο για το Άργος;
tee ora fevyee to treno ya to argos

What time is the first train to Lamia?
Τι ώρα φεύγει το πρώτο τραίνο για τη Λαμία;
tee ora fevyee to proto treno ya tee lameea

The next train
Το επόμενο τραίνο
to epomeno treno

The last train
Το τελευταίο τραίνο
to telefteo treno

What time does it arrive (at Lamia)?
Τι ώρα φτάνει (στη Λαμία);
tee ora ftanee (stee lameea)

What time does the train from Larisa arrive?
Τι ώρα φτάνει το τραίνο από τη Λάρισα;
tee ora ftanee to treno apo tee lareesa

The train to Patras, please?
Το τραίνο για την Πάτρα παρακαλώ
to treno ya teem-batra parakalo

Which platform does the train to Thessalonica leave from?
Από ποια αποβάθρα φεύγει το τραίνο για τη Θεσσαλονίκη;
apo pya apovathra fevyee to treno ya tee thesaloneekee

Does this train go to Kalamata?
Στην Καλαμάτα πάει αυτό το τραίνο;
steen-galamata paee afto to treno

Do we have to change trains?
Πρέπει να αλλάξουμε τραίνο;
prepee na alaksoome treno

Where?
Πού;
poo

Tickets

(*see* Time, *page 213*; Numbers, *page 236*)

One/Four to Thessalonica, please
Ενα/Τέσσερα για τη Θεσσαλονίκη παρακαλώ
ena/tesera ya tee thesaloneekee parakalo

One ticket/Two tickets to Lamia, please
Ενα εισιτήριο/Δύο εισιτήρια για τη Λαμία παρακαλώ
ena eeseeteeryo/dheeo eeseeteerya ya tee lameea parakalo

Single
Απλό
aplo

Return
Με επιστροφή
me epeestrofee

For one adult/two adults
Για ένα ενήλικο/δύο ενήλικους
ya ena eneeleeko/dheeo eneeleekoos

(And) one child/two children
(Και) ένα παιδί/δύο παιδιά
(ke) ena pedhee/dheeo pedhya

First/Second class
Πρώτη/Δεύτερη θέση
protee/dhefteree thesee

For the ten o'clock train to Lamia
Για το τραίνο των δέκα για τη Λαμία
ya to treno ton dheka ya tee lameea

I want to reserve a seat/ two seats
Θέλω να κλείσω μια θέση/ δύο θέσεις
thelo na kleeso mya thesee/ dheeo thesees

I want to reserve a sleeper
Θέλω να κλείσω ένα βαγκόν-λι
thelo na kleeso ena vagon-lee

I want to reserve a couchette
Θέλω να κλείσω μια κουκέττα
thelo na kleeso mya kooketa

Can I take my bicycle on the train?
Μπορώ να πάρω το ποδήλατό μου στο τραίνο;
boro na paro to podheelato-moo sto treno

How much is it?
Πόσο κάνει;
poso kanee

Is there a supplement?
Υπάρχει επιβάρυνση;
eeparkhee epeevareensee

Left luggage

Can I leave this?
Μπορώ να αφήσω αυτό;
boro na afeeso afto

Can I leave these two suitcases?
Μπορώ να αφήσω αυτές τις δύο βαλίτσες;
boro na afeeso aftes tees dheeo valeetses

Until three o'clock
Μέχρι τις τρεις
mekhree tees trees

What time do you close?
Τι ώρα κλείνετε;
tee ora kleenete

How much is it?
Πόσο κάνει;
poso kanee

On the train

I have reserved a seat
Εχω κλείσει μια θέση
ekho kleesee mya thesee

I have reserved a sleeper/
couchette
**Εχω κλείσει ένα βαγκόν-λι/
μια κουκέττα**
*ekho kleesee ena vagon-lee/
mya kooketa*

Is this seat taken?
**Είναι πιασμένη η θέση
αυτή;**
*eene pyazmenee ee thesee
aftee*

Excuse me, may I get by?
Συγγνώμη, μπορώ να περάσω;
seegnomee boro na peraso

Where is the restaurant
car?
Πού είναι το εστιατόριο;
poo eene to estyatoryo

Where is the sleeping-car?
Πού είναι το βαγκόν-λι
poo eene to vagon-lee

Do you mind if I open the
window?
**Επιτρέπεται να ανοίξω το
παράθυρο;**
*epeetrepete na aneekso to
paratheero*

Do you mind if I smoke?
Επιτρέπεται να καπνίσω;
epeetrepete na kapneeso

Where are we?
Πού είμαστε;
poo eemaste

Are we at Lamia?
Είμαστε στη Λαμία;
eemaste stee lameea

How long does the train
stop here?
**Πόση ώρα σταματάει εδώ το
τραίνο;**
*posee ora stamataee edho to
treno*

Can you tell me when we
get to Larisa?
**Μπορείτε να μου πείτε
όταν φτάσουμε στη
Λάρισα;**
*boreete na moo peete otan
ftasoome stee lareesa*

You may hear

Information
(see Time, page 213)

Φεύγει στις δέκα και μισή
fevyee stees dheka ke meesee
It leaves at 10.30

Φτάνει στις τέσσερεις παρά
δέκα
*ftanee stees teserees para
dheka*
It arrives at ten to four

Πρέπει να αλλάξετε τραίνο
στην Αθήνα
*prepee na alaksete treno
steen atheena*
You have to change trains
at Athens

Είναι η αποβάθρα αριθμός
επτά
*eene ee apovathra areethmos
epta*
It's platform number seven

Tickets
(see Time, page 213;
  Numbers, page 236)

Για πότε θέλετε το εισιτήριο;
ya pote thelete to eeseeteeryo
When do you want the ticket
for?

Πότε θέλετε να ταξιδέψετε;
pote thelete na takseedhepsete
When do you want to travel?

Απλό ή με επιστροφή;
aplo ee me epeestrofee
Single or return?

Πότε θέλετε να επιστρέψετε;
pote thelete na epeestrepsete
When do you want to return?

Καπνίζετε;
kapneezete
Do you smoke?

Υπάρχει μόνο πρώτη θέση
eeparkhee mono protee thesee
There's only first class

(Είναι) δύο χιλιάδες
πεντακόσιες δραχμές
*(eene) dheeo kheelyadhes
pendakosyes dhrakhmes*
(It's) 2500 drachmas

Είναι χίλιες διακόσιες
δραχμές επιπλέον
*eene kheelyes dhyakosyes
drakhmes epeepleon*
There is a supplement of
1200 drachmas

BUSES, COACHES AND UNDERGROUND

● Long-distance buses are run by joint associations of bus owners called **ΚΤΕΛ** (*ktel*). They depart from two terminals on the outskirts of Athens which are served by local buses and, of course, by taxis. It is advisable to book in advance to ensure a (numbered) seat, and tickets must in any case be purchased before boarding. Bookings may be made at **ΚΤΕΛ** offices or at the terminals themselves.

● Most villages are served by buses originating from a local town, which often leave very early in the morning.

● In Athens there are electrically-powered trolley-buses as well as the usual urban buses. For both, you need to buy a ticket in advance. Tickets are available, usually in blocks of ten, at some kiosks (see pages 76 and 136) and at special selling points near stops in the city centre. When you get on the bus, or trolley, you push the ticket into a machine that cancels it. There are no conductors, and an inspector may board and want to see the cancelled ticket. If you intend to stay in Athens for a long time and travel a lot by bus and trolley, it may be worth buying a **κάρτα απεριορίστων διαδρομών** (*karta aperyoreeston dhyadhromon*) – a monthly season ticket that entitles you to unlimited travel. There is a fixed fare on buses and trolleys throughout Athens. Children under four travel free.

● There is also a single line of electrified railway running from **Κηφησιά** (*keefeesya*) in the north of Athens to Piraeus, and passing beneath the centre of the city. The central station is beneath Omonoia Square – **Πλατεία Ομόνοιας** (*plateea omonyas*). There is a flat fare, and tickets may be purchased from a machine or ticket office. Tickets have to be cancelled in a machine *before* you go on to the platform (there's a fine for failing to do this).

You may see

ΑΝΟΔΟΣ Ανοδος	Entrance
ΑΠΑΓΟΡΕΥΕΤΑΙ ΤΟ ΚΑΠΝΙΣΜΑ Απαγορεύεται το κάπνισμα	No smoking
ΑΦΕΤΗΡΙΑ Αφετηρία	Terminus
ΕΙΣΙΤΗΡΙΑ ΑΣΤΙΚΩΝ ΣΥΓΚΟΙΝΩΝΙΩΝ ΠΩΛΟΥΝΤΑΙ ΕΔΩ Εισιτήρια αστικών συγκοινωνιών πωλούνται εδώ	Tickets for urban transport sold here
ΕΙΣΟΔΟΣ ΑΠΟ ΤΗΝ ΜΠΡΟΣΤΙΝΗ ΠΟΡΤΑ Είσοδος από την μπροστινή πόρτα	Enter by the front door
ΕΞΟΔΟΣ ΑΠΟ ΤΗΝ ΜΕΣΑΙΑ ΠΟΡΤΑ Εξοδος από την μεσαία πόρτα	Exit by the centre door
ΕΞΟΔΟΣ (ΚΙΝΔΥΝΟΥ) Εξοδος (κινδύνου)	(Emergency) exit

ΗΛΕΚΤΡΙΚΟΣ ΣΙΔΗΡΟΔΡΟΜΟΣ Ηλεκτρικός Σιδηρόδρομος	Electric railway
ΜΗΝ ΟΜΙΛΕΙΤΕ ΣΤΟΝ ΟΔΗΓΟ Μην ομιλείτε στον οδηγό	Do not talk to the driver
ΠΟΥΛΜΑΝ Πούλμαν	Coach
ΣΤΑΘΜΟΣ ΛΕΩΦΟΡΕΙΩΝ Σταθμός λεωφορείων	Bus station
ΣΤΑΣΗ ΛΕΩΦΟΡΕΙΟΥ Στάση λεωφορείου	Bus stop
ΣΤΑΣΗ ΤΡΟΛΛΕΥ Στάση τρόλλεϋ	Trolley stop
ΤΡΟΧΙΑ Ι Τροχιά Ι	Line I
ΥΠΕΡΑΣΤΙΚΟ ΛΕΩΦΟΡΕΙΟ Υπεραστικό λεωφορείο	Long-distance coach

You may want to say

Information

(*for sightseeing bus tours, see* Sightseeing, *page 156*)

Where is the bus stop?
**Πού είναι η στάση
    λεωφορείου;**
*poo eene ee stasee
    leoforeeoo*

Where is the trolley stop?
**Πού είναι η στάση του
    τρόλλεϋ;**
*poo eene ee stasee too
    trole-ee*

Where is the bus station?
Πού είναι ο σταθμός λεωφορείων;
poo eene o stathmos leoforeeon

Is there an underground station around here?
Έχει σταθμό για τον ηλεκτρικό εδώ κοντά;
ekhee stathmo ya ton eelektreeko edho konda

Do you have a map of the underground?
Μήπως έχετε χάρτη του ηλεκτρικού;
meepos ekhete khartee too eelektreekoo

Is there a bus to the beach?
Έχει λεωφορείο για τη πλαζ;
ekhee leoforeeo ya tee plaz

What (number) bus goes to the station?
Ποιο λεωφορείο πάει στο σταθμό;
pyo leoforeeo paee sto stathmo

Do they go often?
Φεύγουν συχνά;
fevgoon seekhna

What time is the bus to Sounion?
Τι ώρα φεύγει το λεωφορείο για το Σούνιο;
tee ora fevyee to leoforeeo ya to soonyo

What time is the first bus to Nafplion?
Τι ώρα φεύγει το πρώτο λεωφορείο για το Ναύπλιο;
tee ora fevyee to proto leoforeeo ya to nafplyo

The next bus
Το επόμενο λεωφορείο
to epomeno leoforeeo

The last bus
Το τελευταίο λεωφορείο
to telefteo leoforeeo

What time does it arrive?
Τι ώρα φτάνει
tee ora ftanee

Where can I buy tickets?
Πού μπορώ να αγοράσω εισιτήρια;
poo boro na agoraso eeseeteerya

Can I book a seat?
Μπορώ να κρατήσω θέση
boro na krateeso thesee

Where does the bus to the
town centre leave from?
Από πού φεύγει το
λεωφορείο για το κέντρο;
*apo poo fevyee to
leoforeeo ya to kendro*

Does the bus to the airport
leave from here?
Από'δώ φεύγει το λεωφορείο
για το αεροδρόμιο;
*apodho fevyee to leoforeeo
ya to aerodhromyo*

Does this go to Larisa?
Στη Λάρισα πάει αυτό;
stee lareesa paee afto

Which stop do I get off at
for Plaka?
Ποια στάση πρέπει να
κατέβω για την Πλάκα;
*pya stasee prepee na
katevo ya teem-blaka*

Does this train go to
Kifisia?
Στην Κηφησιά πάει αυτό το
τραίνο;
*steen-geefeesya paee afto to
treno*

Where are we?
Πού είμαστε;
poo eemaste

I want to get off at the
Archaeological Museum
Θέλω να κατέβω στο
Αρχαιολογικό Μουσείο
*thelo na katevo sto
arkheoloyeeko mooseeo*

Where should I get off?
Πού πρέπει να κατέβω;
poo prepee na katevo

Is this the right stop for the
Acropolis?
Αυτή είναι η στάση για
την Ακρόπολη;
*aftee eene ee stasee ya
teen akropolee*

The next stop, please
Την άλλη στάση παρακαλώ
teen alee stasee parakalo

Can you open the door,
please?
Ανοίξτε παρακαλώ
aneekste parakalo

Excuse me, may I get by?
Συγγνώμη, μπορώ να περάσω;
seegnomee boro na peraso

Tickets

One/Two to the centre,
    please
Eνα/Δύο για το κέντρο
    παρακαλώ
ena/dheeo ya to kendro
    parakalo

A block of (ten) tickets,
    please
Μια δεσμίδα εισιτήρια
    παρακαλώ
mya dhesmeedha eeseeteerya
    parakalo

How much is it?
Πόσο κάνει;
poso kanee

You may hear

Το λεωφορείο για το κέντρο φεύγει από τη στάση εκεί πέρα
to leoforeeo ya to kendro fevyee apo tee stasee ekee pera
The bus to the centre leaves from that stop there

Το πενήντα επτά πάει στο σταθμό
to peneenda epta paee sto stathmo
The 57 goes to the station

Φεύγουν κάθε δέκα λεπτά
fevgoon kathe dheka lepta
They go every ten minutes

Φεύγει στις δέκα και μισή
fevyee stees dheka ke meesee
It leaves at half past ten

Φτάνει στις τρεις και είκοσι
ftanee stees trees ke eekosee
It arrives at twenty past three

Μπορείτε να αγοράσετε εισιτήρια στα περίπτερα
boreete na agorasete eeseeteerya sta pereeptera
You can buy tickets at the kiosks

Θα κατεβείτε εδώ;
tha kateveete edho
Are you getting off here?

Είναι η επόμενη στάση
eene ee epomenee stasee
It's the next stop

Πρέπει να κατεβείτε στην άλλη στάση
prepee na kateveete steen alee stasee
You have to get off at the next stop

Έπρεπε να κατεβείτε στην προηγούμενη στάση
eprepe na kateveete steem-broeegoomenee stasee
You should have got off one stop before

BOATS AND FERRIES

● Frequent boat services operate between Piraeus, the port of Athens, or Rafina on the east coast of Attiki, and most of the islands and coastal towns. There are also other points of origin for boats, such as Thessalonica, Patras, Crete and so on. Hydrofoil services also run from Piraeus to some islands. Boats serving the more distant destinations stop in at other ports of call *en route*, so that it's also possible to travel between certain islands, as well as direct from the mainland.

● Information about departure times can be found in the tourist organisations, the daily press and, of course, the ticket offices. Information should always be checked on the day of departure.

● Tickets can be purchased in Piraeus, or from travel agents and agencies for the ferry boats in central Athens; in smaller ports, tickets are usually sold by the local agent for the boat. Many agencies deal only with tickets for one particular boat, or for a number of boats. It is advisable to find out about which boats are available from some independent source, such as the tourist office or the press.

● There are four classes of travel – first, second, third and deck: πρώτη (*protee*), δεύτερη (*dhefteree*), τρίτη (*treetee*) and κατάστρωμα (*katastroma*). Not all classes are always available. Cabins can usually be had in first and second class, but should be booked in advance.

● Car ferries: on long distance trips, cars should be booked well in advance, especially in the summer. For short crossings, booking is not required.

● There are also organised cruises visiting groups of islands.

You may see

ΑΠΟΒΑΘΡΑ Αποβάθρα	Pier, Quay
ΓΥΡΟΣ ΤΟΥ ΛΙΜΑΝΙΟΥ Γύρος του λιμανιού	Trips round the bay
ΕΚΔΡΟΜΕΣ Εκδρομές	Excursions
ΙΠΤΑΜΕΝΑ ΔΕΛΦΙΝΙΑ Ιπτάμενα δελφίνια	Hydrofoil, Hovercraft
ΚΑΜΠΙΝΕΣ Καμπίνες	Cabins
ΚΑΡΑΒΙΑ Καράβια	Boats
ΚΡΟΥΑΖΙΕΡΕΣ Κρουαζιέρες	Cruises
ΛΙΜΑΝΙ Λιμάνι	Port, Harbour
ΝΑΥΑΓΟΣΩΣΤΙΚΗ ΛΕΜΒΟΣ Ναυαγοσωστική λέμβος	Lifeboat
ΟΝΟΜΑ ΠΛΟΙΟΥ Ονομα πλοίου	Name of boat
ΠΛΟΙΑ Πλοία	Boats
ΠΟΡΘΜΕΙΟ(Ν) Πορθμείο(ν)	Ferry
ΠΡΟΚΥΜΑΙΑ Προκυμαία	Quay
ΠΡΟΟΡΙΣΜΟΣ Προορισμός	Destination
ΣΩΣΙΒΙΟ(Ν) Σωσίβιο(ν)	Lifebelt, Lifejacket

ΦΕΡΡΥ ΜΠΟΤ
Φέρρυ μποτ
ΩΡΑ ΑΝΑΧΩΡΗΣΕΩΣ
Ωρα αναχωρήσεως

Car ferry

Time of departure

You may want to say

Information

(*see* Time, *page 213*)

Is there a boat to Egina (today)?
Έχει καράβι για την Αίγινα (σήμερα);
ekhee karavee ya teen eyeena (seemera)

Is there a car ferry to Milos?
Υπάρχει φέρρυ μποτ για τη Μήλο;
eeparkhee feree-bot ya tee meelo

Are there any boat trips?
Υπάρχουν κρουαζιέρες;
eeparkhoon krooazyeres

What time is the boat to . . .
Τι ώρα φεύγει το καράβι για . . .
tee ora fevyee to karavee ya . . .

What time is the first boat?
Τι ώρα φεύγει το πρώτο καράβι;
tee ora fevyee to proto karavee

The next boat
Το επόμενο καράβι
to epomeno karavee

The last boat
Το τελευταίο καράβι
to telefteo karavee

What time does it arrive?
Τι ώρα φτάνει;
tee ora ftanee

What time does it return?
Τι ώρα γυρίζει;
tee ora yeereezee

How long does the crossing take?
Πόση ώρα κάνει το ταξίδι;
posee ora kanee to takseedhee

Where does the boat to Crete leave from?
Από πού φεύγει το καράβι για την Κρήτη;
apo poo fevyee to karavee ya teen-greetee

Where can I buy tickets?
Από πού μπορώ να αγοράσω εισιτήρια;
apo poo boro na agoraso eeseeteerya

What is the sea like today?
Πώς είναι η θάλασσα σήμερα;
pos eene ee thalasa seemera

Tickets

(*see* Numbers, *page 236*)

Four tickets to Santorini, please
Τέσσερα εισιτήρια για τη Σαντορίνη παρακαλώ
tesera eeseeteerya ya tee sandoreenee parakalo

Two and two children
Δύο και δύο παιδιά
dheeo ke dheeo pedhya

Single
Απλό
aplo

Return
Με επιστροφή
me epeestrofee

I want to book tickets for the ferry to Egina
Θέλω να κλείσω εισιτήρια για το φέρρυ μποτ για την Αίγινα
thelo na kleeso eeseeteerya ya to feree-bot ya teen eyeena

For a car and two passengers
Για ένα αυτοκίνητο και δύο επιβάτες
ya ena aftokeeneeto ke dheeo epeevates

First/Second/Third class
Πρώτη/Δεύτερη/Τρίτη θέση
protee/dhefteree/treetee thesee

Deck class
Κατάστρωμα
katastroma

I want to book a cabin
Θέλω να κρατήσω καμπίνα
thelo na krateeso kabeena

For one person
Για ένα άτομο
ya ena atomo

For two people
Για δύο άτομα
ya dheeo atoma

How much is it?
Πόσο κάνει;
poso kanee

On board

I have reserved a (two-berth) cabin
Έχω κλείσει (δίκλινη) καμπίνα
ekho kleesee (dheekleenee) kabeena

Where are the cabins?
Πού είναι οι καμπίνες;
poo eene ee kabeenes

Where is cabin number 20?
Πού είναι η καμπίνα αριθμός είκοσι;
poo eene ee kabeena areethmos eekosee

Can I go out on deck?
Μπορώ να βγω στο κατάστρωμα;
boro na vgo sto katastroma

You may hear

Έχει καράβι/πλοίο καθε Τρίτη και Παρασκευή
ekhee karavee/pleeo kathe treetee ke paraskevee
There are boats on Tuesdays and Fridays

Το καράβι/πλοίο για την Κρήτη φεύγει στις εννέα
to karavee/pleeo ya teen-greetee fevyee stees enea
The boat to Crete leaves at nine o'clock

Φτάνει στις έξι το πρωί
ftanee stees eksee to proee
It arrives at six in the morning

Γυρίζει στις τεσσερεισήμιση
yeereezee stees tesereeseemeesee
It returns at half past four

Το καράβι/πλοίο για την Κέα φεύγει από τη Ραφήνα
to karavee/pleeo ya teen-gea fevyee apo tee rafeena
The boat to Kea leaves from Rafina

Έχει μπουνάτσα
ekhee boonatsa
The sea is calm

Έχει φουρτούνα
ekhee foortoona
The sea is rough

AT THE TOURIST OFFICE

● The National Tourist Organisation of Greece – **EOT** (*eot*) – has offices in several towns. In Athens it is inside the branch of the National Bank of Greece in Syndagma Square – **Πλατεία Συντάγματος** (*plateea seendagmatos*) or just **Σύνταγμα** (*seendagma*).

These offices have leaflets about sights worth seeing, lists of hotels, plans and maps, and information about opening times and local transport.

● You can make a hotel booking through the main branch in Athens and through some of the other branches.

● In some places there are special tourist police offices to assist visitors, or a member of the police force may be available at a special desk at the police station. The telephone number for the tourist police is 171.

You may want to say

Where is the tourist office?
Πού είναι το τουριστικό γραφείο;
poo eene to tooreesteeko grafeeo

Where is the tourist police?
Πού είναι η τουριστική αστυνομία
poo eene ee tooreesteekee asteenomeea

The tourism section, please (*at the police station*)
Το τμήμα τουρισμού παρακαλώ
to tmeema tooreezmoo parakalo

Do you speak English?
Μιλάτε Αγγλικά;
meelate angleeka

Do you have . . . ?
Μήπως έχετε . . . ;
meepos ekhete . . .

Do you have a plan of the town?
Μήπως έχετε ένα χάρτη της πόλης;
meepos ekhete ena khartee tees polees

Do you have a map of the island?
Μήπως έχετε ένα χάρτη του νησιού;
meepos ekhete ena khartee too neesyoo

Do you have a list of hotels?
Μήπως έχετε μια λίστα με ξενοδοχεία;
meepos ekhete mya leesta me ksenodhokheea

Do you have a list of campsites?
Μήπως έχετε μια λίστα με κάμπιγκ;
meepos ekhete mya leesta me kampeeng

Can you recommend a cheap hotel?
Μπορείτε να συστήσετε ένα φτηνό ξενοδοχείο;
boreete na seesteesete ena fteeno ksenodhokheeo

Can you book a hotel for me, please?
Μπορείτε να μου κλείσετε ένα ξενοδοχείο παρακαλώ;
boreete na moo kleesete ena ksenodhokheeo parakalo

Can you recommend a good restaurant?
Μπορείτε να συστήσετε μια καλή ταβέρνα;
boreete na seesteesete mya kalee taverna

Where can I hire a car?
Πού μπορώ να νοικιάσω ένα αυτοκίνητο;
poo boro na neekyaso ena aftokeeneeto

What is there to see here?
Τι αξιοθέατα έχει εδώ;
tee aksyotheata ekhee edho

Do you have any leaflets?
Μήπως έχετε φυλλάδια;
meepos ekhete feeladhya

What information do you
have about . . . ?
**Τι πληροφορίες έχετε
για . . . ;**
*tee pleeroforee-es ekhete
ya . . .*

Where is the archaeological
museum?
**Πού είναι το αρχαιολογικό
μουσείο;**
*poo eene to arkheoloyeeko
mooseeo*

Can you show me on the
map?
**Μπορείτε να μου δείξετε
στο χάρτη;**
*boreete na moo dheeksete
sto khartee*

When is the museum open?
**Πότε είναι ανοικτό το
μουσείο;**
*pote eene aneekto to
mooseeo*

Are there any excursions?
Υπάρχουν εκδρομές;
eeparkhoon ekdhromes

You may hear

Μπορώ να σας βοηθήσω;
boro na sas voeetheeso
Can I help you?

Είσαστε Αγγλος/Αγγλίδα;
eesaste anglos/angleedha
Are you English?

Γερμανός/Γερμανίδα;
yermanos/yermaneedha
German?

Από πού είσαστε;
apo poo eesaste
Where are you from?

Ορίστε
oreeste
Here you are

Πόσο θα μείνετε εδώ;
poso tha meenete edho
How long are you going to
be here?

**Σε ποιο ξενοδοχείο
μένετε;**
*se pyo ksenodhokheeo
menete*
What hotel are you in?

Τι ξενοδοχείο θέλετε;
tee ksenodhokheeo thelete
What kind of hotel do you
want?

Είναι στην παλαιά πόλη
eene steem-balya polee
It's in the old part of town

ACCOMMODATION

• Hotels in Greece are classified as L (luxury) and category A, B, C, D or E. Those in L, A and B classes will normally have private bathrooms for at least some rooms, and often a restaurant.

In C class hotels, the situation varies. Many hotels do not have a restaurant. D and E class have basic facilities, and sometimes no hot water.

Charges for each category are fixed by the Greek government, and a list of the charges is usually displayed on the inside of the door to the room. The price charged is for the room; one person staying in a double room is usually charged 80% of the double price.

• There are also a number of motels for motorists, and bungalow-type hotels on the coast, in which the rooms take the form of individual 'bungalows'.

• When the hotels are full, it is common practice to find rooms in private houses. During the tourist season, boats are often met by people offering rooms; or information can be had at the local café or from the tourist police officer.

• Youth Hostel accommodation is to be found in Athens and a number of towns. It is open to any member of an organisation affiliated to the International Youth Hostels Federation.

• There are camping sites run by the National Tourist Organisation of Greece, and also a number of private campsites.

• When you book in somewhere you will usually be asked for your passport and to fill in a registration card.

Information requested on a registration card

ONOMA	First name
Ονομα	
ΕΠΩΝΥΜΟΝ	Surname
Επώνυμον	
ΔΙΕΥΘΥΝΣΙΣ/ΟΔΟΣ/	Address/Street/Number
ΑΡΙΘΜΟΣ	
Διεύθυνσις/Οδός/Αριθμός	
ΥΠΗΚΟΟΤΗΤΑ	Nationality
Υπηκοότητα	
ΕΠΑΓΓΕΛΜΑ	Occupation
Επάγγελμα	
ΤΟΠΟΣ ΓΕΝΝΗΣΕΩΣ	Place of birth
Τόπος γεννήσεως	
ΗΜΕΡΟΜΗΝΙΑ	Date of birth
ΓΕΝΝΗΣΕΩΣ	
Ημερομηνία γεννήσεως	
ΑΡΙΘΜΟΣ ΔΙΑΒΑΤΗΡΙΟΥ	Passport number
Αριθμός διαβατηρίου	
ΕΚΔΟΘΗΚΕ	Issued at
Εκδόθηκε	
ΗΜΕΡΟΜΗΝΙΑ	Date
Ημερομηνία	
ΥΠΟΓΡΑΦΗ	Signature
Υπογραφή	

You may see

ΑΙΘΟΥΣΑ ΤΗΛΕΟΡΑΣΕΩΣ Αίθουσα τηλεοράσεως	Television room
ΑΝΔΡΩΝ Ανδρών	Men (toilet)
ΑΝΕΛΚΥΣΤΗΡ Ανελκυστήρ	Lift
ΑΠΑΓΟΡΕΥΕΤΑΙ ΤΟ ΚΑΜΠΙΓΚ Απαγορεύεται το κάμπιγκ	No camping
ΑΠΑΓΟΡΕΥΟΝΤΑΙ ΤΑ ΤΡΟΧΟΣΠΙΤΑ Απαγορεύονται τα τροχόσπιτα	No caravans
ΓΚΑΡΑΖ Γκαράζ	Garage
ΓΥΝΑΙΚΩΝ Γυναικών	Women (toilet)
ΔΕΥΤΕΡΟΣ ΟΡΟΦΟΣ Δεύτερος όροφος	2nd floor
ΕΙΣΟΔΟΣ Είσοδος	Entrance
(ΕΝΟΙΚΙΑΖΟΝΤΑΙ) ΔΩΜΑΤΙΑ (Ενοικιάζονται) δωμάτια	Rooms (to rent)
ΕΞΟΔΟΣ (ΚΙΝΔΥΝΟΥ) Εξοδος (κινδύνου)	(Emergency) exit
ΕΣΤΙΑΤΟΡΙΟ(Ν) Εστιατόριο(ν)	Restaurant
ΗΜΙΔΙΑΤΡΟΦΗ Ημιδιατροφή	Half board
ΙΣΟΓΕΙΟ(Ν) Ισόγειο(ν)	Ground floor

ΚΑΜΠΙΓΚ Κάμπιγκ	Campsite
ΚΡΕΒΑΤΙΑ Κρεβάτια	Beds
ΛΟΥΤΡΟ Λουτρό	Bath(room)
ΜΗΝ ΑΝΑΒΕΤΕ ΦΩΤΙΕΣ Μην ανάβετε φωτιές	Do not light fires
ΜΗ ΡΙΧΝΕΤΕ ΣΚΟΥΠΙΔΙΑ Μη ρίχνετε σκουπίδια	Do not dump rubbish
ΜΟΤΕΛ Μοτέλ	Motel
ΜΠΑΓΚΑΛΑΟΥΣ Μπαγκαλάους	Bungalow hotel
ΝΤΕΜΙ-ΠΑΝΣΙΟΝ Ντεμί-πανσιόν	Half board
ΝΤΟΥΣ Ντους	Showers
ΞΕΝΟΔΟΧΕΙΟ(Ν) Ξενοδοχείο(ν)	Hotel
ΞΕΝΩΝΑΣ ΝΕΟΤΗΤΑΣ Ξενώνας νεότητας	Youth hostel
ΠΑΝΣΙΟΝ Πανσιόν	Hotel, Guest house
ΠΙΣΙΝΑ Πισίνα	Swimming pool
ΠΛΗΡΕΣ Πλήρες	Full up, No vacancies
ΠΛΗΡΗΣ ΔΙΑΤΡΟΦΗ Πλήρης διατροφή	Full board
ΠΛΥΝΤΗΡΙΟ(Ν) Πλυντήριο(ν)	Laundry

ΠΟΣΙΜΟ ΝΕΡΟ Πόσιμο νερό	Drinking water
ΠΡΩΤΟΣ ΟΡΟΦΟΣ Πρώτος όροφος	lst floor
ΡΕΣΕΨΙΟΝ Ρεσεψιόν	Reception
ΡΕΥΜΑ Ρεύμα	Electricity
ΣΑΛΟΝΙ Σαλόνι	Lounge
ΣΚΟΥΠΙΔΙΑ Σκουπίδια	Rubbish
ΤΑΡΙΦΑ Ταρίφα	Charge, Tariff
ΤΟΥΑΛΕΤΕΣ Τουαλέτες	Toilets
ΤΡΑΠΕΖΑΡΙΑ Τραπεζαρία	Dining-room
ΧΤΥΠΗΣΑΤΕ ΤΟ ΚΟΥΔΟΥΝΙ Χτυπήσατε το κουδούνι	Please ring the bell
ΥΠΗΡΕΣΙΑ ΔΩΜΑΤΙΩΝ Υπηρεσία δωματίων	Room service
ΥΠΟΓΕΙΟ(Ν) Υπόγειο(ν)	Basement
ΦΟΥΛ-ΠΑΝΣΙΟΝ Φουλ-πανσιόν	Full board

You may want to say

Booking in and out

I've reserved a room
Έχω κλείσει ένα δωμάτιο
ekho kleesee ena dhomatyo

I've reserved two rooms
Έχω κλείσει δύο δωμάτια
ekho kleesee dheeo dhomatya

I've reserved a place/space
Έχω κλείσει μια θέση
ekho kleesee mya thesee

My name is . . .
Με λένε . . .
me lene . . .

Do you have a room?
Μήπως έχετε δωμάτιο;
meepos ekhete dhomatyo

A single room
Ένα μονόκλινο
ena monokleeno

A double room
Ένα δίκλινο
ena dheekleeno

For one night
Για μία νύχτα
ya meea neekhta

For two nights
Για δύο νύχτες
ya dheeo neekhtes

With bath/shower
Με μπάνιο/ντους
me banyo/doos

Can I see the room?
Μπορώ να δω το δωμάτιο;
boro na dho to dhomatyo

Do you have space for a tent?
Μήπως έχετε θέση για σκηνή;
meepos ekhete thesee ya skeenee

Do you have space for a caravan?
Μήπως έχετε θέση για τροχόσπιτο;
meepos ekhete thesee ya trokhospeeto

How much is it?
Πόσο κάνει;
poso kanee

Per night
Τη νύχτα
tee neekhta

Per week
Την εβδομάδα
teen evdhomadha

Is there a reduction for children?
Εχει έκπτωση για παιδιά;
ekhee ekptosee ya pedhya

Is breakfast included?
Μαζί με το πρωινό;
mazee me to proeeno

It's too expensive
Είναι πολύ ακριβό
eene polee akreevo

Do you have anything cheaper?
Μήπως έχετε κάτι πιο φτηνό;
meepos ekhete katee pyo fteeno

Do you have anything bigger/smaller?
Μήπως έχετε κάτι μεγαλύτερο/μικρότερο;
meepos ekhete katee megaleetero/meekrotero

I'd like to stay another night
Θέλω να μείνω άλλη μία νύχτα
thelo na meeno alee meea neekhta

I am leaving tomorrow morning
Φεύγω αύριο το πρωί
fevgo avryo to proee

The bill, please
Το λογαριασμό παρακαλώ
to logaryazmo parakalo

Do you take credit cards?
Δέχεστε πιστωτικές κάρτες;
dhekheste peestoteekes kartes

Do you take traveller's cheques?
Δέχεστε τραβελερς τσεκ;
dhekheste travelers tsek

Can you recommend a hotel in Kalamata?
Μπορείτε να συστήσετε ένα ξενοδοχείο στην Καλαμάτα;
boreete na seesteesete ena ksenodhokheeo steen-galamata

Can you phone them to make a booking, please?
Μπορείτε να μου κλείσετε δωμάτιο τηλεφωνικώς, παρακαλώ;
boreete na moo kleesete dhomatyo teelefoneekos parakalo

In hotels

(see Problems and complaints, *page 187*; Time, *page 213)*

Where can I park?
Πού μπορώ να παρκάρω;
poo boro na parkaro

Do you have a cot for the baby?
Μήπως έχετε κρεβατάκι για το μωρό;
meepos ekhete krevatakee ya to moro

Is there room service?
Υπάρχει υπηρεσία δωματίων;
eeparkhee eepereseea dhomateeon

Do you have facilities for the disabled?
Εχετε ευκολίες για αναπήρους;
ekhete efkolee-es ya anapeeroos

What time do you serve breakfast?
Τι ώρα σερβίρετε το πρωινό;
tee ora serveerete to proeeno

Can we have breakfast in the room?
Μπορούμε να έχουμε το πρωινό στο δωμάτιο;
boroome na ekhoome to proeeno sto dhomatyo

What time do you serve dinner?
Τι ώρα σερβίρετε το δείπνο;
*tee ora serveerete to **dheepno***

What time does the hotel close?
Τι ώρα κλείνει το ξενοδοχείο;
tee ora kleenee to ksenodhokheeo

I'll be back very late
Θα γυρίσω πολύ αργά
tha yeereeso polee arga

(Key) number 42, please
(Κλειδί) νούμερο σαράντα δύο παρακαλώ
(kleedhee) noomero saranda dheeo parakalo

Are there any messages for me?
Υπάρχουν μηνύματα για μένα;
eeparkhoon meeneemata ya mena

Where is the bathroom?
Πού είναι το μπάνιο;
poo eene to banyo

Where is the dining-room?
Πού είναι η τραπεζαρία;
poo eene ee trapezareea

Can I leave this in the safe?
Μπορώ να αφήσω αυτό στο χρηματοκιβώτιο;
boro na afeeso afto sto khreematokeevotyo

Can you get my things from the safe?
Μπορείτε να μου δώσετε τα πράγματά μου από το χρηματοκιβώτιο;
boreete na moo dhosete ta pragmata-moo apo to khreematokeevotyo

Can you call me at eight o'clock?
Μπορείτε να με ξυπνήσετε στις οχτώ;
boreete na me kseepneesete stees okhto

Can you order me a taxi?
Μπορείτε να μου παραγγείλετε ένα ταξί;
boreete na moo parangeelete ena taksee

For right now
Για τώρα
ya tora

For tomorrow at nine o'clock
Για αύριο στις εννέα
ya avryo stees enea

Can you clean a suit for me?
Μπορείτε να μου καθαρίσετε ένα κοστούμι;
boreete na moo kathareesete ena kostoomee

Can you find me a babysitter?
Μπορείτε να μου βρείτε μια μπεϊμπισίτερ;
boreeta na moo vreete mya be-eebeeseeter

Can you put it on the bill?
Μπορείτε να το βάλετε στο λογαριασμό;
boreete na to valete sto logaryazmo

Room number 21
Δωμάτιο νούμερο είκοσι ένα
dhomatyo noomero eekosee ena

I need another pillow
Χρειάζομαι κι άλλο μαξιλλάρι
khryazome ky-alo makseelaree

I need a towel
Χρειάζομαι πετσέτα
khryazome petseta

At campsites

Is there a campsite around here?
Υπάρχει κάμπιγκ εδώ κοντά;
eeparkhee kampeeng edho konda

Can I camp here?
Μπορώ να κατασκηνώσω εδώ;
boro na kataskeenoso edho

Where can I park?
Πού μπορώ να παρκάρω;
poo boro na parkaro

Where are the showers?
Πού είναι τα ντους;
poo eene ta doos

Where are the toilets?
Πού είναι οι τουαλέτες;
poo eene ee twaletes

Where do we put the rubbish?
Πού βάζουμε τα σκουπίδια;
poo vazoome ta skoopeedhya

Is the water drinkable?
Είναι πόσιμο το νερό;
eene poseemo to nero

Where is the laundry-room?
Πού είναι το πλυντήριο;
poo eene to pleendeeryo

Where is there an electric point?
Πού έχει πρίζα;
poo ekhee preeza

Self-catering accommodation

(*see* Directions, *page 30*; Problems and complaints, *page 187*)

I have rented a villa
Εχω νοικιάσει βίλλα
ekho neekyasee veela

It's called Villa Paradise
Λέγεται η Βίλλα Παράδεισος
leyete ee veela paradheesos

I have rented an apartment
Εχω νοικιάσει διαμέρισμα
ekho neekyasee dhyamereezma

We're in number 11
Είμαστε στο νούμερο έντεκα
eemaste sto noomero endeka

My name is . . .
Με λένε . . .
me lene . . .

What is the address?
Ποια είναι η διεύθυνση;
pya eene ee dhyeftheensee

How do I get there?
Πώς πάω εκεί;
pos pao ekee

Would you give me the
key, please?
**Μου δίνετε το κλειδί
παρακαλώ;**
*moo dheenete to kleedhee
parakalo*

Where is . . . ?
Πού είναι . . . ;
poo eene . . .

Where is the stopcock?
**Πού είναι ο διακόπτης του
νερού;**
*poo eene o dhyakoptees too
neroo*

Where are the fuses?
Πού είναι οι ασφάλειες;
poo eene ee asfalyes

How does the cooker work?
Πώς λειτουργεί η κουζίνα;
pos leetooryee ee koozeena

How does the water-heater
work?
**Πώς λειτουργεί το
θερμοσίφωνο;**
*pos leetooryee to
thermoseefono*

Is there air conditioning?
Εχει κλιματισμό;
ekhee kleemateezmo

Is there a spare gas bottle?
Εχει κι άλλη φιάλη;
ekhee ky-alee fyalee

Is there any spare bedding?
Εχει κι άλλα σκεπάσματα;
ekhee ky-ala skepazmata

What day do they come to
clean?
**Ποια μέρα έρχονται να
καθαρίσουν;**
*pya mera erkhonde na
kathareesoon*

Where do we put the
rubbish?
Πού βάζουμε τα σκουπίδια;
poo vazoome ta skoopeedhya

When do they collect the
rubbish?
**Πότε παίρνουν τα
σκουπίδια;**
*pote pernoon ta
skoopeedhya*

Where can I contact you?
Πού μπορώ να σας βρω;
poo boro na sas vro

You may hear

Μπορώ να σας βοηθήσω;
boro na sas voeetheeso
Can I help you?

Το ονομά σας παρακαλώ;
to onoma-sas parakalo
Your name, please?

Για πόσες νύχτες;
ya poses neekhtes
For how many nights?

Για πόσα άτομα;
ya posa atoma
For how many people?

Με μπάνιο ή χωρίς μπάνιο;
me banyo ee khorees banyo
With bath or without bath?

Είναι μεγάλη η σκηνή, ή μικρή;
eene megalee ee skeenee ee meekree
Is it a large or a small tent?

Λυπάμαι, είμαστε γεμάτοι
leepame eemaste yematee
I'm sorry, we're full

Το διαβατήριό σας παρακαλώ
to dhyavateeryo-sas parakalo
Your passport, please

Υπογράψτε εδώ παρακαλώ
eepograpste edho parakalo
Would you sign here, please?

Το/Την ανάβετε (ανοίγετε) έτσι
to/teen anavete (aneeyete) etsee
You switch (turn) it on like this

Το/Τη σβήνετε (κλείνετε) έτσι
to/tee zveenete (kleenete) etsee
You switch (turn) it off like this

Ερχονται κάθε μέρα
erkhonde kathe mera
They come every day

Ερχονται την Παρασκευή
erkhonde teem-baraskevee
They come on Fridays

TELEPHONES

• There are some phone-boxes (blue for local calls, orange for long-distance), but people mainly make their local calls from the kiosks (see page 136) (or cafés, shops, etc.): you make your call and then pay afterwards. You may have to ask the owner of the kiosk to reset his meter to zero, to give you a line.

Telephone meters are now widely installed, and many (though not all) kiosk owners are prepared to let you make a long-distance call (even abroad) and then pay them for the metered number of units.

Some kiosks and cafés have red phones which currently take 10-drachma coins.

• You can also make your call from an office of the Greek phone company, **OTE** (*ote*). There will be a main **OTE** office in all the larger towns. Here, you make your call from a booth, and then pay afterwards at the counter.

Charges per unit are cheapest at **OTE** offices, slightly more expensive at kiosks and more expensive still in hotels.

Calls are slightly cheaper from 3.00 to 5.00 p.m. and from 8.00 p.m. to 8.00 a.m.

• To call abroad, first dial 00, then the code for the country – for the UK it's 44. Follow this with the town code minus the 0, and then the number you want. For example: for a central London number, dial 00 44 71, then the number.

• The number for the international operator is 161. For Greek directory enquiries, call 151.

Instructions you may see on a public phone

Σηκώστε το ακουστικό και ακούστε το σήμα επιλογής	Lift the receiver and listen for the dialling tone
Ρίξτε ένα δίδραχμο στη σχισμή	Insert a two-drachma piece in the slot (*in fact, you insert a 10-drachma piece!*)
Καλέστε τον αριθμό που θέλετε	Dial the number you require

You may see

ΑΣΤΙΚΟΣ ΝΟΜΙΣΜΑΤΟΔΕΚΤΗΣ Αστικός Νομισματοδέκτης	Local calls coin-box
ΔΕΝ ΛΕΙΤΟΥΡΓΕΙ Δεν λειτουργεί	Out of order
ΔΙΕΘΝΗΣ ΤΗΛΕΦΩΝΙΑ Διεθνής τηλεφωνία	International calls
ΕΔΩ ΤΗΛΕΦΩΝΕΙΤΕ Εδώ τηλεφωνείτε	You can phone from here
ΚΩΔΙΚΟΣ ΑΡΙΘΜΟΣ Κωδικός αριθμός	Code
ΟΤΕ	Greek telephone company
ΤΗΛΕΦΩΝΙΚΟΣ ΚΑΤΑΛΟΓΟΣ Τηλεφωνικός κατάλογος	Telephone directory
ΤΗΛΕΦΩΝΟ(Ν) Τηλέφωνο(ν)	Telephone
ΥΠΕΡΑΣΤΙΚΟΣ ΝΟΜΙΣΜΑΤΟΔΕΚΤΗΣ Υπεραστικός Νομισματοδέκτης	Long-distance coin-box
ΧΡΥΣΟΣ ΟΔΗΓΟΣ Χρυσός Οδηγός	Yellow pages

You may want to say

Is there a telephone?
Υπάρχει τηλέφωνο;
eeparkhee teelefono

Where is the telephone?
Πού είναι το τηλέφωνο;
poo eene to teelefono

Do you have change for the telephone, please?
Μήπως έχετε ψιλά για το τηλέφωνο παρακαλώ;
meepos ekhete pseela ya to teelefono parakalo

Do you have a telephone directory?
Μήπως έχετε τηλεφωνικό κατάλογο;
meepos ekhete teelefoneeko katalogo

Set the meter to zero, please
Μηδενίστε παρακαλώ
meedheneeste parakalo

I want to call England
Θέλω να πάρω την Αγγλία
thelo na paro teen angleea

I want to make a reverse-charge call
Θέλω να κάνω ενα τηλεφώνημα κολέκτ
thelo na kano ena teelefoneema kolekt

Mr Lekkas (Mrs Lekka), please
Τον κύριο Λέκκα (την κυρία Λέκκα) παρακαλώ
ton-geeryo leka (teen-geereea leka) parakalo

Extension 121, please
Εσωτερικό εκατόν είκοσι ένα παρακαλώ
esotereeko ekaton eekosee ena parakalo

My name is . . .
Με λένε . . .
me lene . . .

It's . . . speaking
. . . στο τηλέφωνο
. . . sto teelefono

When will he/she be back?
Πότε θα γυρίσει;
pote tha yeereesee

I'll call later
Θα πάρω αργότερα
tha paro argotera

Can I hold, please?
Μπορώ να περιμένω παρακαλώ;
boro na pereemeno parakalo

Can I leave a message?
Μπορώ να αφήσω μήνυμα;
boro na afeeso meeneema

Please tell him/her that Mr
Watson called
**Πέστε του/της ότι πήρε ο
κύριος Watson**
*peste too/tees otee peere o
keeryos Watson*

I am in the Hilton Hotel
Είμαι στο ξενοδοχείο Χίλτον
*eeme sto ksenodhokheeo
heelton*

My telephone number is . . .
**Ο αριθμός τηλεφώνου μου
είναι . . .**
*o areethmos teelefonoo-moo
eene . . .*

Can you ask him/her to call
me?
**Μπορείτε να του/της πείτε
να με πάρει;**
*boreete na too/tees peete
na me paree*

Can you repeat that, please?
Ξαναπέστε το παρακαλώ
ksanapeste to parakalo

More slowly, please
Πιο αργά παρακαλώ
pyo arga parakalo

Sorry, I've got the wrong
number
**Συγγνώμη, πήρα λάθος
αριθμό**
*seegnomee peera lathos
areethmo*

We have been cut off/The
line went dead
Μας έκοψαν
mas ekopsan

How much is the call?
Πόσο κάνει το τηλεφώνημα;
poso kanee to teelefoneema

Can you give me a number
to call a taxi?
**Μπορείτε να μου δώσετε
έναν αριθμό για ταξί,
παρακαλώ;**
*boreete na moo dhosete
enan areethmo ya taksee
parakalo*

You may hear

Εμπρός
embros
Hello? (*said by person
   answering phone*)

Ο ίδιος (*m.*)/Η ίδια (*f.*)
o eedhyos/ee eedhya
Speaking

Ποιος είναι;
pyos eene
Who's calling?

Ενα λεπτό παρακαλώ
ena lepto parakalo
One moment, please

Περιμένετε παρακαλώ
pereemenete parakalo
Please wait

Σας συνδέω
sas seendheo
I'm putting you through

Μιλάει/Βουίζει
meelaee/vooeezee
The line's engaged

Θέλετε να περιμένετε;
thelete na pereemenete
Do you want to hold on?

Δεν απαντάει
dhen apantaee
There's no answer

Λείπει
leepee
He/She is away

Δεν είναι εδώ
dhen eene edho
He/She is not in

Πήρατε λάθος αριθμό
peerate lathos areethmo
You've got the wrong
   number

Συντομεύετε παρακαλώ
seendomevete parakalo
Be brief please (*said by the
   kiosk owner*)

CHANGING MONEY

● The Greek unit of currency is the drachma – η δραχμή (*ee dhrakhmee*), abbreviated as δρχ. There are coins of 1, 2, 5, 10, 20 and 50 drachmas, and banknotes of 50, 100, 500, 1000 and 5000 drachmas.

● You can change money, traveller's cheques or Eurocheques into drachmas at banks, and other places (hotels, travel agencies, etc.) where you see a ΣΥΝΑΛΛΑΓΜΑ (Συνάλλαγμα) – Exchange – sign.

● Banks are open from 8.00 a.m. to 1.30 p.m. Mondays to Fridays.

● In banks you go first to the ΣΥΝΑΛΛΑΓΜΑ desk where a form is filled in for you to sign. You then get your money from the cashier's (ΤΑΜΕΙΟ(Ν) – Ταμείο(ν)). You will have to give the name of your hotel or the address you're staying at, and produce your passport. In Greece, addresses are given with the street name first and the number afterwards, e.g. Οδός Κόνωνος 4.

● There is a growing network of cash dispensers outside banks, many of which can be operated with credit cards or Eurocheque cards – check with British banks for details.

You may see the following instructions when using a cash dispenser

ΚΑΛΩΣΗΡΘΑΤΕ.
   ΤΟΠΟΘΕΤΗΣΤΕ ΤΗΝ
   ΚΑΡΤΑ ΣΑΣ ΣΤΗΝ
   ΕΠΑΝΩ ΣΧΙΣΜΗ

Welcome. Insert your card
   in the slot at the top

ПЛНКТΡΟΛΟΓΗΣΤΕ ΤΟΝ ΠΡΟΣΩΠΙΚΟ ΣΑΣ ΚΩΔΙΚΟ ΑΡΙΘΜΟ P.I.N.	Key in your PIN
ΠΕΡΙΜΕΝΕΤΕ. ΤΟ ΜΗΧΑΝΗΜΑ ΕΛΕΓΧΕΙ ΤΟΝ ΠΡΟΣΩΠΙΚΟ ΣΑΣ ΚΩΔΙΚΟ ΑΡΙΘΜΟ P.I.N.	Please wait. Your PIN is being checked
ΕΠΙΛΕΞΤΕ ΤΗ ΣΥΝΑΛΛΑΓΗ ΠΟΥ ΕΠΙΘΥΜΕΙΤΕ	Select service you require
ΕΠΙΛΕΞΤΕ ΤΟ ΛΟΓΑΡΙΑΣΜΟ ΑΠΟ ΤΟΝ ΟΠΟΙΟ ΘΑ ΚΑΝΕΤΕ ΑΝΑΛΗΨΗ	Select the account from which you wish to make a withdrawal
ΕΠΙΛΕΞΤΕ ΤΟ ΠΟΣΟ ΤΗΣ ΑΝΑΛΗΨΗΣ	Select the amount you wish to withdraw
ΠΑΡΤΕ ΤΗΝ ΚΑΡΤΑ ΣΑΣ, ΤΑ ΧΡΗΜΑΤΑ ΚΑΙ ΤΗΝ ΑΠΟΔΕΙΞΗ ΣΑΣ	Take your card, the money and your receipt

You may see

ΑΝΟΙΚΤΟ(Ν)	Ανοικτό(ν)	Open
ΕΙΣΟΔΟΣ	Είσοδος	Entrance
ΕΞΟΔΟΣ	Έξοδος	Exit
ΚΛΕΙΣΤΟ(Ν)	Κλειστό(ν)	Closed
ΣΥΝΑΛΛΑΓΜΑ	Συνάλλαγμα	Exchange, Bureau de change
ΤΑΜΕΙΟ(Ν)	Ταμείο(ν)	Cashier
ΤΑΜΙΕΥΤΗ-ΡΙΟ(Ν)	Ταμιευτήριο(ν)	Savings bank
ΤΡΑΠΕΖΑ	Τράπεζα	Bank

You may want to say

I want to change some pounds sterling
Θέλω να αλλάξω μερικές λίρες Αγγλίας
thelo na alakso mereekes leeres angleeas

I want to change some traveller's cheques
Θέλω να αλλάξω μερικά τράβελερς τσεκ
thelo na alakso mereeka travelers tsek

I want to change a Eurocheque
Θέλω να αλλάξω ένα Eurocheque
thelo na alakso ena Eurocheque

I want to get some money with this card
Θέλω να πάρω χρήματα με αυτή την κάρτα
thelo na paro khreemata me aftee teen-garta

What's the exchange rate for sterling?
Ποια είναι η τιμή της λίρας Αγγλίας;
pya eene ee teemee tees leeras angleeas

Can you give me some change, please?
Μπορείτε να μου δώσετε μερικά ψιλά παρακαλώ;
boreete na moo dhosete mereeka pseela parakalo

Can you give me five 1000-drachma notes, please?
Μπορείτε να μου δώσετε πέντε χιλιάρικα, παρακαλώ;
boreete na moo dhosete pende kheelyareeka parakalo

I'm at the Hotel Lux
Είμαι στο ξενοδοχείο Λουξ
eeme sto ksenodhokheeo looks

I'm at the Panselinos apartments
Είμαι στα διαμερίσματα Πανσέληνος
eeme sta dhyamereezmata panseleenos

I'm staying with friends
Μένω με φίλους
meno me feeloos

The address is Odos Sokratous 22
Η διεύθυνση είναι Οδός Σωκράτους είκοσι δύο
ee dhyeftheensee eene odhos sokratoos eekosee dheeo

You may hear

Το διαβατήριό σας παρακαλώ
to dhyavateeryo-sas parakalo
Your passport, please

Πόσο θέλετε να αλλάξετε;
poso thelete na alaksete
How much do you want to change?

Πού μένετε παρακαλώ;
poo menete parakalo
Your address, please

Το όνομα του ξενοδοχείου σας παρακαλώ
to onoma too ksenodhokheeoo-sas parakalo
The name of your hotel, please

Υπογράψτε εδώ παρακαλώ
eepograpste edho parakalo
Sign here, please

Στο ταμείο παρακαλώ
sto tameeo parakalo
Please go to the cashier

EATING AND DRINKING

• To order something, all you need do is name it, and say 'please', adding 'for me', 'for him' or 'for her' if you're ordering for several people to show who wants what.

• In bars and coffee houses you usually pay for all your drinks and so on when you leave, though occasionally you may have to pay when your order is brought to you. (You may want to do this anyway, to avoid waiting a second time to get the waiter's attention.) It's usual to leave some small change as a tip.

In restaurants the bill will usually include service; it's customary to leave a small additional tip on the table for the assistant waiter.

• Meal times in Greece are much later than in Britain. Lunchtime is around 2–3.30 p.m., after the day's work, and Greeks often don't go out to dinner until 10.00 p.m. You should not expect to eat in a ταβέρνα (*taverna*) until 9.00 p.m., though an εστιατόριο (*estyatoryo*) will be open all day from about 11.30 a.m.

• Restaurants fall into two main categories – the ταβέρνα (*taverna*) and the εστιατόριο (*estyatoryo*). The ταβέρνα tends to be open only in the evening, and is a place for a pleasant, social evening out, usually in the company of friends. It specialises in meat, or perhaps fish, cooked on a charcoal grill, and has a wide range of starters – μεζέδες (*mezedhes*) or ορεκτικά (*orekteeka*). There is frequently no menu: either the waiter will recite a list of what's available, or you may be invited into the kitchen to see what takes your fancy. This is quite common for Greeks as well as tourists. The εστιατόριο is likely to be open all day, and offers pre-cooked dishes in large tureens. It's a place to go if you want quick service, and is particularly busy at lunchtime. Here there will almost certainly be a menu – **κατάλογος** (*katalogos*), though again it's perfectly acceptable to wander into the kitchen to see the food. **Εστιατόρια** are classified L (luxury) and category A, B, C, D, or E, like hotels.

A **ταβέρνα** that specialises in fish is called a **ψαροταβέρνα** (*psarotaverna*), and a **ψησταριά** (*pseestarya*) is a restaurant serving only grilled meats and salads.

● If you want to fill a gap with coffee and cake, you should go to a **ζαχαροπλαστείο** (*zakharoplasteeo*). Greeks are very fond of sticky cakes and, again, it's quite common to go in and inspect the range on offer before choosing. The **ζαχαροπλαστείο** also serves beers and spirits, including **ούζο** (*oozo*), the traditional Greek aperitif. In the bigger towns, they also offer sandwiches and snacks.

● The **καφενείο** (*kafeneo*) is a coffee-bar whose clientele is traditionally restricted to men, and is a place where they go to play backgammon or cards, or just talk.

● For a quick snack, there are lots of small snack-bars selling sandwiches – **σάντουιτς** – (*sandweets*) and toasted sandwiches – **τοστ** (*tost*). Here, you will usually find the various fillings laid out on the counter, and you simply choose the ones you want for your sandwich.

There are also a number of snack-bars that serve a limited range of dishes, which are illustrated and accompanied by a number. To order, you simply give the relevant number. They are usually self-service, and a bell rings to tell you your order is ready.

● Greek coffee is served black and strong, in very small cups, and if you want sugar it will already be added. Coffee without sugar is called **σκέτο** (*sketo*), medium coffee is μέτριο (*metryo*), and sweet coffee is γλυκό (*gleeko*). If it's not to your taste, most coffee houses will serve instant coffee – νεσκαφέ (*neskafe*) or νες (*nes*) for short; and in the towns you can usually get French and American coffee, as well as Italian cappuccino and espresso.

● Tea (made with tea-bags) comes on its own – you have to ask for milk or lemon. Herbal teas (e.g. camomile or mint) are also available.

● The resinated ρετσίνα (*retseena*) is the wine most commonly associated with Greece. This can be bought in bottles, but is traditionally better from the barrel. The rosé variety, κοκινέλλι (*kokeenelee*) is particularly popular.

A range of unresinated – αρετσίνωτο (*aretseenoto*) – local wines, both red and white, are also available.

● Lager-type beers are brewed in Greece, and also imported.

● The traditional Greek aperitif is ούζο (*oozo*), a strong, colourless drink tasting of aniseed. It can be drunk either neat, or with added water, which causes it to turn a milky white colour. It is usually served with a μεζέ (*meze*). Μεζέδες (*mezedhes*) are snacks, which may consist of just a slice of cheese or tomato, but can also be a whole plate of titbits that can be a meal on its own.

● Greek restaurants and tavernas have a limited cuisine which, at its best, can be a delightful experience.

Eating out is a fairly informal business, and it is quite common to share dishes. A common pattern is to begin by ordering a range of ορεκτικά (*orekteeka*), or starters, and perhaps a χωριάτικη (*khoryateekee*), or 'Greek' salad, and to nibble at these while considering a main course. Traditional ορεκτικά include ταραμοσαλάτα (*taramosalata*), τζατζίκι (*dzadzeekee*), μελιτζανοσαλάτα (*meleedzano-salata*), τυροπιτάκια (*teeropeetakya*) and ντολμάδες (*dolmadhes*).

This will probably be followed by a piece of grilled meat or fish.

For a sweet, people often move from the restaurant to a ζαχαροπλαστείο. The restaurant itself will probably have only a limited range of sweets, mainly fruit.

Traditionally restaurants did not serve coffee after meals, but an increasing number are doing so to cater for tourist demand.

You may see

ΑΝΑΨΥΚΤΗΡΙΟ(Ν) Αναψυκτήριο(ν)	Bar serving light refreshments
ΑΥΤΟΕΞΥΠΗΡΕΤΗΣΗ Αυτοεξυπηρέτηση	Self-service
ΔΕΧΟΝΤΑΙ ΠΙΣΤΩΤΙΚΕΣ ΚΑΡΤΕΣ Δέχονται πιστωτικές κάρτες	Credit cards accepted
ΕΞΟΧΙΚΟ(Ν) ΚΕΝΤΡΟ(Ν) Εξοχικό(ν) κέντρο(ν)	Country restaurant
ΕΣΤΙΑΤΟΡΙΟ Εστιατόριο	Restaurant
ΖΑΧΑΡΟΠΛΑΣΤΕΙΟ(Ν) Ζαχαροπλαστείο(ν)	Patisserie
ΚΑΒΑ ΠΟΤΑ Κάβα ποτά	Wine cellar; off licence
ΚΑΦΕΝΕΙΟ(Ν) Καφενείο(ν)	Coffee house

ΚΑΦΕΤΕΡΙΑ Καφετερία	Snack-bar
ΜΠΑΡ Μπαρ	Bar
ΟΛΑ ΣΤΑ ΚΑΡΒΟΥΝΑ Ολα στα κάρβουνα	Everything done on the grill
ΟΥΖΕΡΙ Ουζερί	Bar
ΠΙΤΣΑΡΙΑ Πιτσαρία	Pizzeria
ΣΕΛΦ-ΣΕΡΒΙΣ Σελφ-σέρβις	Self-service
ΣΝΑΚ ΜΠΑΡ Σνακ μπαρ	Snack-bar
ΤΑΒΕΡΝΑ Ταβέρνα	Taverna, Restaurant
ΤΟΣΤ Τοστ	Toasted sandwiches
ΤΟΥΑΛΕΤΕΣ Τουαλέτες	Toilets
ΦΑΓΗΤΑ ΣΕ ΠΑΚΕΤΑ Φαγητά σε πακέτα	Take-away
ΧΑΣΑΠΟΤΑΒΕΡΝΑ Χασαποταβέρνα	Taverna associated with a butcher's
ΨΑΡΟΤΑΒΕΡΝΑ Ψαροταβέρνα	Seafood restaurant
ΨΗΣΤΑΡΙΑ Ψησταριά	Grill

You may want to say

General phrases

Are there any inexpensive
restaurants around here?
**Υπάρχουν φτηνά
εστιατόρια εδώ κοντά;**
*eeparkhoon fteena
estyatorya edho konda*

A (One) . . . , please
Ένα/Μία . . . , παρακαλώ
ena/meea . . . parakalo

Another . . . , please
**Αλλο ένα/Αλλη μία . . . ,
παρακαλώ**
*alo ena/alee meea . . .
parakalo*

A little more . . . , please
Λίγο . . . ακόμα, παρακαλώ
leego . . . akoma parakalo

For me
Για μένα
ya mena

For him/her
Γι'αυτόν/Γι'αυτή
yafton/yaftee

This, please
Αυτό παρακαλώ
afto parakalo

Two, please
Δύο παρακαλώ
dheeo parakalo

Do you have . . . ?
Μήπως έχετε . . . ;
meepos ekhete . . .

Is/Are there any . . . ?
**Υπάρχει . . . /
Υπάρχουν . . . ;**
*eeparkhee . . . /
eeparkhoon . . .*

What is there to eat?
Τι έχετε να φάμε;
tee ekhete na fame

Can we see what you have?
Μπορούμε να δούμε τι έχετε;
boroome na dhoome tee ehkete

What desserts do you have?
Τι γλυκά έχετε;
tee gleeka ekhete

What would you recommend?
Τι θα μας συνιστούσατε;
tee tha mas seeneestoosate

Do you have any local dishes?
Εχετε τίποτα τοπικό
ekhete teepota topeeko

What is this?
Τι είναι αυτό;
tee eene afto

Cheers!
Στην υγειά σας!
steen eeyasas

Enjoy your meal!
Καλή όρεξη!
kalee oreksee

Bars and cafés

A medium Greek coffee, please
Ενα μέτριο παρακαλώ
ena metryo parakalo

A sweet Greek coffee, please
Ενα γλυκό παρακαλώ
ena gleeko parakalo

Two Greek coffees without sugar, please
Δυό σκέτους παρακαλώ
dheeo sketoos parakalo

An instant coffee with milk and sugar, please
Ενα νες με γάλα και ζάχαρη παρακαλώ
ena nes me gala ke zakharee parakalo

Where are the toilets?
Πού είναι οι τουαλέτες;
poo eene ee twaletes

Nothing else, thanks
Τίποτ'άλλο, ευχαριστώ
teepotalo efkhareesto

The bill, please
Το λογαριασμό παρακαλώ
to logaryazmo parakalo

A tea with milk/lemon, please
Ενα τσάϊ με γάλα/λεμόνι παρακαλώ
ena tsaee me gala/lemonee parakalo

A camomile tea, please
Ενα χαμομήλι παρακαλώ
ena khamomeelee parakalo

Mineral water, please
Μεταλλικό νερό παρακαλώ
metaleeko nero parakalo

Fizzy/Still
Με ανθρακικό/Χωρίς ανθρακικό
me anthrakeeko/khorees anthrakeeko

A fizzy orange, please
Μία πορτοκαλάδα με ανθρακικό παρακαλώ
meea portokaladha me anthrakeeko parakalo

What fruit juices do you have?
Τι χυμούς έχετε;
tee kheemoos ekhete

An orange juice, please
Ένα χυμό πορτοκάλι παρακαλώ
ena kheemo portokalee parakalo

A beer, please
Μία μπύρα παρακαλώ
meea beera parakalo

Two draught beers, please
Δύο μπύρες από το βαρέλι παρακαλώ
dheeo beeres apo to varelee parakalo

A glass of red wine, please
Ένα ποτηράκι κόκκινο κρασί παρακαλώ
ena poteerakee kokeeno krasee parakalo

A gin and tonic, please
Ένα τζιν τόνικ παρακαλώ
ena dzeen toneek parakalo

With ice
Με παγάκια
me pagakya

Some olives, please
Μερικές ελιές παρακαλώ
mereekes elyes parakalo

Some crisps, please
Τσιπς, παρακαλώ
tseeps parakalo

What sandwiches do you have?
Τι σάντουιτς έχετε;
tee sandweets ekhete

A ham sandwich, please
Ένα σάντουιτς με ζαμπόν παρακαλώ
ena sandweets me zambon parakalo

Two cheese sandwiches, please
Δύο σάντουιτς με τυρί παρακαλώ
dheeo sandweets me teeree parakalo

A toasted sandwich with ham and cheese, please
Ένα τοστ με ζαμπόν και τυρί παρακαλώ
ena tost me zambon ke teeree parakalo

Do you have ice-cream?
Μήπως έχετε παγωτό;
meepos ekhete pagoto

What ice-creams do you have?
Τι παγωτά έχετε;
tee pagota ekhete

A chocolate/vanilla one, please
Ένα σοκολάτα/βανίλια παρακαλώ
ena sokolata/vaneelya parakalo

A strawberry sorbet, please
Μία γρανίτα φράουλα παρακαλώ
meea graneeta fraoola parakalo

Booking a table

I want to reserve a table for two people
Θέλω να κλείσω τραπέζι για δύο άτομα
thelo na kleeso trapezee ya dheeo atoma

For nine o'clock
Για τις εννέα
ya tees enea

For tomorrow at half past ten
Για αύριο στις δέκα και μισή
ya avryo stees dheka ke meesee

I have booked a table
Έχω κλείσει τραπέζι
ekho kleesee trapezee

The name is . . .
Το όνομά μου είναι . . .
to onoma-moo eene . . .

In restaurants

A table for four, please
Ένα τραπέζι για τέσσερα άτομα παρακαλώ
ena trapezee ya tesera atoma parakalo

Outside/On the terrace, if possible
Έξω/Στην ταράτσα, αν έχετε
ekso/steen-daratsa an ekhete

Waiter!
Γκαρσόν!
garson

The menu, please
Τον κατάλογο παρακαλώ
ton-gatalogo parakalo

The wine list, please
Τον κατάλογο κρασιών παρακαλώ
ton-gatalogo krasyon parakalo

Do you have a set menu?
Υπάρχει ταμπλ-ντοτ;
eeparkhee tabl-dot

Do you have anything for vegetarians?
Έχετε τίποτα για χορτοφάγους;
ekhete teepota ya khortofagoos

What starters do you have?
Τι ορεκτικά έχετε;
tee orekteeka ekhete

For the first course . . .
Για πρώτο πιάτο . . .
ya proto pyato . . .

Fish soup, please
Μία ψαρόσουπα παρακαλώ
mya psarosoopa parakalo

A mixed hors-d'œuvres, please
Μία ποικιλία παρακαλώ
meea peekeeleea parakalo

For the main course . . .
Για κύριο πιάτο . . .
ya keeryo pyato . . .

A pork chop, please
Μία μπριζόλα χοιρινή παρακαλώ
meea breezola kheereenee parakalo

Swordfish, please
Ξιφία παρακαλώ
kseefeea parakalo

Are vegetables included?
Γαρνίρεται με χορταρικά;
garneerete me khortareeka

With chips
Με πατάτες τηγανητές
me patates teeganeetes

And a mixed (Greek) salad
Και μία χωριάτικη
ke meea khoryateekee

For dessert . . .
Για γλυκό . . .
ya gleeko . . .

Crème caramel, please
Κρεμ καραμελέ παρακαλώ
krem karamele parakalo

116

(A portion of) watermelon, please
Μία καρπούζι παρακαλώ
meea karpoozee parakalo

What cheeses are there?
Τι τυριά έχετε;
tee teerya ekhete

Excuse me, where is my steak?
Συγγνώμη, πού είναι το φιλέτο μου;
seegnomee, poo eene to feeleto-moo

More bread, please
Κι άλλο ψωμάκι παρακαλώ
ky-alo psomakee parakalo

More chips, please
Κι άλλες πατάτες τηγανητές παρακαλώ
ky-ales patates teeganeetes parakalo

A glass/A jug of water
Ένα ποτήρι/Μία καράφα νερό παρακαλώ
ena poteeree/meea karafa nero parakalo

Half a litre of red house wine
Μισόκιλο κόκκινο κρασί, από το δικό σας
meesokeelo kokeeno krasee, apo to dheeko-sas

Half a bottle of white wine
Ένα μικρό μπουκάλι άσπρο κρασί
ena meekro bookalee aspro krasee

(for ordering coffee, see page 113)

It's very good
Είναι πολύ καλό
eene polee kalo

It's really delicious
Είναι πολύ νόστιμο
eene polee nosteemo

This is burnt
Σας έχει καεί
sas ekhee kaee

This is not cooked
Αυτό δεν είναι καλά ψημένο
afto dhen eene kala pseemeno

117

No, I ordered chicken
Όχι, παράγγειλα κοτόπουλο
okhee, parangeela kotopoolo

The bill, please
Το λογαριασμό παρακαλώ
to logaryazmo parakalo

Do you accept credit cards?
Δέχεστε πιστωτικές κάρτες;
dhekheste peestoteekes kartes

Do you accept traveller's
cheques?
Δέχεστε τράβελερς τσεκ;
dhekheste travelers tsek

Excuse me, there is a
mistake here
Με συγχωρείτε, λάθος
έγινε εδώ
*me seenkhoreete lathos
eyeene edho*

You may hear

Bars and cafés

Τι θέλετε;
tee thelete
What would you like?

Τι θα πάρετε;
tee tha parete
What would you like to
have?

Μήπως θέλετε παγάκια;
meepos thelete pagakya
Would you like ice?

Με ανθρακικό ή χωρίς
ανθρακικό;
*me anthrakeeko ee khorees
anthrakeeko*
Fizzy or still?

Μεγάλο ή μικρό
megalo ee meekro
Large or small?

Ποιο προτιμάτε;
pyo proteemate
Which do you prefer?

Αμέσως/Έφτασα
amesos/eftasa
Right away

Έχουμε . . .
ekhoome . . .
We have . . .

Restaurants

Πόσοι είσαστε;
posee eesaste
How many are you?

Για πόσα άτομα;
ya posa atoma
For how many people?

Ενα λεπτό
ena lepto
Just a moment

Εχετε κλείσει τραπέζι;
ekhete kleesee trapezee
Have you booked a table?

Θα περιμένετε δέκα λεπτά
tha pereemenete dheka lepta
You will have to wait ten minutes

Θέλετε να περιμένετε;
thelete na pereemenete
Would you like to wait?

Τι θα πάρετε;
tee tha parete
What would you like?

Θέλετε απεριτίφ;
thelete apereeteef
Would you like an aperitif?

Συστήνουμε . . .
seesteenoome . . .
We recommend . . .

Εχουμε . . .
ekhoome . . .
We have . . .

Περάστε να δείτε
peraste na dheete
Come and have a look

Για πρώτο πιάτο . . .
ya proto pyato . . .
For the first course . . .

Για κύριο πιάτο . . .
ya keeryo pyato . . .
For the main course . . .

Τι θα πιείτε;
tee tha pyeete
What will you drink?

Πού πάει ο/η/το . . . ;
poo paee o/ee/to . . .
Who is the . . . for?

Τελειώσατε;
telyosate
Have you finished?

Μήπως θέλετε γλυκό, καφέ;
meepos thelete gleeko kafe
Would you like dessert, or coffee?

Τίποτ'άλλο;
teepotalo
Anything else?

MENU READER

General phrases

ΑΝΑΨΥΚΤΙΚΑ	Αναψυκτικά	*anapseekteeka*
		Soft drinks
ΑΠΕΡΙΤΙΦ	Απεριτίφ	*apereeteef*
		Aperitifs
ΓΕΥΜΑ	Γεύμα	*yevma*
		Lunch
ΔΕΙΠΝΟ(Ν)	Δείπνο(ν)	*dheepno*
		Dinner
ΕΝΤΡΑΔΕΣ	Εντράδες	*endradhes*
		Main dishes
ΖΥΜΑΡΙΚΑ	Ζυμαρικά	*zeemareeka*
		Pasta and rice dishes
ΘΑΛΑΣΣΙΝΑ	Θαλασσινά	*thalaseena*
		Seafood
ΚΑΤΑΛΟΓΟΣ	Κατάλογος	*katalogos*
		Menu
ΚΡΑΣΙΑ	Κρασιά	*krasya*
		Wines
(ΑΣΠΡΟ, ΚΟΚΚΙΝΟ, ΡΟΖΕ)	(άσπρο, κόκκινο, ροζέ)	*(aspro, kokeeno, roze)* (white, red, rosé)
ΚΡΕΑΣ	Κρέας	*kreas*
		Meat
ΚΥΜΑΔΕΣ	Κυμάδες	*keemadhes*
		Dishes with mince
ΚΥΝΗΓΙ	Κυνήγι	*keeneeyee*
		Game

ΛΑΔΕΡΑ	Λαδερά	*ladhera* Dishes cooked in oil
ΛΑΧΑΝΙΚΑ	Λαχανικά	*lakhaneeka* Vegetables
ΜΕΖΕΔΑΚΙΑ	Μεζεδάκια	*mezedhakya* Hors d'œuvres
ΜΕΖΕΔΕΣ	Μεζέδες	*mezedhes* Hors d'œuvres
ΜΕΤΑΛΛΙΚΑ ΝΕΡΑ	Μεταλλικά νερά	*metaleeka nera* Mineral waters
ΜΠΥΡΕΣ	Μπύρες	**beeres** Beers
ΟΙΝΟΙ	Οίνοι	*eenee* Wines
ΟΡΕΚΤΙΚΑ	Ορεκτικά	*orekteeka* Starters
ΠΑΓΩΤΑ	Παγωτά	*pagota* Ice creams
ΠΕΡΙΛΑΜΒΑ-ΝΕΤΑΙ ΦΠΑ	Περιλαμβάνεται ΦΠΑ	*pereelamvanete fee pee alfa* VAT included
ΠΙΑΤΟ ΤΗΣ ΜΕΡΑΣ	Πιάτο της μέρας	*pyato tees meras* Dish of the day
ΠΟΤΑ	Ποτά	*pota* (Alcoholic) drinks
ΠΟΥΛΕΡΙΚΑ	Πουλερικά	*poolereeka* Poultry
ΠΡΩΙΝΟ	Πρωινό	*proeeno* Breakfast
ΣΑΛΑΤΕΣ	Σαλάτες	*salates* Salads
ΣΟΥΠΕΣ	Σούπες	*soopes* Soups

ΤΥΡΙΑ	Τυριά	*teerya*
		Cheeses
ΦΡΟΥΤΑ	Φρούτα	*froota*
		Fruit
ΨΑΡΙΑ	Ψάρια	*psarya*
		Fish

Drinks

Αρετσίνωτος [*aretseenotos*] unresinated
Αφρώδης/ης/ες [*afrodhees/ees/es*] sparkling
Βερμούτ [*vermoot*] vermouth
Βότκα [*vodka*] vodka
Βυσσινάδα [*veeseenadha*] cherryade
Γκαζόζα [*gazoza*] mineral water
Γλυκός/ή/ό [*gleekos/ee/o*] sweet

Εισαγωγής/ής/ες [*eesagogees/ees/es*] imported
Εμφιαλωμένος/η/ο [*emfyalomenos/ee/o*] bottled
Επιτραπέζιος/η/ο [*epeetrapezyos/ee/o*] table (wine)
Ημιαφρώδης/ης/ες [*eemyafrodhees/ees/es*] semi-sparkling
Ημίγλυκος/η/ο [*eemeegleekos/ee/o*] semi-sweet
Καλαμάκι [*kalamakee*] straw
Καράφα [*karafa*] carafe
Καρτρούτσο [*kartrootso*] small container of draught wine
Καφέ [*kafe*] coffee
    βαρύγλυκο [*vareegleeko*] very sweet
    γλυκό [*gleeko*] sweet
    ελληνικό [*eleeneeko*] Greek
    εσπρέσσο [*espreso*] espresso
    καπουτσίνο [*kapootseeno*] cappuccino
    με γάλα [*me gala*] with milk
    με καϊμάκι [*me kaeemakee*] with cream
    μέτριο [*metryo*] medium
    ντεκαφεϊνέ [*dekafe-eene*] decaffeinated
    σκέτο [*sketo*] without milk or sugar

Κόκα κόλα [*koka-kola*] Coca cola

Κονιάκ [*konyak*] brandy

Κουμ κουατ [*koom kwat*] brandy made from oranges, drunk on Corfu

Λεμονάδα [*lemonadha*] lemonade

Λικέρ [*leeker*] liqueur

Μάρκα [*marka*] brand

Μαύρη (μπύρα) [*mavree (beera)*] dark (beer)

Με ανθρακικό [*me anthrakeeko*] fizzy

Μέντα [*menda*] mint tea

Μεταλλικό νερό [*metaleeko nero*] mineral water

Μη οινοπνευματώδη ποτά [*mee eenopnevmatodhee pota*] non-alcoholic drinks

Μισό κιλό [*meeso keelo*] half-kilo

Μπουκάλι [*bookalee*] bottle

Μπρούσκο (κρασί) [*broosko (krasee)*] dry (wine)

Μπύρα [*beera*] beer

   εμφιαλωμένη [*emfyalomenee*] bottled

   από το βαρέλι [*apo to varelee*] draught, from the barrel

Νεσκαφέ [*neskafe*] instant coffee

Νεσκαφέ φραππέ [*neskafe frape*] iced coffee

Ντόπιος/α/ο [*dopyos/a/o*] local

Ξανθή (μπύρα) [*ksanthee (beera)*] light (beer)

Ξηρός/ή/ό [*kseeros/ee/o*] dry

Οίνος [*eenos*] wine (*written only*)

Ούζο [*oozo*] ouzo

Ουίσκι [*weeskee*] whisky

   με παγάκια [*me pagakya*] with ice

   με σόδα [*me sodha*] with soda

Παγωμένος/η/ο [*pagomenos/ee/o*] chilled

Πορτοκαλάδα [*portokaladha*] orangeade

Ποτηράκι [*poteerakee*] glass (*wine*)

Ποτήρι [*poteeree*] glass (*water*)

Ρετσίνα [*retseena*] retsina

Ροζέ [*roze*] rosé

Ρούμι [*roomee*] rum

Σαμπάνια [*sambanya*] champagne
Σκέτος/η/ο [*sketos/ee/o*] neat
Τέταρτο [*tetarto*] quarter-kilo (*wine*)
Τζιν [*dzeen*] gin
Τζιν-τόνικ [*dzeen-toneek*] gin and tonic
Τόνικ [*toneek*] tonic
Τσάϊ [*tsaee*] tea
  με ζάχαρη [*me zakharee*] with sugar
  με λεμόνι [*me lemonee*] with lemon
Τσάϊ του βουνού [*tsaee too voonoo*] herbal tea
  χαμομήλι [*khamomeelee*] camomile
Τσέρι [*tseree*] sherry
Χύμα [*kheema*] draught
Χυμός [*kheemos*] (fruit) juice
  χυμός ανανά [*kheemos anana*] pineapple juice
  χυμός γκρέϊπφρουτ [*kheemos gre-eepfroot*] grapefruit
   juice

  χυμός λεμόνι [*kheemos lemonee*] lemon juice
  χυμός μήλο [*kheemos meelo*] apple juice
  χυμός ντομάτα [*kheemos domata*] tomato juice
  χυμός πορτοκάλι [*kheemos portokalee*] orange juice
Χωρίς [*khorees*] without
Χωρίς ανθρακικό [*khorees anthrakeeko*] non-fizzy, still

Food

The Greek dishes are shown without the article ('the').
You can order 'one . . .' of most Greek dishes by saying
'**μία**' (*meea*) . . .' e.g. **μία κοτόπουλο** (*meea kotopoolo*); the
word **μερίδα** (*mereedha*) – portion – is understood.

Αβοκάντο [*avokado*] avocado
Αγγούρι [*angooree*] cucumber

Αγγουροντομάτα σαλάτα [*angoorodomata salata*] cucumber and tomato salad

Αγκινάρες [*angeenares*] artichokes

Αθερινά [*athereena*] whitebait

Αλάτι [*alatee*] salt

Ανανάς [*ananas*] pineapple

Αναψυκτικά [*anapseekteeka*] soft drinks

Αρακάς [*arakas*] peas

Αρνάκι [*arnakee*] lamb

Αρνάκι γάλακτος [*arnakee galaktos*] sucking lamb

Αρνί γιουβέτσι [*arnee yoovetsee*] lamb with noodles

Αρνί κοκκινιστό [*arnee kokeeneesto*] lamb in oil and tomato sauce

Αρνί λεμονάτο [*arnee lemonato*] lamb in lemon sauce

Αρνί μακαρόνια [*arnee makaronya*] lamb with spaghetti

Αρνι πατάτες τηγανητές [*arnee patates teeganeetes*] lamb with chips

Αρνί πατάτες φούρνου [*arnee patates foornoo*] lamb with baked potatoes

Αρνί πιλάφι [*arnee peelafee*] lamb and rice

Αρνί ραγού [*arnee ragoo*] lamb ragout

Αρνί φρικασέ [*arnee freekase*] lamb fricassee

Αστακός [*astakos*] lobster

Αυγά [*avga*] eggs

Αυγά μάτια [*avga matya*] fried eggs

Αυγά μελάτα [*avga melata*] soft-boiled eggs

Αυγά μπρουγέ [*avga brooye*] scrambled eggs

Αυγά ποσέ [*avga pose*] poached eggs

Αυγά σφιχτά [*avga sfeekhta*] hard-boiled eggs

Αχινός [*akheenos*] sea-urchin

Αχλάδι [*akhladhee*] pear

Βερύκοκκο [*vereekoko*] apricot

Βλήτα [*vleeta*] dark green leaf vegetable

Βοδινό [*vodheeno*] beef

Βότανα [*votana*] herbs

Βούτυρο [*vooteero*] butter

Βραστός/ή/ό [*vrastos/ee/o*] boiled
Γάλα [*gala*] milk
Γαλακτομπούρεκο [*galaktobooreko*] pastry filled with custard and syrup
Γαλέος [*galeos*] lamprey
Γαλόπουλο [*galopoolo*] turkey
Γαρίδες [*gareedhes*] shrimps
Γαριδοσαλάτα [*gareedhosalata*] shrimp salad
Γαύρος [*gavros*] sort of fish
Γεμιστός/ή/ό [*yemeestos/ee/o*] stuffed
Γιαούρτι [*yaoortee*] yoghurt
Γίγαντες γιαχνί [*yeegantes yakhnee*] broad beans in tomato sauce
Γιουβαρλάκια [*yoovarlakya*] meat and rice balls
Γιουβέτσι [*yoovetsee*] baked Greek noodles
Γκρέϊπφρουτ [*gre-eepfroot*] grapefruit
Γλυκά [*gleeka*] sweets

Γλυκάδια [*gleekadhya*] sweetbread
Γλυκά του κουταλιού [*gleeka too kootalyoo*] preserved fruit
Γλώσσα [*glosa*] sole
Γόπες [*gopes*] large sardines
Γουρουνόπουλο [*gooroonopoolo*] sucking pig
Γραβιέρα [*gravyera*] Greek gruyère
Γρανίτα [*graneeta*] sorbet
Γύρος [*yeeros*] doner kebab
Δαμάσκηνο [*dhamaskeeno*] plum
Διάφορα [*dhyafora*] assorted
Ελιές [*elyes*] olives
Εντρεκότ [*endrekot*] rib steak
Επιδόρπιο [*epeedhorpyo*] dessert
Εσκαλόπ [*eskalop*] cutlet
Ζαμπόν [*zambon*] ham
Ζάχαρη [*zakharee*] sugar
Ιμάμ μπαϊλντί [*eemam baeeldee*] aubergine stuffed with tomatoes
Καβούρι [*kavooree*] crab

Κακαβιά [*kakavya*] spicy fish stew

Καλαμαράκια [*kalamarakya*] baby squid

Καλαμάρι [*kalamaree*] squid

Καλαμπόκι [*kalabokee*] sweetcorn

Καλοψημένος/η/ο [*kalopseemenos/ee/o*] well done

Καπόνι [*kaponee*] capon

Καπνιστός/ή/ό [*kapneestos/ee/o*] smoked

Καραβίδες [*karaveedhes*] crawfish

Καρδιά [*kardhya*] heart

Καρότα [*karota*] carrots

Καρπούζι [*karpoozee*] water melon

Καρρέ [*kare*] rack

Καρύδι [*kareedhee*] walnut

Καρυδόπιττα [*kareedhopeeta*] walnut bar

Κασέρι [*kaseree*] hard yellow cheese

Καταΐφι [*kataeefee*] shredded pastry, walnuts and honey

Κατεψυγμένος/η/ο [*katepseegmenos/ee/o*] frozen

Κατσίκι [*katseekee*] kid

127

Κέϊκ [*ke-eek*] cake

Κεράσι [*kerasee*] cherry

Κεφάλι [*kefalee*] head

Κέφαλος [*kefalos*] mullet

Κεφαλοτύρι [*kefaloteeree*] salty yellow cheese

Κεφτεδάκια [*keftedhakya*] small meat balls

Κεφτέδες [*keftedhes*] meat balls

Κοκκινιστός/ή/ό [*kokeeneestos/ee/o*] cooked in a tomato sauce

Κοκορέτσι [*kokoretsee*] grilled sheep's entrails

Κολοκυθάκια [*kolokeethakya*] courgettes

Κομπόστα [*kombosta*] stewed fruit

Κόντρα φιλέτο [*kondra feeleto*] steak

Κοτόπιττα [*kotopeeta*] chicken pie

Κοτόπουλο [*kotopoolo*] chicken

Κοτόπουλο ψητό [*kotopoolo pseeto*] roast chicken

Κοτόσουπα [*kotosoopa*] chicken soup

Κουκιά [*kookya*] broad beans

Κουνέλι [*koonelee*] rabbit

Κουνουπίδι [*koonoopeedhee*] cauliflower

Κουραμπιέδες [*koorabyedhes*] biscuits, cookies

Κρασάτος/η/ο [*krasatos/ee/o*] cooked in wine

Κρεατόπιττα [*kreatopeeta*] meat pie

Κρεατόσουπα [*kreatosoopa*] meat soup

Κρεμ καραμελέ [*krem karamele*] crème caramel

Κρεμμυδάκι [*kremeedhakee*] spring onion

Κρεμμύδι [*kremeedhee*] onion

Κρέπες [*krepes*] crèpes

Κριθαράκι γιουβέτσι [*kreetharakee yoovetsee*] Greek
  noodles

Κρύος/η/ο [*kreeos/ee/o*] cold

Κυδώνι [*keedhonee*] quince

Κυμά [*keema*] mince

Κυνήγι [*keeneeyee*] game

Λαγός [*lagos*] hare

Λαγός σιβέ [*lagos seeve*] jugged hare

Λάδι [*ladhee*] oil

Λαδολέμονο [*ladholemono*] oil and lemon dressing

Λαδόξυδο [*ladhokseedho*] oil and vinegar dressing

Λακέρδα [*lakerdha*] salted tuna

Λαχανάκια Βρυξελλών [*lakhanakya vreekselon*] Brussels
  sprouts

Λαχανικά [*lakhaneeka*] vegetables

Λάχανο [*lakhano*] cabbage

Λεμόνι [*lemonee*] lemon

Λιθρίνι [*leethreenee*] grey/red mullet

Λουκάνικο [*lookaneeko*] sausage

Λουκουμάδες [*lookoomadhes*] doughnuts fried in oil

Λουκούμι [*lookoomee*] Turkish delight

Μαγειρίτσα [*mayeereetsa*] easter soup (of lamb's entrails)

Μαγιονέζα [*mayoneza*] mayonnaise

Μαϊντανός [*maeedanos*] parsley

Μακαρόνια [*makaronya*] spaghetti

Μακαρόνια κυμά [*makaronya keema*] spaghetti and mince
Μανιτάρια [*maneetarya*] mushrooms
Μανούρι [*manooree*] soft cheese
Μανταρίνι [*mandareenee*] mandarin
Μαρίδες [*mareedhes*] fried smelt
Μαρούλι [*maroolee*] lettuce
Μαστίχα [*masteekha*] sweet or liqueur made from mastic
Μελιτζάνες [*meleedzanes*] aubergines
Μελιτζανοσαλάτα [*meleedzanosalata*] aubergine salad
Μελομακάρονο [*melomakarono*] honey and nut biscuit
Μερίδα [*mereedha*] portion
Μετά φιλοδωρήματος [*meta feelodhoreematos*] with service charge
Μέτριος/α/ο [*metryos/a/o*] medium
Μήλο [*meelo*] apple
Μηλόπιττα [*meelopeeta*] apple pie
Μούσμουλα [*moosmoola*] medlars: slightly sour fruit
Μοσχάρι [*moskharee*] veal

Μοσχάρι γιουβέτσι [*moskharee yoovetsee*] veal with Greek noodles
Μοσχάρι κολοκυθάκια [*moskharee kolokeethakya*] veal with courgettes
Μοσχάρι μακαρόνια [*moskharee makaronya*] veal with spaghetti
Μοσχάρι πατάτες φούρνου [*moskharee patates foornoo*] veal with baked potatoes
Μοσχάρι πιλάφι [*moskharee peelafee*] veal with rice
Μοσχάρι ψητό [*moskharee pseeto*] roast veal
Μους [*moos*] mousse
Μουσακάς [*moosakas*] mousaka
Μουστάρδα [*moostardha*] mustard
Μπακαλιάρος [*bakalyaros*] cod
Μπακλαβά [*baklava*] flaky pastry with nuts and honey
Μπάμιες [*bamyes*] okra (ladies' fingers)
Μπανάνα [*banana*] banana

Μπαρμπούνι [*barboonee*] red mullet

Μπαχαρικά [*bakhareeka*] spices

Μπέϊκον [*be-eekon*] bacon

Μπεκάτσα [*bekatsa*] woodcock

Μπιζέλια [*beezelya*] peas

Μπιντόκ αλα ρους [*beendok ala roos*] grilled burger with fried

Μπισκότο [*beeskoto*] biscuit

Μπιφτέκι [*beeftekee*] grilled burger

Μπον φιλέ [*bon feele*] bon filet

Μπουγάτσα [*boogatsa*] flaky pastry filled with custard

Μπουρεκάκια [*boorekakya*] small cheese (meat) pies

Μπούτι [*bootee*] leg

Μπριάμ [*bryam*] ratatouille

Μπριζόλες [*breezoles*] chops, cutlets

Μπριζόλες μοσχαρίσιες [*breezoles moskhareesyes*] veal
chops

Μπριζόλες χοιρινές [*breezoles kheereenes*] pork chops

Μυαλό [*myalo*] brain

Μύδια [*meedhya*] mussels

Μυζήθρα [*meezeethra*] white goat's or ewe's milk cheese

Νεράκι [*nerakee*] water

Νερό [*nero*] water

Νεφρά [*nefra*] kidneys

Ντολμαδάκια αυγολέμονο [*dolmadhakya avgolemono*]
stuffed vine leaves in egg and lemon sauce

Ντολμάδες [*dolmadhes*] stuffed vine leaves

Ντομάτα σαλάτα [*domata salata*] tomato salad

Ντομάτες γεμιστές [*domates yemeestes*] stuffed tomatoes

Ξιφίας [*kseefeeas*] swordfish

Ξύδι [*kseedhee*] vinegar

Ομελέτα [*omeleta*] omelette

Ορεκτικά [*orekteeka*] starters

Ορτύκι [*orteekee*] quail

Ουρά βοδινή [*oora vodheenee*] ox tail

Παγωμένος/η/ο [*pagomenos/ee/o*] chilled

Παγωτό [*pagoto*] ice cream
  βανίλια [*vaneelya*] vanilla
  κασάτα [*kasata*] cassata
  σικάγο [*seekago*] mixture of chocolate and vanilla
  σοκολάτα [*sokolata*] chocolate
  φράουλα [*fraoola*] strawberry
Παϊδάκια [*paeedhakya*] lamb chops
Παντζάρια [*pandzarya*] beetroot
Παπάκι [*papakee*] duckling
Πάπια [*papya*] duck
Παπουτσάκια [*papootsakya*] aubergine dish with bechamel
  sauce
Πάστα [*pasta*] cake
Παστέλι [*pastelee*] sesame and honey bar
Παστίτσιο [*pasteetsyo*] baked macaroni and mince
Παστουρμάς [*pastoormas*] highly spiced cured meat
Πατάτες φούρνου [*patates foornoo*] oven-baked potatoes
Πατάτες τηγανητές [*patates teeganeetes*] chips

Πατέ [*pate*] paté
Πατσάς [*patsas*] tripe soup
Πεπόνι [*peponee*] honeydew melon
Πέρδικα [*perdheeka*] partridge
Πέρκα [*perka*] perch
Περιστέρι [*pereesteree*] pigeon
Πες μελμπά [*pes melba*] peach melba
Πέστροφα (καπνιστή) [*pestrofa (kapneestee)*] trout
  (smoked)
Πιάτο της μέρας [*pyato tees meras*] dish of the day
Πιλάφι κυμά [*peelafee keema*] rice and mince
Πιλάφι σάλτσα [*peelafee saltsa*] rice with sauce
Πιπεράτος/η/ο [*peeperatos/ee/o*] cooked with pepper
Πιπεριές [*peeperyes*] peppers (green, red)
Πιπεριές γεμιστές [*peeperyes yemeestes*] stuffed peppers
Πλάτη [*platee*] shoulder
Ποικιλία [*peekeeleea*] mixed (hors d'œuvres)

Πορτοκάλι [*portokalee*] orange
Πουντίγκα [*poodeenga*] pudding
Πουρέ [*poore*] mashed (potato)
Πρασόρυζο [*prasoreezo*] leeks and rice
Πράσα [*prasa*] leeks
Ρέγγα [*renga*] herring
Ραδίκια [*radheekya*] chicory (endive)
Ραπανάκια [*rapanakya*] radishes
Ρεβίθια [*reveethya*] chick-peas
Ρόδι [*rodhee*] pomegranate
Ροδάκινο [*rodhakeeno*] peach
Ροκφόρ [*rokfor*] blue cheese
Ρυζόγαλο [*reezogalo*] rice pudding
Ρώσσικη σαλάτα [*roseekee salata*] Russian salad
Σαγανάκι [*saganakee*] fried cheese
Σαινιάν [*senyan*] rare (steak)
Σαλάμι [*salamee*] salami
Σαλάτα της εποχής [*salata tees epokhees*] salad of the
    season
Σάντουιτς [*sandweets*] sandwich
Σαργοί [*saryee*] sea bream
Σαρδέλλα [*sardhela*] sardine
Σατωπριάν [*satobryan*] thick fillet
Σέλινο [*seleeno*] celery
Σέλλα [*sela*] saddle
Σκορδαλιά [*skordhalya*] garlic sauce
Σκόρδο [*skordho*] garlic
Σκουμπρί [*skoobree*] mackerel
Σνίτσελ [*sneetsel*] schnitzel
Σούβλα [*soovla*] skewer
Σούπα [*soopa*] soup
Σούπα αυγολέμονο [*soopa avgolemono*] egg-lemon soup
Σολομός (καπνιστός) [*solomos (kapneestos)*] salmon
    (smoked)
Σουπιά [*soopya*] cuttlefish

Σουτζουκάκια [*soodzookakya*] meatballs in sauce
Σπανάκι [*spanakee*] spinach
Σπανακόπιττα [*spanakopeeta*] spinach pie
Σπανακόρυζο [*spanakoreezo*] spinach and rice
Σπαράγγια [*sparangya*] asparagus
Σπετσοφάϊ [*spetsofaee*] spicy dish with sausages, peppers
   etc. in sauce
Σπιτικό [*speeteeko*] home-cooked
Σπλήνα [*spleena*] spleen
Σπληνάντερο [*spleenandero*] sheep's intestines, spleen etc.
   cooked on spit
Στα κάρβουνα [*sta karvoona*] charcoaled
Σταφίδα [*stafeedha*] raisin
Σταφύλι [*stafeelee*] grape
Στήθος [*steethos*] breast
Στιφάδο [*steefadho*] meat and onion stew
Στο φούρνο [*sto foorno*] baked
Στρείδια [*streedhya*] oysters
Σύκο [*seeko*] fig
Συκωτάκια [*seekotakya*] liver
Συκώτι [*seekotee*] liver
Συναγρίδα [*seenagreedha*] sea-bream
Σφυρίδα [*sfeereedha*] sea-bream
Ταραμοσαλάτα [*taramosalata*] fish-roe salad
Τζατζίκι [*dzadzeekee*] yoghurt, cucumber and garlic salad
Τηγανητός/ή/ό [*teeganeetos/ee/o*] fried
Της κατσαρόλας [*tees katsarolas*] casseroled
Της σχάρας [*tees skharas*] grilled
Της ώρας [*tees oras*] freshly cooked
Τόννος [*tonos*] tuna
Τοστ [*tost*] toasted sandwich
Τουρσί [*toorsee*] pickle
Τούρτα σοκολάτα [*toorta sokolata*] chocolate cake
Τριμμένος/η/ο [*treemenos/ee/o*] grated
Τσιπούρα [*tseepoora*] gifthead fish

Τσιπς [*tseeps*] crisps
Τυρόπιττα [*teeropeeta*] cheese pie
Τυροπιττάκια [*teeropeetakya*] small cheese pies
Φάβα [*fava*] pease-pudding
Φαγγρί [*fangree*] sea-bream
Φακές [*fakes*] lentils
Φασολάδα [*fasoladha*] bean soup
Φασολάκια [*fasolakya*] green beans
Φασόλια [*fasolya*] haricot beans
Φασόλια γιαχνί [*fasolya yakhnee*] beans in tomato sauce
Φασόλια ξερά [*fasolya ksera*] dried beans
Φασιανός [*fasyanos*] pheasant
Φέτα [*feta*] cheese of ewe's milk
Φιλέτο [*feeleto*] fillet
Φουντούκι [*foondookee*] hazel nut
Φράουλες [*fraooles*] strawberries
Φρέσκος/η/ο [*freskos/ee/o*] fresh
Φρικασέ [*freekase*] fricassee
Φρούτα [*froota*] fruit
Φρουτοσαλάτα [*frootosalata*] fruit salad
Φτερούγα [*fterooga*] wing
Χαβιάρι [*khavyaree*] caviar
Χαλβάς [*khalvas*] sweetmeat with chopped almonds and honey
Χάμπουργερ [*khamboorger*] hamburger
Χέλι [*khelee*] eel
Χήνα [*kheena*] goose
Χόρτα [*khorta*] dark green leaf vegetable
Χορτόσουπα [*khortosoopa*] vegetable soup
Χοτ ντογκ [*khot dog*] hot dog
Χουρμάς [*khoormas*] date
Χταπόδι [*khtapodhee*] octopus
Χυλοπίτες [*kheelopeetes*] sort of macaroni
Χωριάτικη σαλάτα [*khoryateekee salata*] mixed ('Greek') salad

Ψαρόσουπα [*psarosoopa*] fish soup

Ψητός/ή/ό [*pseetos/ee/o*] roast

Ψιλοκομμένος/η/ο [*pseelokomenos/ee/o*] finely chopped

Ψωμάκι [*psomakee*] (piece of) bread, roll

Ψωμί [*psomee*] bread

Ωμός/ή/ό [*omos/ee/o*] raw

SHOPPING

• Shop opening hours vary a bit; generally speaking, shops are open 8.00 a.m. to 2.30 p.m. on Mondays, Wednesdays and Saturdays, and 8.00 a.m. to 1.30 p.m. and then 5.30 to 8.30 p.m. on Tuesdays, Thursdays and Fridays. In winter, the times will be slightly different, and they will be more flexible outside Athens.

• Many places have markets – some permanent, some only one day a week; some outdoor, some indoor. Some sell only fruit and vegetables, others sell almost anything.

• In Athens and the larger towns there are some large department stores and supermarket chains, but on the whole Greek shops tend to be smaller, individual ones.

• The περίπτερο (*pereeptero*), or kiosk, is an important feature of Greek life. Kiosks sell a wide variety of goods, including newspapers, cigarettes, postcards, toilet articles, camera film and so on, and often stay open late.

• Greek cigarettes are mostly made with strong black tobacco, but the main foreign brands are also available (though they cost a good deal more).

• The chemist's – το φαρμακείο (*to farmakeeo*) – has a red cross sign outside. Lists of duty chemists that are open late, or for 24 hours, are displayed in the window (and are printed in newspapers).

Chemists sell mainly medicines, baby products and health foods. For toiletries and cosmetics go to a shop selling καλλυντικά (*kaleendeeka*).

• The post office – το ταχυδρομείο (*to takheedhromeeo*) – is generally open from 7.30 a.m. to 8.30 p.m., Mondays to

Fridays and Saturday mornings. Letterboxes (**ΓΡΑΜΜΑ-ΤΟΚΙΒΩΤΙΑ**) are painted yellow. There may be separate slots for mail within Greece (**ΕΣΩΤΕΡΙΚΟΥ**) and abroad (**ΕΞΩΤΕΡΙΚΟΥ**), and also for express mail (**ΕΠΕΙ-ΓΟΝΤΑ**). You can also buy postage stamps at some kiosks.

If you want to receive mail at a *poste restante*, you can have it sent to any post office.

● To ask for something in a shop, all you need do is name it and add 'please' – or just point and say 'some of this, please' or 'two, please'.

● Note that liquids are sometimes sold by weight: you will want half a kilo of draught wine, for example, not half a litre.

● Before you go shopping, try to make a list of what you need and how to pronounce the words in Greek. If you're looking for clothes or shoes, work out what size to ask for and other things like colour, material and so on.

● In some of the tourist shops and shopping areas you may be able to get a better price by bargaining.

● Customers and shopkeepers often exchange greetings and goodbyes, so check up on the correct phrases for the time of day (see inside back cover). Don't be afraid to take the initiative.

You may see

ΑΘΛΗΤΙΚΑ ΕΙΔΗ Αθλητικά είδη	Sports goods
ΑΝΑΜΝΗΣΤΙΚΑ Αναμνηστικά	Souvenirs
ΑΝΘΟΠΩΛΕΙΟ(Ν) Ανθοπωλείο(ν)	Florist
ΑΝΟΙΚΤΟ(Ν) Ανοικτό(ν)	Open
ΑΝΤΙΚΕΣ Αντίκες	Antiques
ΑΡΤΟΠΩΛΕΙΟ(Ν) Αρτοπωλείο(ν)	Baker's
ΑΥΤΟΕΞΥΠΗΡΕΤΗΣΗ Αυτοεξυπηρέτηση	Self-service
ΒΙΒΛΙΟΠΩΛΕΙΟ(Ν) Βιβλιοπωλείο(ν)	Bookshop
ΓΑΛΑΚΤΟΠΩΛΕΙΟ(Ν) Γαλακτοπωλείο(ν)	Dairy
ΓΡΑΜΜΑΤΟΚΙΒΩΤΙΟ(Ν) Γραμματοκιβώτιο(ν)	Postbox
ΔΕΡΜΑΤΙΝΑ ΕΙΔΗ Δερμάτινα είδη	Leather goods
ΔΙΑΝΥΚΤΕΡΕΥΟΝ ΦΑΡΜΑΚΕΙΟ(Ν) Διανυκτερεύον φαρμακείο(ν)	Duty chemist's (Night time)
ΔΙΗΜΕΡΕΥΟΝ ΦΑΡΜΑΚΕΙΟ(Ν) Διημερεύον φαρμακείο(ν)	Duty chemist's (Day time)
ΔΙΣΚΟΙ, ΚΑΣΕΤΕΣ Δίσκοι, Κασέτες	Records, cassettes

ΔΩΡΑ Δώρα	Gifts
ΕΙΔΗ ΔΩΡΩΝ Είδη δωρών	Gifts
ΕΙΔΗ ΚΑΠΝΙΣΤΗ Είδη καπνιστή	Tobacconist's
ΕΙΔΗ ΚΙΓΚΑΛΛΕΡΙΑΣ Είδη κιγκαλλερίας	Ironmonger's
ΕΙΔΙΚΗ ΠΡΟΣΦΟΡΑ Ειδική προσφορά	Special offer
ΕΙΣΟΔΟΣ Είσοδος	Entrance
ΕΚΠΤΩΣΕΙΣ Εκπτώσεις	Sales/Reductions
ΕΜΠΟΡΙΚΟ ΚΕΝΤΡΟ Εμπορικό κέντρο	Shopping centre
ΕΞΟΔΟΣ (ΚΙΝΔΥΝΟΥ) Εξοδος (κινδύνου)	(Emergency) exit
ΕΠΙΠΛΑ Επιπλα	Furniture
ΕΤΟΙΜΑ ΕΝΔΥΜΑΤΑ Ετοιμα ενδύματα	Clothes (off the peg)
ΖΑΧΑΡΟΠΛΑΣΤΕΙΟ(Ν) Ζαχαροπλαστείο(ν)	Patisserie
ΗΛΕΚΤΡΙΚΑ ΕΙΔΗ Ηλεκτρικά είδη	Electrical goods
ΙΧΘΥΟΠΩΛΕΙΟ(Ν) Ιχθυοπωλείο(ν)	Fishmonger's
ΚΑΒΑ ΠΟΤΑ Κάβα ποτά	Wine cellar; off licence
ΚΑΛΛΥΝΤΙΚΑ Καλλυντικά	Drugstore/Perfumery
ΚΛΕΙΣΤΟ(Ν) Κλειστό(ν)	Closed

ΚΟΜΜΩΤΗΡΙΟ(Ν) Κομμωτήριο(ν)	Hairdresser's
ΚΟΣΜΗΜΑΤΟΠΩΛΕΙΟ(Ν) Κοσμήματοπωλείο(ν)	Jeweller's
ΚΡΕΟΠΩΛΕΙΟ(Ν) Κρεοπωλείο(ν)	Butcher's
ΛΙΑΝΙΚΗ ΤΙΜΗ Λιανική τιμή	Retail price
ΜΑΝΑΒΙΚΟ Μανάβικο	Greengrocer's
ΜΟΔΑ Μόδα	Fashionwear
ΜΠΑΚΑΛΙΚΟ Μπακάλικο	Groceries
ΟΠΤΙΚΑ Οπτικά	Optician's
ΠΑΙΓΝΙΔΙΑ Παιγνίδια	Toys
ΠΑΝΤΟΠΩΛΕΙΟ(Ν) Παντοπωλείο(ν)	Groceries
ΠΟΛΥΚΑΤΑΣΤΗΜΑ Πολυκατάστημα	Department store
ΠΩΛΟΥΝΤΑΙ ΓΡΑΜΜΑΤΟΣΗΜΑ Πωλούνται γραμματόσημα	Stamps on sale
ΡΟΛΟΓΑΣ Ρολογάς	Watchmaker's
ΡΟΥΧΑ (ΓΥΝΑΙΚΕΙΑ/ ΑΝΔΡΙΚΑ/ΠΑΙΔΙΚΑ) Ρούχα (γυναικεία/ανδρικά/ παιδικά)	Clothes (ladies'/men's/ children's)
ΣΕΛΦ ΣΕΡΒΙΣ Σελφ σέρβις	Self-service

ΣΙΔΗΡΙΚΑ Σιδηρικά	Ironmonger's/Hardware
ΣΟΥΒΕΝΙΡ Σουβενίρ	Souvenirs
ΣΟΥΠΕΡΜΑΡΚΕΤ Σουπερμάρκετ	Supermarket
ΣΤΕΓΝΟΚΑΘΑΡΙΣΤΗΡΙΟ(Ν) Στεγνοκαθαριστήριο(ν)	Dry-cleaner's
ΤΑΜΕΙΟ(Ν) Ταμείο(ν)	Cashier
ΤΑΧΥΔΡΟΜΕΙΟ(Ν) Ταχυδρομείο(ν)	Post office
ΥΓΙΕΙΝΕΣ ΤΡΟΦΕΣ Υγιεινές τροφές	Health foods
ΥΠΕΡΑΓΟΡΑ Υπεραγορά	Hypermarket
ΥΠΟΓΕΙΟ(Ν) Υπόγειο(ν)	Basement
ΥΠΟΔΗΜΑΤΑ Υποδήματα	Footwear
ΦΑΡΜΑΚΕΙΟ(Ν) Φαρμακείο(ν)	Chemist's
ΦΟΥΡΝΟΣ Φούρνος	Baker's
ΦΡΟΥΤΑ Φρούτα	Fruit/Fruiterer's
ΧΑΡΤΙΚΑ Χαρτικά	Stationer's
ΨΑΡΑΔΙΚΟ Ψαράδικο	Fishmonger's
ΨΑΡΙΑ Ψάρια	Fish

General phrases

(*see also* Directions, *page 30*; Problems and complaints, *page 187*; Numbers, *page 236*)

Where is the main shopping area?

Πού είναι τα μαγαζιά;
poo eene ta magazya

Where is the chemist's?

Πού είναι το φαρμακείο;
poo eene to farmakeeo

Is there a grocer's shop around here?

Υπάρχει μπακάλικο εδώ κοντά;
eeparkhee bakaleeko edho konda

Where can I buy batteries?

Πού μπορώ να αγοράσω μπαταρίες;
poo boro na agoraso bataree-es

What time does the baker's open?

Τι ώρα ανοίγει ο φούρνος;
tee ora aneeyee o foornos

What time does the post office close?

Τι ώρα κλείνει το ταχυδρομείο;
tee ora kleenee to takheedromeeo

What time do you open in the morning?

Τι ώρα ανοίγετε το πρωί;
tee ora aneeyete to proee

What time do you close this evening?

Τι ώρα κλείνετε απόψε;
tee ora kleenete apopse

Do you have . . . ?

Μήπως έχετε . . . ;
meepos ekhete . . .

Do you have stamps?

Μήπως έχετε γραμματόσημα;
meepos ekhete gramatoseema

Do you have any wholemeal bread?

Μήπως έχετε χωριάτικο ψωμί;
meepos ekhete khoryateeko psomee

How much is it?
Πόσο κάνει;
poso kanee

Altogether
Ολα μαζί
ola mazee

How much is this?
Πόσο κάνει αυτό;
poso kanee afto

How much are these?
Πόσο κάνουν αυτά;
poso kanoon afta

I don't understand
Δεν κατάλαβα
dhen-gatalava

Can you write it down, please?
Μπορείτε να το γράψετε παρακαλώ;
boreete na to grapsete parakalo

It's too expensive
Είναι πολύ ακριβό
eene polee akreevo

Have you got anything cheaper?
Εχετε τίποτα πιο φτηνό;
ekhete teepota pyo fteeno

I don't have enough money
Δεν έχω αρκετά χρήματα
dhen ekho arketa khreemata

Can you keep it for me?
Μπορείτε να μου το κρατήσετε;
boreete na moo to krateesete

I'm just looking
Απλώς χαζεύω
aplos khazevo

This one, please
Αυτό παρακαλώ
afto parakalo

That one, please
Εκείνο παρακαλώ
ekeeno parakalo

Two, please
Δύο παρακαλώ
dheeo parakalo

Three, please
Τρία παρακαλώ
treea parakalo

Not that one – this one
Οχι εκείνο, αυτό εδώ
okhee ekeeno afto edho

There's one in the window
Υπάρχει ένα στη βιτρίνα
eeparkhee ena stee veetreena

That's fine
Αυτό είναι εντάξει
afto eene endaksee

Nothing else, thank you
Τίποτ'άλλο ευχαριστώ
teepotalo efkhareesto

I'll take it
Θα το πάρω
tha to paro

I'll think about it
Θα το σκεφτώ
tha to skefto

Do you have a bag, please?
**Μήπως έχετε σακκούλα
παρακαλώ;**
*meepos ekhete sakoola
parakalo*

Can you wrap it, please?
**Μπορείτε να το τυλίξετε
παρακαλώ;**
*boreete na to teeleeksete
parakalo*

With plenty of paper
Με μπόλικο χαρτί
me boleeko khartee

I'm taking it to England
Θα το πάρω στην Αγγλία
tha to paro steen angleea

It's a gift
Είναι για δώρο
eene ya dhoro

Where do I pay?
Πού πληρώνω;
poo pleerono

Do you take credit cards?
**Δέχεστε πιστωτικές
κάρτες;**
*dhekheste peestoteekes
kartes*

Do you take traveller's
cheques?
Δέχεστε τράβελερς τσεκ;
dhekheste travelers tsek

I'm sorry, I don't have any
change
Συγγνώμη, δεν έχω ψιλά
seegnomee dhen ekho pseela

Can you give me a receipt
please?
**Μπορείτε να μου δώσετε
μια απόδειξη παρακαλώ;**
*boreete na moo dhosete mya
apodheeksee parakalo*

Buying food and drink

A kilo of . . .
Ένα κιλό . . .
ena keelo . . .

A kilo of grapes, please
**Ένα κιλό σταφύλια
παρακαλώ**
ena keelo stafeelya parakalo

Two kilos of oranges, please
Δύο κιλά πορτοκάλια παρακαλώ
dheeo keela portokalya parakalo

Half a kilo of tomatoes, please
Μισόκιλο ντομάτες παρακαλώ
meesokeelo domates parakalo

A hundred grams of . . .
Εκατό γραμμάρια . . .
ekato gramarya . . .

A hundred grams of feta cheese, please
Εκατό γραμμάρια φέτα παρακαλώ
ekato gramarya feta parakalo

Two hundred grams of spicy sausage, please
Διακόσια γραμμάρια λουκάνικο χωριάτικο παρακαλώ
dhyakosya gramarya lookaneeko khoryateeko parakalo

In a piece
Σε ένα κομμάτι
se ena komatee

Sliced
Σε φέτες
se fetes

A piece of cheese, please
Λίγο τυρί παρακαλώ
leego teeree parakalo

Five slices of ham, please
Πέντε φέτες ζαμπόν παρακαλώ
pende fetes zambon parakalo

Half a kilo of white wine, please
Μισόκιλο άσπρο κρασί παρακαλώ
meesokeelo aspro krasee parakalo

A bottle of water, please
Ενα μπουκάλι νερό παρακαλώ
ena bookalee nero parakalo

A small (carton of) milk, please
Ενα μικρό γάλα παρακαλώ
ena meekro gala parakalo

Two cans of beer, please
Δύο μπύρες σε κουτί παρακαλώ
dheeo beeres se kootee parakalo

A bit of that, please
Λίγο απ'αυτό παρακαλώ
leego apafto parakalo

What is this?
Τι είναι αυτό;
tee eene afto

A bit more
Λίγο ακόμα
leego akoma

What is there in this?
Τι περιέχει αυτό;
tee peryekhee afto

A bit less
Πιο λίγο
pyo leego

Can I try it?
Μπορώ να το δοκιμάσω;
boro na to dhokeemaso

At the chemist's

Aspirins, please
Ασπιρίνες παρακαλώ
aspeereenes parakalo

Plasters, please
Λευκοπλάστη παρακαλώ
lefkoplastee parakalo

Do you have something for . . . ?
Μήπως έχετε κάτι για . . . ;
meepos ekhete katee ya . . .

Do you have something for diarrhoea?
Μήπως έχετε κάτι για την ευκοιλιότητα;
meepos ekhete katee ya teen efkeelyoteeta

Do you have something for insect bites?
Μήπως έχετε κάτι για τσίμπημα εντόμου;
meepos ekhete katee ya tseembeema endomoo

Do you have something for period pains?
Μήπως έχετε παυσίπονο για την περίοδο;
meepos ekhete pafseepono ya teem-bereeodho

Buying clothes and shoes

I want a skirt/a shirt
**Θέλω μια φούστα/ένα
πουκάμισο**
*thelo mya foosta/ena
pookameeso*

I want some sandals
Θέλω πέδιλα
thelo pedheela

Size 40
Νούμερο σαράντα
noomero saranda

Can I try it on?
Μπορώ να το δοκιμάσω;
boro na to dhokeemaso

Do you have a mirror?
Έχετε καθρέφτη;
ekhete kathreftee

I like it
Μ'αρέσει
maresee

I like them
Μ'αρέσουν
maresoon

I don't like it
Δεν μ'αρέσει
dhen maresee

I don't like them
Δεν μ'αρέσουν
dhen maresoon

I don't like the colour
Δεν μ'αρέσει το χρώμα
dhen maresee to khroma

Do you have it in other
colours?
**Μήπως υπάρχει σε άλλα
χρώματα;**
*meepos eeparkhee se ala
khromata*

It's too big/small
Είναι πολύ μεγάλο/μικρό
eene polee megalo/meekro

They're too big/small
Είναι πολύ μεγάλα/μικρά
eene polee megala/meekra

Have you got a smaller
size?
**Μήπως έχετε πιο μικρό
νούμερο;**
*meepos ekhete pyo meekro
noomero*

Have you got a bigger size?
**Μήπως έχετε πιο μεγάλο
νούμερο;**
*meepos ekhete pyo megalo
noomero*

Miscellaneous

Five stamps for England,
please
**Πέντε γραμματόσημα για
την Αγγλία παρακαλώ**
*pende gramatoseema ya teen
angleea parakalo*

For postcards/letters
Για καρτ-ποστάλ/γράμματα
ya kart-postal/gramata

Three postcards, please
**Τρεις καρτ-ποστάλ
παρακαλώ**
trees kart-postal parakalo

A box of matches, please
**Ένα κουτί σπίρτα
παρακαλώ**
ena kootee speerta parakalo

A film like this, please
Ένα τέτοιο φιλμ παρακαλώ
ena tetyo feelm parakalo

For this camera
Γι'αυτή τη μηχανή
yaftee tee meekhanee

Do you have any English
newspapers?
**Μήπως έχετε Αγγλικές
εφημερίδες;**
*meepos ekhete angleekes
efeemereedhes*

You may hear

Μπορώ να σας βοηθήσω;
boro na sas voeetheeso
May I help you?

Τι θέλετε;
tee thelete
What would you like?

Πόσο θέλετε;
poso thelete
How much would you like?

Πόσα/Πόσους/Πόσες θέλετε;
posa/posoos/poses thelete
How many would you like?

Εντάξει;
endaksee
Is that all right?

Τίποτ'άλλο;
teepotalo
Anything else?

Λυπάμαι, τελείωσαν
leepame teleeosan
I'm sorry, we're sold out

**Λυπάμαι, αλλά τώρα
είμαστε κλειστά**
*leepame ala tora eemaste
kleesta*
I'm sorry, we're closed now

Θέλετε να σας το τυλίξω;
thelete na sas to teeleekso
Do you want me to wrap it
for you?

Στο ταμείο παρακαλώ
sto tameeo parakalo
Please go to the cashier

Μήπως έχετε ψιλά;
meepos ekhete pseela
Do you have any change?

**Χρειάζεται συνταγή
γιατρού**
khryazete seendayee yatroo
You need a prescription

Τι νούμερο φοράτε;
tee noomero forate
What size are you?

**Για καρτ-ποστάλ ή για
γράμμα;**
ya kart-postal ee ya grama
For postcard or letter?

Τι (είδος) . . . ?
tee (eedhos) . . .
What sort of . . . ?

**Τι (είδος) μηχανή(ς)
έχετε;**
*tee (eedhos) meekhanee(s)
ekhete*
What sort of camera do you
have?

Τι (είδος) φιλμ θέλετε;
tee (eedhos) feelm thelete
What sort of film do you
want?

BUSINESS TRIPS

- You'll probably be doing business with the help of interpreters or in a language everyone speaks, but you may need a few Greek phrases to cope at a company's reception desk.

- When you arrive for an appointment, all you need do is say who you've come to see and give your name or hand over your business card. However, if you're not expected you may need to make an appointment or leave a message.

You may see

1ΟΣ ΟΡΟΦΟΣ 1ος όροφος	1st floor
2ΟΣ ΟΡΟΦΟΣ 2ος όροφος	2nd floor
ΑΝΕΛΚΥΣΤΗΡ Ανελκυστήρ	Lift
ΑΠΑΓΟΡΕΥΕΤΑΙ Η ΕΙΣΟΔΟΣ Απαγορεύεται η είσοδος	No entry
ΑΠΑΓΟΡΕΥΕΤΑΙ Η ΕΙΣΟΔΟΣ ΣΤΟΥΣ ΜΗ ΕΧΟΝΤΑΣ ΕΡΓΑΣΙΑ Απαγορεύεται η είσοδος στους μη έχοντας εργασία	No entry to unauthorised persons
ΑΠΑΓΟΡΕΥΕΤΑΙ ΤΟ ΚΑΠΝΙΣΜΑ Απαγορεύεται το κάπνισμα	No smoking

ΔΕΝ ΛΕΙΤΟΥΡΓΕΙ	Out of order
Δεν λειτουργεί	
ΕΙΣΟΔΟΣ	Entrance
Είσοδος	
ΕΞΟΔΟΣ (ΚΙΝΔΥΝΟΥ)	(Emergency) exit
Εξοδος (κινδύνου)	
ΕΠΕ = Εταιρία **Περιορισμένης** **Ευθύνης**	Limited liability company
ΕΤΑΙΡ(Ε)ΙΑ	Company
Εταιρ(ε)ία	
ΙΣΟΓΕΙΟ(Ν)	Ground floor
Ισόγειο(ν)	
ΚΛΙΜΑΚΟΣΤΑΣΙΟ(Ν)	Stairs
Κλιμακοστάσιο(ν)	
ΡΕΣΕΨΙΟΝ	Reception
Ρεσεψιόν	

You may want to say

(*See also* Days, months, dates, *page 209*; Time, *page 213*)

Mr Sklirakis, please
Τον κύριο Σκληράκη
   παρακαλώ
ton-geeryo skleerakee
   parakalo

Mrs Zapheiropoulos,
   please
Την κυρία Ζαφειροπούλου
   παρακαλώ
teen-geereea zafeeropooloo
   parakalo

Miss Veremis, please
Τη δεσποινίδα Βερέμη
   παρακαλώ
tee dhespeeneedha veremee
   parakalo

The manager, please
Τον διευθυντή παρακαλώ
ton dhyeftheendee parakalo

My name is . . .
Το όνομά μου είναι . . .
to onoma-moo eene . . .

My company is . . .
Η εταιρία μου είναι . . .
ee etereea-moo eene . . .

I have an appointment with Mr Thanos Pandis
Έχω ραντεβού με τον κύριο Θάνο Παντή
*ekho randevoo me ton-geeryo **thano** pandee*

I don't have an appointment
Δεν έχω ραντεβού
dhen ekho randevoo

I'd like to make an appointment with Miss Papadopoulos
Θα ήθελα να κλείσω ραντεβού με τη δεσποινίδα
  Παπαδοπούλου
*tha eethela na **kleeso** randevoo me tee dhespee**needha***
  *papado**pooloo***

I am free this afternoon at five o'clock
Είμαι ελεύθερος/ελεύθερη/σήμερα το απόγευμα στις
  πέντε
*eeme eleftheros/eleftheree seemera to apoyevma stees **pende***

I'd like to talk to the export manager
Θα ήθελα να μιλήσω στον υπεύθυνο εξαγωγών
*tha eethela na meeleeso ston eepeftheeno eksago**gon***

What is his/her name?
Πώς τον/τη λένε;
*pos ton/tee **lene***

When will he/she be back?
Πότε θα επιστρέψει;
pote tha epeestrepsee

Can I leave a message?
Μπορώ να αφήσω μήνυμα;
boro na afeeso meeneema

Can you ask him/her to call me?
Μπορείτε να του/της πείτε να μου τηλεφωνήσει;
boreete na too/tees peete na moo teelefoneesee

My telephone number is . . .
Ο αριθμός τηλεφώνου μου είναι . . .
o areethmos teelefonoo-moo eene . . .

I am staying at the Hotel Paradise
Μένω στο ξενοδοχείο Παράδεισος
meno sto ksenodhokheeo paradheesos

Where is his/her office?
Πού είναι το γραφείο του/της;
poo eene to grafeeo-too/tees

I am here for the exhibition/trade fair
Είμαι εδώ για την έκθεση/εμπορική έκθεση
eeme edho ya teen ektheesee/emboreekee ektheesee

I am here for the conference
Είμαι εδώ για το συνέδριο
eeme edho ya to seenedhryo

I have to make a phone call (to Britain)
Πρέπει να τηλεφωνήσω (στη Μεγάλη Βρετανία)
prepee na teelefoneeso (stee megalee vretaneea)

I have to send a telex
Πρέπει να στείλω ένα τέλεξ
prepee na steelo ena teleks

I have to send this by fax
Πρέπει να στείλω αυτό με fax
prepee na steelo afto me fax

I need someone to type a letter for me
Χρειάζομαι κάποιον να μου δακτυλογραφήσει ένα γράμμα
khryazome kapyon na moo dhakteelografeesee ena grama

I want to send this by post/courier
Θέλω να στείλω αυτό με το ταχυδρομείο/κούριερ
thelo na steelo afto me to takheedhromeeo/kooryer

I need a photocopy (of this)
Χρειάζομαι φωτοτυπία (από αυτό)
khryazome fototeepeea (apo afto)

I need an interpreter
Χρειάζομαι διερμηνέα
khryazome dhyermeenea

You may hear

Το όνομά σας παρακαλώ;
to onoma-sas parakalo
Your name, please?

Πώς σας λένε, παρακαλώ;
pos sas lene parakalo
What are you called,
  please?

**Το όνομα της εταιρίας
  σας παρακαλώ;**
*to onoma tees etereeas-sas
  parakalo*
The name of your
  company, please?

Έχετε ραντεβού;
ekhete randevoo
Do you have an
  appointment?

Έχετε κάρτα;
ekhete karta
Do you have a card?

Σας περιμένει;
sas pereemenee
Is he/she expecting you?

**(Περιμένετε) ένα λεπτό
  παρακαλώ**
*(pereemenete) ena lepto
  parakalo*
(Wait) one moment, please

**Θα του/της πω ότι είσαστε
  εδώ**
*tha too/tees po otee eesaste
  edho*
I'll tell him/her you're here

Έρχεται
erkhete
He/She is coming

Καθήστε παρακαλώ
katheeste parakalo
Please sit down

Περάστε παρακαλώ
peraste parakalo
Go in, please

Ελάτε από'δώ παρακαλώ
elate apodho parakalo
Come this way, please

Ο κύριος Πάνος δεν είναι εδώ
o keeryos panos dhen eene edho
Mr Panos is not here

Η δεσποινίδα Σκούρου λείπει
ee dhespeeneedha skooroo leepee
Miss Skouros is out

Η κυρία Καλογεροπούλου θα επιστρέψει στις έντεκα
ee keereea kaloyeropooloo tha epeestrepsee stees endeka
Mrs Kaloyeropoulos will be back at eleven o'clock

Σε μισή ώρα/μία ώρα
se meesee ora/meea ora
In half an hour/an hour

Πάρτε το ασανσέρ στον τρίτο όροφο
parte to asanser ston-dreeto orofo
Take the lift to the third floor

Προχωρείτε στο διάδρομο
prokhoreete sto dhyadhromo
Go along the corridor

Είναι η πρώτη/δεύτερη πόρτα
eene ee protee/dhefteree porta
It's the first/second door

Αριστερά/δεξιά
areestera/dheksya
On the left/right

Δωμάτιο νούμερο τριακόσια είκοσι
dhomatyo noomero tryakosya eekosee
Room number 320

Εμπρός!
embros
Come in!

SIGHTSEEING

• You can get information about all the sights worth seeing from the National Tourist Organisation of Greece (address, page 235) and from local tourist offices. The latter can also tell you about the sightseeing tours by coach that are available in many cities and tourist areas, often with English-speaking guides.

• Opening hours vary for archaeological sites, museums, galleries and so on, and they often close quite early in the afternoon; it is always worth checking the opening times in advance, particularly when you're visiting a site that's some way away. Most sites and museums shut on either Mondays or Tuesdays.

You may see

ΑΝΟΙΚΤΟ(Ν) Ανοικτό(ν)	Open
ΑΠΑΓΟΡΕΥΕΤΑΙ Η **ΕΙΣΟΔΟΣ** Απαγορεύεται η είσοδος	No entry
ΙΔΙΩΤΙΚΟΣ ΧΩΡΟΣ Ιδιώτικος χώρος	Private area
ΚΛΕΙΣΤΟ(Ν) Κλειστό(ν)	Closed
ΜΗΝ ΑΓΓΙΖΕΤΕ Μην αγγίζετε	Do not touch
ΜΗΝ ΠΑΤΑΤΕ ΤΟ **ΠΡΑΣΙΝΟ** Μην πατάτε το πράσινο	Keep off the grass
ΞΕΝΑΓΗΣΕΙΣ Ξεναγήσεις	Guided tours

You may want to say

(See also At the tourist office, page 83, for asking for information, brochures, etc.)

Opening times

(see Time, page 213)

When is the museum open?
Πότε είναι ανοικτό το μουσείο;
pote eene aneekto to mooseeo

What time does the Acropolis open?
Τι ώρα ανοίγει η Ακρόπολη;
tee ora aneeyee ee akropolee

What time does the museum close?
Τι ώρα κλείνει το μουσείο;
tee ora kleenee to mooseeo

Is it open on Sundays?
Είναι ανοικτό την Κυριακή;
eene aneekto teen-geeryakee

Can we visit the monastery?
Επιτρέπεται να επισκεφτούμε το μοναστήρι;
epeetrepete na epeeskeftoome to monasteeree

Is it open to the public?
Είναι ανοικτό στο κοινό;
eene aneekto sto keeno

157

Visiting places

One/Two, please
Ένα/Δύο παρακαλώ
ena/dheeo parakalo

For two adults and one child
Για δύο ενήλικους και ένα παιδί
ya dheeo eneeleekoos ke ena pedhee

Are there reductions for children?

Υπάρχουν εκπτώσεις για παιδιά;

eeparkhoon ekptosees ya pedhya

For students

Για φοιτητές

ya feeteetes

For pensioners

Για συνταξιούχους

ya seendaksyookhoos

For the disabled

Για αναπήρους

ya anapeeroos

For groups

Για ομάδες

ya omadhes

Are there guided tours (in English)?

Υπάρχει ξενάγηση (στα Αγγλικά);

eeparkhee ksenayeesee (sta angleeka)

Can I take photos?

Επιτρέπεται να πάρω φωτογραφίες;

epeetrepete na paro fotografee-es

Would you mind taking a photo of us, please

Έχετε την καλωσύνη να μας πάρετε μια φωτογραφία;

ekhete teen-galoseenee na mas parete mya fotografeea

When was this built?

Πότε χτίστηκε αυτό;

pote khteesteeke afto

Who painted that picture?

Ποιος έκανε αυτόν τον πίνακα

pyos ekane afton tom-beenaka

In what year? (*see* Days, months, dates, *page 209*)

Ποια χρονιά;

pya khronya

What is this flower called?

Πώς το λένε αυτό το λουλούδι;

pos to lene afto to looloodhee

What is that bird called?

Πώς το λένε αυτό το πουλί;

pos to lene afto to poolee

Sightseeing excursions

What tourist excursions are there?

Τι εκδρομές υπάρχουν για τουρίστες;

tee ekdhromes eeparkhoon ya tooreestes

Are there any excursions to Delphi?

Υπάρχουν εκδρομές για τους Δελφούς;

eeparkhoon ekdhromes ya toos dhelfoos

What time does it leave?

Τι ώρα φεύγει;

tee ora fevyee

How long does it last?

Πόση ώρα κρατάει;

posee ora krataee

What time does it get back?

Τι ώρα γυρίζει;

tee ora yeereezee

Where does it leave from?

Από πού φεύγει;

apo poo fevyee

Does the guide speak English?

Ο/Η ξεναγός μιλάει Αγγλικά;

o/ee ksenagos meelaee angleeka

How much is it?

Πόσο κάνει;

poso kanee

You may hear

Το μουσείο είναι ανοικτό κάθε μέρα πλην της Τρίτης
to mooseeo eene aneekto kathe mera pleen tees treetees
The museum is open every day except Tuesday

Είναι κλείστο κάθε Τρίτη
eene kleesto kathe treetee
It is closed on Tuesdays

Ο ναός χτίστηκε στην κλασσική εποχή
o naos khteesteeke steen-glaseekee epokhee
The temple was built in the Classical period

Το κάστρο χτίστηκε στό δέκατο τρίτο αιώνα
to kastro khteesteeke sto dhekato treeto eona
The castle was built in the thirteenth century

Είναι μια εικόνα του Δαμασκηνού
eene mya eekona too dhamaskeenoo
It's an icon by Damaskinos

Υπάρχουν εκδρομές κάθε Τρίτη και Πέμπτη
eeparkhoon ekdhromes kathe treetee ke pemptee
There are excursions every Tuesday and Thursday

Το πούλμαν φεύγει στις δέκα από την Πλατεία Αίγυπτου
to poolman fevyee stees dheka apo teem-blateea eyeeptoo
The coach leaves at ten o'clock from Plateia Egyptou

ENTERTAINMENTS

• Greece's most popular spectator sports are basketball and football. Most professional sports fixtures take place on Sundays.

• Evening performances at theatres, cinemas, musical events, etc. usually start late – around 10.30 or 11.00 p.m. It is customary to give a small tip to theatre and cinema ushers.

• Films are categorised as suitable for general viewing, or for people over thirteen or eighteen. Some may be labelled as not recommended for those under thirteen or eighteen.

Many American and British films are shown in Greek cinemas, usually subtitled (με υποτίτλους – *me eepoteetloos*).

• In the summer, performances of theatre, both ancient and modern, music and dance are held in the open-air ancient theatre of Herodes Atticus in Athens (το Ηρώδειο – *to eerodhyo*). Tickets can be obtained either at the theatre, or from the National Tourist Organisation of Greece office.

• Performances of folk dance are held throughout the summer in the Dora Stratou theatre on Philopappos Hill, near the Acropolis, in Athens.

• Outside Athens, there are performances of ancient drama in the ancient theatre at Epidavros. These are in Modern Greek translation, but well worth a visit for the experience even if you can't follow the play, in which case you should see a comedy for preference.

• Athens has a number of nightclubs (κέντρα – *kendra*), in which popular singers can be heard, and also some tavernas in which traditional music and dance is performed. Most of these will be closed during the summer months, when indoor activities are avoided.

You may see

ΑΙΘΟΥΣΑ ΣΥΝΑΥΛΙΩΝ Αίθουσα συναυλιών	Concert hall
ΑΚΑΤΑΛΛΗΛΟ ΓΙΑ ΠΑΙΔΙΑ ΚΑΤΩ ΤΩΝ 13 ΕΤΩΝ Ακατάλληλο για παιδιά κάτω των 13 ετών	Not recommended for under-13s
ΑΠΑΓΟΡΕΥΕΤΑΙ Η ΕΙΣΟΔΟΣ ΜΕΤΑ ΤΗΝ ΕΝΑΡΞΗ ΤΗΣ ΠΑΡΑΣΤΑΣΗΣ Απαγορεύεται η είσοδος μετά την έναρξη της παράστασης	No entry once the performance has begun
ΑΠΟΓΕΥΜΑΤΙΝΗ ΠΑΡΑΣΤΑΣΗ Απογευματινή παράσταση	Matinee
ΒΕΣΤΙΑΡΙΟ(Ν) Βεστιάριο(ν)	Cloakroom
ΒΡΑΔΥΝΗ ΠΑΡΑΣΤΑΣΗ Βραδυνή παράσταση	Evening performance
ΔΕΝ ΕΧΕΙ ΔΙΑΛΕΙΜΜΑ Δεν έχει διάλειμμα	There is no interval
ΕΙΣΙΤΗΡΙΑ ΓΙΑ ΤΗ ΣΗΜΕΡΙΝΗ ΠΑΡΑΣΤΑΣΗ Εισιτήρια για τη σημερινή παράσταση	Tickets for today's performance

ΕΞΑΝΤΛΗΘΗΚΑΝ Εξαντλήθηκαν	Sold out
ΕΞΕΔΡΑ Εξέδρα	Stand, grandstand
ΕΞΩΣΤΗΣ Εξώστης	Balcony, circle
ΘΕΑΤΡΟ(Ν) Θέατρο(ν)	Theatre
ΘΕΣΗ Θέση	Seat
ΘΕΩΡΕΙΑ Θεωρεία	Boxes
ΙΠΠΟΔΡΟΜΟΣ Ιππόδρομος	Racecourse
ΚΑΤΑΛΛΗΛΟ ΑΠΟ 13 ΕΤΩΝ ΚΑΙ ΑΝΩ Κατάλληλο από 13 ετών και άνω	Suitable for over-13s only
ΚΙΝΗΜΑΤΟΓΡΑΦΙΚΗ ΛΕΣΧΗ Κινηματογραφική Λέσχη	Film club
ΛΥΡΙΚΗ ΣΚΗΝΗ Λυρική σκηνή	Opera house
ΜΕ ΕΛΛΗΝΙΚΟΥΣ ΥΠΟΤΙΤΛΟΥΣ Με Ελληνικούς υποτίτλους	With Greek subtitles
ΝΤΙΣΚΟΤΕΚ Ντισκοτέκ	Discothèque
ΠΛΑΤΕΙΑ Πλατεία	Stalls seats
ΠΟΡΤΑ Πόρτα	Door

ΠΡΟΠΩΛΗΣΗ ΕΙΣΙΤΗΡΙΩΝ	Advance booking
Προπώληση εισιτηρίων	
ΣΕΙΡΑ	Row
Σειρά	
ΣΙΝΕΜΑ	Cinema
Σινεμά	
ΣΤΑΔΙΟ(Ν)	Stadium
Στάδιο(ν)	
ΣΥΝΕΧΗΣ ΠΑΡΑΣΤΑΣΗ	Continuous performance
Συνεχής παράσταση	
ΤΣΙΡΚΟΣ	Circus
Τσίρκος	
ΩΡΕΣ ΕΝΑΡΞΕΩΣ 6, 9, 12	Separate performances at 6,
Ωρες ενάρξεως 6, 9, 12	9 and 12

You may want to say

What's on

(*see* Time, *page 213*)

What is there to do in the
evenings?
**Τι μπορεί να κάνει κανείς
τα βράδυα;**
*tee boree na kanee kanees ta
vradhya*

Is there a discothèque
around here?
**Υπάρχει ντισκοτέκ εδώ
κοντά;**
*eeparkhee deeskotek edho
konda*

Is there any entertainment
for children?
**Υπάρχει διασκέδαση για
παιδιά;**
*eeparkhee dhyaskedhasee
ya pedhya*

What's on tonight?
Τι παίζει απόψε;
tee pezee apopse

What's on tomorrow?
Τι παίζει αύριο;
tee pezee avryo

At the cinema
Στο σινεμά
sto seenema

At the theatre
Στο θέατρο
sto theatro

Who is playing?
Ποιος παίζει;
pyos pezee

Who is singing?
Ποιος τραγουδάει;
pyos tragoodhaee

Does the film have subtitles?
Η ταινία έχει υποτίτλους;
ee teneea ekhee eepoteetloos

Is there a football match on Sunday?
Εχει ποδόσφαιρο την Κυριακή;
ekhee podhosfero teen-geeryakee

Who are playing?
Ποιοι παίζουν;
pyee pezoon

What time does the show start?
Τι ώρα αρχίζει η παράσταση;
tee ora arkheezee ee parastasee

What time does the concert start?
Τι ώρα αρχίζει η συναυλία;
tee ora arkheezee ee seenavleea

How long does the performance last?
Πόση ώρα κρατάει η παράσταση;
posee ora krataee ee parastasee

When does it end?
Τι ώρα τελειώνει;
tee ora telyonee

Tickets

Where can I get tickets?
Πού μπορώ να πάρω εισιτήρια;
poo boro na paro eeseeteerya

Can you get me tickets for the concert?
Μπορείτε να μου πάρετε εισιτήρια για τη συναυλία;
boreeta na moo parete eeseeteerya ya tee seenavleea

For the football match
Για τον αγώνα
ya ton agona

For the theatre
Για το θέατρο
ya to theatro

Two, please
Δύο παρακαλώ
dheeo parakalo

Two for tonight, please
Δύο για απόψε παρακαλώ
dheeo ya apopse parakalo

Two for the eleven o'clock screening, please
Δύο για την παράσταση των έντεκα παρακαλώ
dheeo ya teem-barastasee ton endeka parakalo

Are there any seats left for Saturday?
Υπάρχουν θέσεις για το Σάββατο;
eeparkhoon thesees ya to savato

I want to book a box for four people
Θέλω να κλείσω ένα θεωρείο για τέσσερα άτομα
thelo na kleeso ena theoreeo ya tesera atoma

I want to book two seats
Θέλω να κλείσω δύο θέσεις
thelo na kleeso dheeo thesees

For Friday
Για την Παρασκευή
ya teem-baraskevee

In the stalls
Στην πλατεία
steem-blateea

In the balcony
Στον εξώστη
ston eksostee

What price are the tickets?
Ποια είναι η τιμή του εισιτηρίου;
pya eene ee teemee too eeseeteereeoo

Do you have anything
cheaper?
**Μήπως έχετε κάτι πιο
φτηνό;**
*meepos ekhete katee pyo
fteeno*

That's fine
Πολύ καλά
polee kala

At the show/game

Where is this seat, please?
(*showing your ticket*)
**Πού είναι αυτή η θέση
παρακαλώ;**
*poo eene aftee ee thesee
parakalo*

Where is the cloakroom?
Πού είναι η γκαρνταρόμπα;
poo eene ee gardaroba

Where is the bar?
Πού είναι το μπαρ;
poo eene to bar

Where are the toilets?
Πού είναι οι τουαλέτες;
poo eene ee twaletes

A programme, please
Ενα πρόγραμμα παρακαλώ
ena programa parakalo

Where can I get a
programme?
**Πού μπορώ να πάρω ένα
πρόγραμμα;**
*poo boro na paro ena
programa*

A cushion, please
Ενα μαξιλλάρι παρακαλώ
ena makseelaree parakalo

Is there an interval?
Εχει διάλειμμα;
ekhee dhyaleema

You may hear

Μπορείτε να αγοράσετε
  εισιτήρια εδώ στο
  ξενοδοχείο
*boreete na agorasete
  eeseeteerya edho sto
  ksenodhokheeo*
You can buy tickets here in
  the hotel

Στο τουριστικό γραφείο
sto tooreesteeko grafeeo
At the tourist office

Στο στάδιο
sto stadhyo
At the stadium

Αρχίζει στις οκτώ
arkheezee stees okto
It begins at eight o'clock

Κρατάει δύο ώρες και ένα
  τέταρτο
*krataee dheeo ores ke ena
  tetarto*
It lasts two and a quarter
  hours

Τελειώνει στις εννιάμιση
telyonee stees enyameesee
It ends at half past nine

Έχει διάλειμμα δεκαπέντε
  λεπτών
*ekhee dhyaleema
  dhekapende lepton*
There is a fifteen-minute
  interval

Για πότε τα θέλετε;
ya pote ta thelete
When would you like them
  for?

Πλατεία, εξώστης;
plateea eksostees
In the stalls, in the
  balcony?

Υπάρχουν δύο εδώ, στην
  πλατεία μπροστά
  (*indicating on seating
  plan*)
*eeparkhoon dheeo edho
  steem-blateea brosta*
There are two here, in the
  orchestra stalls

Λυπάμαι, τα εισιτήρια
  εξαντλήθηκαν
*leepame ta eeseeteerya
  eksandleetheekan*
I'm sorry, the tickets are
  sold out

Μπορώ να δω το εισιτήριό
  σας;
*boro na dho to
  eeseeteeryo-sas*
May I see your ticket?

SPORTS AND ACTIVITIES

- Water-sports are widely practised in Greece, especially in the summer. Tackle for both angling and underwater fishing can often be hired, and there are an increasing number of resorts offering water-skiing and windsurfing facilities.

- For swimming, the National Tourist Organisation of Greece runs a large number of organised beaches, with changing rooms, cafés, beach sports and other facilities.

- There is some provision for skiing (in the mountains of central Greece), golf, riding and tennis; for information, consult the National Tourist Organisation of Greece.

- Greece has a lot of mountainous terrain, and walking and climbing can be a great pleasure.

You may see

ΑΘΛΗΤΙΚΟ ΚΕΝΤΡΟ Αθλητικό κέντρο	Sports centre
ΑΠΑΓΟΡΕΥΕΤΑΙ ΤΟ **ΚΟΛΥΜΠΙ** Απαγορεύεται το κολύμπι	No swimming
ΑΠΑΓΟΡΕΥΕΤΑΙ ΤΟ **ΨΑΡΕΜΑ** Απαγορεύεται το ψάρεμα	No fishing
ΓΗΠΕΔΟ ΓΚΟΛΦ Γήπεδο γκολφ	Golf course
ΓΗΠΕΔΟ ΠΟΔΟΣΦΑΙΡΟΥ Γήπεδο ποδοσφαίρου	Football pitch

ΕΝΟΙΚΙΑΣΗ ΣΑΝΙΔΩΝ ΓΙΑ ΓΟΥΙΝΤΣΕΡΦ	Sailboards for hire
Ενοικίαση σανίδων για γουίντσερφ	
ΕΝΟΙΚΙΑΣΗ ΣΚΑΦΩΝ	Boat hire
Ενοικίαση σκαφών	
ΕΝΟΙΚΙΑΣΗ ΣΚΙ	Ski hire
Ενοικίαση σκι	
ΙΔΙΩΤΙΚΗ ΠΛΑΖ	Private beach
Ιδιωτική πλαζ	
ΚΙΝΔΥΝΟΣ	Danger
Κίνδυνος	
(ΚΛΕΙΣΤΟ(Ν)) ΚΟΛΥΜΒΗΤΗΡΙΟ(Ν)	(Indoor) swimming pool
(Κλειστό(ν)) κολυμβητήριο(ν)	
ΠΛΑΖ	Beach
Πλαζ	
ΣΧΟΛΗ ΓΟΥΙΝΤΣΕΡΦ	Windsurfing school
Σχολή γουίντσερφ	
ΤΕΛΕΦΕΡΙΚ	Cable car
Τελεφερίκ	
ΤΕΝΙΣ	Tennis
Τένις	

You may want to say

General phrases

Can I/we . . . ?
Μπορώ να/Μπορούμε να . . . ;
boro na/boroome na . . .

Can we hire bikes?
**Μπορούμε να νοικιάσουμε
  ποδήλατα;**
*boroome na neekyasoome
  podheelata*

Can I go fishing?
Μπορώ να πάω για ψάρεμα;
boro na pao ya psarema

Can I go horse-riding?
Μπορώ να κάνω ιππασία;
boro na kano eepaseea

Where can I/we . . . ?
**Πού μπορώ να/μπορούμε
  να . . . ;**
*poo boro na/boroome
  na . . .*

Where can we play tennis?
**Πού μπορούμε να παίξουμε
  τένις;**
*poo boroome na peksoome
  tenees*

Where can I go climbing?
**Πού μπορώ να κάνω
  ορειβασία;**
*poo boro na kano
  oreevaseea*

I don't know how to . . .
Δεν ξέρω να . . .
dhen-gsero na . . .

I don't know how to ski
Δεν ξέρω να κάνω σκι
dhen-gsero na kano skee

Do you give lessons?
Δίνετε μαθήματα;
dheenete matheemata

I'm a beginner
Είμαι αρχάριος (*m.*)/
  αρχάρια (*f.*)
eeme arkharyos/arkharya

I'm quite experienced
Εχω κάποια πείρα
ekho kapya peera

How much is it per hour?
Πόσο κοστίζει η ώρα;
poso kosteezee ee ora

How much is it for the
  whole day?
**Πόσο κοστίζει ολόκληρη η
  μέρα;**
*poso kosteezee olokleeree ee
  mera*

How much is it per game?
Πόσο κοστίζει το παιχνίδι;
poso kosteezee to pekhneedhee

Are there special rates for children?
Υπάρχουν ειδικές τιμές για παιδιά;
eeparkhoon eedheekes teemes ya pedhya

Can I hire equipment?
Μπορώ να νοικιάσω τον εξοπλισμό;
boro na neekyaso ton eksopleezmo

Can I hire rackets?
Μπορώ να νοικιάσω ρακέτες;
boro na neekyaso raketes

Can I hire clubs?
Μπορώ να νοικιάσω μπαστούνια;
boro na neekyaso bastoonya

Is a licence needed?
Χρειάζεται άδεια;
khryazete adhya

Where can I get a licence?
Πού μπορώ να πάρω άδεια;
poo boro na paro adhya

Is it necessary to be a member?
Χρειάζεται να είναι κανείς μέλος;
khryazete na eene kanees melos

Beach and pool

Can I swim here?
Μπορώ να κολυμπήσω εδώ;
boro na koleembeeso edho

Can I swim in the sea?
Μπορώ να κολυμπήσω στη θάλασσα;
boro na koleembeeso stee thalasa

Is it dangerous?
Είναι επικίνδυνο;
eene epeekeendheeno

Is it safe for small children?
Είναι ασφαλές για μικρά παιδιά;
eene asfales ya meekra pedhya

You may hear

Είσαστε αρχάριος; (*m.*)
eesaste arkharyos
Are you a beginner?

Είσαστε αρχάρια; (*f.*)
eesaste arkharya
Are you a beginner?

Ξέρετε να κάνετε σκι;
kserete na kanete skee
Do you know how to ski?

Ξέρετε να κάνετε γουίντσερφ;
kserete na kanete weendserf
Do you know how to windsurf?

Κάνει 2000 δραχμές την ώρα
kanee dheeo kheelyadhes drakhmes teen ora
It's 2000 drachmas per hour

Πρέπει να δώσετε 1000 δραχμές προκαταβολή
prepee na dhosete kheelyes drakhmes prokatavolee
You have to pay a deposit of 1000 drachmas

Λυπάμαι, είμαστε συμπληρωμένοι
leepame eemaste seembleeromenee
I'm sorry, we're booked up

Πρέπει να ξανάρθετε αργότερα
prepee na ksanarthete argotera
You'll have to come back later

Τι νούμερο φοράτε;
tee noomero forate
What size are you?

Χρειάζεται μια φωτογραφία
khryazete mya fotografeea
You need a photograph

HEALTH

Medical details – to show to a doctor

(Tick boxes or fill in details)

	Self Εγώ	Other members of family/party		
Blood group **Ομάδα αίματος**				
Asthmatic **Ασθματικός/ή**				
Blind **Τυφλός/ή**				
Deaf **Κουφός/ή**				
Diabetic **Διαβητικός/ή**				
Epileptic **Επιληπτικός/ή**				
Handicapped **Ειδικές ανάγκες**				
Heart condition **Καρδιακή πάθηση**				
High blood pressure **Υψηλή πίεση**				
Pregnant **Εγκυος**				

Allergic to **Αλλεργικός/ή σε:**				
Antibiotics **Αντιβιωτικά**				
Penicillin **Πενικιλλίνη**				
Cortisone **Κορτιζόνη**				

Medicines **Φάρμακα**

Self **Εγώ** _____

Others **Αλλοι** _____

- The Department of Health has a leaflet *Health Advice for Travellers Inside the European Community*. Within the EC you can obtain the local equivalent of NHS treatment by producing the required form – you will probably have to pay first and reclaim the payment when you return to Britain.

- Chemists can often give medical advice and first aid, and provide medicines without a prescription.

- If you need an ambulance, call either the police or the Greek Red Cross (**ο Ερυθρός Σταυρός** – *o ereethros stavros*).

- To indicate where the pain is you can simply point and say 'it hurts here' (**πονάει εδώ** – *ponaee edho*). Otherwise you'll need to look up the Greek for the appropriate part of the body (see page 185).

You may see

ΑΝΑΚΑΤΕΨΕΤΕ ΠΡΙΝ ΑΠΟ ΤΗ ΧΡΗΣΗ Ανακατέψετε πριν από τη χρήση	Shake before use
ΔΗΛΗΤΗΡΙΟ(Ν)! Δηλητήριο(ν)!	Poison!
ΕΚΤΑΚΤΑ ΠΕΡΙΣΤΑΤΙΚΑ Εκτακτα περιστατικά	Emergency services
ΙΑΤΡΟΣ/ΙΑΤΡΕΙΟ(Ν) Ιατρός/Ιατρείο(ν)	Doctor
ΚΛΙΝΙΚΗ Κλινική	Clinic, hospital
ΜΟΝΟ ΓΙΑ ΕΞΩΤΕΡΙΚΗ ΧΡΗΣΗ Μόνο για εξωτερική χρήση	For external use only

ΝΟΣΟΚΟΜΕΙΟ(Ν) Νοσοκομείο(ν)	Hospital
ΟΔΗΓΙΕΣ ΧΡΗΣΕΩΣ Οδηγίες χρήσεως	Instructions for use
ΟΔΟΝΤΙΑΤΡΟΣ/ ΟΔΟΝΤΙΑΤΡΕΙΟ(Ν) Οδοντίατρος/ Οδοντιατρείο(ν)	Dentist
ΠΡΩΤΕΣ ΒΟΗΘΕΙΕΣ Πρώτες βοήθειες	First aid post
ΣΤΑΘΜΟΣ ΑΣΘΕΝΟΦΟΡΩΝ Σταθμός ασθενοφόρων	Ambulance station
ΣΤΑΘΜΟΣ ΠΡΩΤΩΝ ΒΟΗΘΕΙΩΝ Σταθμός πρώτων βοηθειών	First aid post, casualty hospital
ΤΜΗΜΑ ΕΚΤΑΚΤΩΝ ΠΕΡΙΣΤΑΤΙΚΩΝ Τμήμα εκτάκτων περιστατικών	Casualty department
ΩΡΕΣ ΙΑΤΡΕΙΟΥ Ωρες ιατρείου	Surgery hours

You may want to say

At the doctor's

I need a doctor
Χρειάζομαι ιατρό
khryazome yatro

Please call a doctor
Παρακαλώ, φωνάξτε ένα ιατρό
parakalo fonakste ena yatro

Quickly
Γρήγορα
greegora

Does anyone here speak English?
Υπάρχει κανείς εδώ πού μιλάει Αγγλικά;
eeparkhee kanees edho poo meelaee angleeka

Can I make an appointment?
Μπορώ να κλείσω ραντεβού;
boro na kleeso randevoo

It's my son
Είναι ο γιός μου
eene o yos-moo

It's my husband
Είναι ο άντρας μου
eene o andras-moo

It's my daughter
Είναι η κόρη μου
eene ee koree-moo

It's my wife
Είναι η γυναίκα μου
eene ee yeeneka-moo

How much will it cost?
Πόσο θα κοστίσει;
poso tha kosteesee

It's my friend
Είναι ο φίλος μου (*m.*)/
  η φίλη μου (*f.*)
eene o feelos-moo/
  ee feelee-moo

Your symptoms

Someone else's symptoms

I don't feel well
Δεν αισθάνομαι καλά
dhen esthanome kala

He/She doesn't feel well
Δεν αισθάνεται καλά
dhen esthanete kala

He/She is unconscious
Είναι αναίσθητος/η
eene anestheetos/ee

It hurts here
Πονάει εδώ
ponaee edho

It hurts here
Πονάει εδώ
ponaee edho

My . . . hurts
Πονάει ο/η/το . . . μου
ponaee o/ee/to . . . moo

His . . . hurts
Πονάει ο/η/το . . . του
ponaee o/ee/to . . . too

Her . . . hurts
Πονάει ο/η/το . . . της
ponaee o/ee/to . . . tees

My stomach hurts
Πονάει το στομάχι μου
ponaee to stomakhee-moo

His stomach hurts
Πονάει το στομάχι του
ponaee to stomakhee-too

My back hurts
Πονάει η πλάτη μου
ponaee ee platee-moo

Her back hurts
Πονάει η πλάτη της
ponaee ee platee-tees

My . . . hurt
Πονάνε οι/τα . . . μου
ponane ee/ta . . . moo

His . . . hurt
Πονάνε οι/τα . . . του
ponane ee/ta . . . too

Her . . . hurt
Πονάνε οι/τα . . . της
ponane ee/ta . . . tees

My eyes hurt
Πονάνε τα μάτια μου
ponane ta matya-moo

His eyes hurt
Πονάνε τα μάτια του
ponane ta matya-too

My feet hurt
Πονάνε τα πόδια μου
ponane ta podhya-moo

Her feet hurt
Πονάνε τα πόδια της
ponane ta podhya-tees

I have a sore throat
Πονάει ο λαιμός μου
ponaee o lemos-moo

He has a sore throat
Πονάει ο λαιμός του
ponaee o lemos-too

I have a temperature
Εχω πυρετό
ekho peereto

He/She has a temperature
Εχει πυρετό
ekhee peereto

I have diarrhoea
Εχω διάρροια
ekho dhyarya

He/She has diarrhoea
Εχει διάρροια
ekhee dhyarya

I feel dizzy/sick
Εχω ζαλάδα/ναυτία
ekho zaladha/nafteea

He/She feels dizzy/sick
Εχει ζαλάδα/ναυτία
ekhee zaladha/nafteea

I have been sick
Εκανα εμετό
ekana emeto

He/She has been sick
Εκανε εμετό
ekane emeto

I can't sleep
Δεν μπορώ να κοιμηθώ
dhem-boro na keemeetho

I can't breathe
Δεν μπορώ να ανασαίνω
dhem-boro na anaseno

I can't move my . . .
**Δεν μπορώ να κινήσω τον/
τη/το . . . μου**
*dhem-boro na keeneeso ton/
tee/to . . . moo*

My . . . is bleeding
Αιμορραγεί ο/η/το . . . μου
emorayee o/ee/to . . . moo

He/She is bleeding
Αιμορραγεί
emorayee

It's my . . .
Είναι ο/η/το . . . μου
eene o/ee/to . . . moo

It's his . . .
Είναι ο/η/το . . . του
eene o/ee/to . . . too

It's her . . .
Είναι ο/η/το . . . της
eene o/ee/to . . . tees

It's my arm
Είναι το χέρι μου
eene to kheree-moo

It's his ankle
Είναι ο αστράγαλός του
eene o astragalos-too

It's my wrist
Είναι ο καρπός μου
eene o karpos-moo

It's her leg
Είναι το πόδι της
eene to podhee-tees

I think that . . .
Νομίζω ότι . . .
nomeezo otee . . .

It's broken	It's broken
Είναι σπασμένος/η/ο	**Είναι σπασμένος/η/ο**
eene spazmenos/ee/o	*eene spazmenos/ee/o*
I've sprained it	He's/She's sprained it
Το έχω στραμπουλίξει	**Το έχει στραμπουλίξει**
to ekho strambooleeksee	*to ekhee strambooleeksee*
I have cut myself	He/She has cut himself/ herself
Κόπηκα	**Κόπηκε**
kopeeka	*kopeeke*
I have burnt myself	He/She has burnt himself/ herself
Κάηκα	**Κάηκε**
kaeeka	*kaeeke*
I have been stung by an insect	He/She has been stung by an insect
Με τσίμπησε ένα έντομο	**Τον/Τη τσίμπησε ένα έντομο**
me tseembeese ena endomo	*ton/tee tseembeese ena endomo*
I have been bitten by a dog	He/She has been bitten by a dog
Με δάγκωσε ενα σκυλί	**Τον/Τη δάγκωσε ένα σκυλί**
me dhangose ena skeelee	*ton/tee dhangose ena skeelee*

You may hear

Τι έχετε;
tee ekhete
What's wrong?

Πού πονάει;
poo ponaee
Where does it hurt?

Πονάει εδώ;
ponaee edho
Does it hurt here?

Πολύ; Λίγο;
polee leego
A lot? A little?

Από πότε αισθάνεστε έτσι;
apo pote esthaneste etsee
How long have you been
feeling like this?

Πόσων χρονών είσαστε;
poson khronon eesaste
How old are you?

Πόσων χρονών είναι;
poson khronon eene
How old is he/she?

Ανοίξτε το στόμα σας
παρακαλώ
*aneekste to stoma-sas
parakalo*
Open your mouth, please

Γδυθείτε παρακαλώ
gdheetheete parakalo
Get undressed, please

Ξαπλώστε εκεί πέρα
παρακαλώ
ksaploste ekee pera parakalo
Lie down over there, please

Παίρνετε φάρμακα;
pernete farmaka
Are you taking any
medicines?

Είσαστε αλλεργικός/ή σε
φάρμακα;
*eesaste aleryeekos/ee se
farmaka*
Are you allergic to any
medicines?

Έχετε κάνει
αντιτετανικό εμβόλιο;
*ekhete kanee
andeetetaneeko emvolyo*
Have you been vaccinated
against tetanus?

Τι φάγατε σήμερα;
tee fagate seemera
What have you eaten
today?

Θα σας δώσω μια συνταγή
tha sas dhoso mya seendayee
I am going to give you a
prescription

Πάρτε ένα χάπι τρεις
φορές την ημέρα
*parte ena khapee trees fores
teen-eemera*
Take a tablet three times a
day

Πριν/Μετά το φαγητό
preen/meta to fayeeto
Before/After meals

Πριν πάτε για ύπνο
preen pate ya eepno
Before you go to bed

Εχει μόλυνση
ekhee moleensee
There's an infection

Πρέπει να σας κάνω ένεση
prepee na sas kano enesee
I have to give you an
injection

Πρέπει να το ράψω
prepee na to rapso
I have to give you some
stitches

Πρέπει να βγάλουμε πλάκα
prepee na vgaloome plaka
We have to do an X-ray

Θέλω ένα δείγμα του
αίματος/των ούρων
*thelo ena dheegma too
ematos/ton ooron*
I need a blood/urine sample

Εχετε τροφική
δηλητηρίαση
*ekhete trofeekee
dheeleeteereeasee*
You have food poisoning

Είναι καρδιακή προσβολή
eene kardhyakee prozvolee
It's a heart attack

Πρέπει να αναπαυθείτε
prepee na anapaftheete
You must rest

Πρέπει να μείνετε στο
κρεβάτι για τρεις
μέρες
*prepee na meenete sto
krevatee ya trees meres*
You must stay in bed for
three days

Πρέπει να γυρίσετε σε
πέντε μέρες
*prepee na yeereesete se
pende meres*
You must come back in five
days' time

Πρέπει να πίνετε πολλά
υγρά
prepee na peeneete pola eegra
You must drink plenty of
liquids

Δεν πρέπει να φάτε τίπτοτα
dhem-brepee na fate teepota
You should eat nothing

Θα πρέπει να πάτε στο νοσοκομείο
tha prepee na pate sto nosokomeeo
You will have to go to hospital

Δεν είναι τίποτα σοβαρό
dhen eene teepota sovaro
It is nothing serious

Δεν έχετε τίποτα
dhen ekhete teepota
There is nothing wrong with you

Μπορείτε να ντυθείτε
boreete na deetheete
You can get dressed

You may want to say

At the dentist's

I need a dentist
Χρειάζομαι οδοντίατρο
khryazome odhondeeatro

I have toothache
Έχω πονόδοντο
ekho ponodhondo

This tooth hurts
Πονάει αυτό το δόντι
ponaee afto to dhondee

I have broken a tooth
Έσπασα ένα δόντι
espasa ena dhondee

I have lost a filling
Έφυγε ένα σφράγισμα
efeeye ena sfrayeezma

I have lost a crown/cap
Έφυγε μια κορώνα
efeeye mya korona

He/She has toothache
Πονάει το δόντι του/της
ponaee to dhondee-too/tees

He/She has broken a tooth
Έσπασε ένα δόντι
espase ena dhondee

He/She has lost a filling
Του/Της έφυγε ένα σφράγισμα
too/tees efeeye ena sfrayeezma

He/She has lost a crown/ cap
Του/Της έφυγε μια κορώνα
too/tees efeeye mya korona

Can you fix it temporarily?
Μπορείτε να το σφραγίσετε προσωρινά;
boreete na to sfrayeesete prosoreena

Can you give me an injection?
Μπορείτε να μου δώσετε μια ένεση;
boreete na moo dhosete mya enesee

Can you give him/her an injection?
Μπορείτε να του/της δώσετε μια ένεση;
boreete na too/tees dhosete mya enesee

This denture is broken
Εσπασε αυτή η μασέλα
espase aftee ee masela

Can you repair it?
Μπορείτε να τη φτιάξετε;
boreete na tee ftyaksete

How much will it cost?
Πόσο θα κοστίσει;
poso tha kosteesee

You may hear

Ανοίξτε το στόμα σας παρακαλώ
aneekste to stoma-sas parakalo
Open your mouth, please

Χρειάζεστε σφράγισμα
khryazeste sfrayeezma
You need a filling

Πρέπει να το βγάλω
prepee na to vgalo
I have to extract it

Θα σας κάνω μια ένεση
tha sas kano mya enesee
I'm going to give you an injection

Parts of the body

ankle	ο αστράγαλος	o astragalos
appendix	η σκωληκοειδής	ee skoleekoeedhees
arm	το χέρι	to kheree
back	η πλάτη	ee platee
lower back	η μέση	ee mesee
bladder	η κύστη	ee keestee
blood	το αίμα	to ema
body	το σώμα	to soma
bone	το κόκκαλο	to kokalo
bottom	ο πισινός	o peeseenos
bowels	τα έντερα	ta endera
breast	ο μαστός	o mastos
buttock	ο γλουτός	o glootos
cartilage	ο χόνδρος	o khondros
chest	το στήθος	to steethos
chin	το πηγούνι	to peegoonee
ear	το αυτί	to aftee
elbow	ο αγκώνας	o angonas
eye	το μάτι	to matee
face	το πρόσωπο	to prosopo
finger	το δάκτυλο	to dhakteelo
foot	το πόδι	to podhee
genitals	τα γεννητικά όργανα	ta yeneeteeka organa
gland	ο αδένας	o adhenas
hair	τα μαλλιά	ta malya
hand	το χέρι	to kheree
head	το κεφάλι	to kefalee
heart	η καρδιά	ee kardhya
heel	η φτέρνα	ee fterna
hip	το ισχίο	to eeskheeo
jaw	το σαγόνι	to sagonee
joint	η άρθρωση	ee arthrosee

kidney	το νεφρό	to nefro
knee	το γόνατο	to gonato
leg	το πόδι	to podhee
ligament	ο σύνδεσμος	o seendhezmos
lip	το χείλι	to kheelee
liver	το συκώτι	to seekotee
lung	ο πνεύμονας	o pnevmonas
mouth	το στόμα	to stoma
muscle	ο μυς	o mees
nail	το νύχι	to neekhee
neck	ο λαιμός	o lemos
nerve	το νεύρο	to nevro
nose	η μύτη	ee meetee
penis	το πέος	to peos
private parts	το αιδοία	to edheea
rectum	ο πρώκτος	o proktos
rib	το πλευρό	to plevro
shoulder	ο ώμος	o omos
skin	το δέρμα	to dherma
spine	η σπονδυλική στήλη	ee spondheeleekee steelee
stomach	το στομάχι	to stomakhee
tendon	ο τένωνας	o tenonas
testicles	οι ορχείς	ee orkhees
thigh	το μηρός	to meeros
throat	ο λαιμός	o lemos
thumb	ο αντίχειρας	o andeekheeras
toe	το δάκτυλο του ποδιού	to dhakteelo too podhyoo
tongue	η γλώσσα	ee glosa
tonsils	οι αμυγδαλές	ee ameegdhales
tooth	το δόντι	to dhondee
vagina	ο κόλπος	o kolpos
wrist	ο καρπός	o karpos

PROBLEMS AND COMPLAINTS

(*For car breakdowns, see page 46; see also* Emergencies, *page 379*)

● There is a single police force (**η Ελληνική Αστυνομία** – *ee eleeneekee asteenomeea*) responsible for law and order throughout Greece. They wear light blue uniforms, and some carry arms.

● Traffic control comes under a division of the police force – **η Τροχαία** (*ee trokhea*). Police on traffic control duty wear a white diagonal band across the chest.

● If your number plates are removed for illegal parking, you should contact the **Τροχαία**.

You may see

ΑΣΤΥΝΟΜΙΑ	Police station
Αστυνομία	
ΔΕΝ ΛΕΙΤΟΥΡΓΕΙ	Out of order
Δεν λειτουργεί	
ΥΠΗΡΕΣΙΑ ΠΕΛΑΤΩΝ	Customer services
Υπηρεσία πελατών	

You may want to say

General phrases

Can you help me?	Can you fix it (immediately)?
Μπορείτε να με βοηθήσετε;	**Μπορείτε να το φτιάξετε (αμέσως);**
boreete na me voeetheesete	*boreete na to ftyaksete (amesos)*

When can you fix it?
Πότε μπορείτε να το φτιάξετε;
pote boreete na to ftyaksete

Can I speak to the manager?
Μπορώ να μιλήσω στο διευθυντή;
boro na meeleeso sto dhyeftheendee

There's a problem with . . .
Υπάρχει ένα πρόβλημα με . . .
eeparkhee ena provleema me . . .

There isn't any . . .
Δεν υπάρχει . . .
dhen eeparkhee . . .

There aren't any . . .
Δεν υπάρχουν . . .
dhen eeparkhoon . . .

I need . . .
Χρειάζομαι . . .
khryazome . . .

The . . . doesn't work
Δεν λειτουργεί ο/η/το . . .
dhen leetooryee o/ee/to . . .

The . . . is broken
Ο/η/το . . . είναι χαλασμένος/η/ο
o/ee/to . . . eene khalazmenos/ee/o

I can't . . .
Δεν μπορώ να . . .
dhem-boro na . . .

It wasn't my fault
Δεν φταίω εγώ
dhen fteo ego

I have forgotten . . .
Ξέχασα . . .
ksekhasa . . .

I/We have lost . . .
Έχασα/Χάσαμε . . .
ekhasa/khasame . . .

Someone has stolen . . .
Κάποιος έκλεψε . . .
kapyos eklepse . . .

The . . . has disappeared
Εξαφανίστηκε ο/η/το . . .
eksafaneesteeke o/ee/to . . .

The . . . isn't here
Ο/η/το . . . δεν είναι εδώ
o/ee/to . . . dhen eene edho

Something is missing
Κάτι λείπει
katee leepee

The . . . is missing
Ο/η/το . . . λείπει
o/ee/to . . . leepee

This isn't mine
Αυτό δεν είναι δικό μου
afto dhen eene dheeko-moo

Where you're staying

There isn't any (hot) water
Δεν έχει (ζεστό) νερό
dhen ekhee (zesto) nero

There isn't any toilet paper
Δεν έχει χαρτί τουαλέτας
dhen ekhee khartee twaletas

There isn't any electricity
Δεν έχει ρεύμα
dhen ekhee revma

There aren't any towels
Δεν έχει πετσέτες
dhen ekhee petsetes

I need another pillow
Χρειάζομαι κι άλλο
μαξιλλάρι
*khryazome ky-alo
makseelaree*

I need another blanket
Χρειάζομαι κι άλλη
κουβέρτα
*khryazome ky-alee
kooverta*

I need a light bulb
Χρειάζομαι μια λάμπα
khryazome mya lamba

The light doesn't work
Το φως δεν λειτουργεί
to fos dhen leetooryee

The shower doesn't work
Το ντους δεν λειτουργεί
to doos dhen leetooryee

The lock is broken
Η κλειδαριά είναι
χαλασμένη
*ee kleedharya eene
khalazmenee*

The switch on the lamp is
broken
Ο διακόπτης στη λάμπα
είναι χαλασμένος
*o dhyakoptees stee lamba
eene khalazmenos*

I can't open the window
Δεν μπορώ ν'ανοίξω το
παράθυρο
*dhem-boro naneekso to
paratheero*

I can't turn the tap off
Δεν μπορώ να κλείσω τη
βρύση
*dhem-boro na kleeso tee
vreesee*

The toilet doesn't flush
Δεν λειτουργεί το
καζανάκι
*dhen leetooryee to
kazanakee*

The wash-basin is blocked
Ο νιπτήρας είναι
βουλωμένος
*o neepteeras eene
voolomenos*

The wash-basin is dirty
**Ο νιπτήρας είναι
βρώμικος**
*o neepteeras eene
vromeekos*

The room is . . .
Το δωμάτιο είναι . . .
to dhomatyo eene . . .

The room is too dark
**Το δωμάτιο είναι πολύ
σκοτεινό**
*to dhomatyo eene polee
skoteeno*

The room is too small
**Το δωμάτιο είναι πολύ
μικρό**
*to dhomatyo eene polee
meekro*

It's too hot in the room
**Κάνει πολύ ζέστη στο
δωμάτιο**
*kanee polee zestee sto
dhomatyo*

The bed is very
uncomfortable
**Το κρεβάτι είναι πολύ
άβολο**
to krevatee eene polee avolo

There's a lot of noise
Εχει πολύ θόρυβο
ekhee polee thoreevo

There's a smell of gas
Μυρίζει υγραέριο
meereezee eegraeryo

In bars and restaurants

This isn't cooked
Αυτό δεν ψήθηκε καλά
afto dhen pseetheeke kala

This is burnt
Αυτό είναι καμένο
afto eene kameno

This is cold
Αυτό είναι κρύο
afto eene kreeo

I didn't order this, I
ordered . . .
**Δεν παράγγειλα αυτό,
παράγγειλα . . .**
*dhem-barangeela afto,
parangeela . . .*

This glass is cracked
Αυτό το ποτήρι είναι ραγισμένο
afto to poteeree eene rayeezmeno

This is dirty
Αυτό είναι βρώμικο
afto eene vromeeko

This smells bad
Αυτό μυρίζει άσχημα
afto meereezee askheema

This tastes strange
Αυτό έχει μια περίεργη γεύση
afto ekhee mya peree-eryee yefsee

There is a mistake on the bill
Έγινε λάθος στο λογαριασμό
eyeene lathos sto logaryazmo

In shops

I bought this here (yesterday)
Αυτό το αγόρασα εδώ εχτές
afto to agorasa edho ekhtes

Can you change this for me?
Μπορείτε να μου το αλλάξετε;
boreete na moo to alaksete

I want to return this
Θέλω να επιστρέψω αυτό
thelo na epeestrepso afto

Can you refund me the money?
Μπορείτε να μου επιστρέψετε τα χρήματα;
boreete na moo epeestrepsete ta khreemata

Here is the receipt
Να η απόδειξη
na ee apodheeksee

It has a flaw
Έχει ένα ελάττωμα
ekhee ena elatoma

It has a hole
Έχει μια τρύπα
ekhee mya treepa

It has a stain/mark
Εχει ένα λεκέ/σημάδι
ekhee ena leke/seemadhee

This isn't fresh
Αυτό δεν είναι φρέσκο
afto dhen eene fresko

This is off/rotten
Αυτό είναι μπαγιάτικο
afto eene bayateeko

The lid is missing
Λείπει το καπάκι
leepee to kapakee

Forgetting and losing things and theft

I have forgotten my ticket
Ξέχασα το εισιτήριό μου
ksekhasa to eeseeteeryo-moo

I have forgotten the key
Ξέχασα το κλειδί
ksekhasa to kleedhee

I have lost my wallet
Εχασα το πορτοφόλι μου
ekhasa to portofolee-moo

I have lost my driving licence
Εχασα την άδεια οδηγήσεως
ekhasa teen adhya odheeyeeseos

We have lost our rucksacks
Χάσαμε τους σάκκους μας
khasame toos sakoos-mas

Where is the lost property office?
Πού είναι το γραφείο απολεσθέντων αντικειμένων;
poo eene to grafeeo apolosthendon andeekeemenon

Where is the police station?
Πού είναι το (αστυνομικό) τμήμα;
poo eene to (asteenomeeko) tmeema

Someone has stolen my bag
Κάποιος μου έκλεψε την τσάντα μου
kapyos moo eklepse teendsanda-moo

Someone has stolen the car
Κάποιος μου έκλεψε το αυτοκίνητο
kapyos moo eklepse to aftokeeneeto

Someone has stolen my money
Κάποιος μου έκλεψε τα χρήματά μου
kapyos moo eklepse ta khreemata-moo

If someone is bothering you

Please leave me alone
Αφήστε με ήσυχο (*m.*)**/ήσυχη** (*f.*) **παρακαλώ**
afeeste-me eeseekho/eeseekhee parakalo

Go away, or I'll call the police
Φύγε, αλλιώς θα φωνάξω την αστυνομία
feeye alyos tha fonakso teen asteenomeea

There is someone
  bothering me
Κάποιος μ'ενοχλεί
kapyos menokhlee

There is someone following
  me
Κάποιος μ'ακολουθεί
kapyos makeloothee

You may hear

Helpful and unhelpful replies

Ενα λεπτό/Μια στιγμή
  παρακαλώ
ena lepto/mya steegmee
  parakalo
Just a moment, please

Φυσικά
feeseeka
Of course

Ορίστε
oreeste
Here you are

Θα σας φέρω άλλο/άλλη
tha sas fero alo/alee
I'll bring you another one

Θα σας φέρω αμέσως
tha sas fero amesos
I'll bring you one
  immediately

Αμέσως/Εφτασα
amesos/eftasa
Right away

Θα σας το φτιάξω αύριο
tha sas to ftyakso avryo
I'll fix it for you tomorrow

Λυπάμαι, δεν γίνεται
leepame dhen yeenete
I'm sorry, it's not possible

Λυπάμαι, δεν μπορώ να κάνω τίποτα
leepame dhem-boro na kano teepota
I'm sorry, there's nothing I can do

Εγώ δεν είμαι ο υπεύθυνος/ η υπεύθυνη
ego dhen eeme o eepeftheenos/ ee eepeftheenee
I am not the person responsible

Δεν είμαστε υπεύθυνοι
dhen eemaste eepeftheenee
We are not responsible

Πρέπει να το δηλώσετε στην αστυνομία
prepee na to dheelosete steen asteenomeea
You should report it to the police

Το καλύτερο πού έχετε να κάνετε είναι . . .
to kaleetero poo ekhete na kanete eene . . .
The best thing you can do is . . .

Questions you may be asked

Πότε το αγοράσατε;
pote to agorasete
When did you buy it?

Μήπως έχετε την απόδειξη;
meepos ekhete teen apodheeksee
Do you have the receipt?

Πότε έγινε;
pote eyeene
When did it happen?

Πού το/τη χάσατε;
poo to/tee khasate
Where did you lose it?

Πού το/την έκλεψαν;
poo to/teen eklepsan
Where was it stolen?

Πώς είναι η τσάντα σας;
pos eene ee tsanda-sas
What does your bag look like?

Πώς είναι το αυτοκίνητό σας;
pos eene to aftokeeneeto-sas
What does your car look like?

Τι μάρκα είναι;
tee marka eene
What make is it?

Ποιος είναι ο αριθμός του αυτοκινήτου σας;
pyos eene o areethmos too aftokeeneetoo-sas
What is the registration number of your car?

Πώς σας λένε;
pos sas lene
What's your name?

Πού μένετε;
poo menete
Where are you staying?

Ποια είναι η διεύθυνσή σας;
pya eene ee dhyeftheensee-sas
What is your address?

Ποιος είναι ο αριθμός του δωματίου σας;
pyos eene o areethmos too dhomateeoo-sas
What is your room number?

Ποιος είναι ο αριθμός του διαμερίσματός σας;
pyos eene o areethmos too dhyamereezmatos-sas
What is the number of your apartment?

Σε ποια βίλλα μένετε;
se pya veela menete
Which villa are you in?

Ποιος είναι ο αριθμός του διαβατηρίου σας;
pyos eene o areethmos too dhyavateereeoo-sas
What is your passport number?

Εχετε ασφάλεια;
ekhete asfalya
Are you insured?

Παρακαλώ, συμπληρώσετε αυτό το έντυπο
parakalo seembleerosete afto to endeepo
Please fill in this form

BASIC GRAMMAR

Nouns

All Greek nouns have a gender – masculine, feminine or neuter.

Most masculine nouns end in -ος, -ης, -ας or -ες.

Most feminine nouns end in -α or -η.

Most neuter nouns end in -ο, -ι, -α or -ος.

In the Dictionary, nouns are given with the definite article (see below) to show their gender.

Nouns have the endings above when they are the subject of a sentence (this form is called the nominative case). When they are used as the object (accusative case), masculine nouns drop the final -ς; feminine and neuter nouns with the above endings don't change.

	nominative	*accusative*	
masculine	ο αδελφός	τον αδελφό	brother
	ο επιβάτης	τον επιβάτη	passenger
	ο μπαμπάς	τον μπαμπά	dad
	ο πατέρας	τον πατέρα	father
	ο καφές	τον καφέ	coffee
feminine	η μητέρα	τη μητέρα	mother
	η γιαγιά	τη γιαγιά	grandmother
	η αδελφή	την αδελφή	sister
neuter	το θέατρο	το θέατρο	theatre
	το αγόρι	το αγόρι	boy
	το γράμμα	το γράμμα	letter
	το λάθος	το λάθος	mistake

The endings also change to show possession (genitive case). Masculine nouns change to -ου, -η, -α or -ε.
Feminine nouns change to -ας or -ης.
Neuter nouns change to -ου, -ιού, -ατος or -ους.

	nominative	genitive
masculine	ο αδελφός	του αδελφού
	ο επιβάτης	του επιβάτη
	ο πατέρας	του πατέρα
	ο καφές	του καφέ
feminine	η μητέρα	της μητέρας
	η αδελφή	της αδελφής
neuter	το θέατρο	του θεάτρου
	το αγόρι	του αγοριού
	το γράμμα	του γράμματος
	το λάθος	του λάθους

e.g.:

ο Αγγλος (the Englishman) – η βαλίτσα του Αγγλου (the Englishman's suitcase)

η Μαρία (Mary) – το αυτοκίνητο της Μαρίας (Mary's car)

το παιδί (the child) – το όνομα του παιδιού (the child's name)

When you're addressing someone directly, you use a fourth case, called the vocative. In practice, this is mainly the same as the accusative, and means that you leave off the final -ς of masculine words: Νίκο!, when you're addressing Νίκος, etc. Masculine nouns ending in -ος sometimes have a separate form ending in -ε: this is most commonly found with κύριος (Mr), which becomes κύριε, e.g.:

Καλημέρα κύριε Παππά! – Good morning Mr Pappas!

Plurals

The endings of nouns change in the plural. The endings for
the nominative case change as follows:

	singular	plural	example	
masculine	-ος	-οι	ο αδελφός	οι αδελφοί
	-ης	-ες	ο επιβάτης	οι επιβάτες
	-ας	-ες	ο πατέρας	οι πατέρες
	or	-άδες	ο μπαμπάς	οι μπαμπάδες
	-ες	-έδες	ο καφές	οι καφέδες
feminine	-α	-ες	η μητέρα	οι μητέρες
	or	-άδες	η γιαγιά	οι γιαγιάδες
	-η	-ες	η αδελφή	οι αδελφές
neuter	-ο	-α	το θέατρο	τα θέατρα
	-ι	-ια	το αγόρι	τα αγόρια
	-α	-ατα	το γράμμα	τα γράμματα
	-ος	-η	το λάθος	τα λάθη

Articles

The Greek words for 'a' or 'an' (indefinite article) and 'the'
(definitive article) also vary according to the gender (masculine, feminine or neuter) and case (nominative, accusative, genitive) of the noun they are used with.

Indefinite article

	masculine	feminine	neuter
nominative	ένας	μια	ένα
accusative	ένα	μια	ένα
genitive	ενός	μιας	ενός

Definite article

This varies also according to number (singular or plural):

	masculine	feminine	neuter
singular			
nominative	o	η	το
accusative	το, τον*	τη, την*	το
genitive	του	της	του
plural			
nominative	οι	οι	τα
accusative	τους	τις	τα
genitive	τους	τους	τους

* The forms τον and την are used when the noun begins with a vowel, or κ, π, or τ. The κ, π, τ are then pronounced 'g', 'b', 'd' (see page 11), e.g.:

τον άνδρα (man)   τον κατάλογο (menu)
την Αθήνα (Athens)   την Τρίτη (Tuesday)

The definite article is used much more than in English – especially with the names of people, towns, countries, etc., e.g.:

ο Γιάννης (*o yanees*) – John
η κυρία Παππά (*ee keereea papa*) – Mrs Pappas
η Αθήνα (*ee atheena*) – Athens
η Ελλάδα (*ee eladha*) – Greece

Σε

When σε, meaning 'to', 'at', 'in', is followed by the definite article, it fuses with it to make the following forms: στο(v), στη(v), στο, στους, στις, στα:

στον Αγγλο – to the Englishman
στην Αθήνα – to Athens
στο ξενοδοχείο Παράδεισος – in/at the Paradise Hotel

Adjectives

Adjectives 'agree' with their noun – that is, they have the same gender, number and case, with different endings.

Most adjectives have the endings of masculine nouns in -ος, feminine nouns in -η or -α, and neuter nouns in -ο:

	masculine	feminine	neuter
singular	-ος	-η or -α	-ο
plural	-οι	-ες	-α

In the Dictionary, adjectives are shown with the three nominative singular endings, e.g.:

μεγάλος/η/ο (big)
ωραίος/α/ο (nice)

The normal position for the adjective is between the article and the noun:

ο ψηλός Άγγλος (the tall Englishman)

But demonstrative adjectives – 'this', 'that', 'these', 'those' – come before the article:

αυτός ο άνδρας (this man)
εκείνη η πόρτα (that door)

Comparatives and superlatives ('more', 'the most')

'More' is πιο, and comes before the adjective; it also gives the sense of 'taller', etc.:

πιο ακριβός (more expensive)
πιο ψηλός (taller)

'Less' is λιγώτερο:
λιγώτερο ψηλός (less tall)

'Than' is από, and is followed by the accusative case:
Η Μαρία είναι πιο ψηλή από το Γιάννη (Mary is taller than John)

'Smaller' and 'bigger' are μικρότερος (*meekroteros*) and μεγαλύτερος (*megaleeteros*), but you can also say πιο μικρός and πιο μεγάλος.

'Better' and 'worse' are καλύτερος (*kaleeteros*) and χειρότερος (*kheeroteros*).

The superlative form (tallest, biggest, etc.) is formed by putting the definite article in front of the comparative form: ο πιο ψηλός, ο πιο μικρός, ο μεγαλύτερος, etc.

Subject pronouns

I	εγώ
you (*singular*)	εσύ
he, it (*masculine*)	αυτός
she, it (*feminine*)	αυτή
it (*neuter*)	αυτό
we	εμείς
you (*plural*)	εσείς
they	αυτοί (*masculine*), αυτές (*feminine*), αυτά (*neuter*)

The subject pronouns are not routinely used with verbs, since the ending of the verb shows whether it's 'I', 'you' etc. They are mainly added for emphasis, or to avoid confusion.

'You'

In English there is only one way of addressing people using the word 'you'. In Greek there are two ways – one is more polite/formal, the other more casual/informal.

The informal way is used between friends and relatives, between people of the same age group, and to children. The part of the verb used is the second person singular, and the pronoun also second person singular – i.e. εσύ, σε, εσένα or σου.

The formal way uses the second person plural of the verb, and the pronouns εσείς, σας or εσάς.

Direct object pronouns

There are two kinds of direct object pronouns, called 'weak' and 'strong'.

weak forms

me	με
you (*singular*)	σε
him, it (*masculine*)	τον
her, it (*feminine*)	τη(ν)
it (*neuter*)	το
us	μας
you (*plural*)	σας
them	τους (*masculine*), τις (*feminine*), τα (*neuter*)

These forms are used as the object of a verb, and come before it:

σε βλέπω – I see you

μας ακούει – he is listening to us

strong forms

me	εμένα *or* μένα
you (*singular*)	εσένα *or* σένα
him, it (*masculine*)	αυτόν
her, it (*feminine*)	αυτή(ν)
it (*neuter*)	αυτό
us	εμάς *or* μας
you (*plural*)	εσάς *or* σας
them	αυτούς (*masculine*), αυτές (*feminine*), αυτά (*neuter*)

Strong forms are used after prepositions such as **από** (from), **σε** (to), etc.:

από μένα (from me)
σ'αυτούς (to them)

Indirect object pronouns

These are the equivalent of 'to/for me', 'to/for you', etc. The forms are:

to/for me	**μου**
to/for you (*singular*)	**σου**
to/for him, it (*masculine*)	**του**
to/for her, it (*feminine*)	**της**
to/for it (*neuter*)	**του**
to/for us	**μας**
to/for you (*plural*)	**σας**
to/for them (*all genders*)	**τους**

Possessives ('my', 'your', 'his', 'her', etc.)

The possessive pronouns have the same forms as the indirect object pronouns above. To indicate possession, the possessive pronoun is placed after the noun. When this happens, the noun and the pronoun are pronounced together as one word:

ο πατέρας μου (*o pateras-moo*) – my father
το βιβλίο της (*to veevleeo-tees*) – her book
το σπίτι τους (*to speetee-toos*) – their house

If a noun is stressed three syllables from the end, it is given an extra stress on the final syllable when it is followed by a possessive:

το αυτοκίνητο (*to aftokeeneeto*) – **το αυτοκίνητό μου** (*to aftokeeneeto-moo*)

To stress it's 'my . . .', 'your . . .', 'his . . .', use the adjective **δικός** together with the pronoun, before the noun, as follows:

ο δικός μου πατέρας – *my* father
το δικό της βιβλίο – *her* book

'Mine' is **δικός μου** (etc.) on its own. The answer to the question 'whose book is this?' might be **δικό μου** (mine) or **δικό τους** (theirs).

Verbs

Greek verbs have different endings according to (i) the subject of the verb, and (ii) the tense. Subject pronouns are not generally used (see above).

Present tense

The largest category have the same endings as the verb **έχω** (I have):

		endings
I have	έχω	-ω
you have (*singular*)	έχεις	-εις
he, she, it has	έχει	-ει
we have	έχουμε	-ουμε
you have (*plural*)	έχετε	-ετε
they have	έχουν *or* έχουνε*	-ουν *or* -ούνε*

*You'll hear both forms used.

Other common groups are like **μιλάω** (I speak), **μπορώ** (I can) and **έρχομαι** (I come):

		endings
I speak	**μιλάω**	-άω
you speak (*singular*)	**μιλάς**	-άς
he, she, it speaks	**μιλάει**	-άει
we speak	**μιλάμε**	-άμε
you speak (*plural*)	**μιλάτε**	-άτε
they speak	**μιλούν** or **μιλάνε***	-ούν or -άνε*

I can	**μπορώ**	-ώ
you can (*singular*)	**μπορείς**	-είς
he, she, it can	**μπορεί**	-εί
we can	**μπορούμε**	-ούμε
you can (*plural*)	**μπορείτε**	-είτε
they can	**μπορούν** or **μπορούνε***	-ούν or ούνε*

* You'll hear both forms used.

		endings
I come	**έρχομαι**	-ομαι
you come (*singular*)	**έρχεσαι**	-εσαι
he, she, it comes	**έρχεται**	-εται
we come	**ερχόμαστε**	-όμαστε
you come (*plural*)	**έρχεστε**	-εστε
they come	**έρχονται**	-ονται

The Greek present tense corresponds to the English 'I . . .' and 'I am . . . ing' forms, e.g. **μιλάω** means both 'I speak' and 'I am speaking'.

In the Dictionary verbs are given in the first person singular 'I' form – just substitute the endings above for 'you', 'we', etc.

Irregular verbs

The verbs **λέω** (I say), **ακούω** (I hear) and **τρώω** (I eat) have the following present tenses:

say	hear	eat
λέω	ακούω	τρώω
λες	ακούς	τρως
λέει	ακούει	τρώει
λέμε	ακούμε	τρώμε
λέτε	ακούτε	τρώτε
λένε	ακούνε	τρώνε

Θα

The word **θα** is used (i) before a verb stem to form a future tense: **τι θα φάτε;** (what will you eat?), and (ii) with a past tense to mean 'would': **θα ήθελα μία μπύρα** (I would like a beer).

Να

The word **να** comes between two verbs used together. In English the second verb would often be an infinitive ('to . . . '), but in Greek there is no infinitive, so the endings of the second verb also change, e.g.:

Θέλουμε να πάμε στην Ελλάδα – We want to go to Greece
Μπορώ να τραγουδάω – I can sing
Του αρέσει να κολυμπάει – He likes to swim
Πρέπει να φύγουμε – We have to leave

To be

The verb 'to be' has the following forms in the present and past tenses:

I am	είμαι
you are (*singular*)	είσαι
he, she, it is	είναι
we are	είμαστε
you are (*plural*)	είσαστε *or* είστε
they are	είναι

I was*	ήμουν(α)
you were (*singular*)	ήσουν(α)
he, she, it was	ήταν(ε)
we were	ήμαστε
you were (*plural*)	ήσαστε
they were	ήταν(ε)

* The past tense also means 'I used to be', etc.

Other verb tenses

A few verbs in other tenses that you may find useful:

πάω (I go)	I went	πήγα
(*or* πηγαίνω)	we went	πήγαμε
	I used to go	πήγαινα
	we used to go	πηγαίναμε
έχω (I have)	I had/used to have	είχα
	we had/used to have	είχαμε
έρχομαι (I come)	I came	ήρθα
	we came	ήρθαμε
	I used to come	ερχόμουν
	we used to come	ερχόμαστε
	I shall come	θάρθω
	we shall come	θαρθούμε

Negatives

To make a verb negative, put δεν (*dhen*) in front of it, e.g.:

δεν έχω – I don't have

δεν μιλάω Ελληνικά – I don't speak Greek

In Greek, two negatives don't cancel out:

δεν έχω τίποτα (τίποτα = nothing) means 'I don't have anything'.

Questions

When a question does not begin with a question word ('where?', 'how?', 'why?', etc.), the word order is the same as it would be in a statement. The intonation of the voice changes to make it a question, e.g.:

Υπάρχει περίπτερο στην πλατεία – There is a kiosk in the square

Υπάρχει περίπτερο στην πλατεία; – Is there a kiosk in the square?

Notice that the Greek question mark is the same as the English semi-colon.

DAYS, MONTHS, DATES

With days and months, the article is very frequently used. Most of the time the words are found in the accusative (see Basic grammar, page 196), because you're saying, or meaning, 'on Monday', 'in June', etc.). This is the form given below. If you need the nominative of a day of the week, just change the article from τη to η (το Σάββατο stays the same); for the nominative of a month, change the article from το(ν) to ο, and add ς to the end of the word, e.g.: **τον Ιούλιο** *(ton yoolyo)* becomes **ο Ιούλιος** *(ο yoolyos)*.

Finally, when you want to say e.g. 'of July', the ending of the word changes from -ο to -ου, and the stress moves one syllable nearer the end of the word: 'on the 15th of July' is **στις 15 Ιουλίου** *(stees dhekapende yooleeoo)*.

Days

Monday	τη Δευτέρα	*tee dheftera*
Tuesday	την Τρίτη	*teen-dreetee*
Wednesday	την Τετάρτη	*teen-detartee*
Thursday	την Πέμπτη	*teem-bemptee*
Friday	την Παρασκευή	*teem-baraskevee*
Saturday	το Σάββατο	*to savvato*
Sunday	την Κυριακή	*teen-geeryakee*

Months

January	τον Ιανουάριο	*ton yanwaryo*
February	το Φεβρουάριο	*to fevrooaryo*
March	το Μάρτιο	*to martyo*
April	τον Απρίλιο	*ton apreelyo*
May	το Μάιο	*to mayo*
June	τον Ιούνιο	*ton yoonyo*

July	τον Ιούλιο	ton yoolyo
August	τον Αύγουστο	ton avgoosto
September	το Σεπτέμβριο	to septemvryo
October	τον Οκτώβριο	ton oktovryo
November	το Νοέμβριο	to noemvryo
December	το Δεκέμβριο	to dhekemvryo

Seasons

spring	η άνοιξη	ee aneeksee
summer	το καλοκαίρι	to kalokeree
autumn	το φθινόπωρο	to ftheenoporo
winter	ο χειμώνας	o kheemonas

General phrases

day	η μέρα	ee mera
week	η εβδομάδα	ee evdhomadha
fortnight	το δεκαπενθήμερο	to dhekapenthee-mero
month	ο μήνας	o meenas
year	ο χρόνος	o khronos
today	σήμερα	seemera
tomorrow	αύριο	avryo
day after tomorrow	μεθαύριο	methavryo
yesterday	(ε)χτές	(e)khtes
day before yesterday	προχθές	prokhthes
(in) the morning	το πρωί	to proee
(in) the afternoon	το απόγευμα	to apoyevma
(in) the evening	το βράδυ	to vradhee
(at) night	τη νύχτα	tee neekhta

this morning	σήμερα το πρωί	*seemera to proee*
this afternoon	σήμερα το απόγευμα	*seemera to apoyevma*
this evening	σήμερα το βράδυ	*seemera to vradhee*
tonight	απόψε	*apopse*
tomorrow morning	αύριο το πρωί	*avryo to proee*
yesterday afternoon	χτες το απόγευμα	*khtes to apoyevma*
yesterday evening	χτες το βράδυ	*khtes to vradhee*
last night	χτες τη νύχτα	*khtes tee neekhta*
on Monday	τη Δευτέρα	*tee dheftera*
on Tuesdays	την Τρίτη	*teen-dreetee*
every Wednesday	κάθε Τετάρτη	*kathe tetartee*
in August/in spring	τον Αύγουστο/ την άνοιξη	*ton avgoosto/ teen aneeksee*
at the beginning of March	στις αρχές Μαρτίου	*stees arkhes marteeoo*
in the middle of June	στα μέσα Ιουνίου	*sta mesa yooneeoo*
at the end of September	στο τέλος Σεπτεμβρίου	*sto telos septemvreeoo*
in six months' time	σε έξι μήνες	*se eksee meenes*
during the summer	κατά τη διάρκεια του καλοκαιριού	*kata tee dhyarkya too kalokeryoo*
two years ago	πριν δύο χρόνια	*preen dheeo khronya*
in the 'nineties	στη δεκαετία του ενενήντα	*stee dhekaeteea too eneneenda*

last . . .	περασμένος/ περασμένη/ περασμένο	perazmenos/ perazmenee/ perazmeno
last Monday	την περασμένη Δευτέρα	teem-berazmenee dheftera
last week	την περασμένη εβδομάδα	teem-berazmenee evdhomadha
last month	τον περασμένο μήνα	tom-berazmeno meena
last year	πέρυσι	pereesee
this year	φέτος	fetos
next . . .	τον άλλο/την άλλη . . .	ton alo/teen alee . . .
next Tuesday	την άλλη Τρίτη	teen alee treetee
next week	την άλλη εβδομάδα	teen alee evdhomadha
next month	τον άλλο μήνα	ton alo meena
next year	του χρόνου	too khronoo
What day is it today?	Τι μέρα είναι σήμερα;	tee mera eene seemera
What is the date today?	Πόσες έχουμε σήμερα;	poses ekhoome seemera
When is your birthday?	Πότε είναι τα γενέθλιά σου;	pote eene ta yenethlya-soo
When is your saint's day?*	Πότε γιορτάζεις;	pote yortazees
(on) the first of January	(την) πρώτη Ιανουαρίου	(teen) protee yanwareeoo
(on) Saturday 10th May	(το) Σάββατο, δέκα Μαΐου	(to) savato dheka maeeoo
(in) the 15th century	το δέκατο πέμπτο αιώνα	to dhekato pempto eona

* Greeks celebrate the saint's day corresponding to their Christian name

TIME

Note that 'a.m.' is **π.μ. (Π.Μ.)** and 'p.m.' is **μ.μ. (Μ.Μ.)**.

one o'clock	**μία (η ώρα)**	*meea (ee ora)*
two o'clock	**δύο (η ώρα)**	*dheeo (ee ora)*
three o'clock	**τρεις (η ώρα)**	*trees (ee ora)*
four o'clock	**τέσσερεις (η ώρα)**	*teserees (ee ora)*
twelve o'clock	**δώδεκα (η ώρα)**	*dhodheka (ee ora)*
quarter past . . .	**. . . και τέταρτο**	*ke tetarto*
half past . . .	**. . . και μισή**	*ke meesee*
five past . . .	**. . . και πέντε**	*ke pende*
twenty-five past . . .	**. . . και εικοσιπέντε**	*ke eekoseepende*
quarter to . . .	**. . . πάρα τέταρτο**	*para tetarto*
ten to . . .	**. . . πάρα δέκα**	*para dheka*
twenty to . . .	**. . . πάρα είκοσι**	*para eekose*
in the morning	**το πρωί**	*to proee*
in the afternoon	**το απόγευμα**	*to apoyevma*
in the evening	**το βράδυ**	*to vradhee*
at night	**τη νύχτα**	*tee neekhta*
in the early morning	**πρωί-πρωί**	*proee proee*
noon/midday	**δώδεκα το μεσημέρι**	*dhodheka to meseemeree*
midnight	**τα μεσάνυχτα**	*ta mesaneekhta*
a quarter of an hour	**ένα τέταρτο**	*ena tetarto*
three quarters of an hour	**τρία τέταρτα**	*treea tetarta*
half an hour	**μισή ώρα**	*meesee ora*

The following forms are frequently used for 'half past . . .':

half past one	μιάμιση	*myameesee*
half past two	δυόμιση	*dhyomeesee*
half past three	τρεισήμιση	*treeseemeesee*
half past four	τεσσερεισήμιση	*tesereeseemeesee*
half past five	πεντέμιση	*pendemeesee*
half past six	εξήμιση	*ekseemeesee*
half past seven	εφτάμιση	*eftameesee*
half past eight	οχτώμιση	*okhtomeesee*
half past nine	εννιάμιση	*enyameesee*
half past ten	δέκα και μισή	*dheka ke meesee*
half past eleven	εντεκάμιση	*endekameesee*
half past twelve	δωδεκάμιση	*dhodhekameesee*

24-hour clock

0000	ώρα μηδέν	*ora meedhen*
0900	εννέα (η ώρα)	*enea (ee ora)*
1300	δεκατρείς (η ώρα)	*dhekatrees (ee ora)*
1430	δεκατέσσερεις και τριάντα	*dhekateserees ke tryanda*
2149	είκοσι μία και σαράντα εννέα	*eekosee meea ke saranda enea*

General phrases

exactly/precisely two o'clock	δύο ακριβώς	*dheeo akreevos*
just after four	τέσσερεις και	*teserees ke*
about half past six	εξήμιση περίπου	*ekseemeesee pereepoo*

approximately eight o'clock	γύρω στις οκτώ	*yeero stees okto*
just before ten	δέκα παρά	*dheka para*
nearly quarter to five	σχεδόν πέντε πάρα τέταρτο	*skhedhon pende para tetarto*
soon	σε λίγο	*se leego*
early	νωρίς	*norees*
late	αργά	*arga*
on time	στην ώρα του/ της/τους	*steen ora too/ tees/toos*
earlier on	νωρίτερα	*noreetera*
later on	αργότερα	*argotera*
half an hour ago	πριν μισή ώρα	*preen meesee ora*
in ten minutes' time	σε δέκα λεπτά	*se dheka lepta*
What time is it?	Τι ώρα είναι;	*tee ora eene*
It's . . .	Είναι . . .	*eene . . .*
It's one o'clock	Είναι μία (η ώρα)	*eene meea (ee ora)*
It's six o'clock	Είναι έξι (η ώρα)	*eene eksee (ee ora)*
It's quarter past eight	Είναι οκτώ και τέταρτο	*eene okto ke tetarto*
What time . . .?	Τι ώρα . . .;	*tee ora . . .*
At . . .	Στις . . .	*stees . . .*
(*with 'one'*):	Στη . . .	*stee . . .)*
At half past one	Στη μιάμιση	*stee myameesee*
At quarter to seven	Στις εφτά πάρα τέταρτο	*stees efta para tetarto*
At 2055	Στις είκοσι και πενήντα πέντε	*stees eekosee ke peneenda pende*

215

COUNTRIES AND NATIONALITIES

There are special adjectives for people, e.g.: η Αγγλίδα (*ee angleedha*) – the Englishwoman; ο Αγγλος πρωθυπουργός (*o anglos protheepoorgos*) – the English prime minister.

In all other cases, use the adjective in the first column, usually ending in -ικός for the masculine singular. The endings for feminine and neuter are -ή and -ό. For plural endings see page 198. E.g. Αγγλικό διαβατήριο (*angleeko dhyavateeryo*) – an English passport; Αγγλική εφημερίδα (*angleekee efeemereedha*) – an English newspaper.

The name of the language is the same as the neuter plural of the adjective, i.e. with the ending -α: τα Ελληνικά (*ta eleeneeka*) – Greek.

Country/ Adjective	Nationality (masculine, feminine)
Africa **η Αφρική** *ee afreekee* **αφρικανικός/ή/ό** *afreekaneekos/ee/o*	**ο Αφρικανός** *o afreekanos* **η Αφρικάνα** *ee afreekana*
Albania **η Αλβανία** *ee alvaneea* **αλβανικός/ή/ό** *alvaneekos/ee/o*	**ο Αλβανός** *o alvanos* **η Αλβανίδα** *ee alvaneedha*

America
η Αμερική / o Αμερικανός
ee amereekee / *o amereekanos*
αμερικανικός/ή/ό / **η Αμερικανίδα**
amereekaneekos/ee/o / *ee amereekaneedha*

Asia
η Ασία / o Ασιάτης
ee aseea / *o asyatees*
ασιατικός/ή/ό / **η Ασιάτισσα**
asyateekos/ee/o / *ee asyateesa*

Australia
η Αυστραλία / o Αυστραλός
ee afstraleea / *o afstralos*
αυστραλιανός/ή/ό / **η Αυστραλέζα**
afstralyanos/ee/o / *ee afstraleza*

Austria
η Αυστρία / o Αυστριακός
ee afstreea / *o afstryakos*
αυστριακός/ή/ό / **η Αυστριακή**
afstryakos/ee/o / *ee afstryakee*

Belgium
Το Βέλγιο / o Βέλγος
to velyo / *o velgos*
βελγικός/ή/ό / **η Βελγίδα**
velyeekos/ee/o / *ee velyeedha*

Bulgaria
η Βουλγαρία / o Βούλγαρος
ee voolgareea / *o voolgaros*
βουλγαρικός/ή/ό / **η Βουλγάρα**
voolgareekos/ee/o / *ee voolgara*

Canada
ο Καναδάς   **ο Καναδός**
ο kanadhas   *ο kanadhos*
καναδέζικος/η/ο   **η Καναδέζα**
kanadhezeekos/ee/o   *ee kanadheza*

China
η Κίνα   **ο Κινέζος**
ee keena   *keenezos*
κινέζικος/η/ο   **η Κινέζα**
keenezeekos/ee/o   *ee keeneza*

Cyprus
η Κύπρος   **ο Κύπριος**
ee keepros   *ο keepryos*
κυπριακός/ή/ό   **η Κυπραία**
keepreeakos/ee/o   *ee keeprea*

Czechoslovakia
η Τσεχοσλοβακία   **ο Τσεχοσλοβακός**
ee tsekhoslovakeea   *ο tsekhoslovakos*
τσεχοσλοβακικός/ή/ό   **η Τσεχοσλοβάκα**
tsekhoslovakeekos/ee/o   *ee tsekhoslovaka*

Denmark
η Δανία   **ο Δανός**
ee dhaneea   *ο dhanos*
δανικός/ή/ό   **η Δανέζα**
dhaneekos/ee/o   *ee dhaneza*

Egypt
η Αίγυπτος   **ο Αιγύπτιος**
ee eyeeptos   *ο eyeeptyos*
αιγυπτιακός/ή/ό   **η Αιγυπτία**
eyeeptyakos/ee/o   *ee eyeepteea*

England
η Αγγλία   ο Αγγλος
ee angleea   *o anglos*
αγγλικός/ή/ό   η Αγγλίδα
angleekos/ee/o *ee angleedha*

Europe
η Ευρώπη   ο Ευρωπαίος
ee evropee   *o evropeos*
ευρωπαϊκός/ή/ό   η Ευρωπαία
evropaeekos/ee/o *ee evropea*

France
η Γαλλία   ο Γάλλος
ee galeea   *o galos*
γαλλικός/ή/ό   η Γαλλίδα
galeekos/ee/o   *ee galeedha*

Germany
η Γερμανία   ο Γερμανός
ee yermaneea   *o yermanos*
γερμανικός/ή/ό   η Γερμανίδα
yermaneekos/ee/o *ee yermaneedha*

Great Britain
η Μεγάλη Βρετανία
megalee vretaneea
βρετανικός/ή/ό
vretaneekos/ee/o

Greece
η Ελλάδα   ο Ελληνας
ee eladha   *o eleenas*
ελληνικός/ή/ό   η Ελληνίδα
eleeneekos/ee/o *ee eleeneedha*

Hungary
η Ουγγαρία
ee oongareea
ουγγρικός/ή/ό
oongreekos/ee/o

ο Ούγγρος
o oongros
η Ουγγρίδα
ee oongreedha

India
η Ινδία
ee eendheea
ινδικός/ή/ό
eendheekos/ee/o

ο Ινδιάνος
o eendhyanos
η Ινδιάνα
ee eendhyana

Ireland
η Ιρλανδία
ee eerlandheea
ιρλανδικός/ή/ό
eerlandheekos/ee/o

ο Ιρλανδός
o eerlandhos
η Ιρλανδέζα
ee eerlandheza

Israel
το Ισραήλ
to eezraeel
ισραηλινός/ή/ό
eezraeeleenos/ee/o

ο Ισραηλινός
o eezraeeleenos
η Ισραηλινή
ee eezraeeleenee

Italy
η Ιταλία
ee eetaleea
ιταλικός/ή/ό
eetaleekos/ee/o

ο Ιταλός
o eetalos
η Ιταλίδα
ee eetaleedha

Japan
η Ιαπωνία
ee yaponeea
ιαπωνικός/ή/ό
yaponeekos/ee/o

ο Ιαπωνός
o yaponos
η Ιαπωνέζα
ee yaponeza

Lebanon
το Λίβανο   **ο Λιβανέζος**
to leevano   *o leevanezos*
λιβανικός/ή/ό   **η Λιβανέζα**
leevaneekos/ee/o   *ee leevaneza*

Netherlands
η Ολλανδία   **ο Ολλανδός**
ee olandheea   *o olandhos*
ολλανδικός/ή/ό   **η Ολλανδέζα**
olandheekos/ee/o   *ee olandheza*

New Zealand
η Νεαζηλανδία   **ο Νεαζηλανδός**
ee neazeelandheea   *o neazeelandhos*
νεαζηλανδικός/ή/ό   **η Νεαζηλανδέζα**
neazeelandheekos/ee/o   *ee neazeelandheza*

Northern Ireland
η Βορειοϊρλανδία
ee voryoeerlandheea
βορειοϊρλανδικός/ή/ό
voryoeerlandheekos/ee/o

Norway
η Νορβηγία   **ο Νορβηγός**
ee norveeyeea   *o norveegos*
νορβηγικός/ή/ό   **η Νορβηγίδα**
norveeyeekos/ee/o   *ee norveeyeedha*

Poland
η Πολωνία   **ο Πολωνός**
ee poloneea   *o polonos*
πολωνικός/ή/ό   **η Πολωνίδα**
poloneekos/ee/o   *ee poloneedha*

Portugal
η Πορτογαλία
ee portogaleea
πορτογαλικός/ή/ό
portogaleekos/ee/o

ο Πορτογάλος
o portogalos
η Πορτογαλίδα
ee portogaleedha

Romania
η Ρουμανία
ee roomaneea
ρουμανικός/ή/ό
roomaneekos/ee/o

ο Ρουμανός
o roomanos
η Ρουμανίδα
ee roomaneedha

Russia
η Ρωσσία
ee roseea
ρωσσικός/ή/ό
roseekos/ee/o

ο Ρώσσος
o rosos
η Ρωσσίδα
ee roseedha

Scotland
η Σκωτία
ee skoteea
σκωτσέζικος/η/ο
skotsezeekos/ee/o

ο Σκωτσέζος
o skotsezos
η Σκωτσέζα
ee skotseza

South Africa
η Νοτιοαφρική
ee notyoafreekee
νοτιοαφρικανικός/ή/ό
notyoafreekaneekos/ee/o

ο Νοτιοαφρικανός
o notyoafreekanos
η Νοτιοαφρικανίδα
ee notyoafreekaneedha

South America
η Νοτιοαμερική
ee notyoamereekee
νοτιοαμερικανικός/ή/ό
notyoamereekaneekos/ee/o

ο Νοτιοαμερικανός
o notyoamereekanos
η Νοτιοαμερικανίδα
ee notyoamereekaneedha

Soviet Union
η Σοβιέτικη Ενωση
ee sovyeteekee enosee

Spain
η Ισπανία
ee eespaneea
ισπανικός/ή/ό
eespaneekos/ee/o

ο Ισπανός
o eespanos
η Ισπανίδα
ee eespaneedha

Sweden
η Σουηδία
ee sweedheea
σουηδικός/ή/ό
sweedheekos/ee/o

ο Σουηδός
o sweedhos
η Σουηδέζα
ee sweedheza

Switzerland
η Ελβετία
ee elveteea
ελβετικός/ή/ό
elveteekos/ee/o

ο Ελβετός
o elvetos
η Ελβετίδα
ee elveteedha

Turkey
η Τουρκία
ee toorkeea
τουρκικός/ή/ό
toorkeekos/ee/o

ο Τούρκος
o toorkos
η Τούρκισσα
ee toorkeesa

United Kingdom
το Ηνωμένο Βασίλειο
to eenomeno vaseelyo

United States
οι Ηνωμένες Πολιτείες
ee eenomenes poleetee-es

Wales
η Ουαλλία
ee waleea
ουαλλικός/ή/ό
waleekos/ee/o

ο Ουαλλός
o walos
η Ουαλλέζα
ee waleza

Yugoslavia
η Γιουγκοσλαβία
ee yoogoslaveea
γιουγκοσλαβικός/ή/ό
yoogoslaveekos/ee/o

ο Γιουγκοσλάβος
o yoogoslavos
η Γιουγκοσλάβα
ee yoogoslava

GENERAL SIGNS AND NOTICES

ΑΙΘΟΥΣΑ ΑΝΑΜΟΝΗΣ Αίθουσα αναμονής	Waiting room
ΑΝΑΚΟΙΝΩΣΗ Ανακοίνωση	Announcement
ΑΝΑΛΩΣΗ ΜΕΧΡΙ ΚΑΙ Ανάλωση μέχρι και	Consume before
ΑΝΑΧΩΡΗΣΕΙΣ Αναχωρήσεις	Departures
ΑΝΔΡΩΝ Ανδρών	Gentlemen
ΑΝΕΛΚΥΣΤΗΡ Ανελκυστήρ	Lift
ΑΝΟΙΚΤΟ(Ν) Ανοικτό(ν)	Open
ΑΠΑΓΟΡΕΥΕΤΑΙ Η ΕΙΣΟΔΟΣ (ΕΙΣ ΤΟΥΣ ΜΗ ΕΧΟΝΤΑΣ ΕΡΓΑΣΙΑ) Απαγορεύεται η είσοδος (εις τους μη έχοντας εργασία)	No entry (to unauthorised personnel)
ΑΠΑΓΟΡΕΥΕΤΑΙ Η ΕΙΣΟΔΟΣ ΣΕ . . . Απαγορεύεται η είσοδος σε . . .	. . . not admitted
ΑΠΑΓΟΡΕΥΕΤΑΙ ΝΑ ΡΙΧΝΕΤΕ ΣΚΟΥΠΙΔΙΑ Απαγορεύεται να ρίχνετε σκουπίδια	No litter
ΑΠΑΓΟΡΕΥΕΤΑΙ ΤΟ ΚΑΠΝΙΣΜΑ Απαγορεύεται το κάπνισμα	No smoking

ΑΠΕΡΓΙΑ	Strike
Απεργία	
ΑΡΧΑΙΟΛΟΓΙΚΟΣ ΧΩΡΟΣ	Archaeological site
Αρχαιολογικός χώρος	
ΑΦΙΞΕΙΣ	Arrivals
Αφίξεις	
ΓΡΑΜΜΑΤΟΚΙΒΩΤΙΟ(Ν)	Postbox
Γραμματοκιβώτιο(ν)	
ΓΥΝΑΙΚΩΝ	Ladies
Γυναικών	
ΔΕΝ ΛΕΙΤΟΥΡΓΕΙ	Out of order
Δεν λειτουργεί	
ΔΙΑΤΗΡΕΙΤΑΙ ΕΝΤΟΣ ΨΥΓΕΙΟΥ	To be kept in a refrigerator
Διατηρείται εντός ψυγείου	
ΔΙΑΤΗΡΕΙΤΕ ΚΑΘΑΡΗ ΤΗΝ ΑΚΤΗ	Keep the beach clean
Διατηρείτε καθαρή την ακτή	
ΕΙΣΙΤΗΡΙΑ	Ticket office
Εισιτήρια	
ΕΙΣΟΔΟΣ	Entrance
Είσοδος	
ΕΚΠΤΩΣΕΙΣ	Sales, Reductions
Εκπτώσεις	
ΕΛΕΥΘΕΡΗ ΕΙΣΟΔΟΣ	Free admission
Ελεύθερη είσοδος	
ΕΛΕΥΘΕΡΟ(Ν)	Free, Vacant
Ελεύθερο(ν)	
(Ε)ΝΟΙΚΙΑΖΕΤΑΙ/ (Ε)ΝΟΙΚΙΑΖΟΝΤΑΙ	To let
(Ε)νοικιάζεται/ (Ε)νοικιάζονται	

ΕΞΟΔΟΣ (ΚΙΝΔΥΝΟΥ) Εξοδος (κινδύνου)	(Emergency) exit
ΕΥΚΑΙΡΙΕΣ Ευκαιρίες	Bargains
ΖΕΣΤΟ Ζεστό	Hot
ΗΜΕΡΟΜΗΝΙΑ ΛΗΞΕΩΣ Ημερομηνία λήξεως	Expiry date
ΗΣΥΧΙΑ Ησυχία	Silence
ΙΣΟΓΕΙΟ(Ν) Ισόγειο(ν)	Ground floor
ΙΣΤΟΡΙΚΟΣ ΧΩΡΟΣ Ιστορικός χώρος	Historical area
ΚΑΘΥΣΤΕΡΗΣΗ Καθυστέρηση	Delay
ΚΑΠΝΙΖΟΝΤΕΣ Καπνίζοντες	Smokers
ΚΑΤΕΙΛΗΜΜΕΝΟΣ Κατειλημμένος	In use (*lift*)
ΚΙΝΔΥΝΟΣ (ΘΑΝΑΤΟΥ) Κίνδυνος (θανάτου)	Danger (of death)
ΚΙΝΔΥΝΟΣ ΠΥΡΚΑΙΑΣ Κίνδυνος πυρκαϊάς	Fire hazard
ΚΛΕΙΣΤΟ(Ν) (ΛΟΓΩ ΔΙΑΚΟΠΩΝ) Κλειστό(ν) (λόγω διακοπών)	Closed (for holidays)
ΜΗ ΚΑΠΝΙΖΕΤΕ Μη καπνίζετε	No smoking
ΜΗ ΚΑΠΝΙΖΟΝΤΕΣ Μη καπνίζοντες	Non-smokers
ΜΗ ΚΛΕΙΝΕΤΕ ΤΗΝ ΕΙΣΟΔΟ Μη κλείνετε την είσοδο	Do not obstruct entrance

ΜΗΝ ΑΓΓΙΖΕΤΕ	Do not touch
Μην αγγίζετε	
ΜΗΝ ΟΜΙΛΕΙΤΕ ΣΤΟΝ ΟΔΗΓΟ	Do not talk to the driver
Μην ομιλείτε στον οδηγό	
ΜΗ ΠΑΤΑΤΕ ΤΟ ΠΡΑΣΙΝΟ	Keep off the grass
Μη πατάτε το πράσινο	
ΜΗ ΣΚΥΒΕΤΕ ΕΞΩ	Do not lean out
Μη σκύβετε έξω	
ΟΔΗΓΙΕΣ ΧΡΗΣΕΩΣ	Instructions for use
Οδηγίες χρήσεως	
ΟΡΟΦΟΣ	Floor
Οροφος	
ΠΑΡΑΚΑΛΩ (ΜΗ) . . .	Please (do not) . . .
Παρακαλώ (μη) . . .	
ΠΙΑΣΜΕΝΟΣ	Reserved
Πιασμένος	
ΠΛΥΣΙΜΟ ΜΕ ΤΟ ΧΕΡΙ	Hand wash
Πλύσιμο με το χέρι	
ΠΟΣΙΜΟ ΝΕΡΟ	Drinking water
Πόσιμο νερό	
ΠΡΟΣΕΧΕΤΕ	Caution, Take care
Προσέχετε	
ΠΡΟΣΕΧΕΤΕ ΤΟ ΣΚΑΛΟΠΑΤΙ	Mind the step
Προσέχετε το σκαλοπάτι	
ΠΡΟΣΟΧΗ	Caution
Προσοχή	
ΠΡΟΣΟΧΗ ΣΚΥΛΟΣ	Beware of the dog
Προσοχή σκύλος	
ΠΡΟΣΟΧΗ ΤΡΑΙΝΑ	Beware of the trains
Προσοχή τραίνα	

ΠΡΟΣΟΧΗ ΧΡΩΜΑ Προσοχή χρώμα	Wet paint
ΠΩΛΕΙΤΑΙ/ΠΩΛΟΥΝΤΑΙ Πωλείται/Πωλούνται	For sale
ΠΩΛΟΥΝΤΑΙ ΓΡΑΜΜΑΤΟΣΗΜΑ Πωλούνται γραμματόσημα	Stamps sold
ΣΥΜΠΛΗΡΩΜΕΝΟ Συμπληρωμένο	Full, No vacancies
ΣΥΡΑΤΕ Σύρατε	Pull
ΤΑΜΕΙΟ(N) Ταμείο(ν)	Cash desk, Cashier
ΤΟ ΔΙΚΑΙΩΜΑ ΕΙΣΟΔΟΥ ΕΛΕΓΧΕΤΑΙ ΑΠΟ ΤΗ ΔΙΕΥΘΥΝΣΗ Το δικαίωμα εισόδου ελέγχεται από τη διεύθυνση	The management reserves the right of admission
ΤΟΥΑΛΕΤΕΣ Τουαλέτες	Toilets
ΥΠΟΓΕΙΟ(N) Υπόγειο(ν)	Basement
ΧΤΥΠΗΣΑΤΕ ΤΟ ΚΟΥΔΟΥΝΙ Χτυπήσατε το κουδούνι	Ring the bell
ΩΘΗΣΑΤΕ Ωθήσατε	Push
ΩΡΕΣ ΕΠΙΣΚΕΨΕΩΣ Ώρες επισκέψεως	Visiting hours
ΩΡΕΣ ΓΡΑΦΕΙΟΥ Ώρες γραφείου	Office hours

CONVERSION TABLES
(approximate equivalents)

Linear measurements

centimetres	εκατοστά (εκ)	*ekatosta*
metres	μέτρα (μ)	*metra*
kilometres	χιλιόμετρα (χμ)	*kheelyometra*

10 cm = 4 inches	1 inch = 2.45 cm
50 cm = 19.6 inches	1 foot = 30 cm
1 metre = 39.37 inches	1 yard = 0.91 m
(just over 1 yard)	
100 metres = 110 yards	
1 km = 0.62 miles	1 mile = 1.61 km

To convert: km to miles: divide by 8 and multiply by 5
miles to km: divide by 5 and multiply by 8

Miles		Kilometres
0.6	1	1.6
1.2	2	3.2
1.9	3	4.8
2.5	4	6.4
3	5	8
6	10	16
12	20	32
19	30	48
25	40	64
31	50	80
62	100	161
68	110	177
75	120	193
81	130	209

Liquid measures

litre	λίτρο	*leetro*

1 litre = 1.8 pints   1 pint = 0.57 litre
5 litres = 1.1 gallons   1 gallon = 4.55 litres

'A litre of water's a pint and three quarters'

Gallons		Litres
0.2	1	4.5
0.4	2	9
0.7	3	13.6
0.9	4	18
1.1	5	23
2.2	10	45.5

Weights

gram	γραμμάριο (γρ)	*gramaryo*
100 grams	εκατό γραμμάρια	*ekato gramarya*
200 grams	διακόσια γραμμάρια	*dyakosya gramarya*
kilo	κιλό/χιλιόγραμμο (χλγ)	*keelo/kheelyogramo*

100 g = 3.5 oz   1 oz = 28 g
200 g = 7 oz   ¼ lb = 113 g
½ kilo = 1.1 lb   ½ lb = 227 g
1 kilo = 2.2 lb   1 lb = 454 g

Pounds		Kilos (Grams)
2.2	1	0.45 (450)
4.4	2	0.9 (900)
6.6	3	1.4 (1400)
8.8	4	1.8 (1800)
11	5	2.3 (2300)
22	10	4.5 (4500)

Area

The Greek unit of area is the stremma – το στρέμμα
(4 stremmata = 1 acre)

Clothing and shoe sizes

Women's dresses and suits

UK	10	12	14	16	18	20
Continent	36	38	40	42	44	46

Men's suits and coats

UK	36	38	40	42	44	46
Continent	46	48	50	52	54	56

Men's shirts

UK	14	14½	15	15½	16	16½	17
Continent	36	37	38	39	41	42	43

Shoes

UK	2	3	4	5	6	7	8	9	10	11
Continent	35	36	37	38	39	41	42	43	44	45

Waist and chest measurements

inches	28	30	32	34	36	38	40	42	44	46	48	50
centimetres	71	76	81	87	91	97	102	107	112	117	122	127

Tyre pressures

lb/sq in	15	18	20	22	24	26	28	30	33	35
kg/sq cm	1.1	1.3	1.4	1.5	1.7	1.8	2.0	2.1	2.3	2.5

NATIONAL HOLIDAYS

η Πρωτοχρονιά *ee protokhronya*	New Year's Day	1 January
τα Θεοφάνεια *ta theofanya*	Epiphany	6 January
η Καθαρή Δευτέρα *ee katharee dheftera*	Shrove Monday	
η Εικοσή πέμπτη Μαρτίου *ee eekosee pemptee marteeoo*	Independence Day; Annunciation	25 March
η Μεγάλη Παρασκευή *ee megalee paraskevee*	Good Friday	
το Μεγάλο Σάββατο *to megalo savato*	Easter Saturday	
το Πάσχα *to paskha*	Easter Sunday	
η Δευτέρα του Πάσχα *ee dheftera too paskha*	Easter Monday	
η Πρωτομαγιά *ee protomaya*	May Day	1 May
η Ανάληψη *ee analeepsee*	Ascension Day	
το Δεκαπενταύγουστο *to dhekapendavgoosto*	Assumption of the Virgin	15 August
Οχι *okhee*	'No' day (rejection of Italian ultimatum, 1940)	28 October
τα Χριστούγεννα *ta khreestooyena*	Christmas Day	25 December

234

USEFUL ADDRESSES

In the UK and Ireland

National Tourist Organisation of Greece
4 Conduit Street, London W1R 9TG
Tel: 071-409 1992

Greek Embassy
1A Holland Park, London W11 3TP
Tel: 071-727 8040

Greek Embassy
1 Upper Pembroke Street, Dublin 2
Tel: 767 254/5

In Greece

National Tourist Organisation of Greece
Karageorgi Servias 2, Syndagma Square, Athens
Tel: 3222 545

British Embassy
Ploutarchou 1, GR-106 75 Athens
Tel: 7236 211

There are British consulates in: Crete, Corfu, Patras, Rhodes and Thessalonica.

Irish Embassy
Vasileos Konstandinou 7, GR-106 74 Athens
Tel: 7232 771

NUMBERS

0	μηδέν	*meedhen*
1	ένας, μία, ένα	*enas, meea, ena*
2	δύο	*dheeo*
3	τρεις, τρία	*trees, treea*
4	τέσσερεις, τέσσερα	*teserees, tesera*
5	πέντε	*pende*
6	έξι	*eksee*
7	επτά (εφτά)	*epta (efta)*
8	οκτώ (οχτώ)	*okto (okhto)*
9	εννέα (εννιά)	*enea (enya)*
10	δέκα	*dheka*
11	έντεκα	*endeka*
12	δώδεκα	*dhodheka*
13	δεκατρείς, δεκατρία	*dhekatrees, dhekatreea*
14	δεκατέσσερεις, δεκατέσσερα	*dhekateserees, dhekatesera*
15	δεκαπέντε	*dhekapende*

16	δεκαέξι (δεκάξι)
	dhekaeksee (dhekaksee)
17	δεκαεπτά
	dhekaepta
18	δεκαοκτώ
	dhekaokto
19	δεκαεννέα
	dhekaenea
20	είκοσι
	eekosee
21	είκοσι ένας, είκοσι μία, είκοσι ένα
	eekosee enas, eekosee meea, eekosee ena
22	είκοσι δύο
	eekosee dheeo
23	είκοσι τρεις, είκοσι τρία
	eekosee trees, eekosee treea
24 etc.	είκοσι τέσσερεις, είκοσι τέσσερα
	eekosee teserees, eekosee tesera

30	τριάντα
	tryanda
31	τριάντα ένας, μία, ένα
	tryanda enas, meea, ena
32 etc.	τριάντα δύο
	tryanda dheeo
40	σαράντα
	saranda
50	πενήντα
	peneenda
60	εξήντα
	ekseenda
70	εβδομήντα
	evdhomeenda
80	ογδόντα
	ogdhonda
90	ενενήντα
	eneneenda

100	**εκατό(ν)**	
	ekato(n)	
101 etc.	**εκατόν ένας/μία/ένα**	
	ekaton enas/meea/ena	
123	**εκατόν είκοσι τρεις/τρία**	
	ekaton eekosee trees/treea	
200	**διακόσιοι, διακόσιες, διακόσια**	
	dhyakosyee, dhyakosyes, dhyakosya	
300	**τριακόσιοι, τριακόσιες, τριακόσια**	
	tryakosyee, tryakosyes, tryakosya	
400	**τετρακόσιοι, τετρακόσιες, τετρακόσια**	
	tetrakosyee, tetrakosyes, tetrakosya	
500	**πεντακόσιοι, πεντακόσιες, πεντακόσια**	
	pendakosyee, pendakosyes, pendakosya	
600	**εξακόσιοι, εξακόσιες, εξακόσια**	
	eksakosyee, eksakosyes, eksakosya	
700	**επτακόσιοι, επτακόσιες, επτακόσια**	
	eptakosyee, eptakosyes, eptakosya	
800	**οκτακόσιοι, οκτακόσιες, οκτακόσια**	
	oktakosyee, oktakosyes, oktakosya	
900	**εννιακόσιοι, εννιακόσιες, εννιακόσια**	
	enyakosyee, enyakosyes, enyakosya	
1000	**χίλιοι, χίλιες, χίλια**	
	kheelyee, kheelyes, kheelya	
2000	**δύο χιλιάδες**	
	***dheeo** kheelyadhes*	
3000	**τρεις χιλιάδες**	
	trees kheelyadhes	
4000 etc.	**τέσσερεις χιλιάδες**	
	teserees kheelyadhes	
1 000 000	**ένα εκατομύριο**	
	ena ekatomeeryo	
2 000 000	**δύο εκατομύρια**	
	dheeo ekatomeerya	
3 000 000	**τρία εκατομύρια**	
	***treea** ekatomeerya*	

4 000 000 etc.	τέσσερα εκατομύρια
	tesera ekatomeerya
1 000 000 000	ένα δισεκατομύριο
	ena dheesekatomeeryo
3 000 000 000	τρία δισεκατομύρια
	treea dheesekatomeerya

The number one has three different forms for masculine, feminine and neuter nouns – ένας, μία and ένα; three and four have one form for masculine and feminine nouns and one for neuter (τρεις and τρία, τέσσερεις and τέσσερα). All compound numbers involving one, two and three also have these different forms, as follows:

	masculine	*feminine*	*neuter*
13	δεκατρείς	δεκατρείς	δεκατρία
21	είκοσι ένας	είκοσι μία	είκοσι ένα
134	εκατόν τριάντα τέσσερεις	εκατόν τριάντα τέσσερεις	εκατόν τριάντα τέσσερα

and so on.

The numbers 200, 300 . . . 1000 are plural adjectives, and also have different forms for masculine, feminine and neuter nouns.

If the number is on its own, as when you're counting, or asking for your room number, you use the neuter. But when you're dealing with money, you use the feminine, because 'drachma' (η δραχμή) is a feminine noun.

With some numbers there are two slightly different forms, one rather more formal than the other. In the list, the less formal one is given in brackets.

Years:	1992	χίλια εννιακόσια ενενήντα δύο
		kheelya enyakosya eneneenda dheeo
	1821	χίλια οκτακόσια είκοσι ένα
		kheelya oktakosya eekosee ena

DICTIONARY

Greek nouns are given with the definite article ('the') to show their gender: **o** for masculine, **η** for feminine, **το** for neuter (**οι, οι, τα** in the plural).

Adjectives are shown with different endings for masculine, feminine and neuter: **μεγάλος/η/ο** (big) or **ωραίος/α/ο** (nice). A few of the adjectives in this list do not fit this pattern; for these, the masculine, feminine and neuter forms are shown in full, e.g. **πολύς, πολλή, πολύ** (much).

For plurals and other endings of nouns, see Basic grammar (page 196).

Verbs are shown in the first person singular 'I' form of the present tense; for other endings see page 204.

Abbreviations used are: (*m.*) = masculine; (*f.*) = feminine; (*n.*) = neuter; (*pl.*) = plural; (*adj.*) = adjective.

Greek–English

Words for food and drink are in the Menu reader, page 120. See also General signs and notices, page 225, and the 'You may see' lists in the individual sections.

A, α

άβολος/η/ο [*avolos/ee/o*] uncomfortable; inconvenient
αγαπάω, αγαπώ [*agapao, agapo*] I love
η **αγάπη** [*ee agapee*] love
αγγίζω [*angeezo*] I touch
Αγγλικός/ή/ό [*angleekos/ee/o*] English
το **αγγούρι** [*to angooree*] cucumber
η **αγελάδα** [*ee ayeladha*] cow
αγενής, αγενής, αγενές [*ayenees, ayenees, ayenes*] rude

ο άγιος [*o ayos*] saint

η αγκράφα [*ee agrafa*] fastener; buckle

άγνωστος/η/ο [*agnostos/ee/o*] unknown

η αγορά [*ee agora*] market

αγοράζω [*agorazo*] I buy

το αγοράκι [*to agorakee*] little boy

το αγόρι [*to agoree*] boy

άγριος/α/ο [*agryos/a/o*] wild

ο αγώνας [*o agonas*] competition

    ο αγώνας δρόμου [*o agonas dhromoo*] (running) race

η άδεια [*ee adhya*] licence, permit

    η άδεια οδηγήσεως [*ee adhya odheeyeeseos*] driving
    licence

άδειος/α/ο [*adhyos/a/o*] empty

η αδελφή [*ee adhelfee*] sister

ο αδελφός [*o adhelfos*] brother

τα αδέρφια [*ta adherfya*] brothers and sisters

το αδιάβροχο [*to adhyavrokho*] raincoat

αδιάβροχος/η/ο [*adhyavrokhos/ee/o*] waterproof

αδύνατος/η/ο [*adheenatos/ee/o*] thin; weak; impossible

241

ο αέρας [*o aeras*] air

το αεροδρόμιο [*to aerodhromyo*] airport

ο αερολιμένας [*o aeroleemenas*] airport

το αεροπλάνο [*to aeroplano*] aeroplane

ο/η αεροσυνοδός [*o/ee aeroseenodhos*] air steward, stewardess

ο αθλητισμός [*o athleeteezmos*] athletics; sport

η αίθουσα [*ee ethoosa*] hall; room

το αίμα [*to ema*] blood

αισθάνομαι [*esthanome*] I feel

το αίσθημα [*to estheema*] sense; feeling

ο αιώνας [*o eonas*] century

ακόμα [*akoma*] yet, still, more, even

ακούω [*akoo-o*] I hear, listen (to)

ακριβός/ή/ό [*akreevos/ee/o*] expensive, dear; precise, exact

ακριβώς [*akreevos*] exactly, precisely

η ακρόαση [*ee akroasee*] hearing

η ακτή [*ee aktee*] coast

το αλάτι [*to alatee*] salt

η αλήθεια [*ee aleethya*] truth

αλήθεια; [*aleethya*] really?

αλλά [ala] but

αλλάζω [alazo] I change

άλλη μια φορά [alee mya fora] once more, again

άλλη φορά [alee fora] some other time

αλλοιώτικος/η/ο [alyoteekos/ee/o] different

άλλος/η/ο [alos/ee/o] another, other

αλμυρός/ή/ό [almeeros/ee/o] salty; savoury

το άλογο [to alogo] horse

η αλυσίδα [ee aleeseedha] chain

η Αμερική [ee amereekee] America

αμέσως [amesos] immediately, right away

η αμμουδιά [ee amoodhya] sand

το αμπέλι [to ambelee] vineyard

το αμφιθέατρο [to amfeetheatro] amphitheatre

αν, εάν [an, ean] if; whether

ανάβω [anavo] I light; I switch/turn on

η ανάγκη [ee anangee] need, necessity

ανακαλύπτω [anakaleepto] I discover

η ανακοίνωση [ee anakeenosee] announcement

αναλόγως [analogos] accordingly

ανάμεσα (σε) [anamesa (se)] among; between

ανάμικτος/η/ο [anameektos/ee/o] mixed

η ανάπαυση [ee anapafsee] rest

ανάπηρος/η/ο [anapeeros/ee/o] disabled, handicapped

ανάποδα [anapodha] upside down, inside out, wrong way round

ο αναπτήρας [o anapteeras] (cigarette) lighter

η ανατολή [ee anatolee] east

ανατολικός/ή/ό [anatoleekos/ee/o] eastern

αναφέρω [anafero] I report

η αναφορά [ee anafora] report

η αναχώρηση [ee anakhoreesee] departure

το αναψυκτήριο [to anapseekteeryo] bar selling light refreshments

τα αναψυκτικά [ta anapseekteeka] refreshments; soft drinks

ανδρικός/ή/ό [andhreekos/ee/o] of a man; men's

ανεβαίνω [aneveno] I come/go up; I get on (bus etc.)

ο ανελκυστήρ [o anelkeesteer] lift

ο άνεμος [o anemos] wind

η ανεργία [ee aneryeea] unemployment

άνεργος/η/ο [anergos/ee/o] unemployed

άνευ [anev] without

η ανεψιά [ee anepsya] niece

ο ανεψιός [o anepsyos] nephew

ανήσυχος/η/ο [aneeseekhos/ee/o] worried

ο ανήφορος [o aneeforos] uphill slope

ο άνθρωπος [o anthropos] man; human being

ανοίγω [aneego] I open; switch/turn on

ανοικτός/ή/ό [aneektos/ee/o] open; light (coloured)

η άνοιξη [ee aneeksee] spring (season)

το ανοιχτήρι [to aneekhteeree] opener (for cans, bottles etc.)

το ανταλλακτικό [to andalakteeko] spare part; refill

αντί για [andee ya] instead of

οι αντίκες [ee andeekes] antiques

αντίο [adeeo] goodbye

το αντισυλληπτικό [to andeeseeleepteeko] contraceptive

ο αντίχειρας [o andeekheeras] thumb

η αντλία [ee andleea] pump

ο άντρας [o andras] man; husband

ανώμαλος/η/ο [anomalos/ee/o] rough, uneven

αξίζει [akseezee] it's worth (it)

    αξίζει τον κόπο [akseezee ton-gopo] it's worth it (the trouble)

απαγορεύεται [apagorevete] it is prohibited, forbidden

απαλός/ή/ό [apalos/ee/o] smooth; mild; gentle

απαντάω [apandao] I answer

η απάντηση [ee apandeesee] answer, reply

απάνω [apano] up; upstairs; above

απαραίτητος/η/ο [apareteetos/ee/o] essential

απασχολημένος/η/ο [apaskholeemenos/ee/o] engaged; busy

ο απατεώνας [o apateonas] swindler, rogue, scoundrel

απέναντι (από) [apenandee (apo)] opposite

η απεργία [ee aperyeea] strike

απλός/ή/ό [aplos/ee/o] simple; single, one way (ticket)

από [apo] of; from; about

    από καιρό σε καιρό [apo kero se kero] from time to time, occasionally

η αποβάθρα [ee apovathra] pier, jetty; platform

το απόγευμα [to apoyevma] afternoon

απογευματινός/ή/ο [apoyevmateenos/ee/o] (of the) afternoon

η **απόδειξη** [ee apodheeksee] receipt

αποκλείεται [apoklee-ete] it's out of the question

απολύτως [apoleetos] completely

οι **αποσκευές** [ee aposkeves] luggage, baggage

το **αποτέλεσμα** [to apotelezma] result

αποτελεσματικός/ή/ό [apotelezmateekos/ee/o] effective

απότομος/η/ο [apotomos/ee/o] steep

η **απόφαση** [ee apofasee] decision

αποφασίζω [apofaseezo] I decide

απόψε [apopse] this evening

απροσδόκητος/η/ο [aprozdhokeetos/ee/o] unexpected

ο **Αραβας** [o aravas] Arab

η **αράχνη** [ee arakhnee] spider

αργά [arga] slowly; late

άργησα [argeesa] I'm late

αργήσατε [aryeesate] you're late

η **αργία** [ee aryeea] (public) holiday

αργός/ή/ό [argos/ee/o] slow

αργότερα [argotera] later

αρέσω: μ'αρέσει, μ'αρέσουν [areso: maresee, maresoon] I like

   σ'αρέσει, σ'αρέσουν [saresee, saresoon] you like (s., informal)

   σας αρέσει, σας αρέσουν [sas aresee, sas aresoon] you like (pl., formal)

   του/της αρέσει/αρέσουν [too/tees aresee/aresoon] he/she/it likes

αρετσίνωτος/η/ο [aretseenotos/ee/o] unresinated

το **άρθρο** [to arthro] article (newspaper, grammar); clause

η **άρθρωση** [ee arthrosee] joint (body)

ο **αριθμός** [o areethmos] number

ο **αριθμός αυτοκινήτου** [o areethmos aftokeeneetoo] car registration number

αριστερά [areestera] on the left, to the left etc.

αριστερός/ή/ό [areesteros/ee/o] left

αρκετά [arketa] quite, fairly; enough

το **αρνί** [to arnee] lamb

η **αρραβωνιαστικιά** [ee aravonyasteekya] fiancée

ο αρραβωνιαστικός [*o aravonyasteekos*] fiancé

άρρωστος/η/ο [*arostos/ee/o*] ill

τα αρχαία [*ta arkhea*] ancient ruins

η αρχαιολογία [*ee arkheoloyeea*] archaeology

αρχαιολογικός/ή/ό [*arkheoloyeekos/ee/o*] archaeological

αρχαίος/α/ο [*arkheos/a/o*] ancient

ο αρχάριος, η αρχάρια [*o arkharyos, ee arkharya*] beginner

η αρχή [*ee arkhee*] beginning

αρχίζω [*arkheezo*] I begin

ο/η αρχιτέκτονας [*o/ee arkheetektonas*] architect

η αρχιτεκτονική [*ee arkheetektoneekee*] architecture

το άρωμα [*to aroma*] scent, perfume

ας . . . [*as . . .*] let's . . .

    ας πούμε [*as poome*] let's say

το ασανσέρ [*to asanser*] lift

ασημένιος/α/ο [*aseemenyos/a/o*] (made of) silver

το ασήμι [*to aseemee*] silver

η ασπιρίνη [*ee aspeereenee*] aspirin

άσπρος/η/ο [*aspros/ee/o*] white

το αστείο [*to asteeo*] joke

αστείος/α/ο [*asteeos/a/o*] funny

το αστέρι [*to asteree*] star

η αστυνομία [*ee asteenomeea*] police

ασυνήθιστος/η/ο [*aseeneetheestos/ee/o*] unusual

η ασφάλεια [*ee asfalya*] safety; insurance; fuse; safety catch;
    security police

ασφαλής, ασφαλής, ασφαλές [*asfalees, asfalees, asfales*]
    sure; certain; safe

ασφαλώς [*asfalos*] certainly

άσχημα [*askheema*] badly; unwell

άσχημος/η/ο [*askheemos/ee/o*] ugly

η ατζέντα [*ee adzenta*] diary

ο ατμός [*o atmos*] steam

η ατμόσφαιρα [*ee atmosfera*] atmosphere

το ατσάλι [*to atsalee*] steel

το αυγό [*to avgo*] egg

αυριανός/ή/ό [*avryanos/ee/o*] of tomorrow, tomorrow's

αύριο [*avryo*] tomorrow

το αυτί [*to aftee*] ear

αυτοί, αυτές, αυτά [*aftee, aftes, afta*] they; them, these

το **αυτοκίνητο** [*to aftokeeneeto*] car

ο **αυτοκινητόδρομος** [*o aftokeeneetodhromos*] motorway

αυτός/ή/ό [*aftos/ee/o*] he, she, it; this

αφαιρώ [*afero*] I remove, take away

το **αφεντικό** [*to afendeeko*] boss, head, chief

αφήνω [*afeeno*] I leave

η **άφιξη** [*ee afeeksee*] arrival

η **αφίσσα** [*ee afeesa*] advertisement

αφού [*afoo*] since, because; after, when

ο **αφρός** [*o afros*] foam

άχρηστος/η/ο [*akhreestos/ee/o*] useless

Β, β

το **βαγόνι** [*to vagonee*] (train) carriage

το **βάζο** [*to vazo*] jar

βάζω [*vazo*] I put; place; insert

ο **βαθμός** [*o vathmos*] degree, rank, mark

βαθύς, βαθειά, βαθύ [*vathees, vathya, vathee*] deep

η **βαλίτσα** [*ee valeetsa*] suitcase

το **βαμβάκι** [*to vamvakee*] cotton

βαρετός/ή/ό [*varetos/ee/o*] boring, tedious

βαριέμαι [*varyeme*] I am/get bored

η **βάρκα** [*ee varka*] (small) boat

το **βάρος** [*to varos*] weight

βαρυς, βαρειά, βαρύ [*varees, varya, varee*] heavy

ο **βασιλιάς** [*o vaseelyas*] king

βασιλικός/ή/ό [*vaseeleekos/ee/o*] royal

η **βασίλισσα** [*ee vaseeleesa*] queen

βγάζω [*vgazo*] I get/take out; take off

βγαίνω [*vyeno*] I come/go out

βέβαια, βεβαίως [*vevea, veveos*] certainly, of course

η **βελόνα** [*ee velona*] needle

η **βενζίνη** [*ee venzeenee*] petrol

η **βεράντα** [*ee veranda*] veranda

το **βερνίκι** [*to verneekee*] polish

ο **βήχας** [*o veekhas*] cough

βιάζομαι [*vyazome*] I am in a hurry

βιαστικός/ή/ό [*vyasteekos/ee/o*] urgent, in a hurry

το **βιβλίο** [*to veevleeo*] book

η **βιβλιοθήκη** [*ee veevlyotheekee*] library

το **βιβλιοπωλείο** [*to veevlyopoleeo*] bookshop

η **βίδα** [*ee veedha*] screw

το **βιολί** [*to vyolee*] violin

η **βιτρίνα** [*ee veetreena*] shop window

βλέπω [*vlepo*] I see

βοηθάω [*voeethao*] I help

βολεύει: δεν με βολεύει [*volevee: dhen me volevee*] it doesn't suit me, it's not convenient

βολικός/ή/ό [*voleekos/ee/o*] comfortable; convenient

η **βόλτα** [*ee volta*] walk; ride

η **βόμβα** [*ee vomva*] bomb

ο **βορράς** [*o voras*] north

βουλωμένος/η/ο [*voolomenos/ee/o*] blocked up

το **βουνό** [*to voono*] mountain

η **βούρτσα** [*ee voortsa*] brush

το **βραβείο** [*to vraveeo*] prize

το **βραδάκι** [*to vradhakee*] early evening

το **βράδυ** [*to vradhee*] evening

το **βραδυνό** [*to vradheeno*] evening meal

βραδυνός/ή/ό [*vradheenos/ee/o*] (of the) evening

βραστός/ή/ό [*vrastos/ee/o*] boiled

το **βραχιόλι** [*to vrakhyolee*] bracelet

βρεγμένος/η/ο [*vregmenos/ee/o*] wet

βρέχει [*vrekhee*] it's raining, it rains

βρέχω [*vrekho*] I wet

βρήκα [*vreeka*] I found

βρίσκω [*vreesko*] I find

η **βροχή** [*ee vrokhee*] rain

η **βρύση** [*ee vreesee*] tap; fountain

βρώμικος/η/ο [*vromeekos/ee/o*] dirty

Γ, γ

το **γαϊδούρι** [*to gaeedhooree*] donkey

το **γάλα** [*to gala*] milk

γαλάζιος/α/ο [*galazyos/a/o*] (sky) blue

το **γαλακτοπωλείο** [*to galaktopoleeo*] dairy shop

ο γάμος [*o gamos*] marriage, wedding

ο γαμπρός [*o gambros*] son-in-law; brother-in-law; bridegroom

το γάντι [*to gandee*] glove

το γαρύφαλλο [*to gareefalo*] carnation

ο γάτος, η γάτα [*o gatos, ee gata*] cat

το γεγονός [*to yegonos*] fact

γειά σας!, γειά σου! [*yasas, yasoo*] hello!; cheers!

ο γείτονας, η γειτόνισσα [*o yeetonas, ee yeetoneesa*] neighbour

η γειτονιά [*ee yeetonya*] neighbourhood

γελάω [*yelao*] I laugh

το γέλοιο [*to yelyo*] laugh

η γελοιογραφία [*ee yelyografeea*] cartoon

γεμάτος/η/ο [*yematos/ee/o*] full, crowded

γεμίζω [*yemeezo*] I fill

γεμιστός/ή/ό [*yemeestos/ee/o*] stuffed, full

τα γενέθλια [*ta yenethlya*] birthday

τα γένεια [*ta yenya*] beard

γενικά [*yeneeka*] generally

γενναίος/α/ο [*yeneos/a/o*] brave

γέρασα [*yerasa*] I'm old (*past tense of* γερνάω)

γερνάω [*yernao*] I grow old

γερός/ή/ό [*yeros/ee/o*] strong, stout

γέρος/η/ο [*yeros/ee/o*] old

ο γέρος [*o yeros*] old man

η γέφυρα [*ee yefeera*] bridge

το γεύμα [*to yevma*] lunch

η γεύση [*ee yefsee*] taste

η γη [*ee yee*] earth, land

για [*ya*] for

για παράδειγμα [*ya paradheegma*] for example

η γιαγιά [*ee yaya*] grandmother

το γιαούρτι [*to yaoortee*] yoghurt

γιατί [*yatee*] because

γιατί; [*yatee*] why?

ο γιατρός [*o yatros*] doctor

το γιλέκο [*to yeeleko*] waistcoat

γιορτάζω [*yortazo*] I celebrate (*name-day, festival*)

η γιορτή [*ee yortee*] holiday, festival, name-day

ο γιος [*o yos*] son

η γκαλερί [*ee galeree*] gallery

το γκαράζ [*to garaz*] garage

η γκαρνταρόμπα [*ee gardaroba*] cloakroom

το γκαρσόν [*to garson*] waiter

η γλάστρα [*ee glastra*] flower-pot

το γλέντι [*to glendee*] party, festival

γλυκός, γλυκειά, γλυκό [*gleekos, gleekya, gleeko*] sweet

η γλώσσα [*ee glosa*] tongue; language; sole (*fish*)

η γνώμη [*ee gnomee*] opinion

γνωρίζω [*gnoreezo*] I know; am acquainted with

η γνωριμία [*ee gnoreemeea*] acquaintance

γνωστός/ή/ό [*gnostos/ee/o*] known; an acquaintance

η γόμα [*ee goma*] eraser

οι γονείς [*ee gonees*] parents

το γουρούνι [*to gooroonee*] pig

η γραβάτα [*ee gravata*] tie

το γράμμα [*to grama*] letter

το γραμματοκιβώτιο [*to gramatokeevotyo*] letterbox, postbox

το γραμματόσημο [*to gramatoseemo*] stamp

η γραμμή [*ee gramee*] line

το γρατσούνιασμα [*to gratsoonyasma*] scratch

γρατσουνίζω [*gratsooneezo*] I scratch

το γραφείο [*to grafeeo*] office; desk

η γραφομηχανή [*ee grafomeekhanee*] typewriter

γράφω [*grafo*] I write

γρήγορα [*greegora*] quickly

γρήγορος/η/ο [*greegoros/ee/o*] fast

η γριά [*ee grya*] old woman

γρίζος/η/ο [*greezos/ee/o*] grey

η γρίππη [*ee greepee*] flu

η γροθιά [*ee grothya*] fist; punch

το γυαλί [*to yalee*] glass

τα γυαλιά [*ta yalya*] glasses, spectacles

γυαλιστερός/ή/ό [*yaleesteros/ee/o*] slippery, shiny

το γυμνάσιο [*to yeemnasyo*] junior high school

γυμνός/ή/ό [*yeemnos/ee/o*] naked, nude

η γυναίκα [*ee yeeneka*] woman, wife

γυναικείος/α/ο [*yeenekeeos/a/o*] of a woman, women's

γυρίζω [*yeereezo*] I return; turn

γύρω (από) [*yeero (apo)*] around

ο γύφτος, η γύφτισσα [*o yeeftos, ee yeefteesa*] gypsy

η γωνία [*ee goneea*] corner

Δ, δ

το δάκτυλο [*to dhakteelo*] finger

το δάκτυλο του ποδιού [*to dhakteelo too podhyoo*] toe

ο δάσκαλος, η δασκάλα [*o dhaskalos, ee dhaskala*] (primary school) teacher

το δάσος [*to dhasos*] wood, forest

το δαχτυλίδι [*to dhakhteeleedhee*] ring

το δείγμα [*to dheegma*] sample

το δείπνο [*to dheepno*] dinner

δείχνω [*dheekhno*] I show

το δεκάρικο [*to dhekareeko*] ten drachma coin

δέκατος/η/ο [*dhekatos/ee/o*] tenth

το δέμα [*to dhema*] parcel, package; bundle

το δέντρο [*to dhendro*] tree

δεν [*dhen*] not (makes a verb negative)

    δεν επιτρέπεται [*dhen epeetrepete*] it is not allowed

    δεν κατάλαβα [*dhen-gatalava*] I don't understand

    δεν μ'εννοιάζει [*dhen menyazee*] I don't care

    δεν νομίζω [*dhen nomeezo*] I don't think so

    δεν ταιριάζει [*dhen-deryazee*] it doesn't fit

η δεξαμενή [*ee dheksamenee*] reservoir

η δεξιά [*ee dheksya*] right

δεξιά [*dheksya*] on the right, to the right *etc.*

δεξιός/ά/ό [*dheksyos/a/o*] right

το δέρμα [*to dherma*] skin; hide; leather

η δεσποινίς, η δεσποινίδα [*ee dhespeenees, ee dhespeeneedha*] Miss

δεύτερος/η/ο [*dhefteros/ee/o*] second

δέχομαι [*dhekhome*] I accept, receive

δηλαδή [*dheeladhee*] that's to say

το δηλητήριο [*to dheeleeteeryo*] poison

το δημαρχείο [*to dheemarkheeo*] town hall

ο δήμαρχος [*o dheemarkhos*] mayor

ο δημοσιογράφος [*o dheemosyografos*] journalist

δημόσιος/α/ο [*dheemosyos/a/o*] public

τα δημοτικά τραγούδια [*ta dheemoteeka tragoodhya*] folk
   songs
το δημοτικό [*to dheemoteeko*] primary school
   δημοτικός/ή/ό [*dheemoteekos/ee/o*] municipal
   διά [*dhya*] through; across
   διαβάζω [*dhyavazo*] I read
το διάβασμα [*to dhyavazma*] reading
το διαβατήριο [*to dhyavateeryo*] passport
 ο διαγωνισμός [*o dhyagoneezmos*] competition
 η διαδήλωση [*ee dhyadheelosee*] demonstration (*protest*)
 ο διάδρομος [*o dhyadhromos*] corridor; aisle
 η δίαιτα [*ee dhee-eta*] diet
 ο διαιτητής [*o dhyeteetees*] referee
οι διακοπές [*ee dhyakopes*] holiday(s)
 ο διακόπτης [*o dhyakoptees*] switch
το διάλειμμα [*to dhyaleema*] interval; half-time
το διαμάντι [*to dhyamandee*] diamond
το διαμέρισμα [*to dhyamereezma*] apartment, flat; quarter
 η διαμονή [*ee dhyamonee*] stay
 η διανομή [*ee dhyanomee*] distribution
   διάσημος/η/ο [*dhyaseemos/ee/o*] famous
   διασκεδαστικός/ή/ό [*dhyaskedhasteekos/ee/o*] funny,
      amusing
 η διάσταση [*ee dhyastasee*] dimension
 η διασταύρωση [*ee dhyastavrosee*] crossroads; junction
το διάστημα [*to dhyasteema*] space; interval; distance
 η διαφάνεια [*ee dhyafanya*] transparency, slide
 η διαφήμιση [*ee dhyafeemeesee*] advertisement
   διαφορετικός/ή/ό [*dhyaforeteekos/ee/o*] different
   διδάσκω [*dheedhasko*] I teach
 η διεύθυνση [*ee dhyeftheensee*] direction; address;
   management
 ο διευθυντής, η διευθύντρια [*o dhyeftheendees, ee
   dhyeftheendrya*] manager
ο/η δικηγόρος [*o/ee dheekeegoros*] lawyer
το δίκιο [*to dheekyo*] right
   έχω δίκιο [*ekho dheekyo*] I am right
το δίκλινο [*to dheekleeno*] double room
   δικός/ή/ό [*dheekos/ee/o*] my, your etc. (*see page 203*)
το δίκτυ [*to dheektee*] net

δίνω [*dheeno*] I give

τα διόδια [*ta dhyodhya*] toll

διορθώνω [*dhyorthono*] I repair

διότι [*dhyotee*] because

δίπλα (σε) [*dheepla (se)*] beside, next to

διπλός/ή/ό [*dheeplos/ee/o*] double

το δίπλωμα [*to dheeploma*] diploma; permit, licence

ο δίσκος [*o dheeskos*] disc, record; tray

διστάζω [*dheestazo*] I hesitate

διψάω [*dheepsao*] I am thirsty

δοκιμάζω [*dhokeemazo*] I taste, sample

το δόντι [*to dhondee*] tooth

δος μου . . . [*dhos moo . . .*] give me . . .

η δουλειά [*ee dhoolya*] work, job

δουλεύω [*dhoolevo*] I work

το δοχείο [*to dhokheeo*] pot, container

η δραστηριότητα [*ee dhrasteeryoteeta*] activity

η δραχμή [*ee dhrakhmee*] drachma

το δρομολόγιο [*to dhromoloyo*] timetable

ο δρόμος [*o dhromos*] roadway

η δύναμη [*ee dheenamee*] strength, power

δυνατός/ή/ό [*dheenatos/ee/o*] strong; loud; possible

δύο [*dheeo*] two

και οι δύο, και τα δύο [*ke ee dheeo, ke ta dheeo*] both

δυσάρεστος/η/ο [*dheesarestos/ee/o*] unpleasant

η δύση [*ee dheesee*] west

δύσκολος/η/ο [*dheeskolos/ee/o*] difficult

το δυστύχημα [*to dheesteekheema*] accident, misfortune

δυστυχισμένος/η/ο [*dheesteekheezmenos/ee/o*] sad, unhappy

δυστυχώς [*dheesteekhos*] unfortunately

δυτικός/ή/ό [*dheeteekos/ee/o*] western

το δωμάτιο [*to dhomatyo*] room

το δώρο [*to dhoro*] gift, present

δώστε μου [*dhoste moo*] give me

E, ε

ο εαυτός μου/σου/του/τους [*o eaftos moo/soo/too/toos*] him/her/itself; themselves η εβδομάδα [*ee evdhomadha*] week

η Εγγλέζα [*ee engleza*] Englishwoman

εγγλέζικος/η/ο [*englezeekos/ee/o*] English

ο Εγγλέζος [*o englezos*] Englishman

η εγγονή [*ee engonee*] granddaughter

τα εγγόνια [*ta engonya*] grandchildren

ο εγγονός [*o engonos*] grandson

το έγκλημα [*to engleema*] crime

έγκυος (*f. adj.*) [*engeeos*] pregnant

εγώ [*ego*] I

το έδαφος [*to edhafos*] land, ground; territory

εδώ [*edho*] here

η Εθνική Οδός [*ee ethneekee odhos*] National Highway

είδα [*eedha*] I saw

οι ειδήσεις [*ee eedheesees*] news (*radio, TV etc.*)

ειδικά [*eedheeka*] especially

ειδικός/ή/ό [*eedheekos/ee/o*] special; particular

το είδος [*to eedhos*] type, kind

το εικοσάρικο [*to eekosareeko*] twenty drachma coin

είμαι [*eeme*] I am

είμαστε [*eemaste*] we are

253

είναι [*eene*] he/she/it is; they are

το έϊντζ [*to e-eeds*] AIDS

η ειρήνη [*ee eereenee*] peace

είσαι [*eese*] you are (*s.*)

είσαστε, είστε [*eesaste, eeste*] you are (*pl., formal*)

το εισιτήριο [*to eeseeteeryo*] ticket

η είσοδος [*ee eesodhos*] entrance, way in

είχα [*eekha*] I had

το εκατοστάρικο [*to ekatostareeko*] hundred drachma note/coin

το εκδοτήριο [*to ekdhoteeryo*] booking office, box office

η εκδρομή [*ee ekdhromee*] excursion

εκεί [*ekee*] there

εκείνοι/ες/α [*ekeenee/es/a*] those

εκείνος/η/ο [*ekeenos/ee/o*] that

η έκθεση [*ee ekthesee*] exhibition

η εκκλησία [*ee ekleeseea*] church

η εκπαίδευση [*ee ekpedhefsee*] education

η έκπληξη [*ee ekpleeksee*] surprise

η έκπτωση [*ee ekptosee*] reduction, discount

εκτός (από) [*ektos (apo)*] apart (from)

έλα [*ela*] come, come along! (*s.*)

ελάτε [*elate*] come, come along! (*pl.*)

ο έλεγχος εισιτηρίων [*o elenkhos eeseeteereeon*] check-in

ελέγχω [*elenkho*] I check

ελεύθερος/η/ο [*eleftheros/ee/o*] free; unoccupied; vacant; unmarried

η ελιά [*ee elya*] olive

η Ελλάδα [*ee eladha*] Greece

ο Έλληνας [*o eleenas*] Greek (man)

η Ελληνίδα [*ee eleeneedha*] Greek (woman)

η Ελληνική Επανάσταση [*ee eleeneekee epanastasee*] Greek War of Independence

Ελληνικός/ή/ό [*eleeneekos/ee/o*] Greek

η ελπίδα [*ee elpeedha*] hope

ελπίζω [*elpeezo*] I hope (for)

εμαγιέ [*emaye*] enamelled

εμπρός! [*embros*] forward; come in!; (*answering phone*) hello!

εμφανίζω [*emfaneezo*] I show; develop (*film*)

εναντίον [*enandeeon*] against

ένας, ένα [*enas, ena*] a/an; one

η ενέργεια [*ee enerya*] energy, power

ενήλικος/η/ο [*eneeleekos/ee/o*] adult

το ενθύμιο [*to entheemyo*] souvenir

ενοχλώ [*enokhlo*] I bother, annoy

εντάξει [*endaksee*] OK

εντελώς [*endelos*] completely

εντυπωσιακός/ή/ό [*endeeposyakos/ee/o*] impressive

εν τω μεταξύ [*en-do metaksee*] meanwhile

ενώ [*eno*] while

εξαντλημένος/η/ο [*eksandleemenos/ee/o*] exhausted, worn out; sold out

εξαργυρώνω [*eksaryeerono*] I cash (*cheque*)

οι εξετάσεις [*ee eksetasees*] exams

εξηγώ [*ekseego*] I explain

η έξοδος [*ee eksodhos*] exit, way out

ο εξοπλισμός [*o eksopleezmos*] equipment

η εξοχή [*ee eksokhee*] countryside

έξυπνος/η/ο [*ekseepnos/ee/o*] clever, intelligent

έξω [*ekso*] outside; abroad

η ΕΟΚ [*eok*] (= η Ευρωπαϊκή Οικονομική Κοινότητα) [*ee evropaeekee eekonomeekee keenoteeta*] EEC

επαναλαμβάνω [*epanalamvano*] I repeat

ΕΠΕ [*epe*] (= Εταιρεία Περιορισμένων Ευθύνων) [*etereea peryoreesmenon eftheenon*] Limited Company, plc

η επέτειος [*ee epetyos*] anniversary

ο επιβάτης [*o epeevatees*] passenger

επιβεβαιώνω [*epeeveveono*] I confirm

η επιβίβαση [*ee epeeveevasee*] boarding, embarkation

το επιδόρπιο [*to epeedhorpyo*] dessert

επικίνδυνος/η/ο [*epeekeendheenos/ee/o*] dangerous

τα έπιπλα [*ta epeepla*] furniture

επιπλωμένος/η/ο [*epeeplomenos/ee/o*] furnished

επίσης [*epeesees*] besides, as well

επισκέπτομαι [*epeeskeptome*] I visit

επιστρέφω [*epeestrefo*] I return; give back; refund

η επιστροφή [*ee epeestrofee*] return

με επιστροφή [*me epeestrofee*] return (ticket)

επιτίθεμαι [*epeeteetheme*] I attack

επιτρέπεται [*epeetrepete*] it is allowed

η επιτυχία [*ee epeeteekheea*] success

η επιχείρηση [*ee epeekheereesee*] firm, business

επόμενος/η/ο [*epomenos/ee/o*] following, next

η εποχή [*ee epokhee*] season

το επώνυμο [*to eponeemo*] surname

το εργαστήριο [*to ergasteeryo*] workshop

το έργο [*to ergo*] work; play (*theatre*)

το εργοστάσιο [*to ergostasyo*] factory

τα ερείπια [*ta ereepya*] ruins

ΕΡΤ [*ert*] Greek National Radio and Television

ερυθρός/ή/ό [*ereethros/ee/o*] red

έρχομαι [*erkhome*] I come/am coming (*see page 205*)

εσάς [*esas*] you (*pl., formal*) (*see page 202*)

εσείς [*esees*] you (*pl., formal*) (*see page 201*)

εσένα [*esena*] you (*s., informal*) (*see page 202*)

το εστιατόριο [*to estyatoryo*] restaurant

εσύ [*esee*] you (*s., informal*) (*see page 201*)

τα εσώρουχα [*ta esrookha*] underwear

η εταιρεία [ee etereea] company
έτοιμος/η/ο [eteemos/ee/o] ready

το έτος [to etos] year
έτσι [etsee] thus, like this/that
   έτσι δεν είναι; [etsee dhen eene] isn't that so?
   έτσι κι αλλιώς [etsee kyalyos] anyway, in any event
ευγενής, ευγενής, ευγενές [evyenees, evyenees, evyenes]
   polite
ευγνώμων [evgnomon] grateful
ευθεία [eftheea] straight, straight on
εύκολος/η/ο [efkolos/ee/o] easy
ευτυχισμένος/η/ο [efteekheezmenos/ee/o] happy
ευτυχώς [efteekhos] fortunately
ευχαριστημένος/η/ο [efkhareesteemenos/ee/o] pleased
ευχάριστος/η/ο [efkhareestos/ee/o] pleasant
ευχαριστούμε [efkhareestoome] (we) thank you
ευχαριστώ [efkhareesto] (I) thank you
ευχαρίστως [efkhareestos] with pleasure
έφαγα [efaga] I ate

η εφημερίδα [ee efeemereedha] newspaper
έφτασα [eftasa] just a minute
έχασα [ekhasa] I've lost, I lost
εχτές [ekhtes] yesterday
έχω [ekho] I have
   έχει να κάνει με . . . [ekhee na kanee me . . .] it's to do
   with . . .
   έχω ανάγκη από . . . [ekho anangee apo . . .] I need . . .

Z, ζ

η ζακέτα [ee zaketa] coat, jacket
ζαλίζομαι [zaleezome] I get dizzy; feel sick

το ζαμπόν [to zambon] ham

η ζάχαρη [ee zakharee] sugar

το ζαχαροπλαστείο [to zakharoplasteeo] patisserie, coffee
   house
ζεσταίνομαι [zestenome] I am hot

η ζέστη [ee zestee] heat
   κάνει ζέστη [kanee zestee] it's hot (weather)

ζεστός/ή/ό [zestos/ee/o] hot

το ζευγάρι [to zevgaree] couple; married couple

η ζημιά [ee zeemya] damage

ζητάω [zeetao] I ask (for)

ζήτω . . . ! [zeeto . . .] long live . . . !, up with . . . !

το ζουμί [to zoomee] juice

ζυγός/ή/ό [zeegos/ee/o] even (not odd)

ζω [zo] I live

η ζωγραφιά [ee zografya] painting

ζωγραφίζω [zografeezo] I paint

ο/η ζωγράφος [o/ee zografos] painter

η ζωή [ee zoee] life

η ζώνη [ee zonee] belt

ζωντανός/ή/ό [zondanos/ee/o] live, alive; vivid, bright

H, η

η [ee] the

ή [ee] or

ή . . . ή [ee . . . ee] either . . . or

ήδη [eedhee] already; now

ήθελα [eethela] I wanted

το ηλεκτρικό [to eelektreeko] underground railway in Athens

ηλεκτρικός/ή/ό [eelektreekos/ee/o] electric

η ηλίαση [ee eeleeasee] sunstroke

η ηλικία [ee eeleekeea] age

το ηλιοβασίλεμα [to eelyovaseelema] sunset

ηλιοκαμένος/η/ο [eelyokamenos/ee/o] (sun-)tanned

ο ήλιος [o eelyos] sun; sunshine

το ημερολόγιο [to eemeroloyo] diary

η ημερομηνία [ee eemeromeeneea] date

ήμερος/η/ο [eemeros/ee/o] calm, quiet

ήμουν(α) [eemoon(a)] I was

ΗΠΑ [eepa] (= οι Ηνωμένες Πολιτείες της Αμερικής) [ee eenomenes poleetee-es tees amereekees] USA, United States of America

ήπια [eepya] I drank

η ησυχία [ee eeseekheea] quiet, peace

ήσυχος/η/ο [eeseekhos/ee/o] quiet, peaceful

Θ, θ

θα [tha] (*indicates future tense, or conditional*)
    θα ήθελα [tha eethela] I would like
    θα θέλατε; [tha thelate] would you like?
    θα πει [tha pee] it means
    θα τα ξαναπούμε [tha ta ksanapoome] see you soon, so
    long
η θάλασσα [ee thalasa] sea
τα θαλασσινά [ta thalaseena] shellfish
το θαύμα [to thavma] wonder, miracle
    θαυμάσιος/α/ο [thavmasyos/a/o] wonderful
η θέα [ee thea] view; sight; scenery
η θεά [ee thea] goddess
το θέαμα [to theama] show, spectacle
το θέατρο [to theatro] theatre
η θεία [ee theea] aunt
ο θείος [o theeos] uncle
    θέλω [thelo] I want
το θέμα [to thema] matter, subject, topic
η θεραπεία [ee therapeea] remedy, cure
το θέρισμα [to thereezma] harvest; vintage
η θέρμανση [ee thermansee] heating
η θερμάστρα [ee thermastra] heater
η θέση [ee thesee] place; seat
ο θόρυβος [o thoreevos] noise
    θυμάμαι [theemame] I remember
    θυμωμένος/η/ο [theemomenos/ee/o] angry, annoyed
    θυμώνω [theemono] I get angry

Ι, ι

η ιδέα [ee eedhea] idea
ο ιδιοκτήτης, η ιδιοκτήτρια [o eedhyokteetees, ee
    eedhyokteetrya] owner; landlady, landlord
    ίδιος/α/ο [eedhyos/a/o] same
    ο ίδιος, η ίδια [o eedhyos, ee eedhya] 'speaking' (*when
    answering phone*)
    το ίδιο κάνει [to eedhyo kanee] it's all the same

ιδιωτικός/ή/ό [*eedhyoteekos/ee/o*] private

το **ιπτάμενο δελφίνι** [*to eeptameno dhelfeenee*] hovercraft, hydrofoil

ίσια [*eesya*] straight on

η **ιστιοπλοΐα** [*ee eestyoploeea*] sailing

η **ιστορία** [*ee eestoreea*] story, history

ίσως [*eesos*] perhaps, maybe

Κ, κ

η **κάβα** [*ee kava*] wine cellar; wine shop

το **κάδρο** [*to kadhro*] picture, painting

καθαρίζω [*kathareezo*] I clean

το **καθαριστήριο** [*to kathareesteeryo*] cleaner's

καθαρός/ή/ό [*katharos/ee/o*] clean; clear

κάθε [*kathe*] each; every

κάθε μέρα [*kathe mera*] every day

κάθε πότε; [*kathe pote*] how often?, how many times?

ο **καθηγητής, η καθηγήτρια** [*o katheeyeetees, ee katheeyeetrya*] teacher; lecturer; professor

το **καθηκάκι** [*to katheekakee*] (child's) potty

το **καθήκον** [*to katheekon*] duty

η **καθημερινή** [*ee katheemereenee*] weekday, working day

καθημερινός/ή/ό [*katheemereenos/ee/o*] daily

καθήστε [*katheeste*] take a seat

το **κάθισμα** [*to katheezma*] seat

καθιστός/ή/ό [*katheestos/ee/o*] sitting (down)

καθόλου [*katholoo*] absolutely not, not at all

κάθομαι [*kathome*] I sit down, am sitting down

ο **καθρέφτης** [*o kathreftees*] mirror

η **καθυστέρηση** [*ee katheestereesee*] delay

καθώς [*kathos*] as, when

καθώς και [*kathos ke*] as well as

και [*ke*] and

το **καΐκι** [*to kaeekee*] caique, fishing boat

καινούριος/α/ο [*kenooryos/a/o*] new

και οι δύο, και τα δύο [*ke ee dheeo, ke ta dheeo*] both

ο **καιρός** [*o keros*] time; weather

καίω [*keo*] I burn

κακός/ή/ό [*kakos/ee/o*] bad
κακώς [*kakos*] badly
καλά, καλώς [*kala, kalos*] well; fine
το **καλάθι** [*to kalathee*] basket
καλημέρα [*kaleemera*] good day, good morning
καληνύχτα [*kaleeneekhta*] goodnight
καλή όρεξη! [*kalee oreksee*] enjoy your meal!, bon appétit!
καλησπέρα [*kaleespera*] good evening
καλή τύχη! [*kalee teekhee*] good luck!
το **καλοκαίρι** [*to kalokeree*] summer
καλός/ή/ό [*kalos/ee/o*] good
το **καλσόν** [*to kalson*] tights
οι **κάλτσες** [*ee kaltses*] socks, stockings
καλύτερος/η/ο [*kaleeteros/ee/o*] better
ο/η/το **καλύτερος/η/ο** [*o/ee/to kaleeteros/ee/o*] best
καμμία (*see* **κανένας**)
καμμιά φορά [*kamya fora*] sometimes
η **καμπάνα** [*ee kambana*] bell (*church etc.*)
η **καμπίνα** [*ee kabeena*] cabin
η **καμπύλη** [*ee kambeelee*] curve
η **κανάτα** [*ee kanata*] jug
κάνει [*kanee*] it costs
κάνει κρύο/ζέστη [*kanee kreeo/zestee*] it's cold/hot
(weather)
κανένας, καμμία, κανένα [*kanenas, kameea, kanena*] any,
anyone; (*after negative*) no, no one
κανονίζω [*kanoneezo*] I arrange; I fix
κάνουν [*kanoon*] they cost
κάνω [*kano*] I do, make
κάνω αίτηση [*kano eetesee*] I apply for
κάνω σκι [*kano skee*] I ski
το **καπάκι** [*to kapakee*] lid
το **καπέλλο** [*to kapelo*] hat
καπνίζω [*kapneezo*] I smoke
το **κάπνισμα** [*to kapneezma*] smoking
καπνιστός/ή/ό [*kapneestos/ee/o*] smoked
το **καπνοπωλείο** [*to kapnopoleeo*] tobacconist's
ο **καπνός** [*o kapnos*] tobacco; smoke
κάποιος/α/ο [*kapyos/a/o*] someone
το **καράβι** [*to karavee*] boat

260

οι **καραμέλες** [*ee karameles*] sweets

το **κάρβουνο** [*to karvoono*] coal

η **καρδιά** [*ee kardhya*] heart

η **καρέκλα** [*ee karekla*] chair

το **καροτσάκι** [*to karotsakee*] push-chair, pram; wheelchair; wheelbarrow

ο **καρπός** [*o karpos*] fruit; wrist

το **καρπούζι** [*to karpoozee*] water melon

η **κάρτα** [*ee karta*] card

η **κάρτα απεριορίστων διαδρομών** [*ee karta aperyoreeston dhyadhromon*] season ticket (*bus, trolley etc.*)

το **καρτόνι** [*to kartonee*] cardboard; carton

η **καρτ-ποστάλ** [*ee kart-postal*] postcard

το **καρφί** [*to karfee*] nail

η **καρφίτσα** [*ee karfeetsa*] pin

η **κασέτα** [*ee kaseta*] cassette

καστανός/ή/ό [*kastanos/ee/o*] brown, chestnut colour

το **κάστρο** [*to kastro*] castle, fortress

κατά [*kata*] according to; towards

   κατά τη γνώμη μου [*kata tee gnomee moo*] in my opinion

   κατά τη διάρκεια του/της [*kata tee dhyarkya too/tees*] during

κατάλαβα [*katalava*] I've understood, I understand

καταλαβαίνω [*katalaveno*] I understand

κατάλληλος/η/ο [*kataleelos/ee/o*] suitable

ο **κατάλογος** [*o katalogos*] menu; list; directory

ο **καταράχτης** [*o katarakhtees*] waterfall

το **κατάστημα** [*to katasteema*] shop

το **κατάστρωμα** [*to katastroma*] deck

καταψυγμένος/η/ο [*katapseegmenos/ee/o*] (deep) frozen

κατεβαίνω [*kateveno*] I come/go down; I get off (*bus etc.*)

ο **κατήφορος** [*o kateeforos*] downhill slope

το **κατσαβίδι** [*to katsaveedhee*] screwdriver

η **κατσαρόλα** [*ee katsarola*] saucepan

η **κατσίκα** [*ee katseeka*] goat

κάτω [*kato*] down; downstairs; below

κάτω (από) [*kato (apo)*] under; underneath

ο **καυγάς** [*o kavgas*] quarrel, row

καφέ [*kafe*] brown

το **καφεδάκι** [*to kafedhakee*] (cup of) coffee

το καφενείο [*to kafeneeo*] coffee house
ο καφές [*o kafes*] coffee
η καφετιέρα [*ee kafetyera*] coffee pot
κενός/ή/ό [*kenos/ee/o*] empty; vacant
το κέντημα [*to kendeema*] embroidery
το κέντρο [*to kendro*] centre; middle
η κεραία [*ee kerea*] aerial
η κεραμεική [*ee kerameekee*] pottery
το κεράσι [*to kerasee*] cherry
κερδίζω [*kerdheezo*] I earn; I win
το κερί [*to keree*] candle
το κεφάλι [*to kefalee*] head
το κέφι [*to kefee*] high spirits
ο κήπος [*o keepos*] garden
το κιλό [*to keelo*] kilo
ο κίνδυνος [*o keendheenos*] danger
η κίνηση [*ee keeneesee*] movement; traffic
κινώ, κινούμαι [*keeno, keenoome*] I move
κίτρινος/η/ο [*keetreenos/ee/o*] yellow
το κλαδί [*to kladhee*] branch (*tree*)
κλαίω [*kleo*] I cry
το κλαρί [*to klaree*] branch (*tree*)
η κλειδαριά [*ee kleedharya*] lock
το κλειδί [*to kleedhee*] key; spanner
κλείνω [*kleeno*] I close; switch/turn off; reserve
κλειστός/ή/ό [*kleestos/ee/o*] closed
η κλήση [*ee kleesee*] call
το κλίμα [*to kleema*] climate
ο κλιματισμός [*o kleemateezmos*] air-conditioning
κόβω [*kovo*] I cut (off)
η κοιλάδα [*ee keeladha*] valley
κοιμάμαι [*keemame*] I sleep
το κοινοβούλιο [*keenovoolyo*] parliament
κοινός/ή/ό [*keenos/ee/o*] common, ordinary
κοίτα [*keeta*] look (s., informal, imperative)
κοιτάζω [*keetazo*] I look (at); I watch
κοίταξε! [*keetakse*] look! (s., informal, imperative)
κοιτάξτε! [*keetakste*] look! (pl., formal, imperative)
το κόκκαλο [*to kokalo*] bone
κόκκινος/η/ο [*kokeenos/ee/o*] red

το **κολάρο** [*to kolaro*] collar

η **κόλαση** [*ee kolasee*] hell

η **κόλλα** [*ee kola*] glue

ο **κόλπος** [*o kolpos*] bay

κολυμπάω [*koleembao*] I swim

το **κολύμπι** [*to koleembee*] swimming

το **κόμμα** [*to koma*] (political) party; comma

το **κομμάτι** [*to komatee*] piece, bit

το **κομπιούτερ** [*to kombyooter*] computer

κομπλέ [*komble*] complete; full (up)

το **κομπολόι** [*to komboloee*] 'worry beads'

η **κονσέρβα** [*ee konserva*] tinned food

κοντά (σε) [*konda (se)*] close (to), near

το **κοντίσιονερ** [*to kondeesyoner*] (hair) conditioner

κοντός/ή/ό [*kondos/ee/o*] short

η **κόρη** [*ee koree*] daughter

το **κοριτσάκι** [*to koreetsakee*] little girl

το **κορίτσι** [*to koreetsee*] girl

ο **κόσμος** [*o kozmos*] world; people

   έχει πολύ κόσμο [*ekhee polee kozmo*] there's a lot of people

κοστίζει [*kosteezee*] it costs

κοστίζουν [*kosteezoon*] they cost

το **κοστούμι** [*to kostoomee*] dress; suit; outfit

το **κοτόπουλο** [*to kotopoolo*] chicken

ο **κουβάς** [*o koovas*] bucket

κουβεντιάζω [*koovendyazo*] I chat, talk

η **κουβέρτα** [*kooverta*] blanket

το **κουδούνι** [*to koodhoonee*] bell

η **κουζίνα** [*ee koozeena*] kitchen; cooker

η **κούκλα** [*ee kookla*] doll

το **κουμπί** [*to koombee*] button

κουρασμένος/η/ο [*koorazmenos/ee/o*] tired

κουραστικός/ή/ό [*koorasteekos/ee/o*] tiring

το **κουρείο** [*to kooreeo*] barber's

το **κουρέλι** [*to koorelee*] rag

η **κουρτίνα** [*ee koorteena*] curtain

το **κουταλάκι** [*to kootalakee*] teaspoon

το **κουτάλι** [*to kootalee*] spoon

το **κουτί** [*to kootee*] tin, can

κουφός/ή/ό [*koofos/ee/o*] deaf

κοφτερός/ή/ό [*kofteros/ee/o*] sharp

το **κραγιόν** [*to krayon*] lipstick

το **κρασί** [*to krasee*] wine

κρατάω [*kratao*] I keep; reserve

το **κράτος** [*to kratos*] state

το **κρέας** [*to kreas*] meat

το **κρεβάτι** [*to krevatee*] bed

η **κρεβατοκάμαρα** [*ee krevatokamara*] bedroom

η **κρέμα** [*ee krema*] cream; lotion

το **κρεμμύδι** [*to kremeedhee*] onion

η **Κρήτη** [*ee kreetee*] Crete

η **κρουασιέρα** [*ee krooazyera*] cruise

το **κρυολόγημα** [*ee kreeoloyeema*] cold (*illness*)

κρυολογώ [*kreeologo*] I have a cold

κρύος/α/ο [*kreeos/a/o*] cold

   κάνει κρύο (*kanee kreeo*) it's cold (*weather*)

κρυώνω [*kreeono*] I am cold

το **κτήμα** [*to kteema*] farm, country estate

το **κτίριο** [*to kteeryo*] building

η **κυβέρνηση** [*ee keeverneesee*] government

η **κυκλοφορία** [*ee keekloforeea*] traffic

το **κυλικείο** [*to keeleekeeo*] buffet

η **κυλότα** [*ee keelota*] panties (*women's*)

το **κύμα** [*to keema*] wave (*sea*)

κυματώδης/ης/ες [*keematodhees/ees/es*] rough (*sea*); wavy

το **κυνήγι** [*to keeneeyee*] hunting; game

η **κυρία** [*ee keereea*] Mrs

κύριε [*keerye*] Mr (*when addressing someone*)

ο **κύριος** [*o keeryos*] Mr

ο **κώδικας** [*o kodheekas*] code

η **κωμωδία** [*ee komodheea*] comedy

Λ, λ

το **λάδι** [*to ladhee*] oil

το **λάθος** [*to lathos*] mistake

   λάθος κάνετε [*lathos kanete*] you are mistaken

έγινε λάθος [*eyeene lathos*] there's been a mistake

τα λαϊκά τραγούδια [*ta laeeka tragoodhya*] popular songs

η λαϊκή αγορά [*ee laeekee agora*] street market

λαϊκός/ή/ό [*laeekos/ee/o*] popular

ο λαιμός [*o lemos*] throat; neck

η λάμπα [*ee lamba*] lamp; light-bulb

ο λαός [*o laos*] people (race); populace

το λαστιχάκι [*to lasteekhakee*] rubber band

το λάστιχο [*to lasteekho*] tyre

το λαχείο [*to lakheeo*] lottery; lottery ticket

λειτουργώ [*leetoorgo*] I work; function

ο λεκές [*o lekes*] stain

η λεμονάδα [*ee lemonadha*] lemonade

το λεμόνι [*to lemonee*] lemon

η λέξη [*ee leksee*] word

το λεπτό [*to lepto*] minute

λεπτός/ή/ό [*leptos/ee/o*] slim, thin

ο λευκοπλάστης [*o lefkoplastees*] sticking plaster

λευκός/ή/ό [*lefkos/ee/o*] white

το λεωφορείο [*to leoforeeo*] bus

η λεωφόρος [*ee leoforos*] avenue

λέω [*leo*] I say, tell (*see page 206*)

λίγο [*leego*] a bit, a little

   σε λίγο [*se leego*] soon

λίγοι/ες/α [*leegee/es/a*] few, not many

λίγος/η/ο [*leegos/ee/o*] little, not much

το λιμάνι [*to leemanee*] port, harbour, docks

το λιμεναρχείο [*to leemenarkheeo*] port authority

η λίμνη [*ee leemnee*] lake

η λίρα (Αγγλίας) [*ee leera (angleeas)*] pound (sterling)

ο λογαριασμός [*o logaryazmos*] bill; account

λογικός/ή/ό [*loyeekos/ee/o*] sensible, reasonable

ο λόγος [*o logos*] reason; speech; word

λόγω [*logo*] because of

λοιπόν [*leepon*] now, well, now then

το Λονδίνο [*to londheeno*] London

η λοσιόν [*ee losyon*] lotion

το λουκάνικο [*to lookaneeko*] sausage

το λουκέτο [*to looketo*] padlock

το λουλούδι [*to looloodhee*] flower

η λουρίδα [*ee looreedha*] lane (*on road*)

ο λόφος [*o lofos*] hill

το λύκειο [*to leekyo*] senior high school

λυπάμαι [*leepame*] I'm sorry

Μ, μ

μα [*ma*] but

το μαγαζί [*to magazee*] shop

ο μάγειρας [*o mayeeras*] cook, chef

μαγειρεύω [*mayeerevo*] I cook

το μαγιό [*to mayo*] bathing costume, swimsuit

μαζί [*mazee*] together

    μαζί (με) [*mazee (me)*] with

    μαζί μου [*mazee moo*] with me

μαθαίνω [*matheno*] I learn

το μάθημα [*to matheema*] lesson

τα μαθηματικά [*ta matheemateeka*] mathematics

ο μαθητής, η μαθήτρια [*o matheetees, ee matheetrya*] pupil

μακριά [*makrya*] far (away)

μακρύς, μακριά, μακρύ [*makrees, makrya, makree*] long

μαλακός/ή/ό [*malakos/ee/o*] soft

μάλιστα [*maleesta*] yes, certainly

τα μαλλιά [*ta malya*] hair

η μαμά [*ee mama*] mum

ο μανάβης [*o manavees*] greengrocer

το μανικέτι [*to maneeketee*] cuff

το μανίκι [*to maneekee*] sleeve

το μαντήλι [*to mandeelee*] handkerchief

το μαξιλλάρι [*to makseelaree*] pillow

η μαξιλλαροθήκη [*ee makseelarotheekee*] pillowcase

η μάρκα [*ee marka*] make, brand

η μαρμελάδα [*ee marmeladha*] jam

ο μάρτυρας [*o marteeras*] witness

το μάτι [*to matee*] eye

μαύρος/η/ο [*mavros/ee/o*] black

το μαχαίρι [*to makheree*] knife

τα μαχαιροπήρουνα [*ta makheropeeroona*] cutlery

με [*me*] with

με [*me*] me (*see page 202*)

η Μεγάλη Βρετανία [*ee megalee vretaneea*] Great Britain
μεγάλος/η/ο [*megalos/ee/o*] big, large; great; grown up
μεγαλύτερος/η/ο [*megaleeteros/ee/o*] bigger (*etc.*)
ο/η/το μεγαλύτερος/η/ο [*o/ee/to megaleeteros/ee/o*] biggest (*etc.*)
το μέγεθος [*to meyethos*] size
οι μεζέδες [*ee mezedhes*] snacks, appetisers
μεθαύριο [*methavryo*] day after tomorrow
μεθυσμένος/η/ο [*metheezmenos/ee/o*] drunk
το μειονέκτημα [*to meeyonekteema*] disadvantage
η μειοψηφία [*ee meeopseefeea*] minority
η μελανιά [*ee melanya*] bruise
μελαχροινός/ή/ό [*melakhreenos/ee/o*] dark (*hair, skin*)
το μέλος [*to melos*] member
μένω [*meno*] I live, reside; stay
η μέρα [*ee mera*] day
μερικές φορές [*mereekes fores*] sometimes
μερικοί/ές/ά [*mereekee/es/a*] several; some
μερικός/ή/ό [*mereekos/ee/o*] partial; incomplete
το μέρος [*to meros*] part
μέσα [*mesa*] indoors
μέσα (σε) [*mesa (se)*] in; inside

τα μέσα [*ta mesa*] means; influence; pull
τα μεσάνυχτα [*ta mesaneekhta*] midnight
η μέση [*ee mesee*] waist; lower back
το μεσημέρι [*to meseemeree*] afternoon (*literally: mid-day*)
το μεσημεριανό [*to meseemeryano*] lunch
μέσω [*meso*] via, by way of
μετά [*meta*] after(wards), later on
μετά (από) [*meta (apo)*] after
ο μετανάστης [*o metanastees*] migrant
το μετάξι [*to metaksee*] silk
μεταξύ [*metaksee*] between; among
μεταξωτός/ή/ό [*metaksotos/ee/o*] silken
η μεταφορά [*ee metafora*] transport; removal
μεταφράζω [*metafrazo*] I translate
η μετάφραση [*ee metafrasee*] translation
ο μετρητής [*o metreetees*] meter
μέτριος/α/ο [*metryos/a/o*] medium (*including steak*)
το μέτρο (*to metro*) metre; measure
το μετρό [*to metro*] metro, underground railway

μέχρι [*mekhree*] until; as far as

ο μήνας [*o meenas*] month

το μήλο [*to meelo*] apple

το μήνυμα [*to meeneema*] message

μήπως . . . [*meepos* . . .] I wonder if . . . ?

μήπως έχετε . . . ; [*meepos ekhete*] do you have . . . ?

η μητέρα [*ee meetera*] mother

το μηχανάκι [*to meekhanakee*] motor bike

η μηχανή [*ee meekhanee*] machine; camera

μία/μια [*meea/mya*] one (f.); a/an (f.)

το μίγμα [*to meegma*] mixture

μικρός/ή/ό [*meekros/ee/o*] small, little; young

μικρότερος/η/ο [*meekroteros/ee/o*] smaller (*etc.*)

ο/η/το μικρότερος/η/ο [*o/ee/to meekroteros/ee/o*] smallest (*etc.*)

μιλάω [*meelao*] I speak, talk

ο μισθός [*o meesthos*] wage

μισός/ή/ό [*meesos/ee/o*] half

μισώ [*meeso*] I hate

η μνήμη [*ee mneemee*] memory

η μόδα [*ee modha*] fashion

η μοκέτα [*ee moketa*] carpet

μόλις [*molees*] hardly, scarcely

το μολύβι [*to moleevee*] lead; pencil

η μόλυνση [*ee moleensee*] pollution

μοναδικός/ή/ό [*monadheekos/ee/o*] unique; only

μοναχός/ή/ό [*monakhos/ee/o*] alone; lonely

το μονόκλινο [*to monokleeno*] single room

το μονοπάτι [*to monopatee*] path, track

μονός/ή/ό [*monos/ee/o*] single (*not double*); odd (*not even*)

μόνος/η/ο [*monos/ee/o*] alone; only

μόνος μου [*monos moo*] on my own

η μορφή [*ee morfee*] form, shape

η μοτοσυκλέτα [*ee motoseekleta*] motor bike

το μουσείο [*to mooseeo*] museum

η μουσική [*ee mooseekee*] music

το μουστάκι [*to moostakee*] moustache

μπαίνω [*beno*] I enter, go in, come in

η μπάλα [*ee bala*] ball; basketball

το μπαμπάκι [*to bambakee*] cotton wool

ο μπαμπάς [*o babas*] dad

το μπάνιο [*to banyo*] bath; bathtub; bathroom

το μπαούλο [*to baoolo*] trunk

το μπαρ [*to bar*] bar

το μπάσκετ [*to basket*] basketball

το μπαστούνι [*to bastoonee*] stick, club

η μπαταρία [*ee batareea*] battery

το μπαχάρικο [*to bakhareeko*] spice

το μπισκότο [*to beeskoto*] biscuit

μπλε [*ble*] blue

μπλε μαρέν [*ble maren*] navy blue

το μπλοκ [*to blok*] notepad, writing pad

μπλοκαρισμένος/η/ο [*blokareezmenos/ee/o*] blocked

η μπλούζα [*ee blooza*] blouse

μπορούσα [*boroosa*] I was able

μπορώ [*boro*] I am able, can

η μπότα [*ee bota*] boot

το μποτιλιάρισμα [*to boteelyareezma*] traffic jam; bottleneck

η μπουάτ [*ee bwat*] nightclub

το μπουκάλι [*to bookalee*] bottle

το μπράτσο [*to bratso*] arm

μπροστά (από) [*brosta (apo)*] in front (of)

η μπύρα [*ee beera*] beer

η μύγα [*ee meega*] fly

το μυθιστόρημα [*to meetheestoreema*] novel

ο μύλος [*o meelos*] mill

μυρίζει [*meereezee*] it smells

η μυρουδιά [*ee meeroodhya*] smell

η μύτη [*ee meetee*] nose

μ. Χ. (= μετά Χριστόν) [*meta khreeston*] AD

το μωρό [*to moro*] baby

N, ν

να [*na*] (*see page 206*)

ναι [*ne*] yes

ο ναός [*o naos*] temple

ο ναύτης [*o naftees*] sailor

ναυτικός/ή/ό [*nafteekos/ee/o*] naval, maritime

τα νέα [*ta nea*] news

νεαρός/ή/ό [*nearos/ee/o*] young

η νεολαία [*ee neolea*] youth

νέος/α/ο [*neos/a/o*] new; young

το νερό [*to nero*] water

το νέφος [*to nefos*] cloud of pollution

η νίκη [*ee neekee*] victory

το νοίκι [*to neekee*] rent

νοικιάζω [*neekyazo*] I rent, hire

ο νοικιαστής [*o neekyastees*] tenant

η νοικοκυρά [*ee neekokeera*] housewife

νομίζω [*nomeezo*] I think; believe

το νόμισμα [*to nomeezma*] currency; coin

ο νόμος [*o nomos*] law

νόστιμος/η/ο [*nosteemos/ee/o*] tasty

ο νότος [*o notos*] south

το νούμερο [*to noomero*] number

το νήμα [*to neema*] thread

το νησί [*to neesee*] island

η νήσος [*ee neesos*] island

νικάω [*neekao*] I defeat, beat

ο νιπτήρας [*o neepteeras*] wash-basin

η ντομάτα [*ee domata*] tomato

ντόπιος/α/ο [*dopyos/a/o*] local

το ντουλάπι [*to doolapee*] cupboard

το ντους [*to doos*] shower

ντύνομαι [*deenome*] I dress

νυστάζω [*neestazo*] I am sleepy

η νύφη [*ee neefee*] bride; daughter-in-law; sister-in-law

η νύχτα [*ee neekhta*] night

η νυχτικιά [*ee neekhteekya*] nightdress

νωρίς [*norees*] early

Ξ, ξ

η ξαδέρφη [*ee ksadherfee*] cousin (f.)

τα ξαδέρφια [*ta ksadherfya*] cousins

ο ξάδερφος [*o ksadherfos*] cousin (m.)

ξανθός/ή/ό [*ksanthos/ee/o*] fair, blond(e)

ξαπλώνω, ξαπλώνομαι [ksaplono, ksaplonome] I lie down; spread out

ξαφνικά [ksafneeka] suddenly

ξεκουράζομαι [ksekoorazome] I rest; relax

η ξεκούραση [ee ksekoorasee] rest

η ξενιτειά [ee kseneetya] foreign parts, abroad

το ξενοδοχείο [to ksenodhokheeo] hotel

ο ξένος [o ksenos] stranger; foreigner; guest

ξερός/ή/ό [kseros/ee/o] dry

ξέρω [ksero] I know; I know how to

ξεχνάω [ksekhnao] I forget

ξοδεύω [ksodhevo] I spend

το ξύλο [to kseelo] wood (material)

ο ξυλουργός [o kseeloorgos] carpenter

ξινός/ή/ό [kseenos/ee/o] sour

ξυπόλυτος/η/ο [kseepoleetos/ee/o] barefoot

το ξυραφάκι [to kseerafakee] razor blade

το ξυράφι [to kseerafee] razor

ξυρίζομαι [kseereezome] I shave (myself)

η ξυριστική μηχανή [ee kseereesteekee meekhanee] shaver

Ο, ο

ο [o] the (see page 199)

ο όγκος [o ongos] volume (mass)

ο οδηγός [o odheegos] driver; guidebook

οδηγώ [odheego] I drive

η οδοντόπαστα [ee odhondopasta] toothpaste

η οδός [ee odhos] street

η οθόνη [ee othonee] screen (cinema, TV etc.)

οι [ee] the (see page 199)

η οικογένεια [ee eekoyenya] family

όλα [ola] everything

ολόκληρος/η/ο [olokleeros/ee/o] whole

όλος/η/ο [olos/ee/o] all, every

όλος ο κόσμος [olos o kozmos] everyone

η ομάδα [ee omadha] group; team

ομαλός/ή/ό [omalos/ee/o] smooth; level; even

η ομίχλη [ee omeekhlee] fog

η ομορφιά [*ee omorfya*] beauty
όμορφος/η/ο [*omorfos/ee/o*] beautiful; handsome; pretty
η ομπρέλα [*ee ombrela*] umbrella
όμως [*omos*] however
το όνειρο [*to oneero*] dream
το όνομα [*to onoma*] name
οξύς, οξειά, οξύ [*oksees, oksya, oksee*] sharp; acute
όπισθεν [*opeesthen*] backwards
οποιοσδήποτε [*opyozdheepote*] any; whichever
όπως [*opos*] as, like
οπωσδήποτε [*opozdheepote*] definitely
η όραση [*ee orasee*] (eye)sight
τα ορεκτικά [*ta orekteeka*] hors d'œuvres, appetizers
ορίστε! [*oreeste*] here you are!
ορίστε; [*oreeste*] pardon?; how can I help you?
η οροσειρά [*ee oroseera*] mountain range
ο όροφος [*o orofos*] floor, storey
ο ΟΣΕ [*o ose*] Greek Railways
όταν [*otan*] when
ο ΟΤΕ [*o ote*] Greek Telecom
το ουζερί [*to oozeree*] bar serving ouzo
τό ούζο [*to oozo*] ouzo
η ουλή [*ee oolee*] scar
η ουρά [*ee oora*] tail; queue
ο ουρανός [*o ooranos*] sky; heaven
ούτε [*oote*] not even
ούτε . . . ούτε [*oote . . . oote*] neither . . . nor
οφείλω [*ofeelo*] I owe
όχι [*okhee*] no; not

Π, π

τα παγάκια [*ta pagakya*] ice (*for drinks*)
ο πάγος [*o pagos*] ice
παγωμένος/η/ο [*pagomenos/ee/o*] frozen; chilled (*of drinks*)
το παγωτό [*to pagoto*] ice cream
η παιδεία [*ee pedheea*] education, learning

το **παιδί** [*to pedhee*] child

παίζω [*pezo*] I play

παίρνω [*perno*] I obtain, get, take; have (to drink)

το **παιχνίδι** [*to pekhneedhee*] game; toy

το **πακέτο** [*to paketo*] packet

το **φαγητό σε πακέτο** [*to fayeeto se paketo*] take-away food

πάλι [*palee*] again

παλιός/ά/ό [*palyos/a/o*] old

το **παλληκάρι** [*to paleekaree*] brave young man

πάμε [*pame*] let's go

πάμε; [*pame*] shall we go?

πάμφτηνος/η/ο [*pamfteenos/ee/o*] very cheap

η **πάνα** [*ee pana*] nappy

η **Παναγία** [*ee panayeea*] Our Lady

πανάκριβος/η/ο [*panakreevos/ee/o*] very expensive

το **πανεπιστήμιο** [*to panepeesteemyo*] university

το **πανηγύρι** [*to paneeyeeree*] festival, holiday

το **πανί** [*to panee*] cloth; nappy

το **πανσιόν** [*to pansyon*] pension; boarding house

πάντα [*panda*] always

273

τα **πάντα** [*ta panda*] everything

το **παντελόνι** [*to pandelonee*] trousers

παντρεμένος/η/ο [*pandremenos/ee/o*] married

το **παντοπωλείο** [*to pandopoleeo*] grocer's, general store

πάνω [*pano*] up; above; upstairs

πάνω από [*pano apo*] above

πάνω (σε) [*pano (se)*] on, on top of

ο **πάπας** [*o papas*] the Pope

ο **παπάς** [*o papas*] priest

ο **παππούς** [*o papoos*] grandfather

το **παπούτσι** [*to papootsee*] shoe

παρά [*para*] to (time, see page 213)

το **παράδειγμα** [*to paradheegma*] example

η **παράδοση** [*ee paradhosee*] handing over, delivery; tradition

το **παράθυρο** [*to paratheero*] window

παρακαλώ [*parakalo*] please; not at all, don't mention it

η **παραλαβή** [*ee paralavee*] point of collection for goods in some stores

η **παραλία** [*ee paraleea*] sea-front

πάρα πολύ [*para polee*] very much; too much

το παράπονο [*to parapono*] complaint

η παράσταση [*ee parastasee*] performance

η παρέα [*ee parea*] company, group of friends

παρκάρω [*parkaro*] I park

το πάρκιγκ [*to parkeeng*] parking, car-park

το πάρκο [*to parko*] park

το παρκόμετρο [*to parkometro*] parking meter

παρ'όλο που [*parolo poo*] although

η πάστα [*ee pasta*] cake, pastry

το Πάσχα [*to paskha*] Easter

ο πατέρας [*o pateras*] father

η πατρίδα [*ee patreedha*] homeland, birthplace

παχαίνω [*pakheno*] I put on weight, get fat

πάω [*pao*] I go

το πεζοδρόμιο [*to pezodhromyo*] pavement

πεζός/ή/ό [*o pezos/ee/o*] pedestrian

πεθαμένος/η/ο [*pethamenos/ee/o*] dead

η πεθερά [*ee pethera*] mother-in-law

ο πεθερός [*o petheros*] father-in-law

πεθυμώ [*petheemo*] I miss, wish for

πεινάω [*peenao*] I am hungry

πειράζει: δεν πειράζει [*peerazee: dhem-beerazee*] it doesn't matter

ο πελάτης, η πελάτισσα [*o pelatees, ee pelateesa*] customer; client

η πελούζα [*ee pelooza*] lawn

το πενηντάρικο [*to peneendareeko*] fifty drachma note/coin

το πεντακοσάρικο [*to pentakosareeko*] five hundred drachma note

το πενταχίλιαρο [*to pentakheelyaro*] five thousand drachma note

το πεπόνι [*to peponee*] honeydew melon

πέρα: εκεί πέρα [*pera: ekee pera*] over there

περάσατε: πώς περάσατε; [*perasate: pos perasate*] what kind of time did you have?

περασμένος/η/ο [*perazmenos/ee/o*] past; last

περάστε [*peraste*] after you; come in

το περιβάλλον [*to pereevalon*] environment

περιγράφω [*pereegrafo*] I describe

περίεργος/η/ο [peree-ergos/ee/o] strange, odd
τα περιεχόμενα [ta peree-ekhomena] contents
περιμένω [pereemeno] I wait (for); I expect
το περιοδικό [to peryodheeko] magazine
η περιοχή [ee peryokhee] region, area
περίπου [pereepoo] approximately
το περίπτερο [to pereeptero] kiosk
τα περίχωρα [ta pereekhora] surrounding area; outskirts
περνάω [pernao] I pass; go through, spend (time)
πέρυσι [pereesee] last year
πετάω [petao] I fly; I throw, throw away
η πέτρα [ee petra] stone
η πετσέτα [ee petseta] towel; napkin, serviette
πήγα [peega] I went
πηγαίνω [peeyeno] I go
πήρα [peera] I took
το πηρούνι [to peeroonee] fork
πιασμένος/η/ο [pyazmenos/ee/o] occupied, taken
το πιατάκι [to pyatakee] saucer
τα πιατικά [ta pyateeka] crockery; dishes
το πιάτο [to pyato] dish; course
η πιάτσα [ee pyatsa] (taxi) rank
πικάντικος/η/ο [peekandeekos/ee/o] hot, spicy
το πικ-άπ [to peek-ap] record player
το πικ νικ [to peek neek] picnic
πικρός/ή/ό [peekros/ee/o] bitter
η πινακίδα [ee peenakeedha] number plate
πίνω [peeno] I drink
πιο [pyo] more (see page 200)
η πιπίλα [ee peepeela] (baby's) dummy
το πιπέρι [to peeperee] pepper
η πιπεριά [ee peeperya] pepper (red, green)
η πισίνα [ee peeseena] swimming pool
η πίστα [ee peesta] court (tennis etc.); track, course
πιστεύω [peestevo] I believe
πίσω [peeso] behind; back; again
πίσω (από) [peeso (apo)] behind
το πίσω μέρος [to peeso meros] rear, back
η πλαζ [ee plaz] beach
η πλατεία [ee plateea] square; (theatre) stalls

η πλειοψηφία [*ee pleeopseefeea*] most, majority

πλένομαι [*plenome*] I wash (myself)

πλένω [*pleno*] I wash

πλένω τα πιάτα [*pleno ta pyata*] I do the washing up

το πλεονέκτημα [*to pleonekteema*] advantage

η πλευρά [*ee plevra*] side

πλην [*pleen*] less; minus

το πλήρωμα [*to pleeroma*] crew

πληρώνω [*pleerono*] I pay (for)

το πλοίο [*to pleeo*] boat, ship

πλούσιος/α/ο [*ploosyos/a/o*] rich

το πλυντήριο [*to pleendeeryo*] laundry

το ποδήλατο [*to podheelato*] bicycle

το πόδι [*to podhee*] foot, leg

με τα πόδια [*me ta podhya*] on foot, walking

το ποδόσφαιρο [*to podhosfero*] football

ποιανού; [*pyanoo*] whose?

ποιος/α/ο; [*pyos/a/o*] who?; which?

η ποιότητα [*ee pyoteeta*] quality

ο πόλεμος [*o polemos*] war

η πόλη [*ee polee*] town, city

η πολιτική [*ee poleeteekee*] politics; policy

πολλές φορές [*poles fores*] often

πολλοί, πολλές, πολλά [*polee, poles, pola*] many, lots (of)

η πολυθρόνα [*ee poleethrona*] armchair

το πολυκατάστημα [*to poleekatasteema*] department store

η πολυκατοικία [*ee poleekateekeea*] apartment building

η πολυτέλεια [*ee poleetelya*] luxury

πολυτέλειας [*poleetelyas*] de luxe, luxury

το πολυτεχνείο [*to poleetekhneeo*] polytechnic university

πολύς, πολλή, πολύ [*polees, polee, polee*] much, a lot, many

πολύ [*polee*] very; a lot of

πάρα πολύ [*para polee*] very much; too much

πονάει [*ponaee*] (it) hurts

πονάω [*ponao*] I hurt

ο πονοκέφαλος [*o ponokefalos*] headache

ο πόνος [*o ponos*] pain, ache

η πόρτα [*ee porta*] door; gate

η πορτοκαλάδα [*ee portokaladha*] orangeade

το πορτοκάλι [*to portokalee*] orange

πορτοκαλής, πορτοκαλιά, πορτοκαλί [*portokalees, portokalya, portokalee*], orange (*colour*)

το πορτοφόλι [*to portofolee*] purse; wallet; briefcase

πορφυρός/ή/ό [*porfeeros/ee/o*] purple

πόσες φορές; [*poses fores*] how many times?

το ποσό [*to poso*] amount

πόσοι/ες/α; [*posee/es/a*] how many?

πόσος/η/ο; [*posos/ee/o*] how much?

το ποσοστό υπηρεσίας [*to pososto eepeereseeas*] service, service charge

πόσων χρονών είναι, είσαστε; [*poson khronon eene, eesaste*] how old is he/she?, how old are you?

το ποτάμι [*to potamee*] river

πότε; [*pote*] when?

ποτέ [*pote*] never

το ποτηράκι [*to poteerakee*] glass (*wine*)

το ποτήρι [*to poteeree*] glass (*water etc.*)

το ποτό [*to poto*] drink (*alcoholic*)

πού; [*poo*] where?

πουθενά [*poothena*] nowhere

το πουκάμισο [*to pookameeso*] shirt

πουλάω [*poolao*] I sell

το πουλί [*to poolee*] bird

το πούλμαν [*to poolman*] coach, long-distance bus

το πουρμπουάρ [*to poorbwar*] tip

το πούρο [*to pooro*] cigar

το πράγμα [*to pragma*] thing

τα πράγματα [*ta pragmata*] luggage

πραγματικά [*pragmateeka*] really, in fact

η πραγματικότητα [*ee pragmateekoteeta*] reality

στην πραγματικότητα [*steem-bragmateekoteeta*] in fact, actually

το πρακτορείο [*to praktoreeo*] agency

η πρασινάδα [*ee praseenadha*] greenery

πράσινος/η/ο [*praseenos/ee/o*] green

η πρεμιέρα [*ee premyera*] first performance

πρέπει [*prepee*] it is necessary

πρέπει να πάω [*prepee na pao*] I must go

η πρεσβεία [*ee prezveea*] embassy

η πρίζα [ee preeza] plug; socket
πριν [preen] ago
πριν (από) [preen (apo)] before
το πρόβατο [to provato] sheep
το πρόβλημα [to provleema] problem
το πρόγραμμα [to programa] programme
ο πρόεδρος [o proedhros] president
η προειδοποίηση [ee proeedhopee-eesee] notice; warning
προειδοποιώ [proeedhopyo] I warn
η προκαταβολή [ee prokatavolee] deposit
προκαταβολικώς [prokatavoleekos] in advance
η προκυμαία [ee prokeemea] quay, pier
προλαβαίνω [prolaveno] I catch (bus, train etc.)
ο προορισμός [o pro-oreezmos] destination
το προ-πο [to pro-po] football pools
προς [pros] towards
προσέξτε [prosekste] look out!
προσέχετε [prosekhete] be careful
η προσοχή [ee prosokhee] attention, caution
η προσπάθεια [ee prospathya] attempt
προσπαθώ [prospatho] I try
το πρόστιμο [to prosteemo] fine
η προσφορά [ee prosfora] offer
το πρόσωπο [to prosopo] face; person
η πρόταση [ee protasee] proposition (e.g. business)
προτιμάω [proteemao] I prefer
το προφυλακτικό [to profeelakteeko] contraceptive
προχθές [prokhthes] day before yesterday
το πρωί [to proee] morning
το πρωινό [to proeeno] breakfast
πρωινός/ή/ό [proeenos/ee/o] (of the) morning
πρώτος/η/ο [protos/ee/o] first
η πτήση [ee pteesee] flight
ο πύργος [o peergos] tower
ο πυρετός [o peeretos] fever, (high) temperature
η πυροσβεστική (υπηρεσία) [ee peerozvesteekee
   (eepeereseea)] fire brigade
π. Χ. (= προ Χριστού) [pro khreestoo] BC
π. χ. (= παραδείγματος χάριν) [paradheegmatos
   khareen] e.g., for example

278

ο πωλητής, η πωλήτρια [*o poleetees, ee poleetrya*] salesman, saleswoman

πως [*pos*] that

πώς; [*pos*] how?

πώς πάει; [*pos paee*] how are things?

πώς σε λένε; [*pos se lene*] what's your name?

Ρ, ρ

ο ραδιοφωνικός σταθμός [*o radhyofoneekos stathmos*] radio station

το ραδιόφωνο [*to radhyofono*] radio

το ραντεβού [*to randevoo*] appointment, engagement

ο ράφτης [*o raftees*] tailor

τα ρέστα [*ta resta*] change (*money*)

η ρετσίνα [*ee retseena*] retsina, resinated wine

το ρεύμα [*to revma*] (electrical) power, current; draught

ρίχνω [*reekhno*] I throw

η ρόδα [*ee rodha*] wheel

το ροδάκινο [*to rodhakeeno*] peach

ροζ [*roz*] pink

ροζέ [*roze*] rosé (wine)

το ρολό [*to rolo*] blind (*drop-down shutter*)

ο ρολογάς [*o rologas*] watchmaker

το ρολόι [*to roloee*] clock; watch

τα ρούχα [*ta rookha*] clothes, clothing

ρωτάω [*rotao*] I ask

Σ, σ

το Σαββατοκύριακο [*to savatokeeryako*] weekend

το σακκάκι [*to sakakee*] jacket

ο σάκκος [*o sakos*] sack; rucksack

η σαλάτα [*ee salata*] salad

το σάλι [*to salee*] shawl

το σαλόνι [*to salonee*] lounge, living-room

σαν [*san*] when, as, like

το **σάντουιτς** [*to sandweets*] sandwich
σάπιος/α/ο [*sapyos/a/o*] rotten

το **σαπούνι** [*to sapoonee*] soap
(ε)σας [*(e)sas*] you (*pl., formal*)

το **σβέρκο** [*to zverko*] neck
σβήνω [*zveeno*] I extinguish; switch off
σγουρός/ή/ό [*zgooros/ee/o*] curly
σε [*se*] you (*s., informal*)
σε [*se*] to; at; in; on

η **σειρά** [*ee seera*] row; turn
η **σελίδα** [*ee seleedha*] page
(ε)σένα [*(e)sena*] you (*s., informal*)

το **σεντόνι** [*to sendonee*] sheet
η **σερβιέτα** [*ee servyeta*] sanitary towel
σερβίρω [*serveero*] I serve

ο **σερβιτόρος** [*o serveetoros*] waiter
σηκώνω [*seekono*] I lift, raise

η **σημασία** [*ee seemaseea*] meaning, significance
το **σημείο** [*to seemeeo*] sign; signal
σήμερα [*seemera*] today
σημερινός/ή/ό [*seemereenos/ee/o*] of today, today's
σιγά [*seega*] slowly
σιγά-σιγά [*seega-seega*] gradually; carefully

το **σίδερο** [*to seedhero*] iron
το **σινεμά** [*to seenema*] cinema
το **σιντριβάνι** [*to seendreevanee*] fountain
το **σιρόπι** [*to seeropee*] syrup
η **σιωπή** [*syopee*] silence
σιωπηλός/ή/ό [*syopeelos/ee/o*] silent

η **σκάλα** [*ee skala*] stairs, staircase
σκάσε! [*skase*] be quiet!, shut up!
σκεπασμένος/η/ο [*skepazmenos/ee/o*] covered
σκέπτομαι [*skeptome*] I think
σκέτος/η/ο [*sketos/ee/o*] neat; plain; without sugar

η **σκηνή** [*ee skeenee*] tent
η **σκιά** [*ee skya*] shade; shadow
σκληρός/ή/ό [*skleeros/ee/o*] hard; rough; stiff
η **σκόνη** [*ee skonee*] dust; powder
το **σκόρδο** [*to skordho*] garlic
η **σκούπα** [*ee skoopa*] broom

τα **σκουπίδια** [ta skoopeedhya] rubbish

σκουριασμένος/η/ο [skooryazmenos/ee/o] rusty

σκούρος/α/ο [skooros/a/o] dark (colour)

το **σκυλί** [to skeelee] dog

το **σλάϊντ** [to slaeed] slide (photo)

το **σλιπ** [to sleep] petticoat, slip

το **σμάλτο** [to zmalto] enamel

σοβαρός/ή/ό [sovaros/ee/o] serious

η **σοκολάτα** [ee sokolata] chocolate

η **σόμπα** [ee somba] stove

το **σουβλάκι** [to soovlakee] kebabs, meat grilled on a skewer

η **σούπα** [ee soopa] soup

το **σουτιέν** [to sootyen] bra

ο **σπάγγος** [o spangos] string

σπάνιος/α/ο [spanyos/a/o] rare

σπασμένος/η/ο [spazmenos/ee/o] broken

σπάω [spao] I break

το **σπήλαιο** [to speeleo] cave

τα **σπίρτα** [ta speerta] matches

το **σπίτι** [to speetee] home; house, household

το **σπορ** [to spor] sport

σπουδάζω [spoodhazo] I study

οι **σπουδές** [ee spoodhes] studies, course

σπρώχνω [sprokhno] I push

στα [sta] to; at; in; on the . . . (n., pl.)

το **στάδιο** [to stadhyo] stadium

η **σταδιοδρομία** [ee stadhyodromeea] career

η **στάθμευση** [ee stathmefsee] parking

σταθμεύω [stathmevo] I park

ο **σταθμός** [o stathmos] station

η **στάλα** [ee stala] drop (water etc.)

σταματάω [stamatao] I stop

η **στάση** [ee stasee] stop

ο **σταυρός** [o stavros] cross

το **σταχτοδοχείο** [to stakhtodhokheeo] ashtray

η **στέγη** [ee steyee] roof; shelter

το **στεγνοκαθαριστήριο** [to stegnokathareesteeryo] dry-cleaners

στεγνός/ή/ό [stegnos/ee/o] dry

στέλνω [stelno] I send

το **στενό** [to steno] side-street

στενός/ή/ό [stenos/ee/o] narrow

στενοχωρεμένος/η/ο [stenokhoremenos/ee/o] sad, upset

το στεφάνι [to stefanee] marriage wreath; wedding

στη(ν) [stee(n)] to; at; in; on the . . . (f., s.)

η στιγμή [ee steegmee] moment

μια στιγμή [mya steegmee] just a moment

στιγμιαίος/α/ο [steegmyeos/a/o] instant

στις [stees] to; at; in; on the . . . (f., pl.)

στο [sto] to; at; in; on the . . . (n., s.)

το στόμα [to stoma] mouth

το στομάχι [to stomakhee] stomach

στο(ν) [sto(n)] to; at; in; on the . . . (m., s.)

στους [stoos] to; at; in; on the . . . (m., pl.)

στραμπουλίζω [strambooleezo] I twist, sprain

το στρέμμα [to strema] stremma (one quarter of an acre)

στρίβω [streevo] I turn

στρογγυλός/ή/ό [strongeelos/ee/o] round

η στροφή [ee strofee] bend, curve

το στρώμα [to stroma] mattress

το στυλό [to steelo] ballpoint pen

ο συγγενής (pl.: οι συγγενείς) [o seengenees (ee seengenees)] relation, relative

συγγνώμη [seegnomee] pardon me, excuse me

συγκινητικός/ή/ό [seengeeneeteekos/ee/o] exciting

η σύγκρουση [ee seengroosee] collision, crash

συγυρισμένος/η/ο [seeyeereezmenos/ee/o] tidy

συγχαρητήρια! [seenkhareeteerya] congratulations!

η συζήτηση [ee seezeeteesee] discussion

η συλλογή [ee seeloyee] collection (stamps etc.); reflection (thought)

συμβαίνει: τι συμβαίνει; [seemvenee: tee seemvenee] what is happening?

συμπαθητικός/ή/ό [seembatheeteekos/ee/o] nice, charming, pleasant

συμπεριλαμβάνω [seembereelamvano] I include
συμπεριλαμβάνεται . . . [seembereelamvanete . . .] . . . included; including . . .

σύμφωνα με [seemfona me] according to

σύμφωνοι! [seemfonee] agreed, fine, very well

συμφωνώ [seemfono] I agree

συν [seen] with
συναντάω [seenandao] I meet
η σύνδεση [ee seendhesee] connection
το συνέδριο [to seenedhryo] conference, congress
η συνέντευξη [ee seenendefksee] interview
ο/η συνέταιρος [olee seeneteros] partner
συνέχεια [seenekhya] continuously
συνεχής, συνεχής, συνεχές [seenekhees, seenekhees, seenekhes] continuous
συνηθίζω [seeneetheezo] I get used to
συνήθως [seeneethos] usually
η συννεφιά [ee seenefya] cloudy weather
συννεφιασμένος/η/ο [seenefyazmenos/ee/o] cloudy
το σύννεφο [to seenefo] cloud
τα σύνορα [ta seenora] border, frontier
η συνταγή [ee seendayee] recipe; prescription
η σύνταξη [ee seendaksee] pension
πήρα σύνταξη [peera seendaksee] I'm a pensioner
ο/η συνταξιούχος [olee seendaksyookhos] pensioner
σύντομα [seendoma] soon
σύρατε [seerate] pull
το συρτάρι [to seertaree] drawer
συστήνω [seesteeno] I introduce; recommend
συχνά [seekhna] often
σφιχτός/ή/ό [sfeekhtos/ee/o] tight
το σφυρί [to sfeeree] hammer
η σχάρα [ee skhara] grill; roof-rack
το σχέδιο [to skhedhyo] drawing; design, pattern
σχεδόν [skhedhon] almost, nearly
το σχήμα [to skheema] shape
σχισμένος/η/ο [skheezmenos/ee/o] torn
το σχοινί [to skheenee] rope
το σχολείο [to skholeeo] school
το σώβρακο [to sovrako] underpants (men's)
σώζω [sozo] I rescue, save
το σώμα [to soma] body
σωστά! [sosta] that's right!
σωστός/ή/ό [sostos/ee/o] fair; just; correct
ο σωφέρ [o sofer] driver, chauffeur

T, τ

τα [*ta*] the (*see page 199*)
το ταβάνι [*to tavanee*] ceiling
η ταβέρνα [*ee taverna*] taverna
η ταινία [*ee teneea*] film; tape; cassette
το τάληρο [*to taleero*] dollar; five drachma coin; five
    thousand drachma note
το ταμείο [*to tameeo*] cash desk; booking office
το ταμιευτήριο [*to tamyefteeryo*] savings bank
η τάξη [*ee taksee*] class, form (*school*); order
το ταξί [*to taksee*] taxi
ταξιδεύω [*takseedhevo*] I travel
το ταξίδι [*to takseedhee*] journey, trip
ο ταξιτζής [*o takseedzees*] taxi-driver
η ταράτσα [*ee taratsa*] terrace
η ταυτότητα [*ee taftoteeta*] identity card
ταυτοχρόνως, ταυτόχρονα [*taftokhronos, taftokhrona*] at
    the same time; simultaneously
το ταχυδρομείο [*to takheedhromeeo*] post office
η ταχύτητα [*ee takheeteeta*] speed
το τείχος [*to teekhos*] (city) wall
τελειώνω [*telyono*] I finish
τελευταία [*teleftea*] lately
τελευταίος/α/ο [*telefteos/a/o*] last; latest
το τελεφερίκ [*to telefereek*] cable car
το τέλος [*to telos*] end
τέλος πάντων [*telos pandon*] finally, after all; anyway
το τελωνείο [*to teloneeo*] customs
τεμπέλης, τεμπέλα [*tembelees, tembela*] lazy
η τέντα [*ee tenda*] awning
τεράστιος/α/ο [*terastyos/a/o*] enormous
το τέταρτο [*to tetarto*] quarter
τέταρτος/η/ο [*tetartos/ee/o*] fourth
τέτοιος/α/ο [*tetyos/a/o*] such
το τετράδιο [*to tetradhyo*] exercise book
η τέχνη [*ee tekhnee*] art
το τηγάνι [*to teeganee*] frying pan
τηγανητός/ή/ό [*teeganeetos/ee/o*] fried
το τηλεγράφημα [*to teelegrafeema*] telegram

η τηλεόραση [*ee teeleorasee*] television

το τηλεφώνημα [*to teelefoneema*] telephone call

το τηλέφωνο [*to teelefono*] telephone

τηλεφωνώ [*teelefono*] I phone

τί; [*tee*] what?, which?

τι κρίμα! [*tee kreema*] what a pity!

η τιμή [*ee teemee*] price; honour

τίνος; [*teenos*] whose?

τίποτα [*teepota*] anything; nothing

   τίποτ'άλλο [*teepotalo*] nothing else

   τίποτ'άλλο; [*teepotalo*] anything else?

το τιρμπουσόν [*to teerbooson*] corkscrew

το τμήμα [*to tmeema*] part, section; police station

   το [*to*] the

ο τοίχος [*o teekhos*] wall

ο τόμος [*o tomos*] volume (*book*)

ο τόννος [*o tonos*] tonne; tuna

ο τόπος [*o topos*] place

τόσο [*toso*] so

τόσοι/ες/α [*tosee/es/a*] so many

τόσος/η/ο [*tosos/ee/o*] so much

τότε [*tote*] then

η τουαλέτα [*ee twaleta*] toilet

τουλάχιστον [*toolakheeston*] at least

ο τουρίστας, η τουρίστρια [*o tooreestas, ee tooreestrya*]
   tourist

η τούρτα [*ee toorta*] cake, gâteau

τραβάω [*travao*] I pull

τραγουδάω [*tragoodhao*] I sing

το τραγούδι [*to tragoodhee*] song

η τραγωδία [*ee tragodheea*] tragedy

το τραίνο [*to treno*] train

η τράπεζα [*ee trapeza*] bank

η τραπεζαρία [*ee trapezareea*] dining-room

το τραπέζι [*to trapezee*] table

τραυματισμένος/η/ο [*travmateezmenos/ee/o*] injured,
   wounded

τρελλός/ή/ό [*trelos/ee/o*] crazy, mad

τρέχω [*trekho*] I run

το τριαντάφυλλο [*to tryandafeelo*] rose

τριγυρισμένος/η/ο (από) [*treeyeereezmenos/ee/o (apo)*] surrounded (by)

το τρίκλινο [*to treekleeno*] room with three beds

τρίτος/η/ο [*treetos/ee/o*] third

το τρόλεϋ [*to trole-ee*] trolley-bus

τρομερός/ή/ό [*tromeros/ee/o*] terrible

η τρόμπα [*ee tromba*] pump

ο τρόπος [*o tropos*] way, manner

η τρύπα [*ee treepa*] hole

τρυφερός/ή/ό [*treeferos/ee/o*] tender, affectionate

τρώω [*tro-o*] I eat

το τσάϊ [*to tsaee*] tea

η τσάντα [*ee tsanda*] bag, handbag

η τσέπη [*ee tsepee*] pocket

το τσιγάρο [*to tseegaro*] cigarette

ο τσιγγάνος, η τσιγγάνα [*o tseenganos, ee tseengana*] gypsy

η τσίχλα [*ee tseekhla*] chewing gum

ο τύπος [*o teepos*] type; kind; the press

το τυρί [*to teeree*] cheese

τυφλός/ή/ό [*teeflos/ee/o*] blind

τυχερός/ή/ό [*teekheros/ee/o*] lucky

τώρα [*tora*] now

286

Υ, υ

η υγεία [*ee eeyeea*] health

υγειής, υγιείς, υγιές [*eeyee-ees, eeyee-ees, eeyee-es*] healthy

ο υδραυλικός [*o eedhravleekos*] plumber

υπαίθριος/α/ο [*eepethryos/a/o*] outdoors, open-air

υπάρχει, υπάρχουν [*eeparkhee, eeparkhoon*] there is, there are

ο ύπνος [*o eepnos*] sleep

το υπόγειο [*to eepoyo*] basement

υπόγειος/α/ο [*eepoyos/a/o*] underground

υπογράφω [*eepografo*] I sign

το υπόθετο [*to eepotheto*] suppository

υποθέτω [*eepotheto*] I suppose

το υποκατάστημα [to eepokatasteema] branch (*bank*)
η υποχρέωση [ee eepokhreosee] obligation
το ύφασμα [to eefazma] cloth, fabric
τα υφαντά [ta eefanda] textiles

Φ, φ

το φαγητό [to fayeeto] food; meal
το φαγητό σε πακέτο [to fayeeto se paketo] take-away food
φαίνομαι [fenome] I seem; am visible
ο φάκελλος [o fakelos] envelope; file (*office*)
ο φακός [o fakos] lens; torch
το φανάρι [to fanaree] street lamp; headlamp; lighthouse
τα φανάρια [ta fanarya] traffic light
   φαρδύς, φαρδειά, φαρδύ [fardhees, fardhya, fardhee]
      broad, wide
το φαρμακείο [to farmakeeo] chemist's, pharmacy
το φασόλι [to fasolee] bean (*haricot*)
το φασολάκι [to fasolakee] bean (*green*)
το φεγγάρι [to fengaree] moon
ο φελός [o felos] cork
   φέρνω [ferno] I bring; carry
η φέτα [ee feta] slice; cheese made of ewe's milk
   φέτος [fetos] this year
   φεύγω [fevgo] I go away; leave, depart
η φήμη [ee feemee] fame; rumour
   φημισμένος/η/ο [feemeezmenos/ee/o] famous
το φθινόπωρο [to ftheenoporo] autumn
η φιλενάδα [ee feelenadha] girlfriend
το φιλί [to feelee] kiss
το φιλμ [to feelm] film
το φιλοδώρημα [to feelodhoreema] tip (*gratuity*)
ο φίλος, η φίλη [o feelos, ee feelee] friend
το φλούδι [to floodhee] shell; rind, peel
το φλυτζάνι [to fleedzanee] cup
   φοβάμαι [fovame] I am afraid
   φοβερός/ή/ό [foveros/ee/o] awful, dreadful
ο φοιτητής, η φοιτήτρια [o feeteetees, ee feeteetrya] student

287

η φορά [*ee fora*] time (*once, twice, three times etc.*)
φοράω [*forao*] I carry; I wear
το φόρεμα [*to forema*] dress
η φόρμα [*ee forma*] tracksuit; mould
το φορτηγάκι [*to forteegakee*] van
το φορτηγό [*to forteego*] lorry
ο φούρνος [*o foornos*] oven; baker's
η φουρτούνα [*ee foortoona*] storm; rough sea
το φουστάνι [*to foostanee*] skirt
ο ΦΠΑ (*fee pee alpha*) VAT
η φράση [*ee frasee*] phrase
φρέσκος/η/ο [*freskos/ee/o*] fresh; cool
φροντίζω [*frondeezo*] I look after
φταίω [*fteo*] I am to blame
φτάνει [*ftanee*] it is enough; that's enough
φτάνω [*ftano*] I arrive (at), reach
φτηνός/ή/ό [*fteenos/ee/o*] cheap
φτιάχνω [*ftyakhno*] I make; fix
φτύνω [*fteeno*] I spit
   φτού (σου)! [*ftoo (soo)*] symbolic spitting to avert evil
   eye
φτωχός/ή/ό [*ftokhos/ee/o*] poor
η φυλακή [*ee feelakee*] prison
το φυλλάδιο [*to feeladhyo*] leaflet, brochure
το φύλλο [*to feelo*] leaf; sheet of paper; thin pastry
το φύλο [*to feelo*] gender, sex
φυσικά [*feeseeka*] of course
το φυτό [*to feeto*] plant
φωνάζω [*fonazo*] I call, shout
η φωνή [*ee fonee*] voice
το φως [*to fos*] light
η φωτιά [*ee fotya*] fire; light (*for cigarette*)
η φωτογραφία [*ee fotografeea*] photograph

Χ, χ

χαίρετε! [*kherete*] hello! goodbye!
χαίρω πολύ [*khero polee*] it's a pleasure (to meet you)
χαλαρός/ή/ό [*khalaros/ee/o*] slack, loose

χαλασμένος/η/ο [*khalazmenos/ee/o*] broken down, out of order

το χαλί [*to khalee*] carpet

τα χάλια [*ta khalya*] bad condition

έχω τα χάλια μου [*ekho ta khalya-moo*] I'm in a bad way

χαμένος/η/ο [*khamenos/ee/o*] lost

χαμηλός/ή/ό [*khameelos/ee/o*] low

το χαμόγελο [*to khamoyelo*] smile

χάνω [*khano*] I lose

το χάπι [*to khapee*] pill

η χαρά [*ee khara*] joy

μια χαρά [*mya khara*] fine! (*response to 'how are you?'*)

ο χάρακας [*o kharakas*] ruler

χάρηκα πολύ [*khareeka polee*] it was a pleasure (meeting you)

ο χάρτης [*o khartees*] map

το χαρτί [*to khartee*] paper

τα χαρτιά [*ta khartya*] papers; playing cards

το χαρτονόμισμα [*to khartonomeezma*] banknote

η χαρτοπαιξία [*ee khartopekseea*] gambling

ο χειμώνας [*o kheemonas*] winter

χειρότερος/η/ο [*kheeroteros/ee/o*] worse

ο/η/το χειρότερος/η/ο [*o/ee/to kheeroteros/ee/o*] worst

το χέρι [*to kheree*] hand; arm

η χήρα [*ee kheera*] widow

ο χήρος [*o kheeros*] widower

το χιλιάρικο [*to kheelyareeko*] thousand drachma note

το χιόνι [*to khyonee*] snow

χιονίζει [*khyoneezee*] it's snowing, it snows

χλωμός/ή/ό [*khlomos/ee/o*] pale

το χοιρινό [*to kheereeno*] pork

το χόμπυ [*to khobee*] pastime, hobby

χοντρός/ή/ό [*khondros/ee/o*] fat; thick

χορεύω [*khorevo*] I dance

ο χορός [*o khoros*] dance

το χορτάρι [*to khortaree*] grass; herb

η χούφτα [*ee khoofta*] handful, fistful

χρειάζεται . . . [*khryazete . . .*] . . . is needed

χρειάζομαι [*khryazome*] I need; I am needed

τα χρήματα [*ta khreemata*] money

το χρηματιστήριο [*to khreemateesteeryo*] stock exchange

χρησιμοποιώ [*khreeseemopyo*] I use

χρήσιμος/η/ο [*khreeseemos/ee/o*] useful

χριστιανός/ή/ό [*khreestyanos/ee/o*] Christian

  ορθόδοξος/η/ο [*orthodoksos/ee/o*] Orthodox

  καθολικός/ή/ό [*katholeekos/ee/o*] Catholic

  διαμαρτυρόμενος/η/ο [*dhyamarteeromenos/ee/o*]
    Protestant

τα Χριστούγεννα [*ta khreestooyena*] Christmas

η χρονολογία [*ee khronoloyeea*] date; chronology

ο χρόνος [*o khronos*] time; year

του χρόνου [*too khronoo*] next year

το χρυσάφι [*to khreesafee*] gold

το χρώμα [*to khroma*] colour

η χτένα [*ee khtena*] comb

  (ε)χτες [*(e)khtes*] yesterday

    χτες το βράδυ [*khtes to vradhee*] last night

  χτεσινός/ή/ό [*khteseenos/ee/o*] of yesterday, yesterday's

το χτύπημα [*to khteepeema*] knock, blow

ο χυμός [*kheemos*] juice

το χώμα [*to khoma*] earth

το χωνάκι [*to khonakee*] ice-cream cone

η χώρα [*ee khora*] country

το χωράφι [*to khorafee*] field

ο χωριάτης [*o khoryatees*] villager

  χωριάτικη σαλάτα [*khoryateekee salata*] Greek salad

το χωριό [*to khoryo*] village

  χωρίς [*khorees*] without

ο χώρος [*o khoros*] space; room

Ψ, ψ

το ψαλίδι [*to psaleedhee*] scissors

ο ψαράς [*o psaras*] fisherman

το ψάρεμα [*to psarema*] fishing

  ψαρεύω [*psarevo*] I fish

το ψάρι [*to psaree*] fish

  ψάχνω [*psakhno*] I look for; search

  ψεύτικος/η/ο [*psefteekos/ee/o*] false, fake; artificial

ψηλός/ή/ό [*pseelos/ee/o*] high; tall
ψήνω [*pseeno*] I roast
ψητός/ή/ό [*pseetos/ee/o*] roast
τα ψιλά [*ta pseela*] (small) change
το ψυγείο [*to pseeyeeo*] refrigerator
το ψωμί [*to psomee*] bread
τα ψώνια [*ta psonya*] shopping
ψωνίζω [*psoneezo*] I go shopping.

Ω, ω

ωθήσατε [*otheesate*] push
ωμός/ή/ό [*omos/ee/o*] raw
η ώρα [*ee ora*] hour; time
η ώρα της αιχμής [*ee ora tees ekhmees*] rush hour
ωραία [*orea*] good, fine!
ωραίος/α/ο [*oreos/a/o*] pretty, nice, lovely
το ωράριο [*to oraryo*] hours of work; timetable
ώριμος/η/ο [*oreemos/ee/o*] mature, ripe
ως [*os*] up to; until; as; like

There is a list of car parts on page 50, and parts of the body on page 185. See also the lists on pages 120–135; 209–224.

A

a/an **ένας, μια, ένα** (*see page 198*) [*enas, mya, ena*]
abbey **το μοναστήρι** [*to monasteeree*]
about (*on the subject of*) **για** [*ya*]
  (*approximately*) **περίπου** [*pereepoo*]
above (*upstairs etc.*) **(ε)πάνω** [*(e)pano*]
  (*on top of*) **πάνω από** [*pano apo*]
abroad **έξω** [*ekso*]
abscess **το απόστημα** [*to aposteema*]
accept: I accept **δέχομαι** [*dhekhome*]
accident **το δυστύχημα** [*to dheesteekheema*]
according to **σύμφωνα με** [*seemfona me*]
account (*bank*) **ο λογαριασμός** [*o logaryazmos*]
accountant **ο λογιστής** [*o loyeestees*]
ache **ο πόνος** [*o ponos*]
acid **το οξύ** [*to oksee*]
across (*on the other side of*) **απέναντι** [*apenandee*]
acrylic **το ακρυλικό** [*to akreeleeko*]
act: I act **ενεργώ** [*energo*]
  (*theatre*) **παίζω** [*pezo*]
activity **η δραστηριότητα** [*ee dhrasteeryoteeta*]
actor **ο ηθοποιός** [*o eethopyos*]
actress **η ηθοποιός** [*ee eethopyos*]
adaptor (*voltage*) **ο μετασχηματιστής** [*o metaskheemateestees*]
  (*multiple plug*) **η πολλαπλή πρίζα** [*ee polaplee preeza*]
address **η διεύθυνση** [*ee dhyeftheensee*]
adhesive tape **το σελοτέϊπ** [*to selote-eep*]
admission (*entrance fee*) **η είσοδος** [*ee eesodhos*]
adopted **υιοθετημένος/η/ο** [*eeyotheteemenos/ee/o*]
adult **ο/η ενήλικος** [*o/ee eneeleekos*]
advance: in advance **μπροστά** [*brosta*]
advanced (*level*) **προχωρημένος/η/ο**
  [*prokhoreemenos/ee/o*]

advertisement η διαφήμιση [*ee dhyafeemeesee*]
advertising η διαφήμιση [*ee dhyafeemeesee*]
aerial η κεραία [*ee kerea*]
aeroplane το αεροπλάνο [*to aeroplano*]
afford: I can't afford it είναι πολύ ακριβό για μένα
   [*eene polee akreevo ya mena*]
afraid: I am afraid φοβάμαι [*fovame*]
after μετά από [*meta apo*]
  afterwards μετά [*meta*]
afternoon το μεσημέρι [*to meseemeree*]
aftershave το αφτερσέϊβ [*to afterse-eev*]
again πάλι [*palee*]
against εναντίον [*enandeeon*]
age η ηλικία [*ee eeleekeea*]
agency το πρακτορείο [*to praktoreeo*]
ago πριν [*preen*]
agree: I agree συμφωνώ [*seemfono*]
agreed σύμφωνοι [*seemfonee*]
AIDS το έϊντς [*to e-eeds*]
air ο αέρας [*o aeras*]
  by air με το αεροπλάνο [*me to aeroplano*]
  by airmail αεροπορικώς [*aeroporeekos*]
air conditioning ο κλιματισμός [*o kleemateezmos*]
air force η αεροπορία [*ee aeroporeea*]
airline η αεροπορική γραμμή [*ee aeroporeekee gramee*]
air mattress το αερόστρωμα [*to aerostroma*]
airport το αεροδρόμιο [*to aerodhromyo*]
aisle ο διάδρομος [*o dhyadhromos*]
  (*church*) το κλίτος [*to kleetos*]
alarm ο συναγερμός [*o seenayermos*]
alarm clock το ξυπνητήρι [*to kseepneeteeree*]
alcohol το οινόπνευμα [*to eenopnevma*]
alcoholic (*drinks etc.*) οινοπνευματώδης/ης/ες
  [*eenopnevmatodhees/ees/es*]
alive ζωντανός/ή/ό [*zondanos/ee/o*]
all όλος/η/ο [*olos/ee/o*]
allergic to αλλεργικός/ή/ό σε [*alergeekos/ee/o se*]
allow: I allow επιτρέπω [*epeetrepo*]
  . . . is allowed επιτρέπεται . . . [*epeetrepete . . .*]
all right εντάξει [*endaksee*]

almond **το αμύγδαλο** [*to ameegdhalo*]

alone **μόνος/η/ο** [*monos/ee/o*]

along (the street) **κατά μήκος (του δρόμου)** [*kata meekos (too dhromoo)*]

already **ήδη** [*eedhee*]

also **επίσης** [*epeesees*]

although **παρ'όλο που** [*parolo poo*]

always **πάντοτε** [*pandote*]

am (*see* to be)

ambition **η φιλοδοξία** [*ee feelodhokseea*]

ambulance **το ασθενοφόρο** [*to asthenoforo*]

among **ανάμεσα σε** [*anamesa se*]

amount **η ποσότητα** [*ee posoteeta*]

amusement park **το λούνα παρκ** [*to loona park*]

anaesthetic **το αναισθητικό** [*to anestheeteeko*]

and **και** [*ke*]

angry **θυμωμένος/η/ο** [*theemomenos/ee/o*]

animal **το ζώο** [*to zo-o*]

anniversary **η επέτειος** [*ee epetyos*]

annoyed **ενοχλημένος/η/ο** [*enokhleemenos/ee/o*]

anorak **το ανοράκ** [*to anorak*]

another (one) **άλλος/η/ο** [*alos/ee/o*]

answer **η απάντηση** [*ee apandeesee*]

answer:I answer **απαντάω** [*apandao*]

antibiotic **το αντιβιωτικό** [*to andeevyoteeko*]

antifreeze **το αντιψυκτικό** [*to andeepseekteeko*]

antique **η αντίκα** [*ee andeeka*]

antiseptic **αντισηπτικός/ή/ό** [*andeeseepteekos/ee/o*]

anyone **κανένας** (*m.*), **καμμία** (*f.*) [*kanenas, kameea*]

anything (*something*) **τίποτα** [*teepota*]
   anything else? **τιποτ'άλλο;** [*teepotalo*]

anyway **έτσι κι αλλιώς** [*etsee kyalyos*]

anywhere **οπουδήποτε** [*opoodheepote*]

apart (from) **εκτός από** [*ektos apo*]

apartment **το διαμέρισμα** [*to dhyamereezma*]

aperitif **το απεριτίφ** [*apereeteef*]

appendicitis **η σκωληκοειδίτιδα** [*ee skoleekoeedheeteedha*]

apple **το μήλο** [*to meelo*]

appointment **το ραντεβού** [*to randevoo*]

approximately **περίπου** [*pereepoo*]

apricot **το βερύκοκκο** [*to vereekoko*]

arch **το τόξο** [*to tokso*]

archaeology **η αρχαιολογία** [*ee arkheoloyeea*]

architect **ο/η αρχιτέκτονας** [*o/ee arkheetektonas*]

architecture **η αρχιτεκτονική** [*ee arkheetektoneekee*]

are (*see* to be)

area (*surface*) **το εμβαδόν** [*to emvadhon*]

   (*region*) **η περιοχή** [*ee peryokhee*]

argument **ο καυγάς** [*o kavgas*]

arm **το χέρι** [*to kheree*]

armbands (*swimming*) **τα μπρατσάκια** [*ta bratsakya*]

army **ο στρατός** [*o stratos*]

around **γύρω (από)** [*yeero (apo)*]

   around the corner **πίσω από τη γωνία** [*peeso apo tee goneea*]

arrange: I arrange **κανονίζω** [*kanoneezo*]

arrest: under arrest **υπό κράτηση** [*eepo krateesee*]

arrival **η άφιξη** [*ee afeeksee*]

arrive: I arrive **φτάνω** [*ftano*]

art **η τέχνη** [*ee tekhnee*]

   fine arts **οι καλές τέχνες** [*ee kales tekhnes*]

art gallery **η πινακοθήκη** [*ee peenakotheekee*]

arthritis **η αρθρίτιδα** [*ee arthreeteedha*]

artichoke **η αγγινάρα** [*ee angeenara*]

article (*object*) **το αντικείμενο** [*to andeekeemeno*]

artificial **τεχνητός/ή/ό** [*tekhneetos/ee/o*]

artist **ο καλλιτέχνης, η καλλιτέχνις** [*o kaleetekhnees, ee kaleetekhnees*]

   (*painter*) **ο/η ζωγράφος** [*o/ee zografos*]

as **όπως** [*opos*]

as far as **μέχρι** [*mekhree*]

ash **η στάχτη** [*ee stakhtee*]

ashtray **το σταχτοδοχείο** [*to stakhtodhokheeo*]

ask: I ask **ρωτάω** [*rotao*]

   I ask for **ζητάω** [*zeetao*]

asparagus **το σπαρράγγι** [*to sparangee*]

aspirin **η ασπιρίνη** [*ee aspeereenee*]

assistant **ο/η βοηθός** [*o/ee voeethos*]

asthma **το άσθμα** [*to asthma*]

at **σε (στον, στην, στο etc.)** (*see page 199*)
   [*se (ston, steen, sto etc.)*]

Athens η Αθήνα [ee atheena]
athletics ο αθλητισμός [o athleeteezmos]
atmosphere η ατμόσφαιρα [ee atmosfera]
attack: I attack κάνω επίθεση [kano epeethesee]
attractive ελκυστικός/ή/ό [elkeesteekos/ee/o]
aubergine η μελιτζάνα [ee meleedzana]
auction ο πλειστηριασμός [o pleesteeryazmos]
aunt η θεία [ee theea]
author ο/η συγγραφέας [o/ee seengrafeas]
automatic αυτόματος/η/ο [aftomatos/ee/o]
autumn το φθινόπωρο [to ftheenoporo]
avalanche η χιονοστιβάδα [ee khyonosteevadha]
avocado το αβοκάντο [to avokado]
avoid: I avoid αποφεύγω [apofevgo]
away: . . . (kilometres) away . . . (χιλιόμετρα) μακριά
    [. . . (kheelyometra) makrya]
awful τρομερός/ή/ό [tromeros/ee/o]

B

baby το μωρό [to moro]
baby cereal η κρέμα για μωρά [ee krema ya mora]
baby food η βρεφική τροφή [ee vrefeekee trofee]
baby's bottle τα μπιμπερό [to beebero]
babysitter η μπεϊμπι-σίτερ [ee be-eebee-seeter]
baby wipes τα μωρομάντηλα [ta moromandeela]
back: at the back πίσω [peeso]
    (reverse side) η πίσω πλευρά [ee peeso plevra]
backwards πίσω [peeso]
bacon το μπέικον [to be-eekon]
bad κακός/ή/ό [kakos/ee/o]
badly άσχημα [askheema]
bag η τσάντα [ee tsanda]
baggage οι βαλίτσες [ee valeetses]
baker ο φούρναρης [o foornarees]
baker's ο φούρνος [o foornos]
balcony το μπαλκόνι [to balkonee]
    (theatre etc.) ο εξώστης [o eksostees]
bald φαλακρός/ή/ό [falakros/ee/o]

ball η μπάλα [*ee bala*]
ballet το μπαλέτο [*to baleto*]
ballpoint pen το στυλό [*to steelo*]
banana η μπανάνα [*ee banana*]
band (*music*) το συγκρότημα [*to seengroteema*]
bandage ο επίδεσμος [*o epeedhezmos*]
bank η τράπεζα [*ee trapeza*]
bar το μπαρ [*to bar*]
barber's το κουρείο [*to kooreeo*]
basement το υπόγειο [*to eepoyo*]
basket το καλάθι [*to kalathee*]
basketball το μπάσκετ [*to basket*]
bath το μπάνιο [*to banyo*]
bath: I have a bath κάνω μπάνιο [*kano banyo*]
bathing costume το μαγιό [*to mayo*]
bathroom το λουτρό [*to lootro*]
battery η μπαταρία [*ee batareea*]
bay ο κόλπος [*o kolpos*]
be: to be (*see page 207*)

   I am είμαι [*eeme*]
   you are (*s.*) είσαι [*eese*]
   he/she/it is είναι [*eene*]
   we are είμαστε [*eemaste*]
   you are (*pl.*) είσαστε [*eesaste*]
   they are είναι [*eene*]

beach η πλαζ [*ee plaz*]
bean το φασόλι [*to fasolee*]
   French/green το φασολάκι [*to fasolakee*]
beard τα γένεια [*ta yenya*]
beautiful όμορφος/η/ο [*omorfos/ee/o*]
because γιατί [*yatee*]
bed το κρεβάτι [*to krevatee*]
bedroom η κρεβατοκάμαρα [*ee krevatokamara*]
bee η μέλισσα [*ee meleesa*]
beef το μοσχάρι [*to moskharee*]
beer η μπύρα [*ee beera*]
beetroot το παντζάρι [*to pandzaree*]
before πριν (από) [*preen (apo)*]
begin: I begin αρχίζω [*arkheezo*]
beginner ο αρχάριος, η αρχάρια [*o arkharyos, ee arkharya*]

beginning η αρχή [ee arkhee]
behind πίσω (από) [peeso (apo)]
beige μπεζ [bez]
believe: I believe πιστεύω [peestevo]
   I believe so/not πιστεύω πως ναι/όχι [peestevo pos ne/okhee]
bell (church) η καμπάνα [ee kambana]
   (doorbell) το κουδούνι [to koodhoonee]
belong: it belongs to ανήκει σε [aneekee se]
   (to be a member of) είμαι μέλος [eeme melos]
below κάτω [kato]
   (beneath) κάτω από [kato apo]
belt η ζώνη [ee zonee]
bend η στροφή [ee strofee]
bent στραβός/ή/ό [stravos/ee/o]
berry ο καρπός [o karpos]
berth η καμπίνα [ee kabeena]
beside (next to) δίπλα σε [dheepla se]
besides εξ άλλου [eks aloo]
best ο/η/το καλύτερος/η/ο [o/ee/to kaleeteros/ee/o]
better καλύτερος/η/ο [kaleeteros/ee/o]
between ανάμεσα σε [anamesa se]
beyond πιο πέρα από [pyo pera apo]
bib η σαλιάρα [ee salyara]
Bible η Βίβλος [ee veevlos]
bicycle το ποδήλατο [to podheelato]
big μεγάλος/η/ο [megalos/ee/o]
bigger μεγαλύτερος/η/ο [megaleeteros/ee/o]
biggest ο/η/το μεγαλύτερος/η/ο [o/ee/to megaleeteros/ee/o]
bill ο λογαριασμός [o logaryazmos]
bin το καλάθι αχρήστων [to kalathee akhreeston]
bin liner η σακκούλα απορριμάτων [ee sakoola aporeematon]
binoculars τα κιάλια [ta kyalya]
biology η βιολογία [ee veeoloyeea]
bird το πουλί [to poolee]
birthday τα γενέθλια [ta yenethlya]
biscuit το μπισκότο [to beeskoto]
bishop ο επίσκοπος [o epeeskopos]
(a) bit λίγο [leego]
bite: I bite δαγκάνω [dhangano]
bitter πικρός/ή/ό [peekros/ee/o]

black **μαύρος/η/ο** [*mavros/ee/o*]
  black and white (*film etc.*) **μαυρόασπρος/η/ο** [*mavroaspros/ee/o*]
  black (*coffee*) **σκέτο** [*sketo*]
blackberry **το βατόμουρο** [*to vatomooro*]
blanket **η κουβέρτα** [*ee kooverta*]
bleach **το λευκαντικό** [*to lefkandeeko*]
bleed: I bleed **αιμορραγώ** [*emorago*]
blind **τυφλός/ή/ό** [*teeflos/ee/o*]
blind (*window*) **το ρολό** [*to rolo*]
blister **η φουσκάλα** [*ee fooskala*]
blocked **βουλωμένος/η/ο** [*voolomenos/ee/o*]
  (*road*) **μπλοκαρισμένος/η/ο** [*blokareezmenos/ee/o*]
blond(e) **ξανθός/ή/ό** [*ksanthos/ee/o*]
blood **το αίμα** [*to ema*]
blouse **η μπλούζα** [*ee blooza*]
blow: I blow **φυσάω** [*feesao*]
blow-dry **το στέγνωμα** [*stegnoma*]
blue **μπλε** [*ble*]
blusher **το ρουζ** [*to rooz*]
boarding **η επιβίβαση** [*ee epeeveevasee*]
boarding card **η κάρτα επιβιβάσεως**
  [*ee karta epeeveevaseos*]
boat **το καράβι** [*to karavee*]
  by boat **με το καράβι** [*me to karavee*]
body **το σώμα** [*to soma*]
boiled **βραστός/ή/ό** [*vrastos/ee/o*]
boiled egg **το αυγό βραστό** [*to avgo vrasto*]
boiler **ο λέβητας** [*o leveetas*]
bomb **η βόμβα** [*ee vomva*]
bone **το κόκκαλο** [*to kokalo*]
book **το βιβλίο** [*to veevleeo*]
book: I book (*tickets etc.*) **κλείνω** [*kleeno*]
booking office (*railway etc.*) **το εκδοτήριο** [*to ekdhoteeryo*]
  (*theatre*) **το ταμείο** [*to tameeo*]
bookshop **το βιβλιοπωλείο** [*to veevlyopoleeo*]
boot **η μπότα** [*ee bota*]
  (*car*) **το πορτ-μπαγκάζ** [*to port-bagaz*]
border (*edge*) **η παρυφή** [*ee pareefee*]
  (*frontier*) **τα σύνορα** [*ta seenora*]
bored: I am bored **πλήττω** [*pleeto*]

boring **βαρετός/ή/ό** [*varetos/ee/o*]

both **και οι δύο** (*m./f.*) **και τα δύο** (*n.*) [*ke ee dheeo, ke ta dheeo*]

bottle **το μπουκάλι** [*to bookalee*]

bottle opener **το ανοιχτήρι** [*to aneekhteeree*]

bottom **το βάθος** [*to vathos*]

   (*body*) **ο πισινός** [*o peeseenos*]

bow (*ship*) **η πλώρη** [*ee ploree*]

bow (*knot*) **ο φιόγκος** [*o fyongos*]

bowl **το μπωλ** [*to bol*]

bowls (*ten-pin*) **το μπόουλιγκ** [*to bo-ooleeng*]

box **το κουτί** [*to kootee*]

   (*theatre*) **το θεωρείο** [*to theoreeo*]

box office **το ταμείο** [*to tameeo*]

boy **το αγόρι** [*to agoree*]

(my) boyfriend **ο φίλος (μου)** [*o feelos (moo)*]

bra **το σουτιέν** [*to sootyen*]

bracelet **το βραχιόλι** [*to vrakhyolee*]

braces **οι τιράντες** [*ee teerandes*]

brain **το μυαλό** [*to myalo*]

branch **το κλαδί** [*to kladhee*]

   (*bank etc.*) **το υποκατάστημα** [*to eepokatasteema*]

brand **η μάρκα** [*ee marka*]

brandy **το κονιάκ** [*to konyak*]

brave **γενναίος/α/ο** [*yeneos/a/o*]

bread **το ψωμί** [*to psomee*]

break: I break **σπάω** [*spao*]

   I have broken **έσπασα** [*espasa*]

breakdown truck **το ρυμουλκό** [*to reemoolko*]

breakfast **το πρωινό** [*to proeeno*]

breathe: I breathe **ανασαίνω** [*anaseno*]

bride **η νύφη** [*ee neefee*]

bridegroom **ο γαμπρός** [*o gambros*]

bridge **η γέφυρα** [*ee yefeera*]

briefcase **η τσάντα** [*ee tsanda*]

bright (*colour*) **ζωηρός/ή/ό** [*zoeeros/ee/o*]

   (*light*) **φωτεινός/ή/ό** [*foteenos/ee/o*]

bring: can you bring me . . . ? **μου φέρνετε . . . ;**
   [*moo fernete . . .*]

British **βρετανικός/ή/ό** [*vretaneekos/ee/o*]

broad **φαρδύς, φαρδειά, φαρδύ** [*fardhees, fardhya, fardhee*] broad bean το **κουκκί** [*to kookee*]

brochure η **μπροσούρα** [*ee brosoora*]

broken **σπασμένος/η/ο** [*spazmenos/ee/o*]

broken down **χαλασμένος/η/ο** [*khalazmenos/ee/o*]

bronchitis η **βρογχίτιδα** [*ee vronkheeteedha*]

bronze ο **μπρούντζος** [*o broondzos*]
(*adj.*) **μπρούντζινος/η/ο** [*broondzeenos/ee/o*]

brooch η **καρφίτσα** [*ee karfeetsa*]

broom η **σκούπα** [*ee skoopa*]

brother ο **αδελφός** [*o adhelfos*]

brother-in-law (*sister's husband*) ο **γαμπρός** [*o gambros*]
(*wife's brother*) ο **κουνιάδος** [*o koonyadhos*]

brown **καφέ** [*kafe*]
(*hair*) **καστανός/ή/ό** (*kastanos/ee/o*)

bruise η **μελανιά** [*ee melanya*]

brush η **βούρτσα** [*ee voortsa*]

bucket ο **κουβάς** [*o koovas*]

budgerigar το **παπαγαλάκι** [*to papagalakee*]

buffet το **κυλικείο** [*to keeleekeeo*]

build: I build **χτίζω** [*khteezo*]

building το **κτήριο** [*to kteeryo*]

bulb (*electric*) η **λάμπα** [*ee lamba*]

301

bumper ο **προφυλακτήρας** [*o profeelakteeras*]

burn το **έγκαυμα** [*to engavma*]

burn: I burn **καίω** [*keo*]

burnt **καμμένος/η/ο** [*kamenos/ee/o*]

bus το **λεωφορείο** [*to leoforeeo*]
by bus **με το λεωφορείο** [*me to leoforeeo*]

bush ο **θάμνος** [*o thamnos*]

business η **επιχείρηση** [*ee epeekheereesee*]

business trip το **επαγγελματικό ταξίδι**
[*to epangelmateeko takseedhee*]

businessman/woman ο/η **επιχειρηματίας**
[*o/ee epeekheereemateeas*]

business studies οι **επιχειρηματικές σπουδές**
[*ee epeekheereemateekes spoodhes*]

bus station ο **σταθμός λεωφορείων** [*o stathmos leoforeeon*]

bus stop η **στάση λεωφορείου** [*ee stasee leoforeeoo*]

busy **απασχολημένος/η/ο** [*apaskholeemenos/ee/o*]

but **αλλά** [*ala*]

butane gas **το πετρογκάζ** [*to petrogaz*]
butcher's **το χασάπικο** [*to khasapeeko*]
butter **το βούτυρο** [*to vooteero*]
butterfly **η πεταλούδα** [*ee petaloodha*]
button **το κουμπί** [*to koombee*]
buy: I buy **αγοράζω** [*agorazo*]
by (*agent*) **από** [*apo*]

C

cabbage **το λάχανο** [*to lakhano*]
cabin **η καμπίνα** [*ee kabeena*]
cable car **το τελεφερίκ** [*to telefereek*]
café **το καφενείο** [*to kafeneeo*]
cake **η πάστα** [*ee pasta*]
cake shop **το ζαχαροπλαστείο** [*to zakharoplasteeo*]
calculator **το κομπιουτεράκι** [*to kombyooterakee*]
call (*phone*) **το τηλεφώνημα** [*to teelefoneema*]
call: I call (*on the telephone*) **τηλεφωνώ σε** [*teelefono se*]
   I am called **με λένε** [*me lene*]
   he/she/it is called **τον/τη/το λένε** [*ton/tee/to lene*]
   what is he/she/it called? **πώς τον/τη/το λένε;** [*pos ton/tee/to lene*]
calm **ήσυχος/η/ο** [*eeseekhos/ee/o*]
camera **η (φωτογραφική) μηχανή** [*ee (fotografeekee) meekhanee*]
camomile tea **το χαμομήλι** [*to khamomeelee*]
camp: I camp **κάνω κάμπινγκ** [*kano kambeeng*]
campbed **η ράντζα** [*ee randza*]
camping **το κάμπινγκ** [*to kambeeng*]
campsite **το κάμπινγκ** [*to kambeeng*]
can (*to be able*): I can **μπορώ (να)** (*see page 205*) [*boro (na)*]
   can you . . .? **μπορείς/μπορείτε . . . ;** [*borees/boreete . . .*]
can (*tin*) **το κουτί** [*to kootee*]
can opener **το ανοιχτήρι** [*to aneekhteeree*]
cancel: I cancel **καταργώ** [*katargo*]
cancer **το καρκίνο** [*to karkeeno*]
candle **το κερί** [*to keree*]
canoe **το κανώ** [*to kano*]
capital (*city*) **η πρωτεύουσα** [*ee protevoosa*]
captain **ο καπετάνιος** [*o kapetanyos*]

302

car **το αυτοκίνητο** [to aftokeeneeto]
  by car **με το αυτοκίνητο** [me to aftokeeneeto]
carafe **η καράφα** [ee karafa]
caravan **το τροχόσπιτο** [to trokhospeeto]
caravan site **το κάμπιγκ για τροχόσπιτο** [to kambeeng ya trokhospeeto]
cardigan **η πλεκτή ζακέτα** [ee plektee zaketa]
care: I take care **προσέχω** [prosekho]
  I don't care **δεν με νοιάζει** [dhen me nyazee]
careful **προσεκτικός/ή/ό** [prosekteekos/ee/o]
careless **απρόσεκτος/η/ο** [aprosektos/ee/o]
car park **το πάρκιγκ** [to parkeeng]
carpenter **ο ξυλουργός** [o kseeloorgos]
carpet **το χαλί** [to khalee]
carriage (railway) **το βαγόνι** [to vagonee]
carrier bag **η σακούλα** [ee sakoola]
carrot **το καρότο** [to karoto]
carry: I carry **κουβαλάω** [koovalao]
car wash **το πλυντήριο αυτοκινήτων** [to pleendeeryo aftokeeneeton]
case: just in case **αν τυχόν** [an teekhon]
cash: I pay cash **πληρώνω μετρητοίς** [pleerono metreetees]
cash (cheque): I cash **εξαργυρώνω** [eksaryeerono]
cash desk **το ταμείο** [to tameeo]
cassette **η κασέτα** [ee kaseta]
cassette player **το κασετόφωνο** [to kasetofono]
castle **το κάστρο** [to kastro]
cat **ο γάτος, η γάτα** [o gatos, ee gata]
catalogue **ο κατάλογος** [o katalogos]
catch (train/bus); I catch **προλαβαίνω** [prolaveno]
cathedral **η μητρόπολη** [ee meetropolee]
Catholic **καθολικός/ή/ό** [katholeekos/ee/o]
cauliflower **το κουνουπίδι** [to koonoopeedhee]
cause: I cause **προκαλώ** [prokalo]
cave **το σπήλαιο** [to speeleo]
ceiling **το ταβάνι** [to tavanee]
celery **το σέλινο** [to seleeno]
cellar **το υπόγειο** [to eepoyio]
  (wine) **η κάβα** [ee kava]
cemetery **το νεκροταφείο** [to nekrotafeeo]
centimetre **το εκατοστό** [to ekatosto]

central **κεντρικός/ή/ό** [kendreekos/ee/o]

central heating η **κεντρική θέρμανση** [ee kendreekee thermansee]

centre το **κέντρο** [to kendro]

century ο **αιώνας** [o eonas]

cereals τα **δημητριακά** [ta dheemeetryaka]

certain **σίγουρος/η/ο** [seegooros/ee/o]

certainly (why not?) **βεβαίως** [veveos]

certificate το **πιστοποιητικό** [to peestopee-eeteeko]

chain η **αλυσίδα** [ee aleeseedha]

chair η **καρέκλα** [ee karekla]

chair lift το **τελεφερίκ** [to telefereek]

champagne η **σαμπάνια** [ee sambanya]

change (small coins) τα **ψιλά** [ta pseela]
   (money due back) τα **ρέστα** [ta resta]

change: I change **αλλάζω** [alazo]

changing room το **αποδυτήριο** [to apodheeteeryo]

chapel το **παρεκκλήσι** [to parekleesee]

charcoal τα **κάρβουνα** [ta karvoona]

charge (price) η **τιμή** [ee teemee]

charter flight το **τσάρτερ** [to tsarter]

cheap **φτηνός/ή/ό** [fteenos/ee/o]

check (pattern) **καρρέ** [kare]

check: I check **ελέγχω** [elenkho]

check-in (desk) ο **έλεγχος εισιτηρίων** [o elenkhos eeseeteereeon]

cheek το **μάγουλο** [to magoolo]

cheeky **θρασύς, θρασειά, θρασύ** [thrasees, thrasya, thrasee]

cheers! **στην υγειά σας!** [steen eeya sas]

cheese το **τυρί** [to teeree]

chef ο **μάγειρας** [o mayeeras]

chemist's το **φαρμακείο** [to farmakeeo]

chemistry η **χημική** [ee kheemeekee]

cheque η **επιταγή** [ee epeetayee]

cherry το **κεράσι** [to kerasee]

chess το **σκάκι** [to skakee]

chestnut το **καρύδι** [to kareedhee]

chewing gum η **τσίχλα** [ee tseekhla]

chicken το **κοτόπουλο** [to kotopoolo]

chickenpox η **ανεμοβλογιά** [ee anemovloya]

child το **παιδί** [to pedhee]

children τα **παιδιά** [ta pedhya]

chimney **ο καπνοδόχος** [*o kapnodhokhos*]

china **η πορσελάνη** [*ee porselanee*]

chips **οι πατάτες τηγανητές** [*ee patates teeganeetes*]

chocolate **η σοκολάτα** [*ee sokolata*]

chocolates **οι σοκολάτες** [*ee sokolates*]

choose: I choose **διαλέγω** [*dhyalego*]

chop (*meat*) **η μπριζόλα** [*ee breezola*]

chops (*lamb*) **τα παϊδάκια** [*ta paeedhakya*]

Christian **χριστιανός/ή/ό** [*khreestyanos/ee/o*]

   (*Orthodox*) **ορθόδοξος/η/ο** [*orthodhoksos/ee/o*]

   (*Catholic*) **καθολικός/ή/ό** [*katholeekos/ee/o*]

   (*Protestant*) **διαμαρτυρόμενος/η/ο** [*dhyamarteeromenos/ee/o*]

Christian name **το μικρό όνομα** [*to meekro onoma*]

Christmas **τα Χριστούγεννα** [*ta khreestooyena*]

Christmas Eve **η παραμονή Χριστουγέννων** [*ee paramonee khreestooyenon*]

church **η εκκλησία** [*ee ekleeseea*]

cigar **το πούρο** [*to pooro*]

cigarette **το τσιγάρο** [*to tseegaro*]

cigarette lighter **ο αναπτήρας** [*o anapteeras*]

cinema **το σινεμά** [*to seenema*]

cinnamon **η κανέλα** [*ee kanela*]

circle **ο κύκλος** [*o keeklos*]

   (*theatre*) **ο εξώστης** [*o eksostees*]

circus **ο τσίρκος** [*o tseerkos*]

city **η πόλη** [*ee polee*]

civil servant **ο/η δημόσιος υπάλληλος** [*o/ee dheemosyos eepaleelos*]

class **η τάξη** [*ee taksee*]

classical music **η κλασσική μουσική** [*ee klaseekee mooseekee*]

clean **καθαρός/ή/ό** [*katharos/ee/o*]

clean: I clean **καθαρίζω** [*kathareezo*]

cleansing cream **η κρέμα καθαρισμού** [*ee krema kathareezmoo*]

clear **καθαρός/ή/ό** [*katharos/ee/o*]

clerk **ο/η υπάλληλος** [*o/ee eepaleelos*]

clever **έξυπνος/η/ο** [*ekseepnos/ee/o*]

cliff **ο γκρεμός** [*o gremos*]

climate **το κλίμα** [*to kleema*]

climb (up): I climb **σκαρφαλώνω** [*skarfalono*]

climber **ο ορειβάτης** [*o oreevatees*]

climbing **η ορειβασία** [*ee oreevaseea*]

clinic η κλινική [ee kleeneekee]

cloakroom η γκαρνταρόμπα [ee gardaroba]

clock το ρολόι [to roloee]

close (by) κοντά [konda]

close to κοντά σε [konda se]

close: I close κλείνω [kleeno]

closed κλειστός/ή/ό [kleestos/ee/o]

cloth (for cleaning) το πανί [to panee]

clothes τα ρούχα [ta rookha]

clothes peg το μανταλάκι [to mandalakee]

cloud το σύννεφο [to seenefo]

cloudy συννεφιασμένος/η/ο [seenefyazmenos/ee/o]

club η λέσχη [ee leskhee]

    (golf) το μπαστούνι (του γκολφ) [to bastoonee (too golf)]

coach το πούλμαν [to poolman]

    (railway) το βαγόνι [to vagonee]

coal το κάρβουνο [to karvoono]

coarse (texture) χοντρός/ή/ό [khondros/ee/o]

    (skin etc.) αδρός/ή/ό [adhros/ee/o]

coast η ακτή [ee aktee]

coat το σακάκι [to sakakee]

coat-hanger η κρεμάστρα [ee kremastra]

cocktail το κοκτέιλ [to kokte-eel]

coffee ο καφές [o kafes]

coin το νόμισμα [to nomeezma]

cold κρύος/α/ο [kreeos/a/o]

    I'm cold κρυώνω [kreeono]

    it's cold (weather) κάνει κρύο [kanee kreeo]

    I have a cold είμαι κρυωμένος/η/ο [eeme kreeomenos/ee/o]

collar το κολάρο [to kolaro]

colleague ο/η συνάδελφος [o/ee seenadhelfos]

collect: I collect συλλέγω [seelego]

collection η συλλογή [ee seeloyee]

college το κολέγιο [to koleyo]

colour το χρώμα [to khroma]

    (in) colour έγχρωμος/η/ο [enkhromos/ee/o]

    I am colour-blind έχω αχρωματοψία [ekho akhromatopseea]

comb η χτένα [ee khtena]

come: I come έρχομαι [erkhome] (see page 205)

    are you coming? έρχεσαι; (s.); έρχεστε; (pl.) [erkhese; erkheste]

come back: I come back γυρίζω [yeereezo]
come down: I come down κατεβαίνω [kateveno]
comedy η κωμωδία [ee komodheea]
come in: I come in μπαίνω [beno]
come in! εμπρός! [embros]
come out: I come out βγαίνω [vyeno]
comfortable αναπαυτικός/ή/ό [anapafteekos/ee/o]
comic (magazine) το κόμικς [to komeeks]
commercial εμπορικός/ή/ό [emboreekos/ee/o]
common κοινός/ή/ό [keenos/ee/o]
communion η επικοινωνία [ee epeekeenoneea]
communism ο κομμουνισμός [o komooneezmos]
communist ο/η κομμουνιστής [o/ee komooneestees]
compact disc το σι-ντι [to see-dee]
company η εταιρεία [ee etereea]
compared with σε σύγκριση με [se seengreese me]
compartment το διαμέρισμα [to dhyamereezma]
compass ο μπούσουλας [o boosoolas]
complain: I complain κάνω παράπονο [kano parapono]
complaint το παράπονο [to parapono]
completely τελείως [teleeos]
complicated περίπλοκος/η/ο [pereeplokos/ee/o]
composer ο συνθέτης [o seenthetees]
compulsory υποχρεωτικός/ή/ό [eepokhreoteekos/ee/o]
computer το κομπιούτερ [to kombyooter]
computer science/studies οι σπουδές πληροφορικής [ee spoodhes pleeroforeekees]
concert η συναυλία [ee seenavleea]
concert hall η αίθουσα συναυλιών [ee ethoosa seenavlyon]
concussion η διάσειση [ee dhyaseese]
condition η κατάσταση [ee katastase]
conditioner (hair) το κοντίσιονερ [to kondeesyoner]
condom το προφυλακτικό [to profeelakteeko]
conference το συνέδριο [to seenedhryo]
confirm: I confirm επιβεβαιώνω [epeeveveono]
connection (travel) η ανταπόκριση [ee andapokreese]
conservation η συντήρηση [ee seendeereese]
conservative συντηρητικός/ή/ό [seendeereeteekos/ee/o]
constipation η δυσκοιλία [ee dheeskeeleea]
consulate το προξενείο [to prokseneeo]

contact: I contact έρχομαι σε επαφή με [erkhome se epafee me]

I want to contact . . . θέλω να έρθω σε επαφή με . . . [thelo na ertho se epafee me . . .]

contact lens ο φακός επαφής [o fakos epafees]

continent η ήπειρος [ee eepeeros]

continue: I continue συνεχίζω [seenekheezo]

contraceptive το αντισυλληπτικό [to andeeseeleepteeko]

contract το συμβόλαιο [to seemvoleo]

convenient βολικός/ή/ό [voleekos/ee/o]

it's not convenient for me δεν με βολεύει [dhen me volevee]

convent το μοναστήρι [to monasteeree]

cook ο μάγειρας [o mayeeras]

cook: I cook μαγειρεύω [mayeerevo]

cooker η κουζίνα [ee koozeena]

cool δροσερός/ή/ό [dhroseros/ee/o]

cool box το φορητό ψυγείο [to foreeto pseeyeeo]

copper το μπακίρι [to bakeeree]

copy το αντίγραφο [to andeegrafo]

(book) το αντίτυπο [to andeeteepo]

Corfu η Κέρκυρα [ee kerkeera]

cork ο φελός [o felos]

corkscrew το τιρμπουσόν [to teerbooson]

corner η γωνία [ee goneea]

correct σωστός/ή/ό [sostos/ee/o]

corridor ο διάδρομος [o dhyadhromos]

cosmetics τα καλλυντικά [ta kaleendeeka]

cost η τιμή [ee teemee]

how much does it cost? πόσο κάνει;, πόσο κοστίζει; [poso kanee, poso kosteezee]

cot το κρεβατάκι [to krevatakee]

cotton το βαμβάκι [to vamvakee]

cotton wool το μπαμπάκι [to bambakee]

couchette η κουκέτα [ee kooketa]

cough ο βήχας [o veekhas]

cough medicine το σιρόπι για το βήχα [to seeropee ya to veekha]

count: I count μετράω [metrao]

counter (shop) ο πάγκος [o pangos]

country (nation) η χώρα [ee khora]

country(side) η εξοχή [ee eksokhee]

couple το ζευγάρι [to zevgaree]

courgette **το κολοκυθάκι** [*to kolokeethakee*]

course (*lessons*) **ο κύκλος μαθημάτων** [*o keeklos matheematon*]

(*food*) **το πιάτο** [*to pyato*]

court (*law*) **το δικαστήριο** [*to dheekasteeryo*]

(*sport*) **η πίστα** [*ee peesta*]

cousin **ο ξάδελφος, η ξαδέλφη** [*o ksadhelfos, ee ksadhelfee*]

cover **η κουβέρτα** [*ee kooverta*]

cover charge **το κουβέρ** [*to koover*]

cow **η αγελάδα** [*ee ayeladha*]

cramp (*medical*) **η κράμπα** [*ee kramba*]

crash (*car*) **το τρακάρισμα** [*to trakareezma*]

crayon **το κραγιόν** [*to krayon*]

crazy **τρελλός/ή/ό** [*trelos/ee/o*]

cream (*food*) **το καϊμάκι** [*to kaeemakee*]

(*lotion*) **η κρέμα** [*ee krema*]

credit card **η πιστωτική κάρτα** [*ee peestoteekee karta*]

Crete **η Κρήτη** [*ee kreetee*]

crisps **τα τσιπς** [*ta tseeps*]

cross **ο σταυρός** [*o stavros*]

Red Cross **ο Ερυθρός Σταυρός** [*o ereethros stavros*]

cross: I cross (*road etc.*) **πάω απέναντι** [*pao apenandee*]

crossing (*sea*) **το ταξίδι** [*to takseedhee*]

crossroads **το σταυροδρόμι** [*to stavrodhromee*]

crowded **γεμάτος/η/ο** [*yematos/ee/o*]

crown **ο στέφανος** [*o stefanos*]

cruise **η κρουασιέρα** [*ee krooazyera*]

crutch **η πατερίτσα** [*ee patereetsa*]

cry: I cry **κλαίω** [*kleo*]

crystal **το κρύσταλλο** [*to kreestalo*]

cucumber **το αγγούρι** [*to angooree*]

cuff **το μανικέτι** [*to maneeketee*]

cup **το φλυτζάνι** [*to fleedzanee*]

cupboard **το ντουλάπι** [*to doolapee*]

cure (*remedy*) **η θεραπεία** [*ee therapeea*]

cure: I cure **θεραπεύω** [*therapevo*]

curling tongs **το ψαλίδι** [*to psaleedhee*]

curly **σγούρος/η/ο** [*sgooros/ee/o*]

current (*electrical*) **το ρεύμα** [*to revma*]

curtain **η κουρτίνα** [*ee koorteena*]

curve **η καμπύλη** [*ee kambeelee*]

cushion το μαξιλλάρι [to makseelaree]
custard η κρέμα [ee krema]
customs το τελωνείο [to teloneeo]
cut η κοπή [ee kopee]
cut (off): I cut (off) κόβω [kovo]
cutlery τα μαχαιροπήρουνα [ta makheropeeroona]
cycling η ποδηλασία [ee podheelaseea]
cyclist ο ποδηλάτης [o podheelatees]
cystitis η κυστίτιδα [ee keesteeteedha]

D

daily καθημερινός/ή/ό [katheemereenos/ee/o]
damaged χαλασμένος/η/ο [khalazmenos/ee/o]
damp η υγρασία [ee eegraseea]
dance ο χορός [o khoros]
dance: I dance χορεύω [khorevo]
danger ο κίνδυνος [o keendheenos]
dangerous επικίνδυνος/η/ο [epeekeendheenos/ee/o]
dark σκοτεινός/ή/ό [skoteenos/ee/o]
  (hair/skin) μελαχροινός/ή/ό [melakhreenos/ee/o]
data (information) τα δεδομένα [ta dhedhomena]
date (day) η ημερομηνία [ee eemeromeeneea]
  (year) η χρονολογία [ee khronoloyeea]
  (fruit) το σύκο [to seeko]
daughter η κόρη [ee koree]
daughter-in-law η νύφη [ee neefee]
day η μέρα [ee mera]
day after/before η επόμενη, η προηγούμενη [ee epomenee, ee proeegoomenee]
day after tomorrow μεθαύριο [methavryo]
day before yesterday προχθές [prokhthes]
dead νεκρός/ή/ό [nekros/ee/o]
deaf κουφός/ή/ό [koofos/ee/o]
dealer ο εμπορικός αντιπρόσωπος [o emboreekos andeeprosopos]
dear (loved) αγαπημένος/η/ο [agapeemenos/ee/o]
  (expensive) ακριβός/ή/ό [akreevos/ee/o]
death ο θάνατος [o thanatos]

debt το χρέος [*to khreos*]

decaffeinated ντεκαφεϊνέ [*dekafe-eene*]

decide: I decide αποφασίζω [*apofaseezo*]

deck το κατάστρωμα [*to katastroma*]

declare: I declare δηλώνω [*dheelono*]

deep βαθύς, βαθειά, βαθύ [*vathees, vathya, vathee*]

deep freeze η κατάψυξη [*ee katapseeksee*]

deer το ελάφι [*to elafee*]

defect το ελάττωμα [*to elatoma*]

definitely! οπωσδήποτε! [*opozdheepote*]

defrost: I defrost ξεπαγώνω [*ksepagono*]

degree (*temperature*) ο βαθμός [*o vathmos*]
  (*university*) το πτυχείο [*to pteekheeo*]

delay η καθυστέρηση [*ee katheestereesee*]

delicate λεπτός/ή/ό [*leptos/ee/o*]

delicious νόστιμος/η/ο [*nosteemos/ee/o*]

demonstration η επίδειξη [*ee epeedheeksee*]
  (*protest*) η διαδήλωση [*ee dhyadheelosee*]

dentist ο/η οδοντίατρος [*o/ee odhondeeatros*]

dentures η μασέλα [*ee masela*]

deodorant το αποσμητικό [*to apozmeeteeko*]

depart: I depart αναχωρώ [*anakhoro*]

department το τμήμα [*to tmeema*]

department store το πολυκατάστημα [*to poleekatasteema*]

departure η αναχώρηση [*ee anakhoreesee*]

departure lounge η αίθουσα αναχωρήσεων [*ee ethoosa anakhoreeseon*]

deposit η προκαταβολή [*ee prokatavolee*]

describe: I describe περιγράφω [*pereegrafo*]

description η περιγραφή [*ee pereegrafee*]

desert η έρημος [*ee ereemos*]

design το σχέδιο [*to skhedhyo*]

design: I design σχεδιάζω [*skhedhyazo*]

designer ο σχεδιαστής [*o skhedhyastees*]

dessert το επιδόρπιο [*to epeedhorpyo*]

destination ο προορισμός [*o pro-oreezmos*]

detail η λεπτομέρεια [*ee leptomerya*]

detergent το απορρυπαντικό [*to aporeepandeeko*]

develop: I develop (*film*) εμφανίζω [*emfaneezo*]

diabetes ο διαβήτης [*o dhyaveetees*]

dial: I dial γυρίζω [*yeereezo*]

dialling code ο τηλεφωνικός κωδικός [*o teelefoneekos kodheekos*]

dialling tone το σήμα επιλογής [*to seema epeeloyees*]

diamond το διαμάντι [*to dhyamandee*]

diarrhoea η διάρροια [*ee dhyarya*]

diary το ημερολόγιο [*to eemeroloyo*]

dice τα ζάρια [*ta zarya*]

dictionary το λεξικό [*to lekseeko*]

die: I die πεθαίνω [*petheno*]

. . . died . . . πέθανε [. . . *pethane*]

diesel το ντήζελ [*to deezel*]

diet η δίαιτα [*ee dhee-eta*]

diet: I am on a diet κάνω δίαιτα [*kano dhee-eta*]

different διαφορετικός/ή/ό [*dhyaforeteekos/ee/o*]

difficult δύσκολος/η/ο [*dheeskolos/ee/o*]

dining room η τραπεζαρία [*ee trapezareea*]

dinner το δείπνο [*to dheepno*]

dinner jacket το σμόκιν [*to smokeen*]

diplomat ο/η διπλωμάτης [*o/ee dheeplomatees*]

direct άμεσος/η/ο [*amesos/ee/o*]

direction η κατεύθυνση [*ee katetheensee*]

director ο διευθυντής [*o dhyeftheendees*]

directory ο κατάλογος [*o katalogos*]

dirty βρώμικος/η/ο [*vromeekos/ee/o*]

disabled ανάπηρος/η/ο [*anapeeros/ee/o*]

disappointed απογοητευμένος/η/ο [*apogoeetevmenos/ee/o*]

disc ο δίσκος [*o dheeskos*]

disco(thèque) η ντισκοτέκ [*ee deeskotek*]

discount η έκπτωση [*ee ekptosee*]

dish το πιάτο [*to pyato*]

dishwasher το πλυντήριο πιάτων [*to pleendeeryo pyaton*]

disinfectant το απολυμαντικό [*to apoleemandeeko*]

dislocate: I have dislocated . . . έχω βγάλει . . . [*ekho vgalee . . .*]

disposable nappies οι πάνες μίας χρήσεως [*ee panes meeas khreeseos*]

distance η απόσταση [*ee apostasee*]

distilled water το νερό μπαταρίας [*to nero batareeas*]

district η περιοχή [*ee peryokhee*]

dive: I dive βουτάω [*vootao*]

diversion (*road*) το παρακαμπτήριο [*to parakambteeryo*]

diving-board η εξέδρα καταδύσεων [ee eksedhra katadheeseon]

divorcé(e) ο ζωντοχήρος, η ζωντοχήρα [o zondokheeros, ee zondokheera]

dizzy ζαλισμένος/η/ο [zaleezmenos/ee/o]

do: I do κάνω [kano]
 you do (s., informal) κάνεις [kanees]
 he/she/it does κάνει [kanee]
 we do κάνουμε [kanoome]
 you do (pl., formal) κάνετε [kanete]
 they do κάνουν(ε) [kanoon(e)]

docks το λιμάνι [to leemanee]

doctor ο γιατρός [o yatros]

document το έγγραφο [to engrafo]

dog ο σκύλος [o skeelos]

doll η κούκλα [ee kookla]

dollar το δολλάριο [to dholaryo]

dome ο τρούλλος [o troolos]

dominoes το ντόμινο [to domeeno]

donkey το γαϊδούρι [to gaeedhooree]

door η πόρτα [ee porta]

double διπλός/ή/ό [dheeplos/ee/o]

double bed το διπλό κρεβάτι [to dheeplo krevatee]

dough η ζύμη [ee zeemee]

down κάτω [kato]

downstairs κάτω [kato]

drachma η δραχμή [ee dhrakhmee]

drain ο οχετός [o okhetos]

drama το δράμα [to dhrama]

draught (air) το ρεύμα [to revma]

draught beer η μπύρα από το βαρέλι [ee beera apo to varelee]

draw: I draw σχεδιάζω [skhedhyazo]

drawer το συρτάρι [to seertaree]

drawing το σχέδιο [to skhedhyo]

drawing-pin η πυναίζα [ee peeneza]

dreadful φοβερός/ή/ό [foveros/ee/o]

dress το φόρεμα [to forema]

dressing (medical) ο επίδεσμος [o epeedhezmos]
 (salad) το λαδολέμονο [to ladholemono]

drink το ποτό [to poto]

drink: I drink πίνω [peeno]

drip: I drip στάζω [stazo]

drive: I drive οδηγώ [odheego]

driver ο/η οδηγός [o/ee odheegos]

driving licence η άδεια οδηγήσεως [ee adhya odheeyeeseos]

drowned πνιγμένος/η/ο [pneegmenos/ee/o]

drug το ναρκωτικό [to narkoteeko]

drug addict ο τοξικομανής [o tokseekomanees]

drum το τύμπανο [to teembano]

drunk μεθυσμένος/η/ο [metheezmenos/ee/o]

dry στεγνός/ή/ό [stegnos/ee/o]

   (wine) ξηρός/ή/ό [kseeros/ee/o]

dry-cleaner's το στεγνοκαθαριστήριο
   [to stegnokathareesteeryo]

dubbed ντουμπλαρισμένος/η/ο [dooblareezmenos/ee/o]

Dublin το Δουβλίνο [to dhoovleeno]

duck η πάπια [ee papya]

dull (weather) μουντός/ή/ό [moondos/ee/o]

dumb βουβός/ή/ό [voovos/ee/o]

dummy (baby's) η πιπίλα [ee peepeela]

during κατά τη διάρκεια του/της . . .
   [kata tee dhyarkya too/tees . . .]

dust η σκόνη [ee skonee]

dustbin ο σκουπιδοντενεκές [o skoopeedhodenekes]

dusty σκονισμένος/η/ο [skoneezmenos/ee/o]

duty (customs) ο δασμός [o dhazmos]

duty-free αφορολόγητος/η/ο [aforoloyeetos/ee/o]

duvet το πάπλωμα [to paploma]

E

each κάθε [kathe]

ear το αυτί [to aftee]

earache: I have earache μου πονάει το αυτί μου [moo ponaee to
   aftee moo]

earlier νωρίτερα [noreetera]

early νωρίς [norees]

earn: I earn κερδίζω [kerdheezo]

earring το σκουλαρίκι [to skoolareekee]

earth η γη [ee yee]

earthquake ο σεισμός [*o seezmos*]

east η ανατολή [*ee anatolee*]

Easter το Πάσχα [*to paskha*]

eastern ανατολικός/ή/ό [*anatoleekos/ee/o*]

easy εύκολος/η/ο [*efkolos/ee/o*]

eat: I eat τρώω (*see page 206*) [*tro-o*]

  I ate έφαγα [*efaga*]

economical οικονομικός/ή/ό [*eekonomeekos/ee/o*]

economics τα οικονομικά [*ta eekonomeeka*]

economy η οικονομία [*ee eekonomeea*]

Edinburgh το Εδιμβούργο [*to edheemvoorgo*]

egg το αυγό [*to avgo*]

either . . . or ή . . . ή [*ee . . . ee*]

elastic band το λαστιχάκι [*to lasteekhakee*]

election οι εκλογές [*ee ekloyes*]

electric ηλεκτρικός/ή/ό [*eelektreekos/ee/o*]

electrician ο ηλεκτρολόγος [*o eelektrologos*]

electricity το ρεύμα [*to revma*]

electronic ηλεκτρονικός/ή/ό [*eelektroneekos/ee/o*]

embarrass: it embarrasses me με φέρνει σε αμηχανία [*me fernee se ameekhaneea*]

embassy η πρεσβεία [*ee prezveea*]

emergency η κρίσιμη περίσταση [*ee kreeseemee pereestasee*]

empty άδειος/α/ο [*adhyos/a/o*]

empty: I empty αδειάζω [*adhyazo*]

enamel ο σμάλτος [*o zmaltos*]

enamel (*adj.*) εμαγιέ [*emagye*]

end το τέλος [*to telos*]

end: I end τελειώνω [*telyono*]

energetic ενεργητικός/ή/ό [*eneryeeteekos/ee/o*]

energy η ενέργεια [*ee enerya*]

engaged (*to be married*) αρραβωνιασμένος/η [*aravonyazmenos/ee*]

  (*occupied*) πιασμένος/η/ο [*pyazmenos/ee/o*]

engine η μηχανή [*ee meekhanee*]

engineer ο μηχανικός [*o meekhaneekos*]

engineering η μηχανική [*ee meekhaneekee*]

England η Αγγλία [*ee angleea*]

English αγγλικός/ή/ό [*angleekos/ee/o*]

Englishman ο Άγγλος [*o anglos*]

Englishwoman η Αγγλίδα [*ee angleedha*]

enough **αρκετός/ή/ό** [*arketos/ee/o*]

enter: I enter **μπαίνω** [*beno*]

entertainment **η διασκέδαση** [*ee dhyaskedhasee*]

enthusiastic **ενθουσιώδης/ης/ες** [*enthoosyodhees/ees/es*]

entrance **η είσοδος** [*ee eesodhos*]

envelope **ο φάκελλος** [*o fakelos*]

environment **το περιβάλλον** [*to pereevalon*]

equal **ίσος/η/ο** [*eesos/ee/o*]

equipment **ο εξοπλισμός** [*o eksopleezmos*]

-er (*e.g. bigger, cheaper: see page 200*) **πιο . . .** [*pyo . . .*]

escalator **η κυλιόμενη σκάλα** [*ee keelyomenee skala*]

especially **ειδικά** [*eedheeka*]

essential **απαραίτητος/η/ο** [*apareeteetos/ee/o*]

estate (*country*) **το κτήμα** [*to kteema*]

estate agent **ο μεσίτης** [*o meseetees*]

evaporated milk **το (γάλα) εβαπορέ** [*to (gala) evapore*]

even (*including*) **ακόμα και** [*akoma ke*]
    (*not odd*) **ζυγός/ή/ό** [*zeegos/ee/o*]

evening **το βράδυ** [*to vradhee*]

evening dress **το βραδυνό φόρεμα** [*to vradheeno forema*]

every (*each*) **κάθε** [*kathe*]
    (*all*) **όλος/η/ο** [*olos/ee/o*]

everyone **όλος ο κόσμος** [*olos o kozmos*]

everything **τα πάντα** [*ta panda*]

everywhere **παντού** [*pandoo*]

exactly **ακριβώς** [*akreevos*]

examination (*school etc.*) **οι εξετάσεις** [*ee eksetasees*]

example **το παράδειγμα** [*to paradheegma*]
    for example **για παράδειγμα** [*ya paradheegma*]

excellent **εξαιρετικός/ή/ό** [*eksereteekos/ee/o*]

except **πλην** [*pleen*]

excess luggage **το υπερβάλλον βάρος αποσκευών** [*to eepervalon varos aposkevon*]

exchange: I exchange **αλλάζω** [*alazo*]

exchange rate **η τιμή συναλλάγματος** [*ee teemee seenalagmatos*]

excited **συγκινημένος/η/ο** [*seengeeneemenos/ee/o*]

exciting **συναρπαστικός/ή/ό** [*seenarpasteekos/ee/o*]

excursion **η εκδρομή** [*ee ekdhromee*]

excuse me **συγγνώμη** [*seegnomee*]

executive ο υπεύθυνος επιχειρήσεως [*o eepeftheenos epeekheereeseos*]

exercise (*physical*) η γυμναστική [*ee yeemnasteekee*] (*practice*) η άσκηση [*ee askeesee*]

exhibition η έκθεση [*ee ekthese*]

exit η έξοδος [*ee eksodhos*]

expect: I expect περιμένω [*pereemeno*]

expensive ακριβός/ή/ό [*akreevos/ee/o*]

experience η πείρα [*ee peera*]

expert ο/η ειδικός [*o/ee eedheekos*]

explain: I explain εξηγώ [*ekseego*]

explosion η έκρηξη [*ee ekreeksee*]

export η εξαγωγή [*ee eksagoyee*]

export: I export εξάγω [*eksago*]

extension (*telephone*) το εσωτερικό [*to esotereeko*]

external εξωτερικός/ή/ό [*eksotereekos/ee/o*]

extra (*in addition*) επί πλέον [*epee pleon*]

eye το μάτι [*to matee*]

eyebrow το φρύδι [*to freedhee*]

eyebrow pencil το μολύβι για τα μάτια [*to moleevee ya ta matya*]

eyelash το βλέφαρο [*to vlefaro*]

eyeliner το αϊλάϊνερ [*to aeelaeener*]

eyeshadow η σκιά για τα μάτια [*ee skya ya ta matya*]

F

fabric το ύφασμα [*to eefazma*]

face το πρόσωπο [*to prosopo*]

face cream η κρέμα προσώπου [*ee krema prosopoo*]

face powder η πούδρα για το πρόσωπο [*ee poodhra ya to prosopo*]

facilities οι ευκολίες [*ee efkolee-es*]

fact το γεγονός [*to yegonos*]

in fact στην πραγματικότα [*steem-bragmateekota*]

factory το εργοστάσιο [*to ergostasyo*]

fail: I fail (*exam/test*) μένω [*meno*]

failure η αποτυχία [*ee apoteekheea*]

faint: I faint λιποθυμώ [*leepotheemo*]

fair (*hair*) ξανθός/ή/ό [*ksanthos/ee/o*]

fair **το πανηγύρι** [*to paneeyeeree*]

   trade fair **η έκθεση** [*ee ekthesee*]

fairly (*quite*) **αρκετά** [*arketa*]

faith **η πίστη** [*ee peestee*]

faithful **πιστός/ή/ό** [*peestos/ee/o*]

fake **ψεύτικος/η/ο** [*psefteekos/ee/o*]

fall: I fall **πέφτω** [*pefto*]

   he/she fell (down) **έπεσε** [*epese*]

false **ψεύτικος/η/ο** [*psefteekos/ee/o*]

   false teeth **η μασέλα** [*ee masela*]

family **η οικογένεια** [*ee eekoyenya*]

famous **διάσημος/η/ο** [*dhyaseemos/ee/o*]

fan **η βεντάλια** [*ee vendalya*]

   (*electric*) **ο ανεμιστήρας** [*o anemeesteeras*]

   (*supporter*) **ο οπαδός** [*o opadhos*]

fantastic (*imaginary*) **φανταστικός/ή/ό** [*fandasteekos/ee/o*]

   (*wonderful*) **καταπληκτικός/ή/ό** [*katapleekteekos/ee/o*]

far (*away*) **μακρυά** [*makrya*]

   is it far? **είναι μακρυά;** [*eene makrya*]

fare **το εισιτήριο** [*to eeseeteeryo*]

farm **το κτήμα** [*to kteema*]

farmer **ο γεωργός** [*o yeorgos*]

fashion **η μόδα** [*ee modha*]

fashionable/in fashion **της μόδας** [*tees modhas*]

fast **γρήγορος/η/ο** [*greegoros/ee/o*]

fat **το λίπος** [*to leepos*]

fat (*large*) **χοντρός/ή/ό** [*khondros/ee/o*]

fatal **θανάσιμος/η/ο** [*thanaseemos/ee/o*]

father **ο πατέρας** [*o pateras*]

father-in-law **ο πεθερός** [*o petheros*]

fault (*defect*) **η βλάβη** [*ee vlavee*]

faulty **ελαττωματικός/ή/ό** [*elatomateekos/ee/o*]

favourite **ο αγαπημένος/η/ο** [*o agapeemenos/ee/o*]

feather **η φτερούγα** [*ee fterooga*]

fed up: I am fed up **βαριέμαι** [*varyeme*]

feed: I feed **ταΐζω** [*taeezo*]

   (*breast feed*) **θηλάζω** [*theelazo*]

feel: I feel **αισθάνομαι** [*esthanome*]

   you feel (*s., informal*) **αισθάνεσαι** [*esthanese*]

   he/she/it feels **αισθάνεται** [*esthanete*]

we feel **αισθανόμαστε** [*esthanomaste*]
you feel (pl., plural) **αισθάνεστε** [*esthaneste*]
they feel **αισθάνονται** [*esthanonde*]
I feel well/unwell **αισθάνομαι καλά/άσχημα** [*esthanome kala/askheema*]

felt-tip pen **το μαρκαδόρο** [*to markadhoro*]
female, feminine **θηλυκός/ή/ό** [*theeleekos/ee/o*]
feminist **ο φεμινιστής, η φεμινίστρια** [*o femeeneestees, ee femeeneestrya*]
fence **η περίφραξη** [*ee pereefraksee*]
ferry **το φέρρυ μποτ** [*to feree-bot*]
festival (village etc.) **το πανηγύρι** [*to paneeyeeree*]
   (film etc.) **το φεστιβάλ** [*to festeeval*]
fever **ο πυρετός** [*o peeretos*]
few **λίγοι** [*leeyee*]
   a few (some) **μερικοί** [*mereekee*]
fiancé(e) **ο αρραβωνιαστικός, η αρραβωνιαστικιά** [*o aravonyasteekos, ee aravonyasteekya*]
fibre **η ίνα** [*ee eena*]
field **το χωράφι** [*to khorafee*]
fig **το σύκο** [*to seeko*]
fight **η μάχη** [*ee makhee*]
file **ο φάκελλος** [*o fakelos*]
   (computer) **το αρχείο** [*to arkheeo*]
   (nail, DIY) **η λίμα** [*ee leema*]
fill: I fill **γεμίζω** [*yemeezo*]
   I fill in **συμπληρώνω** [*seembleerono*]
filling (dental) **το σφράγισμα** [*to sfrayeezma*]
film (cinema) **η ταινία** [*ee teneea*]
   (for camera) **το φιλμ** [*to feelm*]
film star **το σταρ του σινεμά** [*to star too seenema*]
filter **το φίλτρο** [*to feeltro*]
finance **τα οικονομικά** [*ta eekonomeeka*]
find: I find **βρίσκω** [*vreesko*]
fine (weather) **καλός/ή/ό** [*kalos/ee/o*]
   (OK) **εντάξει** [*endaksee*]
fine (penalty) **το πρόστιμο** [*to prosteemo*]
finish: I finish **τελειώνω** [*telyono*]
fire **η φωτιά** [*ee fotya*]
fire brigade **η πυροσβεστική υπηρεσία** [*ee peerozvesteekee eepeereseea*]

fire extinguisher ο πυροσβεστήρας [o peerozvesteeras]

firewood τα ξύλα [ta kseela]

firework το πυροτέχνημα [to peerotekhneema]

firm (company) η εταιρεία [ee etereea]

first πρώτος/η/ο [protos/ee/o]

first aid πρώτες βοήθειες [protes voeethyes]

first aid box/kit το κουτί πρώτων βοηθειών [to kootee proton voeethyon]

fish το ψάρι [to psaree]

fish: I fish/go fishing ψαρεύω [psarevo]

fishing το ψάρεμα [to psarema]

fishing rod το καλάμι [to kalamee]

fishmonger's το ψαράδικο [to psaradheeko]

fit (healthy) σε καλή φόρμα [se kalee forma]

fit: I fit ταιριάζω [teryazo]

fitting room ο θάλαμος πρόβας [o thalamos provas]

fix: I fix φτιάχνω [ftyakhno]

fizzy με ανθρακικό [me anthrakeeko]

flag η σημαία [ee seemea]

flashbulb το φλας [to flas]

flat (apartment) το διαμέρισμα [to dhyamereezma]

flat (level) επίπεδος/η/ο [epeepedhos/ee/o]
  (battery) άδειος/α/ο [adhyos/a/o]

flavour η γεύση [ee yefsee]

flaw το ελάττωμα [to elatoma]

flea η ψείρα [ee pseera]

flight η πτήση [ee pteesee]

flippers τα βατραχοπέδιλα [ta vatrakhopedheela]

flood η πλημμύρα [ee pleemeera]

floor το πάτωμα [to patoma]
  (storey) ο όροφος [o orofos]
  ground floor το ισόγειο [to eesoyo]

flour το αλεύρι [to alevree]

flower το λουλούδι [to looloodhee]

flu η γρίππη [ee greepee]

fluid το υγρό [to eegro]

fly η μύγα [ee meega]

foam ο αφρός [o afros]

fog η ομίχλη [ee omeekhlee]
  it's foggy έχει ομίχλη [ekhee omeekhlee]

foil **το αλουμινόχαρτο** [*to aloomeenokharto*]

folding (*chair etc.*) **πτυσσώμενος/η/ο** [*pteesomenos/ee/o*]

following (*next*) **επόμενος/η/ο** [*epomenos/ee/o*]

food **το φαγητό** [*to fayeeto*]

food poisoning **η τροφική δηλητηρίαση** [*ee trofeekee dheeleeteereeasee*]

foot **το πόδι** [*to podhee*]
  on foot **με τα πόδια** [*me ta podhya*]

football **το ποδόσφαιρο** [*to podhosfero*]

footpath **το πεζοδρόμιο** [*to pezodhromyo*]

for **για** [*ya*]

forbidden (it is) **απαγορεύεται** [*apagorevete*]

foreign **ξένος/η/ο** [*ksenos/ee/o*]

forest **το δάσος** [*to dhasos*]

forget: I forget **ξεχνάω** [*ksekhnao*]

forgive: I forgive **συγχωρώ** [*seenkhoro*]

fork **το πηρούνι** [*to peeroonee*]

form (*document*) **το έντυπο** [*to endeepo*]

fortnight **το δεκαπενθήμερο** [*to dhekapentheemero*]

forward **μπροστά** [*brosta*]

foundation (*make-up*) **η κρέμα βάσης** [*ee krema vasees*]

fountain **το σιντριβάνι** [*to seendreevanee*]

foyer **το φουαγιέ** [*to fwaye*]

fracture **το κάταγμα** [*to katagma*]

fragile **εύθραυστος/η/ο** [*efthrafstos/ee/o*]

frankly **ειλικρινά** [*eeleekreena*]

freckle **η φακίδα** [*ee fakeedha*]

free **ελεύθερος/η/ο** [*eleftheros/ee/o*]

freedom **η ελευθερία** [*ee eleunthereea*]

freeze: I freeze **παγώνω** [*pagono*]

freezer **η κατάψυξη** [*ee katapseeksee*]

frequent **συχνός/ή/ό** [*seekhnos/ee/o*]

fresh **φρέσκος/η/ο** [*freskos/ee/o*]

fridge **το ψυγείο** [*to pseeyeeo*]

fried **τηγανητός/ή/ό** [*teeganeetos/ee/o*]

friend **ο φίλος, η φίλη** [*o feelos, ee feelee*]

frightened **φοβισμένος/η/ο** [*foveezmenos/ee/o*]
  I am frightened **φοβάμαι** [*fovame*]

fringe (*hair*) **η φράντζα** [*ee frandza*]

frog **ο βάτραχος** [*o vatrakhos*]

from από [*apo*]
front: in front (of) μπροστά (από) [*brosta (apo)*]
front door η εξώπορτα [*ee eksoporta*]
frontier τα σύνορα [*ta seenora*]
frost η παγωνιά [*ee pagonya*]
frozen παγωμένος/η/ο [*pagomenos/ee/o*]
fruit το φρούτο [*to frooto*]
fruit shop το μανάβικο [*to manaveeko*]
frying pan το τηγάνι [*to teeganee*]
fuel το καύσιμο [*to kafseemo*]
full γεμάτος/η/ο [*yematos/ee/o*]
full board η πλήρης διατροφή [*ee pleerees dhyatrofee*]
full up γεμάτος/η/ο [*yematos/ee/o*]
funeral η κηδεία [*ee keedheea*]
funfair το λούνα παρκ [*to loona park*]
funny (amusing) διασκεδαστικός/ή/ό [*dhyaskedhasteekos/ee/o*]
    (peculiar) περίεργος/η/ο [*peree-ergos/ee/o*]
fur η γούνα [*ee goona*]
furniture τα έπιπλα [*ta epeepla*]
further on πιο πέρα [*pyo pera*]
fuse η ασφάλεια [*ee asfalya*]

G

gallery η γκαλερί [*ee galeree*]
gambling η χαρτοπαιξία [*ee khartopekseea*]
game το παιχνίδι [*to pekhneedhee*]
    (match) ο αγώνας [*o agonas*]
    (hunting) το κυνήγι [*to keeneeyee*]
garage το γκαράζ [*to garaz*]
    (filling station) το βενζινάδικο [*to venzeenadheeko*]
garden ο κήπος [*o keepos*]
gardener ο κηπουρός [*o keepooros*]
garlic το σκόρδο [*to skordho*]
gas το γκάζι [*to gazee*]
gas bottle/cylinder η φιάλη [*ee fyalee*]
gastritis η γαστρίτιδα [*ee gastreeteedha*]
gate η πόρτα [*ee porta*]
general γενικός/ή/ό [*yeneekos/ee/o*]

generous γενναιόδωρος/η/ο [yeneodhoros/ee/o]

gentle ήμερος/η/ο [eemeros/ee/o]

gentleman ο κύριος [o keeryos]

genuine γνήσιος/α/ο [gneesyos/a/o]

geography η γεωγραφία [ee yeografeea]

get: I get (obtain) παίρνω [perno]

get off: I get off (bus etc.) κατεβαίνω [kateveno]

get on: I get on (bus etc.) ανεβαίνω [aneveno]

gift το δώρο [to dhoro]

gin το τζιν [to dzeen]

gin and tonic το τζιν-τόνικ [to dzeen-toneek]

girl η κοπέλλα [ee kopela]

girlfriend η φιλενάδα [ee feelenadha]

give: I give δίνω [dheeno]

   can you give me . . . ? μου δίνετε . . . ; [moo dheenete . . .]

Glasgow η Γλασκώβη [ee glaskovee]

glass (container) το ποτήρι [to poteeree]

   (material) το γυαλί [to yalee]

glasses τα γυαλιά [ta yalya]

glove το γάντι [to gandee]

glue η κόλλα [ee kola]

go: I go πάω [pao]

   let's go πάμε [pame]

go down: I go down κατεβαίνω [kateveno]

go in: I go in μπαίνω [beno]

go out: I go out βγαίνω [vyeno]

go up: I go up ανεβαίνω [aneveno]

goal (sport) το γκολ [to gol]

goat το κατσίκι [to katseekee]

God ο θεός [o theos]

goggles (diving) τα γυαλιά κατάδυσης [ta yalya katadheesees]

gold το χρυσάφι [to khreesafee]

   (made of) gold χρυσαφένιος/α/ο [khreesafenyos/a/o]

golf το γκολφ [to golf]

golf clubs τα μπαστούνια του γκολφ [ta bastoonya too golf]

golf course το γήπεδο του γκολφ [to yeepedho too golf]

good καλός/ή/ό [kalos/ee/o]

goodbye αντίο [adeeo]

good evening καλησπέρα [kaleespera]

good morning καλημέρα [kaleemera]

goodnight **καληνύχτα** [*kaleeneekhta*]
government **η κυβέρνηση** [*ee keeverneesee*]
gram **το γραμμάριο** [*to gramaryo*]
grammar **η γραμματική** [*ee gramateekee*]
grandchildren **τα εγγόνια** [*ta engonya*]
granddaughter **η εγγονή** [*ee engonee*]
grandfather **ο παππούς** [*o papoos*]
grandmother **η γιαγιά** [*ee yaya*]
grandson **ο εγγονός** [*o engonos*]
grandstand **η εξέδρα** [*ee eksedhra*]
grape **το σταφύλι** [*to stafeelee*]
grapefruit **το γρέιπφρουτ** [*to gre-eepfroot*]
grass **το χορτάρι** [*to khortaree*]
grateful **ευγνώμων** [*evgnomon*]
greasy **λιπαρός/ή/ό** [*leeparos/ee/o*]
great **μεγάλος/η/ο** [*megalos/ee/o*]
great! **θαυμάσια!** [*thavmasya*]
Great Britain **η Μεγάλη Βρετανία** [*ee megalee vretaneea*]
green **πράσινος/η/ο** [*praseenos/ee/o*]
green card **η πράσινη κάρτα** [*ee praseenee karta*]
greengrocer's **το μανάβικο** [*to manaveeko*]
greet: I greet **χαιρετώ** [*khereto*]
grey **γκρίζος/η/ο** [*greezos/ee/o*]
grilled **της σχάρας** [*tees skharas*]
grocer's **το μπακάλικο** [*to bakaleeko*]
ground **το έδαφος** [*to edhafos*]
ground floor **το ισόγειο** [*to eesoyo*]
groundsheet **ο μουσαμάς εδάφους** [*o moosamas edhafoos*]
group **η ομάδα** [*ee omadha*]
  (music) **το συγκρότημα** [*to seengroteema*]
grow: I grow (cultivate) **καλλιεργώ** [*kalyergo*]
  I grow up **μεγαλώνω** [*megalono*]
grown up **μεγάλος/η/ο** [*megalos/ee/o*]
guarantee **η εγγύηση** [*ee engee-eesee*]
guest **ο ξένος, η ξένη** [*o ksenos, ee ksenee*]
guest house **το πανσιόν** [*to pansyon*]
guide **ο/η ξεναγός** [*o/ee ksenagos*]
guidebook **ο οδηγός** [*o odheegos*]
guided tour **η ξενάγηση** [*ee ksenayeesee*]
guilty **ένοχος/η/ο** [*enokhos/ee/o*]

guitar η κιθάρα [ee keethara]
gun το όπλο [to oplo]
gymnastics η γυμναστική [ee yeemnasteekee]

H

habit (custom) το έθιμο [to etheemo]
haemorrhoids οι αιμορροΐδες [ee emoroeedhes]
hail το χιονόνερο [to khyononero]
hair το μαλλιά [ta malya]
hairbrush η βούρτσα [ee voortsa]
hair curlers το μπικουτί [to beekootee]
haircut το κούρεμα [to koorema]
hairdresser's το κομμωτήριο [to komoteeryo]
hairdryer ο στεγνωτήρας [o stegnoteeras]
hairgrip το τσιμπιδάκι [to tseembeedhakee]
hairspray το σπρέϊ για μαλλιά [to spre-ee ya malya]
half το μισό [to meeso]
half μισός/ή/ό [meesos/ee/o]
half an hour μισή ώρα [meesee ora]
half board η ημιδιατροφή [ee eemeedhyatrofee]
half past (see Time, page 213) και μισή [ke meesee]
half price/fare το μισό εισιτήριο [to meeso eeseeteeryo]
hall (in house) το χωλ [to khol]
    (concert) η αίθουσα [ee ethoosa]
ham το ζαμπόν [to zambon]
hamburger το χάμπουργκερ [to khamboorger]
hammer το σφυρί [to sfeeree]
hand το χέρι [to kheree]
handbag η τσάντα [ee tsanda]
hand cream η κρέμα χεριών [ee krema kheryon]
handicapped ανάπηρος/η/ο [anapeeros/ee/o]
handkerchief το μαντήλι [to mandeelee]
handle το χερούλι [kheroolee]
hand luggage οι χειραποσκευές [ee kheeraposkeves]
hand-made χειροποίητος/η/ο [kheeropee-eetos/ee/o]
hangover: I have a hangover έχω βαρύ κεφάλι [ekho varee kefalee]
hang (up): I hang (up) κρεμάω [kremao]
happen: what is happening? τι συμβαίνει; [tee seemvenee]
    what has happened? τι έγινε; [tee eyeene]

happy **ευτυχισμένος/η/ο** [*efteekheezmenos/ee/o*]

harbour **το λιμάνι** [*to leemanee*]

hard **σκληρός/ή/ό** [*skleeros/ee/o*]

   (*difficult*) **δύσκολος/η/ο** [*dheeskolos/ee/o*]

hat **το καπέλλο** [*to kapelo*]

hate: I hate **μισώ** [*meeso*]

have: I have **έχω** [*ekho*]

   do you have . . . ? **μήπως έχετε . . . ;** [*meepos ekhete . . .*]

hay fever **το αλλεργικό σινάχι** [*to aleryeeko seenakhee*]

hazelnut **το φουντούκι** [*to foondookee*]

he **αυτός** [*aftos*] (*see page 201*)

head **το κεφάλι** [*to kefalee*]

   (*boss*) **ο/η προϊστάμενος** [*o/ee proeestamenos*]

headache **ο πονοκέφαλος** [*o ponokefalos*]

headphones **τα ακουστικά** [*ta akoosteeka*]

heal: I heal **θεραπεύω** [*therapevo*]

health **η υγεία** [*ee eeyeea*]

health foods **οι υγιεινές τροφές** [*ee eeyee-eenes trofes*]

healthy **υγιής, υγιής, υγιές** [*eeyee-ees, eeyee-ees, eeyee-es*]

hear: I hear **ακούω** [*akoo-o*]

hearing aid **το ακουστικό** [*to akoosteeko*]

heart **η καρδιά** [*ee kardhya*]

heart attack **η καρδιακή προσβολή** [*ee kardhyakee prozvolee*]

heat **η ζέστη** [*ee zestee*]

heater **η θερμάστρα** [*ee thermastra*]

heating **η θέρμανση** [*ee thermansee*]

heaven **ο ουρανός** [*o ooranos*]

heavy **βαρύς, βαρειά, βαρύ** [*varees, varya, varee*]

heel **η φτέρνα** [*ee fterna*]

   (*shoe*) **το τακούνι** [*to takoonee*]

height **το ύψος** [*to eepsos*]

helicopter **το ελικόπτερο** [*to eleekoptero*]

hell **η κόλαση** [*ee kolasee*]

hello **γειά σας!, γειά σου!** [*yasas, yasoo*]

help **η βοήθεια** [*ee voeethya*]

   help! **βοήθεια!** [*voeethya*]

help: I help **βοηθάω** [*voeethao*]

her **αυτή** [*aftee*] (*see page 203*)

her, hers **δικός/ή/ό της** (*see page 203*) [*dheekos/ee/o tees*]

herb **το βότανο** [*to votano*]

herbal tea το τσάι του βουνού [to tsaee too voonoo]

here εδώ [edho]

hiccups; I have hiccups έχω λόξυγγα [ekho lokseenga]

high ψηλός/ή/ό [pseelos/ee/o]

hijack η αεροπειρατεία [ee aeropeerateea]

hill ο λόφος [o lofos]

him αυτόν [afton] (see page 203)

hire: I hire νοικιάζω [neekyazo]

his δικός/ή/ό του (see page 203) [dheekos/ee/o too]

history η ιστορία [ee eestoreea]

hit: I hit χτυπάω [khteepao]

hitchhike: I hitchhike κάνω ωτοστόπ [kano otostop]

hobby το χόμπυ [to khobee]

hole η τρύπα [ee treepa]

holiday(s) οι διακοπές [ee dhyakopes]
   on holiday σε διακοπές [se dhyakopes]
   public holiday η αργία [ee aryeea]

holy άγιος/α/ο [ayos/a/o]

Holy Week η Μεγάλη Εβδομάδα [ee megalee evdhomadha]

home το σπίτι [to speetee]
   at home σπίτι [speetee]
   I go home πάω σπίτι [pao speetee]

home address η μόνιμη διεύθυνση [ee moneemee dhyeftheensee]

homosexual ο ομοφυλόφιλος [o omofeelofeelos]

honest τίμιος/α/ο [teemyos/a/o]

honeymoon το ταξίδι του μέλιτος [to takseedhee too meleetos]

hope: I hope ελπίζω [elpeezo]
   I hope so/not ελπίζω πως ναι/όχι [elpeezo pos ne/okhee]

horrible φρικτός/ή/ό [freektos/ee/o]

horse το άλογο [to alogo]

horse-riding η ιππασία [ee eepaseea]

hose το λάστιχο [to lasteekho]

hospital το νοσοκομείο [to nosokomeeo]

hot ζεστός/ή/ό [zestos/ee/o]
   I'm hot ζεσταίνομαι [zestenome]
   it's hot (weather) κάνει ζέστη [kanee zestee]

hot (spicy) πικάντικος/η/ο [peekandeekos/ee/o]

hotel το ξενοδοχείο [to ksenodhokheeo]

hour η ώρα [ee ora]

house το σπίτι [to speetee]

housewife η **νοικοκυρά** [*ee neekokeera*]

housework το **νοικοκυριό** [*to neekokeeryo*]

hovercraft το **ιπτάμενο δελφίνι** [*to eeptameno dhelfeenee*]

how? **πώς;** [*pos*]

how are you? **τι κάνετε/κάνεις;** [*tee kanete/kanees*]

how long? **πόσο καιρό;** [*poson-gero*]

how many? **πόσοι/ες/α;** [*posee/es/a*]

how much? **πόσος/η/ο;** [*posos/ee/o*]

how much is it? **πόσο κάνει;** [*poso kanee*]

human **ανθρώπινος/η/ο** [*anthropeenos/ee/o*]

   (*being*) ο **άνθρωπος** [*o anthropos*]

hungry: I am hungry **πεινάω** [*peenao*]

hunt: I hunt **κυνηγάω** [*keeneegao*]

hunting το **κυνήγι** [*to keeneeyee*]

hurry: I hurry **βιάζομαι** [*vyazome*]

hurt: I hurt **πονάω** [*ponao*]

   my . . . hurts **πονάει ο/η/το . . . μου** (*see page 177*) [*ponaee o/ee/to . . . moo*]

husband ο **άντρας** [*o andras*]

hut η **καλύβα** [*ee kaleeva*]

hydrofoil το **ιπτάμενο δελφίνι** [*to eeptameno dhelfeenee*]

hypermarket η **υπεραγορά** [*ee eeperagora*]

I

I **εγώ** (*see page 201*) [*ego*]

ice ο **πάγος** [*o pagos*]

   (*with drink*) τα **παγάκια** [*ta pagakya*]

ice cream το **παγωτό** [*to pagoto*]

ice rink η **πίστα για πατινάζ** [*ee peesta ya pateenaz*]

icy **παγωμένος/η/ο** [*pagomenos/ee/o*]

idea η **ιδέα** [*ee eedhea*]

if **αν** [*an*]

ill **άρρωστος/η/ο** [*arostos/ee/o*]

illness η **αρρώστια** [*ee arostya*]

imagination η **φαντασία** [*ee fandaseea*]

imagine: I imagine **φαντάζομαι** [*fandazome*]

immediately **αμέσως** [*amesos*]

immersion heater το **θερμοσίφωνο** [*to thermoseefono*]

impatient **ανυπόμονος/η/ο** [*aneepomonos/ee/o*]

important **σημαντικός/ή/ό** [*seemandeekos/ee/o*]

impossible **αδύνατος/η/ο** [*adheenatos/ee/o*]

impressive **εντυπωσιακός/ή/ό** [*endeeposyakos/ee/o*]

in **σε** (*see page 199*) [*se*]

included (. . . is included) **συμπεριλαμβάνεται . . .**
    [*seembereelamvanete . . .*]

income **το εισόδημα** [*to eesodheema*]

independent **ανεξάρτητος/η/ο** [*aneksarteetos/ee/o*]

indigestion **η δυσπεψία** [*ee dheespepseea*]

indoors **μέσα (στο σπίτι)** [*mesa (sto speetee)*]

industrial **βιομηχανικός/ή/ό** [*veeomeekhaneekos/ee/o*]

industry **η βιομηχανία** [*veeomeekhaneea*]

infected **μολυσμένος/η/ο** [*moleezmenos/ee/o*]

infection **η μόλυνση** [*ee moleensee*]

infectious **μεταδοτικός/ή/ό** [*metadhoteekos/ee/o*]

inflamed **ερεθισμένος/η/ο** [*eretheezmenos/ee/o*]

inflammation **η φλεγμονή** [*ee flegmonee*]

influenza **η γρίππη** [*ee greepee*]

informal **ανεπίσημος/η/ο** [*anepeeseemos/ee/o*]

information **οι πληροφορίες** [*ee pleeroforee-es*]

information office **το γραφείο πληροφοριών** [*to grafeeo pleeroforyon*]

injection **η ένεση** [*ee enesee*]

injured **τραυματισμένος/η/ο** [*travmateezmenos/ee/o*]

injury **το τραύμα** [*to travma*]

ink **το μελάνι** [*to melanee*]

inner **εσωτερικός/ή/ό** [*esotereekos/ee/o*]

innocent **αθώος/α/ο** [*atho-os/a/o*]

insect **το έντομο** [to *endomo*]

insect bite **το τσίμπημα** [*to tseembeema*]

insecticide **το εντομόκτονο** [*to endomoktono*]

insect repellent **το απωθητικό εντόμων** [*to apotheeteeko endomon*]

inside **μέσα (σε . . .)** [*mesa (se . . .)*]

insist: I insist **επιμένω** [*epeemeno*]

instant coffee **ο στιγμιαίος καφές** [*o steegmyeos kafes*]

instead of **αντί** [*andee*]

instructor **ο δάσκαλος, η δασκάλα** [*o dhaskalos, ee dhaskala*]

insulin **η ινσουλίνη** [*ee eensooleenee*]

insult **η προσβολή** [*ee prozvolee*]

insurance **η ασφάλεια** [*ee asfalya*]

insurance certificate **το πιστοποιητικό ασφάλειας** [*to peestopyeeteeko asfalyas*]

intelligent **έξυπνος/η/ο** [*ekseepnos/ee/o*]

interested: I'm (not) interested in . . . **(δεν) μ'ενδιαφέρει ο/η/το . . .** [*(dhen) mendhyaferee o/ee/to . . .*]

interesting **ενδιαφέρων, ενδιαφέρουσα, ενδιαφέρον** [*endhyaferon, endhyaferoosa, endhyaferon*]

interior **εσωτερικός/ή/ό** [*esotereekos/ee/o*]

international **διεθνής, διεθνής, διεθνές** [*dhyethnees, dhyethnees, dhyethnes*]

interpreter **ο διερμηνέας** [*o dhyermeeneas*]

internal **εσωτερικός/ή/ό** [*esotereekos/ee/o*]

interval (*theatre etc.*) **το διάλειμμα** [*to dhyaleema*]

interview **η συνέντευξη** [*ee seenendefksee*]

into **σε** (*see page 199*) [*se*]

introduce: I introduce **συστήνω** [*seesteeno*]

invite: I invite **προσκαλώ** [*proskalo*]

invitation **η πρόσκληση** [*proskleesee*]

iodine **το ιώδιο** [*to yodhyo*]

Ireland **η Ιρλανδία** [*ee eerlandheea*]

Irish **ιρλανδικός/ή/ό** [*eerlandheekos/ee/o*]

Irishman **ο Ιρλανδός** [*o eerlandhos*]

Irishwoman **η Ιρλανδέζα** [*ee eerlandheza*]

iron **το σίδερο** [*to seedhero*]

iron: I iron **σιδερώνω** [*seedherono*]

ironmonger **ο σιδεράς** [*o seedheras*]

is (*see* to be)

is there . . . ? **υπάρχει . . . ;** [*eeparkhee . . .*]

island **το νησί** [*to neesee*]

it **αυτός/ή/ό** (*see page 201*) [*aftos/ee/o*]

itch **η φαγούρα** [*ee fagoora*]

J

jacket **το σακκάκι** [*to sakakee*]

jam **η μαρμελάδα** [*ee marmeladha*]

jar **το βάζο** [*to vazo*]

jazz **η τζαζ** [*ee dzaz*]

jeans **το τζην** [*to dzeen*]

jelly **το ζελέ** [*to zele*]
jellyfish **η τσούχτρα** [*ee tsookhtra*]
Jesus, Jesus Christ **ο Ιησούς Χριστός** [*o yeesoos khreestos*]
jeweller's **το κοσμηματοπωλείο** [*to kozmeematopoleeo*]
Jew **ο Εβραίος** [*o evreos*]
Jewess **η Εβραία** [*ee evrea*]
Jewish **εβραϊκός/ή/ό** [*evraeekos/ee/o*]
job **η δουλειά** [*ee dhoolya*]
jogging **το τζόγκιν** [*to dzogeen*]
joke **το αστείο** [*to asteeo*]
journalist **ο/η δημοσιογράφος** [*o/ee dheemosyografos*]
journey **το ταξίδι** [*to takseedhee*]
judge **ο δικαστής** [*o dheekastees*]
jug **η κανάτα** [*ee kanata*]
juice **το ζουμί** [*to zoomee*]
  (*fruit*) **ο χυμός** [*o kheemos*]
jump: I jump **πηδάω** [*peedhao*]
jump leads **τα καλώδια μπαταρίας** [*ta kalodhya batareeas*]
jumper **το τρικό** [*to treeko*]
junction (*road*) **η διακλάδωση** [*ee dhyakladhosee*)

just (*only*) **μόνο** [*mono*]

K

keep: I keep **κρατάω** [*kratao*]
kettle **ο βραστήρας** [*o vrasteeras*]
key **το κλειδί** [*to kleedhee*]
key ring **ο κρίκος** [*o kreekos*]
kidney **το νεφρό** [*to nefro*]
kill: I kill **σκοτώνω** [*skotono*]
kilo(gram) **το κιλό** [*to keelo*]
kilometre **το χιλιόμετρο** [*to kheelyometro*]
kind (*sort*) **το είδος** [*to eedhos*]
kind (*generous*) **καλόκαρδος/η/ο** [*kalokardhos/ee/o*]
king **ο βασιλιάς** [*o vaseelyas*]
kiosk **το περίπτερο** [*to pereeptero*]
kiss **το φιλί** [*to feelee*]
kiss: I kiss **φιλώ** [*feelo*]
kitchen **η κουζίνα** [*ee koozeena*]

knickers (*women's*) το σλιπ [*to sleep*]
knife το μαχαίρι [*to makheree*]
knit: I knit πλέκω [*pleko*]
knock: I knock χτυπάω [*khteepao*]
knot ο κόμπος [*o kombos*]
know: I know (*someone*) γνωρίζω [*gnoreezo*]
  I don't know him/her δεν τον/τη γνωρίζω [*dhen ton/tee gnoreezo*]
  (*something*) ξέρω [*ksero*]
  I (don't) know (δεν) ξέρω [(*dhen*) *ksero*]
know (*how to*): I know how to ξέρω [*ksero*]
  I don't know how to . . . δεν ξέρω να . . . [*dhen ksero na . . .*]

L

label η ετικέτα [*ee eteeketa*]
lace η νταντέλα [*ee dandela*]
  (*shoe*) το κορδόνι [*to kordhonee*]
ladder η σκάλα [*ee skala*]
ladies and gentlemen κυρίες και κύριοι [*keeree-es ke keeryee*]
lady η κυρία [*ee keereea*]
lager η μπύρα [*ee beera*]
lake η λίμνη [*ee leemnee*]
lamb το αρνάκι [*to arnakee*]
lamp η λάμπα [*ee lamba*]
lamp post ο στύλος [*o steelos*]
land η γη [*ee yee*]
  (*country*) η χώρα [*ee khora*]
land: I land (*in plane*) προσγειώνομαι [*prosyeeonome*]
  (*from boat*) ξεμπαρκάρω [*ksembarkaro*]
landlady η ιδιοκτήτρια [*ee eedhyokteetrya*]
landlord ο ιδιοκτήτης [*o eedhyokteetees*]
lane (*country road*) ο χωματόδρομος [*o khomatodhromos*]
language η γλώσσα [*ee glosa*]
large μεγάλος/η/ο [*megalos/eelo*]
last τελευταίος/α/ο [*telefteos/a/o*]
  (*preceding*) προηγούμενος/η/ο [*proeegoomenos/ee/o*]
last: it lasts κρατάει [*krataee*]
late αργά [*arga*]
  I am late άργησα [*aryeesa*]
later αργότερα [*argotera*]

laugh το γέλιο [*to yelyo*]

laugh: I laugh γελάω [*yelao*]

launderette το πλυντήριο [*to pleendeeryo*]

laundry το πλυντήριο [*to pleendeeryo*]
  (*clothes for washing*) τα ρούχα για πλύσιμο [*ta rookha ya pleeseemo*]

law ο νόμος [*o nomos*]
  (*study subject*) τα νομικά [*ta nomeeka*]

lawyer ο/η δικηγόρος [*o/ee dheekeegoros*]

laxative το καθαρτικό [*to katharteeko*]

lazy τεμπέλης/α/ο [*tembelees/a/o*]

lead το μολύβδι [*to moleevdhee*]

lead-free αμόλυβδος/η/ο [*amoleevdhos/ee/o*]

leaf το φύλλο [*to feelo*]

leaflet το φυλλάδιο [*to feeladhyo*]

learn: I learn μαθαίνω [*matheno*]

learner ο μαθητής, η μαθήτρια [*o matheetees, ee matheetrya*]

least: at least τουλάχιστον [*toolakheeston*]

leather το δέρμα [*to dherma*]

leave: I leave (*message etc.*) αφήνω [*afeeno*]
  (*depart*) φεύγω [*fevgo*]

___

left αριστερός/ή/ό [*areesteros/ee/o*]
  on/to the left αριστερά [*areestera*]

left luggage (office) η φύλαξη αποσκευών [*ee feelaksee aposkevon*]

left-hand αριστερός/ή/ό [*areesteros/ee/o*]

left-handed αριστερόχειρ [*areesterokheer*]

leg το πόδι [*to podhee*]

legal νόμιμος/η/ο [*nomeemos/ee/o*]

lemon το λεμόνι [*to lemonee*]

lemonade η λεμονάδα [*ee lemonadha*]

lend: I lend δανείζω [*dhaneezo*]

length το μήκος [*to meekos*]
  (*duration*) η διάρκεια [*ee dhyarkya*]

lens ο φακός [*o fakos*]

lesbian η λεσβία [*ee lesveea*]

less λιγότερος/η/ο [*leegoteros/ee/o*]
  less (than) λιγότερο (από) [*leegotero (apo)*]

lesson το μάθημα [*to matheema*]

let: I let (*allow*) αφήνω [*afeeno*]
  (*rent*) νοικιάζω [*neekyazo*]

letter **το γράμμα** [to grama]

letterbox **το γραμματοκιβώτιο** [to gramatokeevotyo]

lettuce **το μαρούλι** [to maroolee]

level (height, standard) **το επίπεδο** [to epeepedho]

level (flat) **επίπεδος/η/ο** [epeepedhos/ee/o]

level crossing **η ισόπεδος διάβαση** [ee eesopedhos dhyavasee]

library **η βιβλιοθήκη** [ee veevlyotheekee]

licence **η άδεια** [ee adhya]

lid **το καπάκι** [to kapakee]

life **η ζωή** [ee zoee]

lifebelt **το σωσίβιο** [to soseevyo]

lifeboat **η ναυαγοσωστική λέμβος** [ee navagososteekee lemvos]

lifeguard **ο ναυαγοσώστης** [o navagosostees]

lifejacket **το σωσίβιο** [to soseevyo]

lift **το ασανσέρ** [to asanser]

light **το φως** [to fos]

light (coloured) **ανοικτός/ή/ό** [aneektos/ee/o]
   (weight) **ελαφρός/ή/ό** [elafros/ee/o]

light: I light (fire etc.) **ανάβω** [anavo]

light bulb **η λάμπα** [ee lamba]

lighter (cigarette) **ο αναπτήρας** [o anapteeras]

lightning **η αστραπή** [ee astrapee]

like (similar to) **όμοιος/α/ο** [omyos/a/o]
   like this/that **έτσι** [etsee]
   what is/are . . . like? **πώς είναι . . .** [pos eene . . .]

like: I like (one thing) **μ'αρέσει** [maresee], (more than one thing)
   μ'αρέσουν [maresoon]
   do you like . . . ? **σ'αρέσει . . . ; σ'αρέσουν . . . ;** (informal)
   [saresee, saresoon] **σας αρέσει . . . ; σας αρέσουν . . . ;**
   (formal) [sas aresee, sas aresoon]

likely **πιθανός/ή/ό** [peethanos/ee/o]

limited **περιορισμένος/η/ο** [peryoreezmenos/ee/o]

line **η γραμμή** [ee gramee]

lion **το λιοντάρι** [to lyondaree]

lipstick **το κραγιόν** [to krayon]

liqueur **το λικέρ** [to leeker]

liquid **το υγρό** [to eegro]

list **ο κατάλογος** [o katalogos]

listen (to): I listen **ακούω** [akoo-o]

litre **το λίτρο** [to leetro]

litter **τα σκουπίδια** [*ta skoopeedhya*]
little (*small*) **μικρός/ή/ό** [*meekros/ee/o*]
   a little **λίγο** [*leego*]
live: I live **ζω** [*zo*]
liver **το συκώτι** [*to seekotee*]
living-room **το σαλόνι** [*to salonee*]
loaf (of bread) **το ψωμί** [*to psomee*]
local **ντόπιος/α/ο** [*dopyos/a/o*]
lock **η κλειδαριά** [*ee kleedharya*]
   (*padlock*) **το λουκέτο** [*to looketo*]
lock: I lock **κλειδώνω** [*kleedhono*]
London **το Λονδίνο** [*to londheeno*]
lonely **μοναχός/ή/ό** [*monakhos/ee/o*]
long **μακρύς, μακρυά, μακρύ** [*makrees, makrya, makree*]
look (at): I look **κοιτάω** [*keetao*]
look after: I look after **φροντίζω** [*frondeezo*]
look for: I look for **ψάχνω** [*psakhno*]
look like: I look like **μοιάζω** [*myazo*]
loose **χαλαρός/ή/ό** [*khalaros/ee/o*]
   (*clothes*) **άνετος/η/ο** [*anetos/ee/o*]

335

lorry **το φορτηγό** [*to forteego*]
lorry-driver **ο οδηγός φορτηγού** [*o odheegos forteegoo*]
lose: I lose **χάνω** [*khano*]
lost property office **το γραφείο απολεσθέντων αντικειμένων** [*to grafeeo apolesthendon andeekeemenon*]
lot: a lot (of) **πολύς, πολλή, πολύ** [*polees, polee, polee*]
lotion **η λοσιόν** [*ee losyon*]
lottery **το λαχείο** [*to lakheeo*]
loud **δυνατός/ή/ό** [*dheenatos/ee/o*]
lounge **το σαλόνι** [*to salonee*]
love **η αγάπη** [*ee agapee*]
love: I love **αγαπάω** [*agapao*]
lovely **όμορφος/η/ο** [*omorfos/ee/o*]
low **χαμηλός/ή/ό** [*khameelos/ee/o*]
lower **χαμηλότερος/η/ο** [*khameeloteros/ee/o*]
lozenge **η παστίλια** [*ee pasteelya*]
lucky **τυχερός/ή/ό** [*teekheros/ee/o*]
luggage **οι αποσκευές** [*ee aposkeves*]
lump **το κομμάτι** [*to komatee*]
lunch **το μεσημεριανό** [*to meseemeryano*]

M

machine η μηχανή [*ee meekhanee*]
machinist η γαζώτρια [*ee gazotrya*]
mad τρελλός/ή/ό [*trelos/ee/o*]
madam η κυρία [*ee keereea*]
magazine το περιοδικό [*to peryodheeko*]
main κύριος/α/ο [*keeryos/a/o*]
make (brand) η μάρκα [*ee marka*]
make: I make φτιάχνω [*ftyakhno*]
make-up το μακιγιάζ [*to makeeyaz*]
male αρσενικός/ή/ό [*arseneekos/ee/o*]
man ο άντρας [*o andras*]
manager ο/η προϊστάμενος [*o/ee proeestamenos*]
managing director ο διευθυντής, η διευθύντρια
    [*o dhyeftheendees, ee dhyeftheendrya*]
many πολλοί/ές/ά [*polee/es/a*]
   not many όχι πολλοί [*okhee polee*]
map ο χάρτης [*o khartees*]
marble το μάρμαρο [*to marmaro*]
margarine η μαργαρίνη [*ee margareenee*]
market η αγορά [*ee agora*]
married παντρεμένος/η/ο [*pandremenos/ee/o*]
mascara η μάσκαρα [*ee maskara*]
masculine αρσενικός/ή/ό [*arseneekos/ee/o*]
mask η μάσκα [*ee maska*]
mass (church) η λειτουργία [*ee leetooryeea*]
match (game) ο αγώνας [*o agonas*]
matches τα σπίρτα [*ta speerta*]
material το υλικό [*to eeleeko*]
   (cloth) το ύφασμα [*to eefazma*]
mathematics τα μαθηματικά [*ta matheemateeka*]
matter: it doesn't matter δεν πειράζει [*dhem-beerazee*]
   what's the matter (with you)? τι έχεις; [*tee ekhees*]
   what's going on? τι συμβαίνει; [*tee seemvenee*]
mattress το στρώμα [*to stroma*]
mature ώριμος/η/ο [*oreemos/ee/o*]
mayonnaise η μαγιονέζα [*ee mayoneza*]
me (ε)μένα, με (see page 202) [*(e)mena, me*]
meadow το λειβάδι [*to leevadhee*]

meal **το φαγητό** [to fayeeto]

mean: what does this mean? **τι σημαίνει αυτό;** [tee seemenee afto]

meanwhile **εν τω μεταξύ** [en-do metaksee]

measles **τα ιλαρά** [ta eelara]

   German measles **τα ερυθρά** [ta ereethra]

measure: I measure **μετράω** [metrao]

measurements **τα μέτρα** [ta metra]

meat **το κρέας** [to kreas]

mechanic **ο μηχανικός** [o meekhaneekos]

medical **ιατρικός/ή/ό** [yatreekos/ee/o]

medicine (*subject*) **η ιατρική** [ee yatreekee]

   (*drug*) **το φάρμακο** [to farmako]

Mediterranean **η Μεσόγειος** [ee mesoyeeos]

medium **μέτριος/α/ο** [metryos/a/o]

medium dry (*wine*) **ημίγλυκος/η/ο** [eemeegleekos/ee/o]

meeting **η συνάντηση** [ee seenandeesee]

melon (honeydew) **το πεπόνι** [to peponee]

   (watermelon) **το καρπούζι** [to karpoozee]

member **το μέλος** [to melos]

mend: I mend **διορθώνω** [dhyorthono]

menu **ο κατάλογος** [o katalogos]

   set menu **το μενού** [to menoo]

message **το μήνυμα** [to meeneema]

metal **το μέταλλο** [to metalo]

meter **ο μετρητής** [o metreetees]

metre **το μέτρο** [to metro]

microwave (oven) **ο φούρνος μικροκυμάτων** [o foornos meekrokeematon]

midday **το μεσημέρι** [to meseemeree]

middle **η μέση** [ee mesee]

middle-aged **μεσήλικας** [meseeleekas]

midnight **τα μεσάνυχτα** [ta mesaneekhta]

migraine **η ημικρανία** [ee eemeekraneea]

mild (*taste*) **ελαφρός/ή/ό** [elafros/ee/o]

   (*temperature*) **ήπιος/α/ο** [eepyos/a/o]

mile **το μίλι** [to meelee]

milk **το γάλα** [ta gala]

milkshake **το μιλκσέϊκ** [to meelkse-eek]

mill **ο μύλος** [o meelos]

mince **ο κυμάς** [o keemas]

mind: do you mind if . . . ? σας ενοχλεί αν . . . ; [*sas enokhlee an . . .*]

I don't mind δεν πειράζει [*dhem-beerazee*]

mine (*possessive*) δικός/ή/ό μου (*see page 203*) [*dheekos/ee/o moo*]

minister ο/η υπουργός [*o/ee eepoorgos*]

minute (*time*) το λεπτό [*to lepto*]

mirror ο καθρέφτης [*o kathreftees*]

Miss (η) δεσποινίδα [*(ee) dhespeeneedha*]

miss: I miss (*bus etc.*) χάνω [*khano*]

   (*someone*) πεθυμώ [*petheemo*]

mist η ομίχλη [*ee omeekhlee*]

mistake το λάθος [*to lathos*]

mistaken λανθασμένος/η/ο [*lanthazmenos/ee/o*]

mixed μικτός/ή/ό [*meektos/ee/o*]

mixture το μίγμα [*to meegma*]

model το μοντέλο [*to modelo*]

   (*original*) το πρωτότυπο [*to prototeepo*]

modern σύγχρονος/η/ο [*seenkhronos/ee/o*]

moisturiser η ενυδατική κρέμα [*ee eneedhateekee krema*]

monastery το μοναστήρι [*to monasteeree*]

money τα χρήματα [*ta khreemata*]

month ο μήνας [*o meenas*]

monument το μνημείο [*to mneemeeo*]

moon το φεγγάρι [*to fengaree*]

moped το μηχανάκι [*to meekhanakee*]

more περισσότερος/η/ο [*pereesoteros/ee/o*]

morning το πρωί [*to proee*]

mortgage η υποθήκη [*ee eepotheekee*]

mosque το τζαμί [*to dzamee*]

mosquito το κουνούπι [*to koonoopee*]

mosquito net η κουνουπιέρα [*ee koonoopyera*]

most (of) ο/η/το περισσότερος/η/ο [*o/ee/to pereesoteros/ee/o*]

mother η μητέρα [*ee meetera*]

mother-in-law η πεθερά [*ee pethera*]

motor η μηχανή [*ee meekhanee*]

motorbike η μοτοσυκλέτα [*ee motoseekleta*]

motorboat η βενζινάκατος [*ee venzeenakatos*]

motor racing οι αυτοκινητοδρομίες [*ee aftokeeneetodhromee-es*]

motorway ο αυτοκινητόδρομος [*ee aftokeeneetodhromos*]

mountain το βουνό [*to voono*]

mountaineering η ορειβασία [*ee oreevaseea*]
moustache το μουστάκι [*to moostakee*]
mouth το στόμα [*to stoma*]
move: I move (*something*) κινώ [*keeno*]
  (*myself*) κινούμαι [*keenoome*]
Mr ο κύριος [*o keeryos*]
  (*as direct address*) κύριε [*keerye*]
Mrs η κυρία [*ee keereea*]
much πολύς, πολλή, πολύ [*polees, polee, polee*]
  not much όχι πολύ [*okhee polee*]
mug η κούπα [*ee koopa*]
museum το μουσείο [*to mooseeo*]
mushroom το μανιτάρι [*to maneetaree*]
music η μουσική [*ee mooseekee*]
musical μουσικός/ή/ό [*mooseekos/ee/o*]
musician ο/η μουσικός [*o/ee mooseekos*]
must: you must . . . πρέπει να . . . [*prepe na . . .*]
mustard η μουστάρδα [*ee moostardha*]
my δικός/ή/ό μου (*see page 203*) [*dheekos/ee/o moo*]

N

nail το καρφί [*to karfee*]
  (*finger/toe*) το νύχι [*to neekhee*]
nail file η λίμα [*ee leema*]
nail polish το βερνίκι [*to verneekee*]
nail polish remover το ασετόν [*to aseton*]
naked γυμνός/ή/ό [*yeemnos/ee/o*]
name το όνομα [*to onoma*]
  my name is . . . με λένε . . . [*me lene . . .*]
  what is your name? πώς σας λένε; [*pos sas lene*]
napkin η πετσέτα [*ee petseta*]
  paper napkin η χαρτοπετσέτα [*ee khartopetseta*]
nappy η πάνα [*ee pana*]
  disposable nappies οι πάνες μίας χρήσεως [*ee panes meeas khreeseos*]
narrow στενός/ή/ό [*stenos/ee/o*]
national εθνικός/ή/ό [*ethneekos/ee/o*]

nationality η εθνικότητα [ee ethneekoteeta]
natural φυσικός/ή/ό [feeseekos/ee/o]
naturally φυσικά [feeseeka]
naughty άτακτος/η/ο [ataktos/ee/o]
navy το ναυτικό [to nafteeko]
navy blue μπλε μαρέν [ble maren]
near (to) κοντά (σε) [konda (se)]
nearly σχεδόν [skhedhon]
necessary απαραίτητος/η/ο [apareteetos/ee/o]
necklace το κολλιέ [to kolye]
need: I need χρειάζομαι [khryazome]
needle η βελόνα [ee velona]
negative (photo) το αρνητικό [to arneeteeko]
neighbour ο γείτονας, η γειτόνισσα [o yeetonas, ee yeetoneesa]
neither . . . nor ούτε . . . ούτε [oote . . . oote]
nephew ο ανεψιός [o anepsyos]
nervous νευρικός/ή/ό [nevreekos/ee/o]
net το δίκτυ [to dheektee]
never ποτέ [pote]

340

new καινούριος/α/ο [kenooryos/a/o]
New Year ο Καινούριος Χρόνος [o kenooryos khronos]
New Year's Day η Πρωτοχρονιά [ee protokhronya]
news τα νέα [ta nea]
   (on TV, radio) οι ειδήσεις [ee eedheesees]
newspaper η εφημερίδα [ee efeemereedha]
newspaper kiosk το περίπτερο [to pereeptero]
next επόμενος/η/ο [epomenos/ee/o]
   next week/month/year (see page 212)
nice (person) συμπαθητικός/ή/ό [seembatheeteekos/ee/o]
   (place etc.) ωραίος/α/ο [oreos/a/o]
niece η ανεψιά [ee anepsya]
night η νύχτα [ee neekhta]
nightclub το (νυχτερινό) κέντρο [to (neekhtereeno) kendro]
nightdress το νυχτικό [to neekhteeko]
no όχι [okhee]
nobody κανένας (m.), καμμία (f.) [kanenas, kameea]
noise ο θόρυβος [o thoreevos]
noisy θορυβώδης/ης/ες [thoreevodhees/ees/es]
non-alcoholic μη οινοπνευματώδης/ης/ες [mee eenopnevmatodhees/ees/es]

none **κανένας, καμμία, κανένα** [*kanenas, kameea, kanena*]

non-smoking **μη καπνίζοντες** [*mee kapneezondes*]

normal **κανονικός/ή/ό** [*kanoneekos/ee/o*]

north **ο βορράς** [*o voras*]

northern **βόρειος/α/ο** [*voryos/a/o*]

nose **η μύτη** [*ee meetee*]

nosebleed **η ρινορραγία** [*ee reenorayeea*]

  I've got a nosebleed **άνοιξε η μύτη μου** [*aneekse ee meetee moo*]

not **δεν** [*dhen*]

note (*bank*) **το χαρτονόμισμα** [*to khartonomeezma*]

notepad **το μπλοκ** [*to blok*]

nothing **τίποτα** [*teepota*]

nothing else **τίποτ'άλλο** [*teepotalo*]

now **τώρα** [*tora*]

nowhere **πουθενά** [*poothena*]

nuclear **πυρηνικός/ή/ό** [*peereeneekos/ee/o*]

nuclear energy **η πυρηνική ενέργεια** [*ee peereeneekee enerya*]

number **ο αριθμός** [*o areethmos*]

nurse **ο νοσοκόμος, η νοσοκόμα** [*o nosokomos, ee nosokoma*]

nut **ο ξηρός καρπός** [*o kseeros karpos*]

  (*for bolt*) **το παξιμάδι** [*to pakseemadhee*]

nylon **το νάυλον** [*to naeelon*]

O

oar **το κουπί** [*to koopee*]

object **το αντικείμενο** [*to andeekeemeno*]

obvious **φανερός/ή/ό** [*faneros/ee/o*]

occasionally **αραιά και πού** [*area ke poo*]

occupied (*seat*) **πιασμένος/η/ο** [*pyazmenos/ee/o*]

odd **περίεργος/η/ο** [*peree-ergos/ee/o*]

  (*not even*) **μονός/ή/ό** [*monos/ee/o*]

of (*see page 203*)

of course **φυσικά** [*feeseeka*]

off (*switched off*) **κλειστός/ή/ό** [*kleestos/ee/o*]

office **το αξίωμα** [*to akseeoma*]

  (*room*) **το γραφείο** [*to grafeeo*]

official **επίσημος/η/ο** [*epeeseemos/ee/o*]

often συχνός/ή/ό [*seekhnos/ee/o*]
   how often? κάθε πόσο; [*kathe poso*]
oil το λάδι [*to ladhee*]
OK εντάξει [*endaksee*]
old γέρος/η/ο [*yeros/ee/o*]
   how old are you? πόσων χρονών είσαστε; [*poson khronon eesaste*]
   (to a child) πόσων χρονών είσαι; [*poson khronon eese*]
   how old is he/she? πόσων χρονών είναι; [*poson khronon eene*]
   I am . . . years old είμαι . . . χρονών [*eeme . . . khronon*]
old-fashioned ντεμοντέ [*demode*]
old woman η γριά [*ee grya*]
olive η ελιά [*ee elya*]
olive oil το λάδι [*to ladhee*]
on (πάνω) σε (*see page 199*) [(*pano*) *se*]
   (switched on) ανοικτός/ή/ό [*aneektos/ee/o*]
once μία φορά [*meea fora*]
onion το κρεμμύδι [*to kremeedhee*]
only μόνο [*mono*]
open ανοικτός/ή/ό [*aneektos/ee/o*]
open: I open ανοίγω [*aneego*]
opera η όπερα [*ee opera*]
operation η εγχείρηση [*ee enkheereesee*]
opinion η γνώμη [*ee gnomee*]
   in my opinion κατά τη γνώμη μου [*kata tee gnomee moo*]
opposite (contrary) αντίθετος/η/ο [*andeethetos/ee/o*]
opposite (to) απέναντι (από) [*apenandee (apo)*]
optician ο οπτικός [*o opteekos*]
or ή [*ee*]
orange (fruit) το πορτοκάλι [*to portokalee*]
   (colour) πορτοκαλής/ιά/ί [*portokalees/ya/ee*]
orangeade η πορτοκαλάδα [*ee portokaladha*]
order (restaurant etc.) η παραγγελία [*ee parangeleea*]
   (command) η εντολή [*ee endolee*]
order: I order (in restaurant) παραγγέλλω [*parangelo*]
ordinary κοινός/ή/ό [*keenos/ee/o*]
organise: I organise κανονίζω [*kanoneezo*]
original (not copied) πρωτότυπος/η/ο [*prototeepos/ee/o*]
   (first) αρχικός/ή/ό [*arkheekos/ee/e*]
other άλλος/η/ο [*alos/ee/o*]
others άλλοι/ες/α [*alee/es/a*]

our, ours **δικός/ή/ό μας** (*see page 203*) [*dheekos/ee/o mas*]
out (of) **έξω (από)** [*ekso (apo)*]
  he/she is out **λείπει** [*leepee*]
outdoors **έξω** [*ekso*]
outside **έξω** [*ekso*]
over (*above*) **πάνω (από)** [*pano (apo)*]
overcast (sky) **συννεφιασμένος/η/ο** [*seenefyazmenos/ee/o*]
overcoat **το παλτό** [*to palto*]
overtake: I overtake **προσπερνάω** [*prospernao*]
owner **ο ιδιοκτήτης, η ιδιοκτήτρια** [*o eedhyokteetees, ee eedhyokteetrya*]

P

package tour **η οργανωμένη εκδρομή** [*ee organomenee ekdhromee*]
packet **το πακέτο** [*to paketo*]
padlock **το λουκέτο** [*to looketo*]
page **η σελίδα** [*ee seleedha*]
pain **ο πόνος** [*o ponos*]
painful: it is painful **πονάει** [*ponaee*]
painkiller **το παυσίπονο** [*to pafseepono*]
paint **το χρώμα** [*to khroma*]
paint: I paint **ζωγραφίζω** [*zografeezo*]
painter **ο/η ζωγράφος** [*o zografos*]
painting (*picture*) **η ζωγραφιά** [*ee zografya*]
  (*art*) **η ζωγραφική** [*zografeekee*]
pair **το ζευγάρι** [*to zevgaree*]
palace **το παλάτι** [*to palatee*]
pale **χλωμός/ή/ό** [*khlomos/ee/o*]
  (*colour*) **ανοικτός/ή/ό** [*aneektos/ee/o*]
pants (*women's panties*) **το σλιπ** [*to sleep*]
paper **το χαρτί** [*to khartee*]
paper clip **ο συνδετήρας** [*o seendheteeras*]
paraffin **το φωτιστικό πετρέλαιο** [*to foteesteeko petreleo*]
parcel **το δέμα** [*to dhema*]
pardon? **ορίστε;** [*oreeste*]
parents **οι γονείς** [*ee gonees*]
park **το πάρκο** [*to parko*]

park: I park παρκάρω [parkaro]
parking το πάρκινγκ [to parkeeng]
parking meter το παρκόμετρο [to parkometro]
parliament το κοινοβούλιο [to keenovoolyo]
part το μέρος [to meros]
parting (hair) η χωρίστρα [ee khoreestra]
partly εν μέρει [en meree]
partner (business) ο/η συνέταιρος [o/ee seeneteros]
party (celebration) η γιορτή [ee yortee]
pass: I pass (salt etc.) δίνω [dheeno]
   (exam/test) περνάω [pernao]
passenger ο/η επιβάτης [o/ee epeevatees]
passport το διαβατήριο [to dhyavateeryo]
past το παρελθόν [to parelthon]
past (time, see page 213) περασμένος/η/ο [perazmenos/ee/o]
pasta τα μακαρόνια [ta makaronya]
pastille η παστίλλια [ee pasteelya]
pastry (cake) η πάστα [ee pasta]
   (very thin) το φύλλο [to feelo]
path το μονοπάτι [to monopatee]

patient (hospital) ο/η ασθενής [o/ee asthenees]
pattern το σχέδιο [to skhedhyo]
pavement το πεζοδρόμιο [to pezodhromyo]
pay: I pay πληρώνω [pleerono]
   I pay cash πληρώνω μετρητοίς [pleerono metreetees]
pea το μπιζέλι [to beezelee]
peace η ειρήνη [ee eereenee]
peach το ροδάκινο [to rodhakeeno]
peanut το αράπικο [to arapeeko]
pear το αχλάδι [to akhladhee]
pedal το πετάλι [to petalee]
pedestrian πεζός/ή/ό [o pezos/ee/o]
pedestrian crossing η διάβαση πεζών [ee dhyavasee pezon]
peel: I peel ξεφλουδίζω [ksefloodheezo]
   (fruit) καθαρίζω [kathareezo]
peg ο γόμφος [o gomfos]
   (clothes) το μανταλάκι [to mandalakee]
pen το στυλό [to steelo]
pencil το μολύβι [to moleevee]
pencil sharpener η ξύστρα [ee kseestra]

penknife ο σουγιάς [o sooyas]

pension η σύνταξη [ee seendaksee]

pensioner ο/η συνταξιούχος [o/ee seendaksyookhos]

people ο κόσμος [o kozmos]

pepper το πιπέρι [to peeperee]
  green/red pepper η πιπεριά [ee peeperya]

peppermint η μέντα [ee menda]

perfect τέλειος/α/ο [telyos/a/o]

performance η παράσταση [ee parastasee]

perfume το άρωμα [to aroma]

perhaps ίσως [eesos]

period (menstrual) η περίοδος [ee pereeodhos]

period pains οι πόνοι της περιόδου [ee ponee tees peryodhoo]

perm η περμανάντ [ee permanant]

permit η άδεια [ee adhya]

permit: I permit επιτρέπω [epeetrepo]

person το πρόσωπο [to prosopo]

personal προσωπικός/ή/ό [prosopeekos/ee/o]

personal stereo το γουακμάν [to wakman]

petrol η βενζίνη [ee venzeenee]

petrol station το βενζινάδικο [to venzeenadheeko]

345

petticoat το μεσοφόρι [to mesoforee]

philosophy η φιλοσοφία [ee feelosofeea]

photocopy η φωτοτυπία [ee fototeepeea]

photocopy: I photocopy κάνω φωτοτυπία [kano fototeepeea]

photograph η φωτογραφία [ee fotografeea]

photographer ο/η φωτογράφος [o/ee fotografos]

photography η φωτογραφική [ee fotografeekee]

phrase book το βιβλίο χρήσιμων φράσεων [to veevleeo khreeseemon fraseon]

physics η φυσική [ee feeseekee]

piano το πιάνο [to pyano]

pick: I pick (choose) διαλέγω [dhyalego]
  (flowers etc.) κόβω [kovo]

pick up: I pick up σηκώνω [seekono]

picnic το πικ νικ [to peek neek]

picture η εικόνα [ee eekona]

piece το κομμάτι [to komatee]

pier η αποβάθρα [ee apovathra]

pig το γουρούνι [to gooroonee]

pill το χάπι [to khapee]
   (the) pill (contraceptive) το χάπι [to khapee]
pillow το μαξιλλάρι [to makseelaree]
pillowcase η μαξιλλαροθήκη [ee makseelarotheekee]
pilot ο πιλότος [o peelotos]
pin η καρφίτσα [ee karfeetsa]
pineapple ο ανανάς [o ananas]
pink ροζ [roz]
pipe (smoking) το τσιμπούκι [to tseembookee]
   (drain etc.) ο σωλήνας [o soleenas]
place το μέρος [to meros]
   (seat) η θέση [ee thesee]
plan (of town) ο χάρτης [o khartees]
plant το φυτό [to feeto]
plaster (sticking) ο λευκοπλάστης [o lefkoplastees]
plastic το πλαστικό [to plasteeko]
plastic bag η σακούλα νάϋλον [ee sakoola naeelon]
plate το πιάτο [to pyato]
platform (station) η αποβάθρα [ee apovathra]

play (theatre) το έργο [to ergo]
play: I play παίζω [pezo]
pleasant ευχάριστος/η/ο [efkhareestos/ee/o]
please παρακαλώ [parakalo]
pleased ευχαριστημένος/η/ο [efkhareesteemenos/ee/o]
plenty (of) άφθονος/η/ο [afthonos/ee/o]
pliers η τανάλια [ee tanalya]
plimsolls τα αθλητικά παπούτσια [ta athleeteeka papootsya]
plug (bath) η τάπα [ee tapa]
   (electrical) το φις [to fees]
plumber ο υδραυλικός [o eedhravleekos]
pneumonia η πνευμονία [ee pnevmoneea]
pocket η τσέπη [ee tsepee]
point το σημείο [to seemeeo]
poison το δηλητήριο [to dheeleeteeryo]
poisonous δηλητηριώδης/ης/ες [dheeleeteeryodhees/ees/es]
pole το κοντάρι [to kondaree]
   (north, south) ο πόλος [o polos]
police η αστυνομία [ee asteenomeea]
police car το περιπολικό [to pereepoleeko]
police station το τμήμα [to tmeema]

polish: I polish γυαλίζω [*yaleezo*]

polite ευγενικός/ή/ό [*evyeneekos/ee/o*]

politician ο/η πολιτικός [*o/ee poleeteekos*]

political πολιτικός/ή/ό [*poleeteekos/ee/o*]

politics η πολιτική [*ee poleeteekee*]

polluted μολυσμένος/η/ο [*moleezmenos/ee/o*]

pollution η μόλυνση [*ee moleensee*]

pool (*swimming*) η πισίνα [*peeseena*]

poor φτωχός/ή/ό [*ftokhos/ee/o*]

pop (*music*) το ποπ [*to pop*]

Pope ο Πάπας [*o papas*]

popular δημοφιλής/ής/ές [*dheemofeelees/ees/es*]

pork το χοιρινό [*to kheereeno*]

port (*harbour*) το λιμάνι [*to leemanee*]

portable φορητός/ή/ό [*foreetos/ee/o*]

porthole το φιλιστρίνι [*to feeleestreenee*]

portrait το πορτραίτο [*to portreto*]

possible δυνατός/ή/ό [*dheenatos/ee/o*]

    as . . . as possible όσο πιο . . . δυνατόν [*oso pyo . . . dheenaton*]

    if possible αν είναι δυνατόν [*an eene dheenaton*]

possibly ίσως [*eesos*]

post (*mail*) τα γράμματα [*ta gramata*]

post: I post ταχυδρομώ [*takheedhromo*]

postbox το γραμματοκιβώτιο [*to gramatokeevotyo*]

postcard η καρτ ποστάλ [*ee kart postal*]

postcode ο ταχυδρομικός κωδικός [*o takheedhromeekos kodheekos*]

poster η αφίσσα [*ee afeesa*]

postman ο ταχυδρόμος [*o takheedhromos*]

post office το ταχυδρομείο [*to takheedhromeeo*]

postpone: I postpone αναβάλλω [*anavalo*]

pot το δοχείο [*to dhokheeo*]

potato η πατάτα [*ee patata*]

pottery η κεραμεική [*ee kerameekee*]

potty (*child's*) το καθηκάκι [*to katheekakee*]

pound (*sterling*) η λίρα [*ee leera*]

pour: I pour (*drinks*) βάζω [*vazo*]

powder η σκόνη [*ee skonee*]

power η δύναμη [*ee dheenamee*]

    (*electrical*) το ρεύμα [*to revma*]

power cut η διακοπή ρεύματος [*ee dhyakopee revmatos*]

pram το **καροτσάκι** [*to karotsakee*]
prefer: I prefer **προτιμώ** [*proteemo*]
pregnant **έγκυος** (*f. adj.*) [*engeeos*]
prepare: I prepare **ετοιμάζω** [*eteemazo*]
prescription η **συνταγή** [*ee seendayee*]
present (*gift*) το **δώρο** [*to dhoro*]
pretty **ωραίος/α/ο** [*oreos/a/o*]
price η **τιμή** [*ee teemee*]
priest ο **παπάς** [*o papas*]
prime minister ο/η **πρωθυπουργός** [*o/ee protheepoorgos*]
prince ο **πρίγκιπας** [*o preengeepas*]
princess η **πριγκίπισσα** [*ee preengeepeesa*]
print (*photo*) η **εκτύπωση** [*ee ekteeposee*]
    (*picture*) η **γκραβούρα** [*ee gravoora*]
prison η **φυλακή** [*ee feelakee*]
private **ιδιωτικός/ή/ό** [*eedhyoteekos/ee/o*]
prize το **βραβείο** [*to vraveeo*]
probably **πιθανόν** [*peethanon*]
problem το **πρόβλημα** [*to provleema*]
producer (*radio/TV*) ο/η **παραγωγός** [*o/ee paragogos*]
profession το **επάγγελμα** [*to epangelma*]
professor ο **καθηγητής**, η **καθηγήτρια** [*o katheeyeetees,*
    ee katheeyeetrya]
profit το **κέρδος** [*to kerdhos*]
program (*computer*) το **πρόγραμμα** [*to programa*]
programme το **πρόγραμμα** [*to programa*]
(it is) prohibited **απαγορεύεται** [*apagorevete*]
promise η **υπόσχεση** [*ee eeposkhesee*]
promise: I promise **υπόσχομαι** [*eeposkhome*]
pronounce: I pronounce **προφέρω** [*profero*]
pronunciation η **προφορά** [*ee profora*]
properly **σωστά** [*sosta*]
property η **ιδιοκτησία** [*ee eedhyokteeseea*]
public **δημόσιος/α/ο** [*dheemosyos/a/o*]
public το **κοινό** [*to keeno*]
public holiday η **αργία** [*ee aryeea*]
pull: I pull **τραβάω** [*travao*]
pump up: I pump up **φουσκώνω** [*fooskono*]
puncture το **τρύπημα** [*to treepeema*]
pure **καθαρός/ή/ό** [*katharos/ee/o*]

purple **πορφυρός/ή/ό** [*porfeeros/ee/o*]
purse **το πορτοφόλι** [*to portofolee*]
push: I push **σπρώχνω** [*sprokhno*]
push-chair **το καροτσάκι** [*to karotsakee*]
put: I put **βάζω** [*vazo*]
pyjamas **η πυτζάμα** [*ee peedzama*]

Q

quality **η ποιότητα** [*ee pyoteeta*]
quarter **το τέταρτο** [*to tetarto*]
 (*of a town*) **η συνοικία** [*ee seeneekeea*]
quay **η προκυμαία** [*ee prokeemea*]
queen **η βασίλισσα** [*ee vaseeleesa*]
question **το ερώτημα** [*to eroteema*]
queue **η ουρά** [*ee oora*]
quick **γρήγορος/η/ο** [*greegoros/ee/o*]
quickly **γρήγορα** [*greegora*]
quiet **ήσυχος/η/ο** [*eeseekhos/ee/o*]
quite (*fairly*) **αρκετά** [*arketa*]
 (*completely*) **τελείως** [*teleeos*]

R

rabbi **ο ραββίνος** [*o raveenos*]
rabbit **το κουνέλι** [*to koonelee*]
rabies **η λύσσα** [*ee leesa*]
race **ο αγώνας δρόμου** [*o agonas dhromoo*]
racecourse/track **το στάδιο** [*to stadhyo*]
 (*horse*) **το ιπποδρόμιο** [*to eepodhromyo*]
races, racing (*track*) **οι αγώνες δρόμου** [*ee agones dhromoo*]
 (*horses*) **οι ιπποδρομίες** [*ee eepodhromee-es*]
 (*cars*) **οι αυτοκινητοδρομίες** [*ee aftokeeneetodhromee-es*]
racket (*tennis*) **η ρακέτα** [*ee raketa*]
radio **το ραδιόφωνο** [*to radhyofono*]
radioactive **ραδιενεργός/ή/ό** [*radhyenergos/ee/o*]
radio station **ο ραδιοφωνικός σταθμός** [*o radhyofoneekos stathmos*]
raft **η σχεδία** [*ee skhedheea*]

railway **ο σιδηρόδρομος** [*o seedheerodhromos*]

railway station **ο (σιδηροδρομικός) σταθμός**
  [*o (seedheerodhromeekos) stathmos*]

rain **η βροχή** [*ee vrokhee*]

  it's raining **βρέχει** [*vrekhee*]

raincoat **το αδιάβροχο** [*to adhyavrokho*]

rainy **βροχερός/ή/ό** [*vrokheros/ee/o*]

rape: I've been raped **με βιάσανε** [*me vyasane*]

rare **σπάνιος/α/ο** [*spanyos/a/o*]

  (steak) **σαινιάν** [*senyan*]

rash **το εξάνθημα** [*to eksantheema*]

raspberry **το σμέουρο** [*to zmeooro*]

rate (speed) **η ταχύτητα** [*ee takheeteeta*]

  (tariff) **η τιμή** [*ee teemee*]

rather (quite) **μάλλον** [*malon*]

raw **ωμός/ή/ό** [*omos/ee/o*]

razor **το ξυράφι** [*to kseerafee*]

razor blade **το ξυραφάκι** [*to kseerafakee*]

reach: I reach (arrive at) **φτάνω** [*ftano*]

read: I read **διαβάζω** [*dhyavazo*]

reading **το διάβασμα** [*to dhyavazma*]

ready **έτοιμος/η/ο** [*eteemos/ee/o*]

real (authentic) **πραγματικός/ή/ό** [*pragmateekos/ee/o*]

really (very) **πραγματικά** [*pragmateeka*]

really? **αλήθεια;** [*aleethya*]

rear **το πίσω μέρος** [*to peeso meros*]

reason **ο λόγος** [*o logos*]

receipt **η απόδειξη** [*ee apodheeksee*]

receiver (telephone) **το ακουστικό** [*to akoosteeko*]

reception **η δεξίωση** [*ee dhekseeosee*]

  (hotel etc.) **η ρεσεψιόν** [*ee resepsyon*]

receptionist **ο/η ρεσεψιονίστ** [*o/ee resepsyoneest*]

recipe **η συνταγή** [*ee seendayee*]

recognise: I recognise **αναγνωρίζω** [*anagnoreezo*]

recommend: I recommend **συστήνω** [*seesteeno*]

record **ο δίσκος** [*o dheeskos*]

record: I record **ηχογραφώ** [*eekhografo*]

record player **το πικ-άπ** [*to peek-ap*]

red **κόκκινος/η/ο** [*kokeenos/ee/o*]

  Red Cross **ο Ερυθρός Σταυρός** [*o ereethros stavros*]

reduction η έκπτωση [*ee ekptosee*]

refill το ανταλλακτικό [*to andalakteeko*]
(pen) η καρτούς [*ee kartoos*]

refrigerator το ψυγείο [*to pseeyeeo*]

refund: I refund επιστρέφω [*epeestrefo*]

region η περιοχή [*ee peryokhee*]

registered (letter) συστημένος/η/ο [*seesteemenos/ee/o*]

registration number ο αριθμός αυτοκινήτου [*o areethmos aftokeeneetoo*]

relation ο/η συγγενής [*o/ee seengenees*]

religion η θρησκεία [*ee threeskeea*]

remain: I remain παραμένω [*parameno*]

remember: I remember θυμάμαι [*theemame*]

remove: I remove αφαίρω [*afero*]

rent: I rent νοικιάζω [*neekyazo*]

rent(al) το νοίκι [*to neekee*]

repair: I repair επισκευάζω [*epeeskevazo*]

repeat: I repeat επαναλαμβάνω [*epanalamvano*]

reply απαντάω [*apandao*]

report (business etc.) η αναφορά [*ee anafora*]
(newspaper) το ρεπορτάζ [*to reportaz*]

report: I report (crime etc.) δηλώνω [*dheelono*]

rescue: I rescue σώζω [*sozo*]

reservation: I make a reservation κλείνω θέση [*kleeno thesee*]

reserve: I reserve κρατάω [*kratao*]

reserved κρατημένος/η/ο [*krateemenos/ee/o*]

responsible υπεύθυνος/η/ο [*eepeftheenos/ee/o*]

rest: I rest ξεκουράζομαι [*ksekoorazome*]

restaurant το εστιατόριο, η ταβέρνα [*to estyatoryo, ee taverna*]

restaurant-car το βαγόν-ρεστωράν [*to vagon-restoran*]

result το αποτέλεσμα [*to apotelezma*]

retire: I retire παίρνω σύνταξη [*perno seendaksee*]

return η επιστροφή [*ee epeestrofee*]
(ticket) με επιστροφή [*me epeestrofee*]

return: I return γυρίζω [*yeereezo*]
(give back) επιστρέφω [*epeestrefo*]

reverse gear το όπισθεν [*to opeesthen*]

reversed charge call το πληρωτέο τηλεφώνημα [*to pleeroteo teelefoneema*]

Rhodes η Ρόδος [*ee rodhos*]

rheumatism **ο ρευματισμός** [*o revmateezmos*]

ribbon **η κορδέλλα** [*ee kordhela*]

rice **το ρύζι** [*to reezee*]

rich **πλούσιος/α/ο** [*ploosyos/a/o*]

ride: I go for a ride **πάω βόλτα** [*pao volta*]

   I ride a bike/in a car **πάω με ποδήλατο/αυτοκίνητο** [*pao me podheelato/aftokeeneeto*]

   I ride a horse **κάνω ιππασία** [*kano eepaseea*]

right **δεξιός/ά/ό** [*dheksyos/a/o*]

   on/to the right **δεξιά** [*dheksya*]

right: you are (not) right **(δεν) έχετε δίκιο** [(*dhen*) *ekhete dheekyo*]

   that's right **σωστά** [*sosta*]

right-hand **δεξιός/ά/ό** [*dheksyos/a/o*]

ring (*jewellery*) **το δαχτυλίδι** [*to dhakhteeleedhee*]

ripe **ώριμος/η/ο** [*oreemos/ee/o*]

river **το ποτάμι** [*to potamee*]

road (*main*) **ο δρόμος** [*o dhromos*]

roadworks **τα έργα** [*ta erga*]

roast **ψητός/ή/ό** [*pseetos/ee/o*]

rob: I've been robbed **με κλέψανε** [*me klepsane*]

robbery **η κλοπή** [*ee klopee*]

roll (*bread*) **το ψωμάκι** [*to psomakee*]

roof **η στέγη** [*ee steyee*]

roof rack **η σχάρα** [*ee skhara*]

room (*house, hotel*) **το δωμάτιο** [*to dhomatyo*]

   (*space*) **ο χώρος** [*o khoros*]

rope **το σχοινί** [*to skheenee*]

rose **το τριαντάφυλλο** [*to tryandafeelo*]

rosé **ροζέ** [*roze*]

rotten **σάπιος/α/ο** [*sapyos/a/o*]

rough (*surface*) **ανώμαλος/η/ο** [*anomalos/ee/o*]

   (*sea etc.*) **κυματώδης/ης/ες** [*keematodhees/ees/es*]

round **στρογγυλός/ή/ό** [*strongeelos/ee/o*]

roundabout (*traffic*) **ο οδικός δακτύλιος** [*o odheekos dhakteelyos*]

   (*funfair*) **τα αλογάκια** [*ta alogakya*]

row (*theatre etc.*) **η σειρά** [*ee seera*]

to row: I row (*boat*) **κάνω κουπί** [*kano koopee*]

rowing boat **η βάρκα** [*ee varka*]

royal **βασιλικός/ή/ό** [*vaseeleekos/ee/o*]

rubber (*material*) το καουτσούκ [*to kaootsook*]
  (*eraser*) η γόμα [*ee goma*]
rubber band το λαστιχάκι [*to lasteekhakee*]
rubbish τα σκουπίδια [*ta skoopeedhya*]
rubbish! σαχλαμάρες! [*sakhlamares*]
rucksack ο σάκκος [*o sakos*]
rude αγενής, αγενής, αγενές [*ayenees, ayenees, ayenes*]
ruins τα ερείπια [*to ereepya*]
  (*ancient*) τα αρχαία [*ta arkhea*]
ruler (*for measuring*) ο χάρακας [*o kharakas*]
rum το ρούμι [*to roomee*]
run: I run τρέχω [*treko*]
rush hour η ώρα αιχμής [*ee ora ekhmees*]
rusty σκουριασμένος/η/ο [*skooryazmenos/ee/o*]

S

sad λυπημένος/η/ο [*leepeemenos/ee/o*]
safe (*strongbox*) το χρηματοκιβώτιο [*to khreematokeevotyo*]
safe ασφαλής/ής/ές, [*asfalees/ees/es*]
safety pin η παραμάνα [*ee paramana*]
sail το πανί [*to panee*]
sailboard το σέϊλμπορντ [*to se-eelbord*]
sailing η ιστιοπλοΐα [*ee eestyoploeea*]
sailing boat το ιστιοφόρο [*to eestyoforo*]
sailor ο ναύτης [*o naftees*]
saint ο άγιος, η άγια [*o ayos, ee aya*]
salad η σαλάτα [*ee salata*]
salami το σαλάμι [*to salamee*]
sale οι εκπτώσεις [*ee ekptosees*]
salesman ο πωλητής [*o poleetees*]
saleswoman η πωλήτρια [*ee poleetrya*]
salmon ο σολομός [*o solomos*]
Salonica η Θεσσαλονίκη [*ee thesaloneekee*]
salt το αλάτι [*to alatee*]
salty αλμυρός/ή/ό [*almeeros/ee/o*]
same ίδιος/α/ο [*eedhyos/a/o*]
sample το δείγμα [*to dheegma*]

sand η αμμουδιά [ee amoodhya]
sandal το πέδιλο [to pedheelo]
sandwich το σάντουιτς [to sandweets]
   toasted sandwich το τοστ [to tost]
sanitary towel η σερβιέτα [ee servyeta]
sauce η σάλτσα [ee saltsa]
saucepan η κατσαρόλα [ee katsarola]
saucer το πιατάκι [to pyatakee]
sauna το σάουνα [to saoona]
sausage το λουκάνικο [to lookaneeko]
save: I save (rescue) σώζω [sozo]
   (money) αποταμιεύω [apotamyevo]
say: I say λέω (see page 206) [leo]
   how do you say it? πώς το λένε; [pos to lene]
   people say that . . . λένε ότι . . . [lene otee . . .]
   that is to say δηλαδή [dheeladhee]
scales η ζυγαριά [ee zeegarya]
scarf το κασκόλ [to kaskol]
scene (theatre) η σκηνή [ee skeenee]

354

   (view) η θεά [ee thea]
scenery (countryside) το τοπίο [to topeeo]
scent το άρωμα [to aroma]
school το σχολείο [to skholeeo]
science η επιστήμη [ee epeesteemee]
   natural/physical sciences οι θετικές επιστήμες [ee theteekes
   epeesteemes]
scientist ο/η θετικός επιστήμων [o/ee theteekos epeesteemon]
scissors το ψαλίδι [to psaleedhee]
score: what's the score? τι είναι το σκορ; [tee eene to skor]
   final score το αποτέλεσμα [to apotelezma]
Scotland η Σκωτία [ee skoteea]
Scotsman ο Σκωτσέζος [o skotsezos]
Scotswoman η Σκωτσέζα [ee skotseza]
Scottish σκωτσέζικος/η/ο [skotsezeekos/ee/o]
scrambled eggs η στραπατσάδα [ee strapatsadha]
scratch η γρατσουνιά [ee gratsoonya]
screen (TV, cinema etc.) η οθόνη [ee othonee]
   (partition) το παραβάν [to paravan]
screw η βίδα [ee veedha]
screwdriver το κατσαβίδι [to katsaveedhee]

sculpture (*object*) το γλυπτό [*to gleepto*]
   (*art*) η γλυπτική [*ee gleepteekee*]
sea η θάλασσα [*ee thalasa*]
seafood τα θαλασσινά [*ta thalaseena*]
seasickness η ναυτία [*ee nafteea*]
season (*of year*) η εποχή [*ee epokhee*]
season ticket η κάρτα απεριορίστων διαδρομών [*ee karta aperyoreeston dhyadhromon*]
seat η θέση [*ee thesee*]
   (*chair*) το κάθισμα [*to katheezma*]
seatbelt η ζώνη ασφαλείας [*ee zonee asfaleeas*]
second δεύτερος/η/ο [*dhefteros/ee/o*]
second (*time*) το δευτερόλεπτο [*to dhefterolepto*]
secret το μυστικό [*to meesteeko*]
secret μυστικός/ή/ό [*meesteekos/ee/o*]
secretary ο/η γραμματέας [*o/ee gramateas*]
section το τμήμα [*to tmeema*]
see: I see βλέπω [*vlepo*]
   I can't see it δεν το βλέπω [*dhen to vlepo*]
seem: I seem φαίνομαι [*fenome*]
   it seems φαίνεται [*fenete*]

self-service η αυτοεξυπηρέτηση [*ee aftoekseepeereeteesee*]
sell: I sell πουλάω [*poolao*]
send: I send στέλνω [*stelno*]
senior citizen ο/η συνταξιούχος [*o/ee seendaksyookhos*]
sensible λογικός/ή/ό [*loyeekos/ee/o*]
sentence η πρόταση [*ee protasee*]
   (*prison*) η καταδίκη [*ee katadheekee*]
separate χωριστός/ή/ό [*khoreestos/ee/o*]
separated χωρισμένος/η/ο [*khoreezmenos/ee/o*]
serious σοβαρός/ή/ό [*sovaros/ee/o*]
serve: I serve σερβίρω [*serveero*]
service (*church*) η λειτουργία [*ee leetooryeea*]
service (*charge/car*) το σερβίς [*to servees*]
set (*group*) η ομάδα [*ee omadha*]
   (*series*) η σειρά [*ee seera*]
   (*hair*) το μιζ αν πλι [*to meez an plee*]
several μερικοί [*mereekee*]
sew: I sew ράβω [*ravo*]
sewing το ράψιμο [*to rapseemo*]

sex (*gender*) **το φύλο** [*to feelo*]
  (*intercourse*) **το σεξ** [*to seks*]

shade (*colour*) **η απόχρωση** [*ee apokhrosee*]

shadow **η σκιά** [*ee skya*]

shampoo **το σαμπουάν** [*to sambwan*]

shampoo and blow-dry **το λούσιμο και στέγνωμα** [*to looseemo ke stegnoma*]

shampoo and set **το λούσιμο και οντουλάρισμα** [*to looseemo ke ondoolareezma*]

sharp (*edge*) **κοφτερός/ή/ό** [*kofteros/ee/o*]
  (*pain*) **οξύς, οξεία, οξύ** [*oksees, okseea, oksee*]

shave: I shave (myself) **ξυρίζομαι** [*kseereezome*]

shaver **η ξυριστική μηχανή** [*ee kseereesteekee meekhanee*]

shaving cream/foam **ο αφρός ξυρίσματος** [*o afros kseereezmatos*]

she **αυτή** (*see page 201*) [*aftee*]

sheep **το πρόβατο** [*to provato*]

sheet **το σεντόνι** [*to sendonee*]

shelf **το ράφι** [*to rafee*]

shell (*egg, nut*) **το τσόφλι** [*to tsoflee*]
  (*sea*) **η αχηβάδα** [*ee akheevadha*]

shellfish **τα θαλασσινά** [*ta thalaseena*]

shelter **το καταφύγιο** [*to katafeeyo*]

shiny **γυαλιστερός/ή/ό** [*yaleesteros/ee/o*]

ship **το καράβι** [*to karavee*]

shirt **το πουκάμισο** [*to pookameeso*]

shock (*surprise*) **η έκπληξη** [*ee ekpleeksee*]

shoe **το παππούτσι** [*to papootsee*]

shoelace **το κορδόνι** [*to kordhonee*]

shoe polish **το βερνίκι** [*to verneekee*]

shoe shop **το υποδηματοπωλείο** [*to eepodheematopoleeo*]

shop **το μαγαζί** [*to magazee*]

shop assistant **ο πωλητής, η πωλήτρια** [*o poleetees, ee poleetrya*]

shopping: I go shopping **πάω για ψώνια** [*pao ya psonya*]

shopping centre **το εμπορικό κέντρο** [*to emboreeko kendro*]

short **κοντός/ή/ό** [*kondos/ee/o*]

shorts **το σορτς** [*to sorts*]

shout: I shout **φωνάζω** [*fonazo*]

show **η έκθεση** [*ee ekthese*]
  (*theatre*) **η παράσταση** [*ee parastasee*]

show: I show **δείχνω** [*dheekhno*]

shower **το ντους** [*to doos*]

shrink: does/will it shrink? **μαζεύει;** [*mazevee*]
  it has shrunk **μάζεψε** [*mazepse*]

shut **κλειστός/ή/ό** [*kleestos/ee/o*]

shutter **το παντζούρι** [*to pandzooree*]
  (*camera*) **το διάφραγμα** [*to dhyafragma*]

sick (*ill*) **άρρωστος/η/ο** [*arostos/ee/o*]

sick: I am sick **κάνω εμετό** [*kano emeto*]
  I feel sick **ζαλίζομαι** [*zaleezome*]

side **η πλευρά** [*ee plevra*]

sieve **το κόσκινο** [*to koskeeno*]

sight (*vision*) **η θεά** [*ee thea*]

sights (*tourist*) **τα αξιοθέατα** [*ta aksyotheata*]

sightseeing **ο τουρισμός** [*o tooreezmos*]

sign (*signpost*) **η πινακίδα** [*ee peenakeedha*]

sign: I sign **υπογράφω** [*eepografo*]

signal **το σήμα** [*to seema*]

signature **η υπογραφή** [*ee eepografee*]

silent **σιωπηλός/ή/ό** [*syopeelos/ee/o*]

silk **το μετάξι** [*to metaksee*]
  made of silk **μεταξωτός/ή/ό** [*metaksotos/ee/o*]

357

silver **το ασήμι** [*to aseemee*]
  made of silver **ασημένιος/α/ο** [*aseemenyos/a/o*]

similar (to) **παρόμοιος/α/ο (με)** [*paromyos/a/o (me)*]

simple **απλός/ή/ό** [*aplos/ee/o*]

since **από** [*apo*]
  (*because*) **επειδή** [*epeedhee*]

sing: I sing **τραγουδάω** [*tragoodhao*]

single (*ticket*) **απλός/ή/ό** [*aplos/ee/o*]
  (*unmarried*) **ελεύθερος/η/ο** [*eleftheros/ee/o*]

single room **το μονόκλινο** [*to monokleeno*]

sink **ο νεροχύτης** [*o nerokheetees*]

sir (*as direct address*) **κύριε** [*keerye*]

sister **η αδελφή** [*ee adhelfee*]

sister-in-law (*brother's wife*) **η νύφη** [*ee neefee*]
  (*husband's sister*) **η κουνιάδα** [*ee koonyadha*]

sit (down): I sit **κάθομαι** [*kathome*]

sitting (down) **καθιστός/ή/ό** [*katheestos/ee/o*]

size **το μέγεθος** [*to meyethos*]
  (*clothes, shoes*) **το νούμερο** [*to noomero*]

skate το πατίνι [*to pateenee*]

skate: I skate κάνω πατινάζ [*kano pateenaz*]

ski το σκι [*to skee*]

ski: I ski κάνω σκι [*kano skee*]

skiing το σκι [*to skee*]

skimmed milk το αποβουτυρωμένο γάλα [*to apovooteeromeno gala*]

skin το δέρμα [*to dherma*]

skindiving (*underwater swimming*) το υποβρύχιο κολύμπι [*to eepovreekhyo koleembee*]

(*underwater fishing*) το υποβρύχιο ψάρεμα [*to eepovreekhyo psarema*]

skirt η φούστα [*ee foosta*]

sky ο ουρανός [*o ooranos*]

sleep: I sleep κοιμάμαι [*keemame*]

sleeper/sleeping-car το βαγόν-λι [*to vagon-lee*]

sleeping bag το σλίπινγκ-μπαγκ [*to sleepeeng-bag*]

sleeve το μανίκι [*to maneekee*]

slice η φέτα [*ee feta*]

sliced σε φέτες [*se fetes*]

slide (*film*) η διαφάνεια [*ee dhyafanya*]

slim λεπτός/ή/ό [*leptos/ee/o*]

slip (*petticoat*) το κομπιναίζον [*to kombeenezon*]

slippery γλιστερός/ή/ό [*gleesteros/ee/o*]

slow αργός/ή/ό [*argos/ee/o*]

slowly αργά [*arga*]

small μικρός/ή/ό [*meekros/ee/o*]

smell η μυρουδιά [*ee meeroodhya*]

smell: it smells bad/good μυρίζει άσχημα/ωραία [*meereezee askheema/orea*]

it smells of . . . μυρίζει . . . [*meereezee . . .*]

smile το χαμόγελο [*to khamoyelo*]

smoke ο καπνός [*o kapnos*]

smoke: I smoke καπνίζω [*kapneezo*]

smoked καπνιστός/ή/ό [*kapneestos/ee/o*]

smooth λείος/α/ο [*leeos/a/o*]

sneeze: I sneeze φτερνίζομαι [*fterneezome*]

snorkel ο αναπνευστικός σωλήνας [*o anapnefsteekos soleenas*]

snow το χιόνι [*to khyonee*]

snow: it's snowing χιονίζει [*khyoneezee*]

so τόσο [toso]
   (thus) έτσι [etsee]
soap το σαπούνι [to sapoonee]
sober νηφάλιος/α/ο [neefalyos/a/o]
socialism ο σοσιαλισμός [o sosyaleezmos]
socialist ο/η σοσιαλιστής [o/ee sosyaleestees]
social worker ο/η κοινωνικός λειτουργός [o/ee keenoneekos leetoorgos]
sociology η κοινωνιολογία [ee keenonyoloyeea]
sock η κάλτσα [ee kaltsa]
socket (electrical) η πρίζα [ee preeza]
soda (water) η σόδα [ee sodha]
soft μαλακός/ή/ό [malakos/ee/o]
   (flabby) πλαδαρός/ή/ό [pladharos/ee/o]
soft drink το αναψυκτικό [to anapseekteeko]
sold out (we've . . .) τελείωσε (one thing), τελείωσαν (more than one thing) [teleeose, teleeosan]
soldier ο στρατιώτης [o stratyotees]
solid στέρεος/α/ο [stereos/a/o]
some λίγος/η/ο [leegos/ee/o]

359

somehow κάπως [kapos]
someone κάποιος/α [kapyos/a]
something κάτι [katee]
sometime κάποτε [kapote]
sometimes μερικές φορές [mereekes fores]
somewhere κάπου [kapoo]
so many τόσοι/ες/α [tosee/es/a]
so much τόσος/η/ο [tosos/ee/o]
son ο γιος [o yos]
song το τραγούδι [to tragoodhee]
son-in-law ο γαμπρός [o gambros]
soon σε λίγο [se leego]
   as soon as possible όσο πιο γρήγορα δυνατόν [oso pyo greegora dheenaton]
sore: I have a sore throat πονάει ο λαιμός μου [ponaee o lemos-moo]
sorry (pardon me) συγγνώμη! [seegnomee]
   I'm sorry λυπάμαι [leepame]
sort το είδος [to eedhos]

sound **ο ήχος** [*o eekhos*]

soup **η σούπα** [*ee soopa*]

sour **ξυνός/ή/ό** [*kseenos/ee/o*]

south **ο νότος** [*o notos*]

southern **νότιος/α/ο** [*notyos/a/o*]

souvenir **το ενθύμιο** [*to entheemyo*]

space (*room*) **ο χώρος** [*o khoros*]

   (*void*) **το κενό** [*to keno*]

   (*outer*) **το διάστημα** [*to dhyasteema*]

spade **το φτυάρι** [*to ftyaree*]

spanner **το κλειδί** [*to kleedhee*]

spare (*available*) **διαθέσιμος/η/ο** [*dhyatheseemos/ee/o*]

   (*left over*) **περιττός/ή/ό** [*pereetos/ee/o*]

spare time **οι ελεύθερες ώρες** [*ee eleftheres ores*]

spare wheel **η ρεζέρβα** [*ee rezerva*]

sparkling (*wine*) **αφρώδης/ης/ες** [*afrodhees/ees/es*]

speak: I speak **μιλάω** [*meelao*]

special **ειδικός/ή/ό** [*eedheekos/ee/o*]

specialist **ο/η ειδικός** [*o/ee eedheekos*]

speciality **η ειδικότητα** [*ee eedheekoteeta*]

special offer **η ειδική προσφορά** [*ee eedheekee prosfora*]

spectacles **τα γυαλιά** [*ta yalya*]

speed **η ταχύτητα** [*ee takheeteeta*]

speed limit **το όριο ταχύτητας** [*to oryo takheeteetas*]

spend: I spend (*money*) **ξοδεύω** [*ksodhevo*]

   (*time*) **περνάω** [*pernao*]

spice **το μπαχαρικό** [*to bakhareeko*]

spicy **πικάντικος/η/ο** [*peekandeekos/ee/o*]

spinach **το σπανάκι** [*to spanakee*]

spirits **τα οινοπνευματώδη ποτά** [*ta eenopnevmatodhee pota*]

splinter **το θραύσμα** [*to thravzma*]

spoil: I spoil **χαλνάω** [*khalnao*]

sponge (*bath*) **το σφουγγάρι** [*to sfoongaree*]

   (*cake*) **το παντεσπάνι** [*to pandespanee*]

spoon **το κουτάλι** [*to kootalee*]

   (*teaspoon*) **το κουταλάκι** [*to kootalakee*]

sport **το σπορ** [*to spor*]

spot **το σπυρί** [*to speeree*]

   (*place*) **το μέρος** [*to meros*]

sprain **το στραμπούλιασμα** [*to stramboolyazma*]

spray **το σπρέϊ** [to spre-ee]

spring (season) **η άνοιξη** [ee aneeksee]

square **η πλατεία** [ee plateea]

square (shape) **το τετράγωνο** [to tetragono]

stadium **το στάδιο** [to stadhyo]

stain **ο λεκές** [o lekes]

stainless steel **το ανοξείδωτο ατσάλι** [to anokseedhoto atsalee]

stairs **η σκάλα** [ee skala]

stalls (theatre) **η πλατεία** [ee plateea]

stamp (postage) **το γραμματόσημο** [to gramatoseemo]

stand (stadium) **η εξέδρα** [ee eksedhra]

standing (up) **όρθιος/α/ο** [orthyos/a/o]

staple **ο συνδετήρας** [o seendheteeras]

stapler **η συρραπτική** [ee seerapteekee]

star **το αστέρι** [to asteree]

start (beginning) **η αρχή** [ee arkhee]

start: I start **αρχίζω** [arkheezo]

starters (food) **οι μεζέδες, τα ορεκτικά** [ee mezedhes, ta orekteeka]

state **το κράτος** [to kratos]

station **ο σταθμός** [o stathmos]

361

station master **ο σταθμάρχης** [o stathmarkhees]

stationer's **το χαρτοπωλείο** [to khartopoleeo]

statue **το άγαλμα** [to agalma]

stay **η διαμονή** [ee dhyamonee]

stay: I'm staying at . . . **μένω σε . . .** [meno se . . .]

steak **το φιλέτο** [to feeleto]

steal: someone has stolen my . . . **κάποιος μου έκλεψε . . .** [kapyos moo eklepse . . .]

steam **ο ατμός** [o atmos]

steel **το ατσάλι** [to atsalee]

steep **απότομος/η/ο** [apotomos/ee/o]

step **το βήμα** [to veema]

  (stair) **το σκαλοπάτι** [to skalopatee]

step-brother **ο ξενάδελφος** [o ksenadhelfos]

step-children **τα προγόνια** [ta progonya]

step-daughter **η προγονή** [ee progonee]

step-father **ο πατριός** [o patreeyos]

step-mother **η μητριά** [ee meetreeya]

step-sister **η ξεναδέλφη** [ee ksenadhelfee]

step-son **ο προγονός** [o progonos]

stereo **το στέρεο** [*to stereo*]

sterling: pound sterling **η λίρα Αγγλίας** [*ee leera angleeas*]

steward/stewardess (*air*) **ο/η αεροσυνοδός** [*o/ee aeroseenodhos*]

stick (*piece of wood*) **το ξύλο** [*to kseelo*]

    (*walking*) **το μπαστούνι** [*to bastoonee*]

stick (*adhesive*): I stick **κολλάω** [*kolao*]

    it is sticky **κολλάει** [*kolaee*]

sticking plaster **ο λευκοπλάστης** [*o lefkoplastees*]

sticky tape **το σελοτέιπ** [*to selote-eep*]

stiff **σκληρός/ή/ό** [*skleeros/ee/o*]

still (*yet*) **ακόμα** [*akoma*]

    (*non-fizzy*) **χωρίς ανθρακικό** [*khorees anthrakeeko*]

sting (*insect*) **το τσίμπημα** [*to tseembeema*]

stock exchange **το χρηματιστήριο** [*to khreemateesteeryo*]

stockings **οι κάλτσες** [*ee kaltses*]

stolen: my . . . has been stolen **μου έκλεψαν . . . μου** [*moo eklepsan . . . moo*]

stomach **το στομάχι** [*to stomakhee*]

    stomach ache: I have a . . . **πονάει το στομάχι μου** [*ponaee to stomakhee-moo*]

    stomach upset **η στομαχική διαταραχή** [*ee stomakheekee dhyatarakhee*]

stone **η πέτρα** [*ee petra*]

stop (*bus*) **η στάση** [*ee stasee*]

stop: I stop **σταματάω** [*stamatao*]

    stop! **σταμάτα!** [*stamata*]

stopcock **ο διακόπτης του νερού** [*o dhyakoptees too neroo*]

storey **ο όροφος** [*o orofos*]

story **η ιστορία** [*ee eestoreea*]

stove (*cooker*) **η κουζίνα** [*ee koozeena*]

straight **ίσιος/α/ο** [*eesyos/a/o*]

straight on **ίσια** [*eesya*]

strange **περίεργος/η/ο** [*peree-ergos/ee/o*]

    (*foreign*) **ξένος/η/ο** [*ksenos/ee/o*]

strap **το λουρί** [*to looree*]

straw (*drinking*) **το καλαμάκι** [*to kalamakee*]

strawberry **η φράουλα** [*ee fraoola*]

stream **το ρεύμα** [*to revma*]

street **η οδός** [*ee odhos*]

street light **το φως του δρόμου** [*to fos too dhromoo*]

stretcher **το φορείο** [*to foreeo*]

strike **η απεργία** [*ee aperyeea*]

   are they on strike? **απεργούν;** [*apergoon*]

string **ο σπάγγος** [*o spangos*]

stripe **η ρίγα** [*ee reega*]

striped **ριγωτός/ή/ό** [*reegotos/ee/o*]

strong **δυνατός/ή/ό** [*dheenatos/ee/o*]

student **ο φοιτητής, η φοιτήτρια** [*o feeteetees, ee feeteetrya*]

studio **το ατελιέ** [*to atelye*]

study: I study **σπουδάζω** [*spoodhazo*]

stupid **κουτός/ή/ό** [*kootos/ee/o*]

style (air) **το ύφος** [*to eefos*]

   (fashion) **η μόδα** [*ee modha*]

styling mousse **το μους κτενίσματος** [*to moos kteneezmatos*]

subtitled **με υπότιτλους** [*me eepoteetloos*]

suburbs **τα προάστεια** [*ta proastya*]

succeed: I succeed **πετυχαίνω** [*peteekheno*]

success **η επιτυχία** [*ee epeeteekheea*]

such **τέτοιος/α/ο** [*tetyos/a/o*]

suddenly **ξαφνικά** [*ksafneeka*]

sugar **η ζάχαρη** [*ee zakharee*]

suit **το κοστούμι** [*to kostoomee*]

suitcase **η βαλίτσα** [*ee valeetsa*]

summer **το καλοκαίρι** [*to kalokeree*]

sun **ο ήλιος** [*o eelyos*]

sunbathe: I sunbathe **κάνω ηλιοθεραπεία** [*kano eelyotherapeea*]

sunburn: I get sunburnt **με καίει ο ήλιος** [*me ke-ee o eelyos*]

sunburnt **ηλιοκαμμένος/η/ο** [*eelyokamenos/ee/o*]

sunglasses **τα γυαλιά ηλίου** [*ta yalya eeleeoo*]

sunshade **η ομπρέλα** [*ee ombrela*]

sunstroke **η ηλίαση** [*ee eeleeasee*]

suntan cream/oil **η κρέμα/το λάδι για τον ήλιο** [*ee krema/to ladhee ya ton eelyo*]

supermarket **το σουπερμάρκετ** [*to soopermarket*]

supper **το δείπνο** [*to dheepno*]

supplement **το συμπλήρωμα** [*to seembleeroma*]

suppose: I suppose so **το υποθέτω** [*to eepotheto*]

suppository **το υπόθετο** [*to eepotheto*]

sure **σίγουρος/η/ο** [*seegooros/ee/o*]

surface **η επιφάνεια** [*ee epeefanya*]

surname το επώνυμο [*to eponeemo*]

surprise η έκπληξη [*ee ekpleeksee*]

surprised έκπληκτος/η/ο [*ekpleektos/ee/o*]

surrounded (by) τριγυρισμένος/η/ο (από)
  [*treeyeereezmenos/ee/o (apo)*]

sweat: I sweat ιδρώνω [*eedhrono*]

sweater το πουλόβερ [*to poolover*]

sweatshirt η φανέλα [*ee fanela*]

sweep: I sweep σκουπίζω [*skoopeezo*]

sweet γλυκός, γλυκειά, γλυκό [*gleekos, gleekya, gleeko*]

sweetener η ζαχαρίνη [*ee zakhareenee*]

sweets οι καραμέλες [*ee karameles*]

swelling το πρήξιμο [*to preekseemo*]

swim: I swim κολυμπάω [*koleembao*]

swimming το κολύμπι [*to koleembee*]

swimming pool η πισίνα [*ee peeseena*]

swimming trunks, swimsuit το μαγιό [*to mayo*]

switch ο διακόπτης [*o dhyakoptees*]

switch off: I switch off κλείνω [*kleeno*]

switch on: I switch on ανοίγω [*aneego*]

swollen πρησμένος/η/ο [*preezmenos/ee/o*]

symptom το σύμπτωμα [*to seemptoma*]

synagogue η συναγωγή [*ee seenagoyee*]

synthetic συνθετικός/ή/ό [*seentheteekos/ee/o*]

system το σύστημα [*to seesteema*]

T

table το τραπέζι [*to trapezee*]

tablet το χάπι [*to khapee*]

table tennis το πινγκ-πόγκ [*to peeng-pong*]

tailor ο ράφτης [*o raftees*]

take: I take παίρνω [*perno*]

take off: I take off (*remove*) βγάζω [*vgazo*]
  (*plane*) it takes off απογειώνεται [*apoyeeonete*]

take out: I take out βγάζω [*vgazo*]

taken (*seat*) πιασμένος/η/ο [*pyazmenos/ee/o*]

talcum powder το ταλκ [*to talk*]

talk: I talk μιλάω [*meelao*]

tall ψηλός/ή/ό [pseelos/ee/o]

tame ήμερος/η/ο [eemeros/ee/o]

tampon το ταμπόν [to tambon]

tap η βρύση [ee vreesee]

tape η ταινία [ee teneea]

tape measure η μεζούρα [ee mezoora]

tape recorder το κασετόφωνο [to kasetofono]

taste η γεύση [ee yefsee]

tasty νόστιμος/η/ο [nosteemos/ee/o]

tax ο φόρος [o foros]

taxi το ταξί [to taksee]

taxi rank η πιάτσα ταξί [ee pyatsa taksee]

tea το τσάι [to tsaee]

teabag το τσάι σε φακελλάκι [to tsaee se fakelakee]

teach: I teach διδάσκω [dheedhasko]

teacher ο δάσκαλος, η δασκάλα [o dhaskalos, ee dhaskala]

team η ομάδα [ee omadha]

teapot η τσαγιέρα [ee tsayera]

tear: I tear σχίζω [skheezo]

teaspoon το κουταλάκι [to kootalakee]

teat (for baby's bottle) το μπιμπερό [to beebero]

tea-towel η πετσέτα [ee petseta]

technical τεχνικός/ή/ό [tekhneekos/ee/o]

technology η τεχνολογία [ee tekhnoloyeea]

teenager ο/η τηνέϊτζερ [o/ee teene-eetzer]

telegram το τηλεγράφημα [to teelegrafeema]

telephone το τηλέφωνο [to teelefono]

telephone: I telephone τηλεφωνώ [teelefono]

telephone directory ο τηλεφωνικός κατάλογος [o teelefoneekos katalogos]

television η τηλεόραση [ee teeleorasee]

tell: I tell λέω (see page 206) [leo]

temperature η θερμοκρασία [ee thermokraseea]
   I have a temperature έχω πυρετό [ekho peereto]

temporary προσωρινός/ή/ό [prosoreenos/ee/o]

tender τρυφερός/ή/ό [treeferos/ee/o]

tennis το τένις [to tenees]

tennis court η πίστα [ee peesta]

tennis shoes τα αθλητικά παπούτσια [ta athleeteeka papootsya]

tent η σκηνή [ee skeenee]

terminal, terminus **το τέρμα** [*to terma*]

terrace **η ταράτσα** [*ee taratsa*]

terrible **τρομερός/ή/ό** [*tromeros/ee/o*]

terrorist **ο/η τρομοκράτης** [*o/ee tromokratees*]

thank you (very much) **ευχαριστώ (πολύ)** [*efkhareesto (polee)*]

that **ότι** [*otee*]

that, that one **εκείνος/η/ο** (see page 200) [*ekeenos/ee/o*]

the (see page 199)

theatre **το θέατρο** [*to theatro*]

their, theirs **δικός/ή/ό τους** (see page 203) [*dheekos/ee/o toos*]

them **αυτούς, αυτές, αυτά** (see page 202) [*aftoos, aftes, afta*]

then **τότε** [*tote*]

  (later on) **μετά** [*meta*]

there **εκεί** [*ekee*]

there is/are **υπάρχει/υπάρχουν** [*eeparkhee/eeparkhoon*]

therefore **γι'αυτό** [*yafto*]

thermometer **το θερμόμετρο** [*to thermometro*]

these **αυτοί, αυτές, αυτά** [*aftee, aftes, afta*]

Thessalonica **η Θεσσαλονίκη** [*ee thesaloneekee*]

they (see page 201)

thick **χοντρός/ή/ό** [*khondros/ee/o*]

thief **ο κλέφτης** [*o kleftees*]

thin **λεπτός/ή/ό** [*leptos/ee/o*]

thing **το πράγμα** [*to pragma*]

think: I think **νομίζω** [*nomeezo*]

  I think so **νομίζω πως ναι** [*nomeezo pos ne*]

  I don't think so **νομίζω πως όχι** [*nomeezo pos okhee*]

  (reflect) **σκέφτομαι** [*skeftome*]

third **τρίτος/η/ο** [*treetos/ee/o*]

thirsty: I am thirsty **διψάω** [*dheepsao*]

this, this one **αυτός/ή/ό** (see page 200) [*aftos/ee/o*]

those **εκείνοι, εκείνες, εκείνα** [*ekeenee, ekeenes, ekeena*]

  (see page 200)

thread **το νήμα** [*to neema*]

throat **ο λαιμός** [*o lemos*]

throat lozenges/pastilles **οι παστίλιες για το λαιμό** [*ee pasteelyes
  ya to lemo*]

through **μέσα από** [*mesa apo*]

throw: I throw **ρίχνω** [*reekhno*]

throw away: I throw away **πετάω** [*petao*]

thumb ο αντίχειρας [*o andeekheeras*]

thunder η βροντή [*ee vrondee*]

ticket το εισιτήριο [*to eeseeteeryo*]

ticket office το εκδοτήριο [*to ekdhoteeryo*]
    (*theatre*) το ταμείο [*to tameeo*]

tide η παλίρροια [*ee paleerya*]

tidy τακτοποιημένος/η/ο [*taktopee-eemenos/ee/o*]

tie η γραβάτα [*ee gravata*]

tie: I tie δένω [*dheno*]

tight σφιχτός/ή/ό [*sfeekhtos/ee/o*]

tights το καλσόν [*to kalson*]

till (*until*) μέχρι [*mekhree*]

time (*once etc.*) η φορά [*ee fora*]

time η ώρα (*see page 213*) [*ee ora*]
    there's no time δεν έχουμε καιρό [*dhen ekhoome kero*]

timetable (*trains etc.*) το δρομολόγιο [*to dhromoloyo*]

tin το κουτί [*to kootee*]

tin foil το αλουμινόχαρτο [*to aloomeenokharto*]

tin opener το ανοιχτήρι [*to aneekhteeree*]

tinned σε κουτί [*se kootee*]

tip (*money*) το φιλοδώρημα [*to feelodhoreema*]

tired κουρασμένος/η/ο [*koorazmenos/ee/o*]

tissues τα χαρτομάντηλα [*ta khartomandeela*]

to σε (*see page 199*) [*se*]

toast, toasted sandwich το τοστ [*to tost*]

tobacco ο καπνός [*o kapnos*]

tobacconist's το καπνοπωλείο [*to kapnopoleeo*]

today σήμερα [*seemera*]

toilet η τουαλέτα [*ee twaleta*]

toilet paper το χαρτί τουαλέτας [*to khartee twaletas*]

toilet water η κολόνια [*ee kolonya*]

toiletries τα καλλυντικά [*ta kaleendeeka*]

toll τα διόδια [*ta dhyodhya*]

tomato η ντομάτα [*ee domata*]

tomorrow αύριο [*avryo*]

tongue η γλώσσα [*ee glosa*]

tonic water το τόνικ [*to toneek*]

tonight απόψε [*apopse*]

too (*also*) επίσης [*epeesees*]

too (*excessively*) πολύ [*polee*]

tool το εργαλείο [*to ergaleeo*]

tooth το δόντι [*to dhondee*]

toothache ο πονόδοντος [*o ponodhondos*]

toothbrush η οδοντόβουρτσα [*ee odhondovoortsa*]

toothpaste η οδοντόκρεμα [*ee odhondokrema*]

toothpick η οδοντογλυφίδα [*ee odhondogleefeedha*]

top το πάνω μέρος [*to pano meros*]

   on top (of) πάνω (σε) [*pano (se)*]

top floor ο τελευταίος όροφος [*o telefteos orofos*]

torch ο φακός [*o fakos*]

torn σχισμένος/η/ο [*skheezmenos/ee/o*]

total το σύνολο [*to seenolo*]

touch: I touch αγγίζω [*angeezo*]

tough (*meat*) σκληρός/ή/ό [*skleeros/ee/o*]

tour (*excursion*) η εκδρομή [*ee ekdhromee*]

   (*visit*) η επίσκεψη [*ee epeeskepsee*]

tourism ο τουρισμός [*o tooreezmos*]

tourist ο τουρίστας, η τουρίστρια [*o tooreestas, ee tooreestrya*]

tourist office το τουριστικό γραφείο [*to tooreesteeko grafeeo*]

368

tow: I tow ρυμουλκώ [*reemoolko*]

tow rope το συρματόσχοινο [*to seermatoskheeno*]

towards προς [*pros*]

towel η πετσέτα [*ee petseta*]

tower ο πύργος [*o peergos*]

town η πόλη [*ee polee*]

town centre το κέντρο πόλεως [*to kendro poleos*]

town hall το δημαρχείο [*to dheemarkheeo*]

toy το παιχνίδι [*to pekhneedhee*]

track (*path*) το μονοπάτι [*to monopatee*]

   (*race*) η πίστα [*ee peesta*]

tracksuit η φόρμα γυμναστικής [*ee forma yeemnasteekees*]

trade union το συνδικάτο [*to seendheekato*]

traditional παραδοσιακός/ή/ό [*paradhosyakos/ee/o*]

traffic η κίνηση [*ee keeneesee*]

traffic jam το μποτιλιάρισμα [*to boteelyareezma*]

traffic lights τα φανάρια [*ta fanarya*]

trailer το τροχόσπιτο [*to trokhospeeto*]

train το τραίνο [*to treno*]

   by train με το τραίνο [*me to treno*]

training shoes, trainers **τα αθλητικά παπούτσια** [*ta athleeteeka papootsya*]

tram **το τραμ** [*to tram*]

tranquilliser **το ηρεμιστικό** [*to eeremeesteeko*]

translate: I translate **μεταφράζω** [*metafrazo*]

translation **η μετάφραση** [*ee metafrasee*]

travel: I travel **ταξιδεύω** [*takseedhevo*]

travel agency **το τουριστικό γραφείο** [*to tooreesteeko grafeeo*]

travel sickness **η ναυτία** [*ee nafteea*]

traveller's cheque **το τράβελερς τσεκ** [*to travelers tsek*]

tray **ο δίσκος** [*o dheeskos*]

treatment **η θεραπεία** [*ee therapeea*]

tree **το δέντρο** [*to dhendro*]

trip **η εκδρομή** [*ee ekdhromee*]

trolley-bus **το τρόλεϋ** [*to trole-ee*]

trousers **το παντελόνι** [*to pandelonee*]

trout **ο σολομός** [*o solomos*]

true: that's true **είναι αλήθεια** [*eene aleethya*]

try (*attempt*): I try **προσπαθώ** [*prospatho*]

try on: I try on **δοκιμάζω** [*dhokeemazo*]

T-shirt **το Τ-σερτ** [*to tee-sert*]

tube **ο σωλήνας** [*o soleenas*]

tuna **ο τόννος** [*o tonos*]

tunnel **το τουνέλι** [*to toonelee*]

turn: I turn **γυρίζω** [*yeereezo*]

turn off: I turn off **κλείνω** [*kleeno*]

turn on: I turn on **ανοίγω** [*aneego*]

turning (*side road*) **το στενό** [*to steno*]

TV **η τηλεόραση** [*ee teeleorasee*]

twice **δύο φορές** [*dheeo fores*]

twin-bedded room **το δίκλινο δωμάτιο** [*to dheekleeno dhomatyo*]

twins **τα δίδυμα** [*ta dheedheema*]

twisted **στριφτός/ή/ό** [*streeftos/ee/o*]

type (*sort*) **το είδος** [*to eedhos*]

type: I type **δακτυλογραφώ** [*dhakteelografo*]

typewriter **η γραφομηχανή** [*ee grafomeekhanee*]

typical **χαρακτηριστικός/ή/ό** [*kharakteereesteekos/ee/o*]

U

ugly **άσχημος/η/ο** [*askheemos/ee/o*]
ulcer **το έλκος** [*to elkos*]
umbrella **η ομπρέλα** [*ee ombrela*]
uncle **ο θείος** [*o theeos*]
uncomfortable **άβολος/η/ο** [*avolos/ee/o*]
under, underneath **κάτω από** [*kato apo*]
underground **υπόγειος/α/ο** [*eepoyos/a/o*]
  (*railway*) **το μετρό** [*to metro*]
underpants (*men's*) **το σώβρακο** [*to sovrako*]
understand: I understand **καταλαβαίνω** [*katalaveno*]
  I don't understand **δεν κατάλαβα** [*dhen-gatalava*]
underwear **τα εσώρουχα** [*ta esorookha*]
underwater **υπόγειος/α/ο** [*eepoyos/a/o*]
unemployed **άνεργος/η/ο** [*anergos/ee/o*]
unfortunately **δυστυχώς** [*dheesteekhos*]
unhappy **δυστυχισμένος/η/ο** [*dheesteekheezmenos/ee/o*]
  (*sad*) **στενοχωρεμένος/η/ο** [*stenokhoremenos/ee/o*]
uniform **η στολή** [*ee stolee*]
university **το πανεπιστήμιο** [*to panepeesteemyo*]
unleaded petrol **η αμόλυβδη βενζίνη** [*ee amoleevdhee venzeenee*]
unless **εκτός αν** [*ektos an*]
unpleasant **δυσάρεστος/η/ο** [*dheesarestos/ee/o*]
unscrew: I unscrew **ξεβιδώνω** [*kseveedhono*]
until **μέχρι** [*mekhree*]
unusual **ασυνήθιστος/η/ο** [*aseeneetheestos/ee/o*]
unwell **άρρωστος/η/ο** [*arostos/ee/o*]
up (ε)πάνω [*(e)pano*]
upper **ανώτερος/η/ο** [*anoteros/ee/o*]
upstairs **πάνω** [*pano*]
urgent **επείγων, επείγουσα, επείγον** [*epeegon, epeegoosa, epeegon*]
urine **τα ούρα** [*ta oora*]
us **μάς** (*see page 202*) [*(e)mas*]
use **η χρήση** [*ee khreesee*]
use: I use **χρησιμοποιώ** [*khreeseemopyo*]
useful **χρήσιμος/η/ο** [*khreeseemos/ee/o*]
useless **άχρηστος/η/ο** [*akhrestos/ee/o*]
usual: as usual **ως συνήθως** [*os seeneethos*]
usually **συνήθως** [*seeneethos*]

V

vacant ελεύθερος/η/ο [*eleftheros/ee/o*]
vacuum cleaner η ηλεκτρική σκούπα [*ee eelektreekee skoopa*]
vacuum flask το θερμός [*to thermos*]
valid έγκυρος/η/ο [*engeros/ee/o*]
   it is not valid δεν ισχύει [*dhen eeskhee-ee*]
valley η κοιλάδα [*ee keeladha*]
valuable πολύτιμος/η/ο [*poleeteemos/ee/o*]
valuables τα αντικείμενα αξίας [*ta andeekeemena akseeas*]
van το φορτηγάκι [*to forteegakee*]
vanilla η βανίλια [*ee vaneelya*]
vase το βάζο [*to vazo*]
VAT ο ΦΠΑ [*o fee pee alfa*]
veal το μοσχάρι [*to moskharee*]
vegetable (*green*) το λαχανικό [*to lakhaneeko*]
vegetarian χορτοφάγος/η/ο [*khortofagos/ee/o*]
vehicle το όχημα [*to okheema*]
vermouth το βερμούτ [*to vermoot*]
very πολύ [*polee*]
very much πάρα πολύ [*para polee*]
vest το φανελάκι [*to fanelakee*]
vet ο κτηνίατρος [*o kteeneeatros*]
via μέσω [*meso*]
video cassette η βίντεο-κασέτα [*ee veedeo-kaseta*]
video recorder το βίντεο [*to veedeo*]
view η θέα [*ee thea*]
villa η βίλλα [*ee veela*]
village το χωριό [*to khoryo*]
vinegar το ξύδι [*to kseedhee*]
vineyard το αμπέλι [*to ambelee*]
virgin η παρθένα [*ee parthena*]
Virgin Mary η Παναγία [*ee panayea*]
visit η επίσκεψη [*ee epeeskepsee*]
visit: I visit επισκέπτομαι [*epeeskeptome*]
visitor ο επισκέπτης [*o epeeskeptees*]
vitamin η βιταμίνη [*ee veetameenee*]
vodka η βότκα [*ee vodka*]
voice η φωνή [*ee fonee*]
volleyball το βόλεϋ [*to vole-ee*]

voltage **η τάση** [*ee tasee*]
vote: I vote **ψηφίζω** [*pseefeezo*]

W

wage **ο μισθός** [*o meesthos*]
waist **η μέση** [*ee mesee*]
waistcoat **το γιλέκο** [*to yeeleko*]
wait (for): I wait (for) **περιμένω** [*pereemeno*]
waiter **το γκαρσόνι** [*to garsonee*]
   waiter! **γκαρσόν!** [*garson*]
waiting room **η αίθουσα αναμονής** [*ee ethoosa anamonees*]
Wales **η Ουαλλία** [*ee waleea*]
walk **η βόλτα** [*ee volta*]
   I go for a walk **πάω βόλτα** [*pao volta*]
   I walk **περπατάω** [*perpatao*]
walking stick **το μπαστούνι** [*to bastoonee*]
wall (*of building*) **ο τοίχος** [*o teekhos*]
   (*of city, fortress*) **το τείχος** [*to teekhos*]
   (*of garden etc.*) **η μάντρα** [*ee mandra*]
wallet **το πορτοφόλι** [*to portofolee*]
walnut **το καρύδι** [*to kareedhee*]
want: I want **θέλω** [*thelo*]
   I would like **θα ήθελα** [*tha eethela*]
war **ο πόλεμος** [*o polemos*]
   Greek War of Independence **η Ελληνική Επανάσταση**
     [*ee eleeneekee epanastasee*]
warm **ζεστός/ή/ό** [*zestos/ee/o*]
wash: I wash **πλένω** [*pleno*]
   I wash (myself) **πλένομαι** [*plenome*]
washable: it is washable **πλένεται** [*plenete*]
wash-basin **ο νιπτήρας** [*o neepteeras*]
washing **η μπουγάδα** [*ee boogadha*]
washing machine **το πλυντήριο** [*to pleendeeryo*]
washing powder **η σκόνη πλυσίματος** [*ee skonee pleeseematos*]
washing-up: I do the washing-up **πλένω τα πιάτα** [*pleno ta pyata*]
washing-up liquid **το υγρό για τα πιάτα** [*to eegro ya ta pyata*]
wasp **η σφήκα** [*ee sfeeka*]
wastepaper basket **ο κάλαθος αχρήστων** [*o kalathos akhreeston*]
watch (*wristwatch*) **το ρολόι** [*to roloee*]

watch (*TV etc.*): I watch βλέπω [*vlepo*]

watchstrap το λουράκι [*to loorakee*]

water το νερό [*to nero*]

water heater το θερμοσίφωνο [*to thermoseefono*]

water melon το καρπούζι [*to karpoozee*]

waterfall ο καταρράχτης [*o katarakhtees*]

waterproof αδιάβροχος/η/ο [*adhyavrokhos/ee/o*]

water-skiing το θαλάσσιο σκι [*to thalasyo skee*]

wave (*sea*) το κύμα [*to keema*]

wax το κερί [*to keree*]

way (*route*) ο δρόμος [*o dhromos*]

    that way από'κεί [*apokee*]

    this way από'δώ [*apodho*]

    (*method*) ο τρόπος [*o tropos*]

way in η είσοδος [*ee eesodhos*]

way out η έξοδος [*ee eksodhos*]

we εμείς (*see page 201*) [*emees*]

weather ο καιρός [*o keros*]

    what's the weather like? τι καιρό κάνει; [*tee kero kanee*]

wedding ο γάμος [*o gamos*]

week η εβδομάδα [*ee evdhomadha*]

weekday η καθημερινή [*ee katheemereenee*]

weekend το Σαββατοκύριακο [*to savatokeeryako*]

weekly εβδομαδιαίος/α/ο [*evdhomadhyeos/a/o*]

    (*each week*) κάθε εβδομάδα [*kathe evdhomadha*]

weigh: I weigh ζυγίζω [*zeeyeezo*]

weight το βάρος [*to varos*]

welcome το καλωσόρισμα [*to kalosoreezma*]

    (*reception*) η υποδοχή [*ee eepodhokhee*]

welcome! καλώς ορίσατε! [*kalos oreesate*]

well (*water*) το πηγάδι [*to peegadhee*]

well καλά [*kala*]

    as well επίσης [*epeesees*]

well done (*steak*) καλοψημένος/η/ο [*kalopseemenos/ee/o*]

Welsh ουαλλικός/ή/ό [*waleekos/ee/o*]

Welshman ο Ουαλλός [*o walos*]

Welshwoman η Ουαλλέζα [*ee waleza*]

west η δύση [*ee dheesee*]

western δυτικός/ή/ό [*dheeteekos/ee/o*]

wet βρεγμένος/η/ο [*vregmenos/ee/o*]

what τι [tee]
what? τι; [tee]
   what is . . . ? τι είναι . . . ; [tee eene . . .]
wheel η ρόδα [ee rodha]
wheelchair το καροτσάκι [to karotsakee]
when όταν [otan]
when? πότε; [pote]
where πού [poo]
where? πού; [poo]
   where is/are . . . ? πού είναι . . . ; [poo eene . . .]
which που [poo]
which? ποιος/α/ο; [pyos/a/o]
while ενώ [eno]
whisky το ουίσκι [to weeskee]
   whisky and soda το ουίσκι με σόδα [to weeskee me sodha]
white άσπρος/η/ο [aspros/ee/o]
   (with milk) με γάλα [me gala]
who που [poo]
who? ποιος/α/ο; [pyos/a/o]

   who is it? ποιος είναι; [pyos eene]
whole ολόκληρος/η/ο [olokleeros/ee/o]
wholemeal bread το μαύρο ψωμί [to mavro psomee]
whose του οποίου [too opeeoo]
whose? ποιανού; [pyanoo]
why? γιατί; [yatee]
why not? γιατί όχι; [yatee okhee]
wide φαρδύς, φαρδειά, φαρδύ [fardhees, fardhya, fardhee]
widow η χήρα [ee kheera]
widower ο χήρος [o kheeros]
wife η γυναίκα [ee yeeneka]
wild άγριος/α/ο [agryos/a/o]
win η νίκη [ee neekee]
win: I win κερδίζω [kerdheezo]
   who won? ποιος κέρδισε; [pyos kerdheese]
wind ο άνεμος [o anemos]
windmill ο ανεμόμυλος [o anemomeelos]
window το παράθυρο [to paratheero]
   (shop) η βιτρίνα [ee veetreena]
windsurfing το γουίντσερφ [to weendserf]
windy: it's windy φυσάει [feesaee]

wine **το κρασί** [*to krasee*]
wine merchant/shop **η κάβα** [*ee kava*]
wing **το φτερό** [*to ftero*]
winter **ο χειμώνας** [*o kheemonas*]
with **με** [*me*]
without **χωρίς** [*khorees*]
woman **η γυναίκα** [*ee yeeneka*]
wonderful **θαυμάσιος/α/ο** [*thavmasyos/a/o*]
wood (*group of trees*) **το δάσος** [*to dhasos*]
   (*material*) **το ξύλο** [*to kseelo*]
wool **το μαλλί** [*to malee*]
word **η λέξη** [*ee leksee*]
work **η δουλειά** [*ee dhoolya*]
I work (*job*) **δουλεύω** [*dhoolevo*]
   (*function*) **λειτουργώ** [*leetoorgo*]
world **ο κόσμος** [*o kozmos*]
world (*of the world*) **παγκόσμιος/α/ο** [*pangozmyos/a/o*]
   World Cup **ο μουντιάλ** [*o moondyal*]
   First/Second World War **Ο Πρώτος/Δεύτερος Παγκόσμιος**
     Πόλεμος [*o protos/dhefteros pangozmyos polemos*]
worried **στενοχωρεμένος/η/ο** [*stenokhoremenos/ee/o*]
worry: don't worry **μη στενοχωριέσαι** [*mee stenokhoryese*]
worse **χειρότερος/η/ο** [*kheeroteros/ee/o*]
worth: it's worth . . . **αξίζει** . . . [*akseezee . . .*]
   it's not worth it **δεν αξίζει** [*dhen akseezee*]
would like (*see* want)
wound (*injury*) **το τραύμα** [*to travma*]
wrap (up): I wrap **τυλίγω** [*teeleego*]
write: I write **γράφω** [*grafo*]
writer **ο/η συγγραφέας** [*o/ee seengrafeas*]
writing pad **το μπλοκ** [*to blok*]
writing paper **το χαρτί αλληλογραφίας** [*to khartee aleelografeeas*]
wrong (*incorrect*) **λανθασμένος/η/ο** [*lanthazmenos/ee/o*]
   you're wrong **λάθος κάνετε/κάνεις** [*lathos kanete/kanees*]
   there's something wrong **κάτι δεν πάει καλά** [*katee dhem-baee kala*]

X

X-ray **η ακτινογραφία** [*ee akteenografeea*]

Y

yacht **το κότερο** [*to kotero*]

yawn: I yawn **χασμουριέμαι** [*khazmooryeme*]

year **ο χρόνος** [*o khronos*]

yellow **κίτρινος/η/ο** [*keetreenos/ee/o*]

yes **ναι** [*ne*]

yesterday **χτες** [*khtes*]

yet **ακόμα** [*akoma*]
    not yet **όχι ακόμα** [*okhee akoma*]

yoghurt **το γιαούρτι** [*to yaoortee*]

you **εσείς** (*formal*), **εσύ** (*informal*) (*see page 201*) [*esees, esee*]

young **νέος/α/ο** [*neos/a/o*]

your, yours **δικός/ή/ό σας** (*formal*), **δικός/ή/ό σου** (*informal*)
    (*see page 203*) [*dheekos/ee/o sas, dheekos/ee/o soo*]

youth **η νεολαία** [*ee neolea*]

youth hostel **ο ξενώνας νιότητας** [*o ksenonas nyoteetas*]

Z

zip **το φερμουάρ** [*to fermwar*]

zoo **ο ζωολογικός κήπος** [*o zo-oloyeekos keepos*]

zoology **η ζωολογία** [*ee zo-oloyeea*]

NOTES

NOTES

378

EMERGENCIES

(*see also* Problems and Complaints, *page 187*)

You may want to say

Phoning the emergency services

(I want) the police, please
(Θέλω) την αστυνομία παρακαλώ
(*thelo*) *teen asteenomeea parakalo*

(I want) the fire brigade
(Θέλω) την πυροσβεστική υπηρεσία παρακαλώ
(*thelo*) *teem-beerozvesteekee eepeereseea parakalo*

(I want) an ambulance
(Θέλω) ένα ασθενοφόρο
(*thelo*) *ena asthenoforo*

There's been a robbery
Έγινε κλοπή
eyeene klopee

There's been a burglary
Έγινε διάρρηξη
eyeene dhyareeksee

There's been an accident
Έγινε δυστύχημα
eyeene dheesteekheema

There's a fire
Έπιασε φωτιά
epyase fotya

I've been attacked/mugged
Με επιτέθηκαν
me epeetetheekan

I've been raped
Με βιάσανε
me vyasane

There's someone ill/injured
Κάποιος είναι άρρωστος/ τραυματισμένος
kapyos eene arostos/ travmateezmenos

It's my husband/son
Είναι ο άντρας μου/ο γιος μου
eene o andras-moo/o yos-moo

It's my wife/daughter
Είναι η γυναίκα μου/η κόρη μου
eene ee yeeneka-moo/ee koree-moo

It's my friend
Είναι ο φίλος μου/η φίλη μου
eene o feelos-moo/ee feelee-moo

Please come immediately
Ελάτε αμέσως
elate amesos

The address is . . .
Η διεύθυνση είναι . . .
ee dhyeftheensee eene . . .

My name is . . .
Με λένε . . .
me lene . . .

My telephone number is . . .
Ο αριθμός τηλεφώνου μου είναι . . .
o areethmos teelefonoo-moo eene . . .

Where is the police station?
Πού είναι το τμήμα;
poo eene to tmeema

Where is the hospital?
Πού είναι το νοσοκομείο;
poo eene to nosokomeeo

At the police station/hospital

Is there anybody here who speaks English?
Υπάρχει κανείς εδώ πού μιλάει Αγγλικά;
eeparkhee kanees edho poo meelaee angleeka

I want to speak to a woman
Θέλω να μιλήσω σε μια γυναίκα
thelo na meeleeso se mya yeeneka

Please call the British Embassy
Τηλεφωνήστε στη Βρετανική Πρεσβεία παρακαλώ
teelefoneeste stee vretaneekee presveea parakalo

I want a lawyer
Θέλω ένα δικηγόρο
thelo ena dheekeegoro

You may hear

When you phone the emergency services

Τι συμβαίνει;
tee seemvenee
What is the matter?

Τι συνέβη;
tee seenevee
What has happened?

Πείτε μου το όνομά σας και
τη διεύθυνσή σας
*peete moo to onoma-sas ke
tee dhyeftheensee-sas*
Tell me your name and
your address

Θα στείλουμε ένα
περιπολικό
*tha steeloome ena
pereepoleeko*
We will send a police car

Ερχεται ένα περιπολικό
erkhete ena pereepoleeko
A police car is on the way

Ερχεται η πυροσβεστική
υπηρεσία
*erkhete ee peerozvesteekee
eepeereseea*
The fire brigade is on the
way

Στέλνω ένα ασθενοφόρο τώρα
stelno ena asthenoforo tora
I am sending an ambulance
now

The police

Πώς σας λένε;
pos sas lene
What is your name?

Τη διεύθυνσή σας;
tee dhyeftheensee-sas
What is your address?

Τι συνέβη;
tee seenevee
What happened?

Πού συνέβη;
poo seenevee
Where did it happen?

Πότε συνέβη;
pote seenevee
When did it happen?

Μπορείτε να περιγράψετε . . . ;
boreete na pereegrapsete . . .
Can you describe . . . ?

Ελάτε μαζί μας στο τμήμα
elate mazee-mas sto tmeema
Come with us to the police
    station

Είστε υπό κράτηση
eeste eepo krateesee
You're under arrest

The doctor

(*see* Health, *page 174*)

Πού πονάει;
poo ponaee
Where does it hurt?

Πόσον καιρό είσαστε έτσι;
poson-gero eesaste etsee
How long have you been like this?

Πόσον καιρό είναι έτσι;
poson-gero eene etsee
How long has he/she been like this?

Θα πρέπει να πάτε στο νοσοκομείο
tha prepee na pate sto nosokomeeo
You will have to go to hospital

Help!
Βοήθεια!
voeethya

Help me!
Βοηθήστε με!
voeetheeste me

Police!
Αστυνομία!
asteenomeea

Stop!
Σταμάτα!
stamata

Stop thief!
Σταμάτα, κλέφτης!
stamata kleftees

Fire!
Φωτιά
fotya

Look out!
Προσέξτε!
prosekste

Danger! Gas!
Κίνδυνος! Γκάζι!
keendheenos gazee

Get out of the way!
Διάδρομο!
dhyadhromo

Call the police
Φωνάξτε την αστυνομία
fonakste teen asteenomeea

Call the fire brigade
Φωνάξτε την πυροσβεστική
fonakste teem-beerozvesteekee

Call an ambulance
Φωνάξτε ένα ασθενοφόρο
fonakste ena asthenoforo

Call a doctor
Φωνάξτε ένα ιατρό
fonakste ena yatro

Get help quickly
Φέρτε βοήθεια, γρήγορα
ferte voeethya greegora

It's an emergency
Είναι επείγον
eene epeegon

Emergency telephone numbers

Police	100
Fire Brigade	199
Forestry Service	191 (for forest fires)
Red Cross	150
Medical assistance	166

ALL-PURPOSE PHRASES

Hello/Goodbye
Γειά σας/Αντίο
yasas/adeeo

Good morning/Good day
Καλημέρα
kaleemera

Good evening
Καλησπέρα
kaleespera

Goodnight
Καληνύχτα
kaleeneekhta

Yes/No
Ναι/Οχι
ne/okhee

Please
Παρακαλώ
parakalo

Thank you (very much)
Ευχαριστώ (πολύ)
efkhareesto (polee)

Don't mention it
Παρακαλώ
parakalo

I don't understand
Δεν κατάλαβα
dhen-gatalava

I speak very little Greek
Μιλάω μόνο λίγα Ελληνικά
meelao mono leega eleeneeka

I don't know
Δεν ξέρω
dhen-gsero

Pardon?
Ορίστε;
oreeste

Would you repeat that, pleas
Ξαναπέστε το, παρακαλώ
ksanapeste to parakalo

More slowly/Again, please
Πιο αργά/Πάλι, παρακαλώ
pyo arga/palee parakalo

Can you show me in the book
**Μπορείτε να μου δείξετε
    στο βιβλίο;**
*boreete na moo dheeksete
    sto veevleeo*

Can you write it down?
Μπορείτε να το γράψετε;
boreete na to grapsete

Do you speak English?
Μιλάτε Αγγλικά;
meelate angleeka

Is there anyone here who
    speaks English?
**Υπάρχει κανείς εδώ που
    μιλάει Αγγλικά;**
*eeparkhee kanees edho poo
    meelaee angleeka*